Reader's
Digest

LONG LIFE

FOR YOUR STUFF

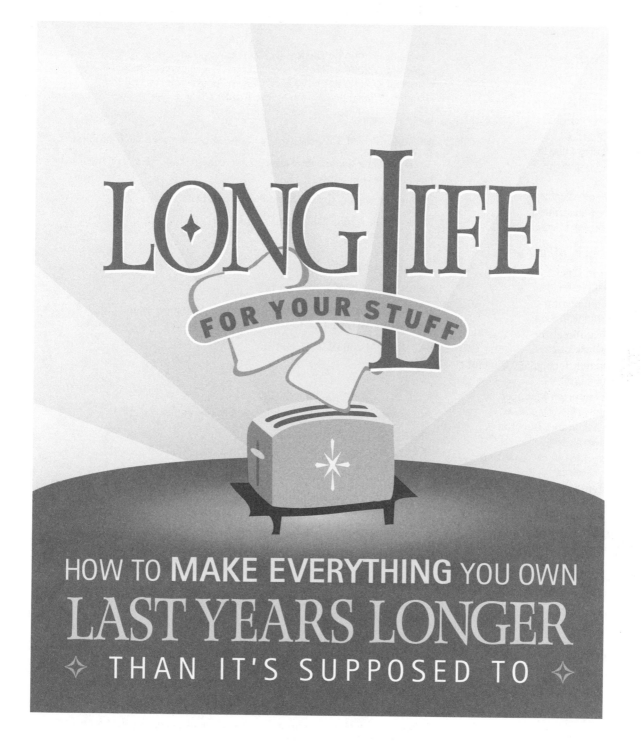

LONG LIFE

FOR YOUR STUFF

HOW TO **MAKE EVERYTHING** YOU OWN
LAST YEARS LONGER
✦ THAN IT'S SUPPOSED TO ✦

Reader's Digest

The Reader's Digest Association

Pleasantville, NY | Montreal

Project Staff

Editor
Don Earnest

Designer
Michele Laseau

Copy Editors
Marilyn Knowlton
Kathryn Phelps

Indexer
Nanette Bendyna

How-to Illustration
© Russell Charpentier

Reader's Digest Books

Editor in Chief
Neil Wertheimer

Managing Editor
Suzanne Beason

Creative Director
Michele Laseau

Production Technology Director
Doug Croll

Manufacturing Manager
John L. Cassidy

Book Marketing Director
Dawn Nelson

Director of Direct Marketing
Lisa Walker

President & Publisher, Trade Books
Harold Clarke

President, U.S. Books & Home Entertainment
Dawn Zier

Reader's Digest Association, Inc.

President, North America & Global Editor-In-Chief
Eric W. Schrier

Text prepared especially for
Reader's Digest by

NAILHAUS PUBLICATIONS, Inc.

Publishing Director
David Schiff

Writers
Beth Kalet, Michael Kaufman,
Joseph Provey, Steven Schwartz,
Anita Selene, Amy Ziffer

Library of Congress Cataloging-in-Publication Data

Reader's Digest long life for your stuff.

    p. cm.

Includes index.

ISBN 0-7621-0703-0 (hdcvr)

1. Home economics. 2. House furnishings—Maintenance and repair. I. Title: Long life for your stuff. II. Reader's Digest Association.

TX158.R376 2005

640—dc22

2005018137

Address any comments about *Long Life for Your Stuff* to:

The Reader's Digest Association, Inc.
Editor-in-Chief, Books and Music
Reader's Digest Road
Pleasantville, NY 10570-7000

To order copies of *Long Life for Your Stuff*, call 1-800-846-2100.

Visit our website at **rd.com**

Printed in the United States of America

1 3 5 7 9 10 8 6 4 2

US 4604/IC

To Our Readers

The information in this book has been carefully researched, and all efforts have been made to ensure its accuracy and safety. Neither Nailhaus Publications, Inc. nor Reader's Digest Association, Inc. assumes any responsibility for any injuries suffered or damages or losses incurred as a result of following the instructions in this book. Before taking any action based on information in this book, study the information carefully and make sure that you understand it fully. Observe all warnings. Test any new or unusual repair or cleaning method before applying it broadly, or on a highly visible area or a valuable item. The mention of any brand or product in this book does not imply an endorsement. All prices and product names mentioned are subject to change and should be considered general examples rather than specific recommendations.

Waste Not, Want Not

We've come a long way since the words above defined our cultural character and the motto of every cost-conscious householder was "use it up, wear it out, make it do, or do without." But we have not gone so far that we can't come home again.

It's true that we've been attracted by the flash of convenience—throw-away products, quick meals, instant everything. We're in a hurry, we say. We deserve a break. Besides, why should we have to work so hard to prepare dinner or pay so much for something—a razor, say, or a mop—when for just pennies, a disposable one does the job just as well?

But those pennies add up dramatically over time, and each toss-away time saver comes with its ugly twin: waste. And hidden in that waste are mounting disposal and environmental costs that we don't want to recognize. Reason tells us that our ultra-disposable lifestyle doesn't make sense. We need to see the shallow promises of convenience products for what they are—empty and unsatisfying. We know there's got to be a better way.

Long Life for Your Stuff is here to provide you with an answer—a myriad of simple solutions to those aggravating household problems caused by wear, tear, heat, cold, planned obsolescence, and the wiles of advertising. This book puts you back in the driver's seat. With every turn of the page, you'll find new and useful information for every item. You're going to experience a lot of "Aha!" moments as you discover hundreds of simple ways to make your life easier without all the waste.

If your trash cans overflow with packaging, junk mail, empty nonrefillable containers, and worn-out goods—from shirts and shoes to pots and pans and VCRs and TVs—that just don't hold up, hang in there. If you've been frustrated because things wear out before you think they ought to, if you're spending too much on repairs or replacement parts, or if you're consigning too many items to the junk heap, you're going to love this book. On each and every page, you'll learn something that you can use right away. You'll find useful common-sense tips and surprising hints, along with lots of old-fashioned make-do wisdom. This book will help you make the most of your possessions, your money, and your time.

We've talked with industry experts, consumer advocates, and savvy householders—regular folks—to bring you the best advice on more than a thousand of the most common problems that shorten the life of your possessions. We cover hundreds of everyday items that you can normally expect to be called upon to replace or repair. And we guarantee you will collect enough hints, tips, advice, and good old down-to-earth know-how to last you a lifetime.

Did you know that your furniture doesn't crave oil—no matter what the furniture polish ads say? The pores of properly finished wood are sealed with finish. You're better off applying a thin coat of wax. And when buying furniture, a good way to tell its quality is to check for finish on all surfaces. If the bottom of a tabletop is not finished, for example, it will absorb more moisture than the finished upper surface. This could cause the top to cup, split, or warp.

And did you know that all you need to do to prolong the life of your hair dryer is to occasionally vacuum the air vent at the back? How many hair dryers have you tossed before their time? A little maintenance goes a long way.

That's what *Long Life for Your Stuff* is all about. Get ready to bookmark pages and highlight your favorites. Did you know that you can prolong the life of your automobile's air-conditioning system by running it a few times throughout the winter? This prevents moving parts in the compressor from seizing and helps keep the seals soft and pliant. And did you know that fabric softener actually makes your towels less useful? It interferes with their absorbency. Instead, try adding a cup of white vinegar to the final rinse cycle. This low-cost pantry product acts as a natural fabric softener, reduces static cling, and helps eliminate extra suds and soap deposits.

If you are tired of all the glossy come-ons that we confront daily in ads and articles, you'll appreciate *Long Life for Your Stuff*. You'll learn time-honored methods of preserving things that have been lost in the hustle and bustle of modern life. You'll not only discover how to make your goods last longer and your money go farther, but you'll also learn how to shop for products that will last.

Take a deep breath and join the growing group of folks who have come to believe it's time to return to a more sensible lifestyle—one in which ease doesn't equate with waste and expense. It's just a matter of learning some old tricks, making some new choices, and exercising a little ingenuity. We promise, you'll be saying "Aha!" an awful lot.

So sit back, get comfortable, and take a look at what we've gathered up for you. We know you'll find this book to be a handy and useful reference you'll turn to time and again. And do us all a favor. Don't keep secrets. Pass along the good advice to family, friends, and neighbors.

—The Editors

Contents

Making Things Last Longer

Conquering the Villains of Long Life

Conquering the Villains of Long Life

You need to understand the main culprits that shorten the life of your belongings so you can mount a defense that ensures that your things will be around to serve you longer.

So how do you make things last longer? Actually, that's the wrong question. The real question is: What causes things to wear out or fall apart before you are ready for their useful days to be over? Interestingly, the number of factors that regularly cause the early demise of our possessions is surprisingly small, and once you know what they are, you'll automatically begin to intuit the precautions you need to take in order to extend the lives of most of the things you own.

Villain 1: Sun

When things begin to age, one of the prime suspects is good old everyday sunshine. You probably know that prolonged sun exposure is bad for your skin, and you should know not to keep a pet in the car on a hot day. Similarly, everyone knows that sun beating down on your house's exterior causes paint to peel and shingles and siding to fade and grow brittle. But the sun can also harm your home's interior. Direct sunlight can fade or dry out painted or papered walls, carpeting and rugs, wooden and upholstered

furniture, and even your drapes and curtains if they are not lined. The solution is to draw the shades on windows that get a lot of sun during the day.

Even the photographs on your walls will fade if regularly exposed to sunlight (or strong room light, for that matter). It's actually a good idea to display copies of valuable family photos and keep the originals safely tucked away. Sunlight will also age documents such as birth certificates, wedding licenses, and diplomas as surely as it yellows newsprint; it just takes longer. Also keep in mind that sunlight causes plastics of all sorts to deteriorate—pliable plastics in particular become stiff and prone to cracking. But even the resin furniture on your deck will last longer if it's kept in the shade.

Sunlight and heat from it are tough on CDs, DVDs, cassettes, and musical instruments—all of which should not be left in direct sunlight or locked in a hot car. If you carry CDs in your car, don't keep them on the dash or the sun visor, where sunlight can ruin them.

Villain 2: Heat

Be wary of heat not only from the sun but from other sources as well. The glue joints on a wood chair or table can dry out quickly if you place the furniture too close to a radiator or heating grille. And appliances such as refrigerators and microwaves need breathing room to vent heat. Don't push them too close to a wall, where the heat can build up and damage the appliance. If you're redesigning your kitchen, don't place the refrigerator next to the stove or a heating source (or in direct sunlight); the heat can trick the compressor into coming on more often than necessary.

Heat is also deadly for the chips and circuitry in electronic equipment—televisions, VCRs, tape decks, DVD players and recorders, stereo components, and computers. Make sure all electronic gear is well ventilated—especially if you keep units in a cabinet. Don't stack them so that the heat from one unit rises to affect the one on top of it. Don't block the vents on your PC's main unit.

Food staples are also affected by heat. Store canned and packaged goods in a cool, dry place—ideally between 50° and 70°F (10° and 21°C). Don't store them in direct sunlight or near hot pipes or heat registers. Never store herbs

Five Everyday Things That Will Last a Lifetime

Outside of a tree, a wedding ring, or an heirloom—a grandfather clock, say—what can you expect to purchase today that you will use for the rest of your life? What can you pass on to your progeny? Here are five useful items that will last you a lifetime.

Cast-iron pan	LOOK FOR a new cast-iron pan with the surface that is uniformly dull gray inside and out and uniformly rough in texture with small grains or "pores." AVOID pans with seams, cracks, or uneven or sharp edges. Buy a cast-iron pan that is all of a piece—not one with a wooden handle. Avoid a ridged bottom; a flat surface conducts heat best.
Chef's knife	LOOK FOR a good-quality chef's knife that you feel comfortable handling. Pick up a knife and see how it feels in your hand. Also buy a steel and use it regularly to keep your knife honed. If you buy a good chef's knife and care for it properly, you should never have to replace it. For more on buying knives, see page 33. AVOID knives that have a serrated cutting edge or those that claim to "never need sharpening." Good knives do need sharpening.
Hand tools	LOOK FOR forged metal, and plastic, fiberglass, or metal handles . A typical basic set includes a 16-ounce claw hammer, a few sizes of screwdrivers (regular flat tip, together with Phillips or Robertsons), an adjustable (Crescent) wrench, slotted pliers, a wide 25-foot (7.5-meter) tape measure, a retractable utility knife, and an 8-point crosscut saw. Good-quality hand tools should last not just one lifetime, but for a couple of generations. For tool care, see page 346. AVOID cheaply made cast-iron tools and tools with wooden handles.
Scrapbook or photo album	LOOK FOR a baby book, photo album, or scrapbook with pages made from dye-free, pH-balanced archival paper. Affix your photos and memorabilia with picture corners or small mounting squares. Check your local crafts store for the latest materials—the scrapbook craft industry is making improvements all the time. AVOID plastic sheets and sticky-backed pages, and don't use regular tape.
Leather handbag or briefcase	LOOK FOR small tight stitches made with heavy thread. Make sure clamps, hinges, or locks are nicely machined and work smoothly. The most durable bags are made of top-grain leather. Leather described as full grain won't necessarily last longer. A top-quality leather handbag or briefcase is actually inexpensive—if you amortize it over the lifetime of use. AVOID trendy designs. Buy a classic style that will endure for a lifetime.

and spices over your stovetop, where they are exposed to both heat and light.

Villain 3: **Moisture**

Like sunlight and heat, another major culprit is moisture. Everyone knows that moisture can cause metal to rust. That's why it's crucial to use stainless steel or galvanized fasteners and fixtures in anything exposed to moisture or high humidity, whether you are building a deck or putting up shelves in the bathroom. And any chips or scratches in most exposed metals should be touched up as quickly as possible. Unfortunately, moisture can cause a host of other problems. It can undermine foundations, cause wood to rot, paint to peel, and encourage mildew to sprout up everywhere from improperly stored clothes and upholstery to the grout lines in your tiles. You even have to be careful mopping; too much water can damage wood and vinyl floor seams. Often, the solution to moisture problems is improving ventilation by installing vents or an exhaust fan or leaving a window cracked open. Sometimes a dehumidifier or air conditioner may be needed.

Humidity can damage any number of other things, from rolls of film to packaged food. Professional photographers store film in sealed containers with moisture-absorbing packets in a refrigerator until it's time to use it. Humidity, together with heat, breaks down the chemicals on the unprocessed film. Dried pantry items such as flour, pasta, and sugar are especially vulnerable to moisture. Dried herbs and spices, too, suffer when exposed to humidity. To keep all of them fresh as long as possible, store them in sealed containers in a low-humidity environment.

Villain 4: **Dirt**

Last, but by no means least, is dirt—in all its forms, from dust and debris to greasy grime. On first thought, it's easy to presume that we keep things clean just for aesthetic and hygienic reasons. But dirt is a real villain when it comes to wearing things out. Walking over a layer of fine grit on your wood or vinyl-tiled floor is practically the same as sanding it with abrasive paper, which is why regular vacuuming or dust-mopping is needed to preserve them. Letting grit build up in a machine or other item with moving parts is a sure way to wear it out, which is why proper maintenance usually involves cleaning and lubricating the parts. And dirt that becomes embedded in any fabric—be it a rug, upholstery, bedding, table linens, clothes, or even garden gloves—causes it to wear out faster, which is why regular vacuuming or washing is needed.

It's not just the friction caused by dirt that creates a problem. Debris that accumulates on the surface of an object can collect and hold moisture, causing the object to rust, peel, or develop mold. More troublesome is dust that accumulates on the vents of appliances and electronic equipment, on heating grates and baseboard radiators, and in furnace and air-conditioning filters. It blocks the circulation of air and produces a buildup of heat that causes motors to work harder and circuitry to overheat. Simply by routinely dusting and vacuuming your appliances, you'll extend their lives.

Sun, heat, moisture, and dirt are by no means the only culprits responsible for shortening the lives of the things you own. Extreme cold can damage plastic, or sudden dramatic shifts in temperature can wreak havoc on metal. And sometimes the absence of enough humidity can cause problems with wood and paper. At times, being too zealous in the pursuit of dirt can wear out a fragile or delicate object. And of course, things do fall apart from excessive or improper use. But day to day, the four sources described above are the ones to control when you want make your things last longer.

Food & Cookware

table of contents

Fruits and Vegetables

It takes very little time and energy to keep your fruits and vegetables fresh. Mostly, it's a matter of being savvy about how to store different kinds of produce—most importantly, if and when to refrigerate (see Should You Refrigerate?).

Prepare your veggie bin

Even though it may be labeled "crisper drawer," you may find that veggies stored inside it quickly become limp and moldy. The culprit is moisture. The solution is simple: Draw the moisture away from the vegetables by lining the drawer with newspaper covered with a layer of paper towel.

Line storage bags

When you get your celery, romaine lettuce, or radishes home, take them out of the plastic bag they came in. Line a re-sealable bag with paper towel, put in the produce, and then squeeze out as much air as you can before sealing the bags. The produce will last up to two weeks.

Be freezer–smart

Your freezer can be a powerful tool for long-term life for most vegetables and some fruits—if you know how to use it. The first problem with freezing produce is that the water inside expands, breaking down the cell walls, so the food is mushy when you defrost it. This usually isn't a big deal with vegetables that will be cooked, since cooking softens them anyway. But it usually precludes freezing fruits that you want to eat raw.

The other problem with freezing is that fresh fruits and vegetables contain enzymes that will cause them to lose nutrients, flavor, and color, even when frozen. So before freezing produce, you'll want to inactivate the enzymes by blanching—giving them a quick dip in boiling water or steam and then an ice-water bath to stop the cooking process.

Freeze celery for seasoning

Chop up extra celery; then microwave it at 10-second intervals on a paper towel until it is dried. It will keep in the freezer for up to a year for use in seasoning soups and other dishes.

Revive your raisins

Are your raisins all dried out and clumped together? Don't chuck 'em. The next time you make oatmeal, throw in a handful a few minutes before the cereal is finished cooking. They'll plump right up. Delicious! To use dried-out raisins in other recipes, just soak them in warm water for a few minutes first.

Freeze extra bananas

Got more ripe bananas than you can use? Slice 'em up and lay them out on a small cookie sheet. Freeze the slices on the cookie sheet; then toss them into a resealable plastic freezer bag. Keep them frozen until it's time for your next smoothie or banana bread.

Save the juice

The next time you open a can of peaches or other fruit, don't pour the liquid down the drain. Pour it into a glass or plastic container, seal it, and store it in the fridge. Then, when you prepare a gelatin dessert, enhance the flavor by using the liquid instead of water in the recipe. Or mix the liquid with an equal amount of milk and freeze it in ice-pop molds to create a treat kids will love.

☛ NO
fruit near potatoes

Don't store potatoes next to apples—or apricots, bananas, avocados, blueberries, cantaloupes, or peaches, for that matter. All these fruits emit ethylene gas, a natural ripening agent that causes potatoes to sprout sooner. And don't refrigerate potatoes. They'll last longer in a place that's dark and cool, not cold.

Choose your berries well

Strawberries do not ripen once they are picked, so be sure to select the brightest and most firm berries. Berry size should not affect flavor, but berries should be intact, not squashed. Look for baskets without stains, and check the bottom of the baskets for bruised, squashed, or mildewed berries.

• Refrigerate to preserve berries for up to three days. If you have room in your refrigerator, lay them out in a single layer to prevent the delicate berries from bumping against one another. Wash right before eating because washing hastens mold growth.

• When strawberries are abundant in early spring, clean, pat dry, and pulse a batch of the berries in your food processor or blender. Freeze the pulp to use later for smoothie drinks or baked goods.

Chop 'n' freeze leftovers

Blanching before freezing is the best way to preserve veggies for the long term. But you don't want to go through that

SHOULD YOU REFRIGERATE?

Some fruits and vegetables last longest if refrigerated; some do better stored out of direct sunlight in a cool, dry place. And then there are those that should be ripened at room temperature and then refrigerated. Here's a list you might want to copy and tape to the fridge:

Refrigerate immediately

Asian pears	Cauliflower	Grapes	Plums
Asparagus	Celery	Kumquats	Radishes
Beans	Cantaloupe	Lettuce	Salad greens
Beets	Citrus	Lychees	Spinach
Berries	Corn	Mushrooms	Summer squash
Broccoli	Cranberries	Okra	
Cabbage	Cucumbers	Peas	
Carrots	Eggplants	Peppers	

Ripen, then refrigerate

Avocado	Kiwi
Bananas	Peaches
Guava	Tomatoes
Papaya	
Pears	

Keep in a cool, dry place

Apples	Potatoes
Honeydew melons	Sweet potatoes
Mangoes	Watermelons
Onions	Winter squash
Pineapples	

Blanching times vary by veggie—from as little as 90 seconds for kohlrabi to as long as 11 minutes for large ears of corn. In the U.S., you can find specific times and procedures by calling the local county office of your state college or university extension service. You'll find it in the government listings of the phone directory under the Department of Agriculture. Also blanching times are listed in most preserving and canning cookbooks. Or check online. Here's a site where you can find detailed advice and charts:

> **National Center for Home Food Preservation**
http://www.uga.edu/nchfp/how/freeze.html

trouble for a leftover piece of pepper or onion. And you know the piece is probably doomed if you just wrap it in plastic and stick it in the fridge. Here's a handy solution that will preserve the leftover piece for at least a few weeks: If you like to stir-fry, slice up the leftovers. Or if you think they might come in handy for adding to a sauce or dip, chop them. Freeze the pieces in a resealable plastic bag or a plastic container with a tight lid. Later, just break off whatever you need from the frozen chunk—there's no need to thaw it before you use it.

Hydrate your asparagus

You probably already are in the habit of snipping the bottoms of cut flower stems before you put them in a vase or wrapping them in damp paper towels for transport. A sharp, fresh cut helps the stems draw water. The same principal works to keep asparagus fresh: Snip the bottoms of asparagus stalks and wrap them in wet paper towels to prolong freshness.

Keep mushrooms fresh

Your mushrooms are starting to wrinkle and discolor, and you haven't even taken the plastic off the basket yet. Well, that was your mistake. They'll last longer

if you take them out of the package as soon as you get home and store them in a brown paper bag in the produce bin of your refrigerator.

Give veggies a new lease on life with lemon

Wait! Before you stuff those wilted vegetables into the garbage disposal, try this: Soak the produce in 1 teaspoon of lemon juice added to 1/2 gallon (2 liters) of water. If the vegetable has a stalk—like celery, asparagus, or broccoli—cut the bottom off before soaking. Slice or chop other veggies, such as peppers or radishes, so the lemon water can soak in. The veggies should perk up in about half an hour.

Cure pumpkin and winter squash

The key to making winter squashes and pumpkins last well into winter is to cure them in a warm, dry place for a few days before putting them into cool storage. You're looking for a curing temperature of about 75° to 85° F (24° to 29° C)—a warm sunny porch or even the attic would do the trick. The key is to let any cuts or abrasions from harvesting heal up. Then store them in a cool, dry place—about 50° F (10° C) is optimum.

Meat and Poultry

With the price of meat and poultry these days, you want to be certain nothing goes to waste. A key to keeping these items fresh is knowing how to wrap them.

No need to rewrap if using immediately

If you plan to use that store-bought beef on the day of purchase or the following day, leave it in its original wrapping and store in the coldest part of your refrigerator.

Save for later use

You can keep roasts and other large cuts of beef in your refrigerator for up to five days after purchase if you remove the store packaging and rewrap loosely in plastic or foil so air can circulate.

Prevent deli meats from drying out

Store these items in your refrigerator for up to a week, wrapped in the packaging from the deli counter. Or place in plastic containers in the fridge.

Follow these freezer dos and don'ts

Don't freeze luncheon or deli meats such as salami, bologna, etc. Do freeze freshly store-bought cuts of meat as soon as possible. If you intend to freeze them, don't store them in the refrigerator first.

Make and freeze burgers

Try making hamburger patties on the lids from coffee cans and using those lids as burger separators. They'll come apart easier than burgers stored on waxed paper. Store your stack of burgers in a freezer bag.

Repackage before freezing

If you're planning to freeze a cut of meat, first unwrap it from its original packaging. If the meat was displayed on a foam base, throw that away. Neither the foam nor the plastic on the meat in the store is meant for long-term or low-temperature storage. Rewrap in a moisture-proof wrapping product, such as heavy-duty foil or freezer paper. This helps the meat retain its moisture. Wrap your meat tightly, and make sure the entire item is sealed in. Use freezer tape if needed, to seal the wrap shut.

Hot dogs can take a month in the freezer

Was there a sale on hot dogs at your local grocer? You can freeze frankfurters for up to a month. First, remove the dogs from the store packaging, which is not meant to withstand long periods in the deep cold. Repackage by double-wrapping in a moisture-proof product, like heavy-duty foil or freezer paper. Wrap tightly, making sure the entire item is sealed in. Use freezer tape if needed, to seal the wrap shut.

Double-wrap pork

When freezing pork roast for more than four or five months, double-wrap it.

? How Long Will Frozen Meat Last?

ANSWER: Up to a year

Solid chunks of meat will keep longer in the freezer than cut-up pieces.

• Store beef roasts and steaks in the freezer for up to a year, but beef cubes for no more than three months.

• Pork roasts can be frozen for up to eight months, but pork chops will last only up to four months. Cubes of pork will last just a few months in the freezer.

Be poultry wise

Whole, uncooked chickens or turkeys can be frozen for up to a year. If you plan to freeze a bird for more than a few months, remove the giblets and freeze separately. Cooked chicken and turkey, properly wrapped, can keep in the freezer for two to three months. Be sure to remove all air from the freezer bag before popping it into the freezer.

Get cooked turkey quickly to the fridge or freezer

According to the Louisiana State University Agriculture Center, you have about two hours from the time you remove a turkey from the oven to safely serve and refrigerate or freeze your leftovers. This includes turkey, stuffing, and gravy. Here's why: Bacteria grow fast. They can multiply to undesirable levels on perishable food left at room temperature for more than two hours and can cause food-borne illness. Here are some more tips on handling turkey or other poultry:

• Before refrigerating or freezing: Remove the meat from the bones. Legs and wings may be left whole.

• If you're freezing turkey and stuffing, wrap each separately, using heavy foil or freezer wrap, or place it in a freezer container.

• For best quality, use frozen turkey and stuffing within a month. It will lose moisture after that, thereby diminishing texture and flavor. Use refrigerated leftovers within three days.

Don't unwrap before thawing

Thaw poultry in its original freezer wrapper. Defrost in the refrigerator or in cold water. Keep the wrapper tight until poultry is defrosted, unwrapping when the job is complete.

Not all frozen meats need to thaw before cooking

Frozen chicken pieces can be held under running water to separate, then cooked as usual, adding just five minutes to the cooking time. Whole roasts, while best if thawed, can be cooked frozen. Lower your cooking temperature by 30 to 50 degrees below what you would use for a fresh roast, then add half the cooking time again onto the time your roast spends in the oven.

❁

Grandma says...

"The wise use of leftovers will benefit your pocketbook. Freeze leftover cooked meats for up to three months to use in stews, hashes, quiches, or stir-fries."

ooo

Dairy Products

You'd be surprised how simple it is to prolong the life of dairy products safely by following some basic advice. You can freeze many dairy products, too. So go ahead, take advantage of that sale on butter or cheese and stock up.

Turn it over

To prevent mold from growing in an opened container of cottage cheese, turn it upside down and give it a shake. Store it this way. Mold grows in the layers of oxygen that gather under the opened lid, but your shake and turn stop the process.

Longer-lasting milk

Good news for those who drink milk infrequently or buy it only for their coffee. You can prolong the life of a container of milk by dropping a pinch or two of baking soda into the container and giving it a shake. The baking soda will reduce the milk's acidity, staving off spoilage.

Stop crystallization

Ice cream kept too long in the freezer forms crystals along the top. After opening a container of ice cream, cover with plastic wrap before replacing the lid.

Freeze butter

When butter goes on sale, buy extra. It will keep in the freezer for up to four months. No special thawing is needed; just place it in the fridge.

Quick-freeze dairy products

Most dairy products are not good candidates for freezing. Fats separate and don't always reintegrate well. You may, however, find that you can freeze milk and even cream for short periods if you follow this method: Pour milk or cream into meticulously cleaned glass jars, leaving 2 inches (5 cm) of headroom for the liquid to expand. Seal jars tightly and place in the coldest part of your freezer. The goal is to freeze the product quickly. Milk should keep for up to five months; cream only for two or three months. Thaw at room temperature for 3 to 4 hours before using.

Freeze cheese

Many cheeses will keep well for up to six months in the freezer. The key is to freeze small pieces that weigh 1 pound (450 grams) or less and that are not more than 1 inch (25mm) thick. It works well with both hard and soft cheeses. Good candidates include brick, cheddar, Camembert, Edam, Gouda, mozzarella, Muenster, Port Salut, provolone, and Swiss. Wrap the cheese tightly in freezer wrap, and store in a freezer bag to keep moisture from developing. You can also grate the cheese first, then store it in freezer bags for several months.

Seal your eggs

Prolong the lifespan of fresh eggs by rubbing the shells with vegetable oil. Now your eggs should last from three to five weeks in the refrigerator.

How to freeze eggs

Frozen eggs will keep for up to six months. You can freeze scrambled whole eggs or can freeze whites or yolks alone.

• Freeze egg whites in airtight containers singly or as called for in recipes you use most often. Leave a little headroom in the container for the whites to expand as they freeze.

• Whole eggs or yolks can become hard when frozen. To avoid this, stabilize them by stirring 1 teaspoon of either salt or honey into 1 cup of eggs—that's about five whole eggs or a dozen yolks. Freeze in an airtight container. Mark which ingredient was added. You'll want to know for cooking purposes later so that you can reduce the salt or sweetener in your recipe. If you like, spoon the scrambled eggs into ice-cube trays for individual portions. When they're frozen, pop the egg cubes out and store them in an airtight freezer bag.

Baked Goods

Nothing says home like home-baked goodies. It's not diffi-
cult to keep those cakes, pies, and cookies fresh until the
last morsel is gobbled up. Mostly, it's a matter of knowing
when to refrigerate and how best to wrap for freshness.

Cool cakes before storing

Many unfrosted cakes will keep
well on your countertop for up
to a week if wrapped in plastic
wrap, kept under a cake dome,
or if the cake is covered in foil.
The key is to cool the cake completely before wrapping—
wrapping before the cake is cool
encourages mold growth in the
pockets of moisture. Set the cake
in the pan on a wire rack to cool
until you can touch it without
hurting your fingers. Then
remove the cake from the pan,
and continue cooling on the
rack. Finally, set it on a cake
dish. Keep the wrapped or
domed cake in an area free from
moisture and humidity.

ProTip

WHIP TOPPING AT LAST MINUTE

Whipped-cream frosting doesn't
hold up more than a day or two in
the fridge. It becomes "weepy" and
loses its consistency. So if you need
to make the cake in advance, don't
whip up the topping until just before
you serve it. You might even serve up
the whipped cream in a nice bowl
and let your guests dollop on their
own frosting.

Refrigerate frosted cakes with dairy-based frosting

If a cake frosting is made with
eggs, custard, whipped cream,
or cream cheese, you'll have to
refrigerate the cake. You can take
it from the refrigerator and
bring it to room temperature
prior to cutting the first time
you serve, of course. Chilling
the cake may lessen the flavors,
so you'll want to remove it from
the refrigerator again before
serving seconds.

Some frostings are nonperishable

Some frostings are safe to keep
out of the fridge. Cakes frosted
with store-bought, canned frostings are usually fine for about
five days on your counter if
properly covered under a dome
or a loose-fitting helmet of foil.

What's inside counts

Cakes with fruit filling or topping, cakes with perishable
ingredients, and cheesecakes
must be refrigerated.

Triple-wrap cakes

To retain that just-baked freshness, you can freeze unfrosted
cakes for several months if you
triple-wrap them first. Once it
has cooled, wrap each layer of
the cake in plastic, then foil.
Next pop the layers into a freezer bag and squeeze out the
excess air. When defrosting, let
the cake come to room temperature before rewrapping.

An instant cake-keeper

If you don't have a cake-keeper
or glass dome, it's easy to
improvise one. Just put a large
bowl upside down over the cake
to protect it.

Give your pies an encore

Baking two pies isn't much
more trouble than baking one.
So when baking a pie for dinner tonight, do yourself a favor
and double the recipe. Once
you've baked and cooled both
pies, wrap the extra one in plastic and foil, and pop it into a
freezer bag for later use.

Keep store-bought pies covered

Got some leftover store-bought
pie? Before you stick it in the
fridge, cover the pie with a
paper plate or an aluminum
pie plate, then wrap the entire
package in a couple of layers
of plastic wrap. This method
allows some air to surround
the pie, rather than smothering
it with plastic. You'll keep the
freshness in for up to a week
or more.

Climate is key to keeping cookies fresh

When storing crisp cookies, the humidity of the climate you live in makes a big difference. If you live in a dry climate, store the cookies in a container or jar with a loose-fitting lid; if you live in a humid climate, cover them tightly.

Grandma says...

"Use an apple wedge to keep your soft cookies fresh. Store the cookies in a tightly covered container and place the apple slice, skin side down, on top before closing the lid. Moisture from the apple helps prevent the cookies from drying out. Replace the apple every two days."

Keep cream cheese and custard cookies cool

Always refrigerate cookies that are made with cream cheese or that have with a custard filling or frosting. If you just cover them loosely with aluminum foil, they should keep for the better part of a week.

Freezing is fine for most cookies

You can store fully baked and cooled cookies in the freezer for several months if you put them in a sealed, airtight container. Unfortunately, freezing is not recommended for cookies with low butterfat content, because they tend to dry out.

Keep your cookie dough

Tightly wrap your homemade cookie dough in plastic, and it will last for up to three or four days in the fridge before it begins to loose its consistency. Need to store it longer? Pop the wrapped dough in the freezer, and it will last for at least a month before the flavor fades and consistency breaks down.

Freeze for the long term

Store-bought sliced soft bread can last in your breadbox or on the shelf for several days. Extend its life by refrigerating the loaf in its bag for up to a week or freeze it for up to six months. So feel free to take advantage of that sale, and you'll always have a loaf handy. Defrost at room temperature.

Refresh crusty breads in the microwave

French and Italian loaves, fresh muffins, and rolls have short life spans. Keep them in a paper bag on the counter or in a breadbox for several days. Refresh a slightly stale muffin or chunk of French or Italian bread by sprinkling it lightly with water and microwaving or baking it briefly in an oven or a toaster oven. Or you can slice it in half and put it in a regular toaster.

Dried breadcrumbs last long

Dried breadcrumbs can be refrigerated for two months or frozen for up to a year. Seal fresh bread crumbs in a plastic bag or tightly closed plastic container and refrigerate for up to two weeks.

Cans and Jars of Food

When purchasing canned goods from the store, always buy those in best condition. Don't buy dented cans. Jars should be rust-free and show no signs of leakage or cracking.

Keep cans cool

Store canned goods in a pantry or shelving system that is cool and dry. Ideal temperatures for canned products are between 50° and 70° F (10° and 21° C). Keep cans out of direct sunlight and away from hot pipes or heat registers. If you must store canned goods in temperatures above 75° F (24° C), use them within a year, rather than two years.

Know what the dates mean

Many nonperishable food products are printed with a "sell by" date, a "best if used by" date, or a "use by" date. They are not safety dates. Except for infant formula and some baby foods, product dating is not required by federal regulations. Furthermore, there is no universally accepted system for food dating in North America. Generally speaking, commercially processed cans in good condition should last up to two years on your pantry shelf. Packaged nonperishable foods stored in the pantry may last a year or more.

These three basic types of dating on canned and other goods should guide your purchase:

• The "sell by" date indicates to the store how long to display the product for sale. Consumers can use this date too. Buy the product before the date expires so you will have time to use it at best quality.

• The "best if used by" date is recommended for best flavor or quality; it is not a purchase or safety date.

• The "use by" date is the last date recommended for the use of the product at its peak quality or flavor, as determined by the manufacturer.

If you see coded dates that are difficult to understand, don't worry that you're missing something. These numbers are used by the manufacturer to rotate stock, and they help them find their merchandise on store shelves in case of a product recall.

☞ DON'T
freeze peanut butter

Freezing breaks down the oils in peanut butter, changing its texture. This makes the peanut butter more difficult to spread, as well as less palatable.

Do refrigerate natural peanut butter

Labels on natural peanut butter advise you to refrigerate them after opening because they have no preservatives to protect them from molds and pests. Refrigeration discourages molds.

Keep the peanut butter flowing

In many households there's no worry about peanut butter going bad; it's eaten up too

❓ How Long Will Canned Foods Last?

ANSWER: **Two years or more**

There is an easy rule of thumb for storage times for canned foods:

• Canned acidic foods, such as tomatoes, are best if used within 18 months of purchase.

• Canned low-acid foods, such as meat or vegetables, will keep two or more years on your shelf, providing your storage area is cool and dry.

✦ BEST ADVICE ✦ **Canned Food**

USE WITHIN 1 1/2 YEARS IF THE FOOD IS ACIDIC, LIKE TOMATOES

KEEP CANS AT ROOM TEMPERATURE OR BELOW

USE WITHIN 2 YEARS IF THE FOOD IS NOT ACIDIC

STORE IN A DARK, DRY CABINET OR PANTRY

quickly. But what often causes family arguments is the question of whether this favorite food needs refrigeration. The answer is no! Refrigerating peanut butter makes it more difficult to spread. However, once the jar is opened, the flavor will begin to break down after a few months, so if you will have it that long, by all means keep it in the fridge. An unopened jar of peanut butter will last on the shelf for several years.

Dried Cooking Staples

Because rice, pasta, grains, beans, baking supplies, and other staples are dried, we think of them as impervious. But the truth is, these staples are delicate and susceptible to insect infestations and mold growth. A little storage sense will prolong their life.

Treat rice right for long life

How you should store rice depends on the type:

• White rice of any variety keeps almost indefinitely as long as it remains unopened in its original package. No refrigeration needed. Once opened, put the rice into a tightly sealed container that will keep out dust, moisture, and insects. Stored like this, rice will keep for several months.

• Brown rice requires more care, as it is a more delicate cousin of white rice. The bran left on the grain contains oils that may spoil the product if it's not properly cared for. Unopened packages will keep for about six months on the pantry shelf and only about two months when opened and transferred to airtight containers. In humid weather, be sure to refrigerate brown rice.

• Wild rice (which is not really rice) is a better keeper than brown rice and should last indefinitely on your pantry shelf in an unopened package. Once opened, wild rice should hold up well if kept in a tightly sealed container.

Barley is tough stuff

The barley you buy in most supermarkets is pearled barley; the bran has been removed and the barley polished. It usually comes in a box, and an unopened box will keep almost indefinitely on the shelf. Once you open the box, transfer the barley to a sealed airtight container, where it will keep for a year.

Preserve your pasta

With spaghetti and other dried pasta, the most important thing is to keep them dry and contained. Dried pastas left sealed in their packages should keep for several months on your pantry shelf. To store pasta longer, place it in a tightly sealed glass or plastic container, and store it in a cool, dry, and dark cabinet for as long as a year.

Keep honey cool and dry

Store honey at room temperature on a dry, dark kitchen shelf. Honey should last a year on your shelf. Do not refrigerate because that will cause the honey to crystallize.

• After using honey, wipe around the lid and make sure the seal is tight to keep moisture and air out.

• If crystallization forms in your honey jar, place the jar in a pot of warm—not boiling—water until the crystals dissolve.

Just keep your beans dry

Once you open a plastic package of dried beans, transfer the contents to a sealed plastic container and store in a cool, dark place, where it is not likely to be affected by moisture. Stored in this manner, dried beans of all types should keep indefinitely.

Herbs and Spices, Nuts and Seeds

Good cooks rely on a well-stocked spice cupboard. When you reach for that dried herb or spice, you want to know it will be full of all the flavor you expect.

Store dried spices and herbs in airtight containers

All herbs and spices need to be stored in a cool, dark, dry place. Dried herbs and spices in the whole or broken form keep longer than ground ones. Once they are ground, they begin to loose their taste and potency immediately. So if you are buying in the whole state, be sure to grind only what you need immediately. Or create something with them and then preserve the spices. Make paste or pesto (herbs in oil) or sauce and then freeze them—or use them in some recipe that you plan to freeze. Always date the container or jar, and check the contents frequently.

Bag fresh herbs

Most fresh herbs should be washed, patted thoroughly dry with paper towels, and slipped into a plastic bag, then stored in the refrigerator, where they will last for up to several days. Fresh herbs are delicate, so they can be tricky to dry. To prevent them from cracking and to minimize loss, let the herbs rest on the paper towel in the bag.

Make a basil bouquet

Keep fresh basil in a jar of water, as if it were a bouquet of flowers, until you're ready to use it. Trim off the bottom of the stems before you put them in the water. Try to buy the basil no more than one to three days before you plan to use it. The same trick works with parsley, watercress, and other leafy herbs.

Make convenient portion cubes

Freeze ice-cube trays filled with chopped fresh herbs. Then pop the cubes into freezer bags so you can defrost just what you need when you need it.

ProTip

CHOP BEFORE FREEZING

Chefs know that if you freeze the entire leaves of fresh herbs such as basil, they'll often crackle, which causes them to loose flavor. You won't have this problem if you wash and dry the herbs, then chop them up before freezing. Freeze your prepared herbs in freezer bags; they'll last for up to six months.

A cool cabinet is nice for spice

Store-bought dried herbs and spices should be kept in a cool, dark cabinet. Most will keep up to about a year before losing their essential nature. Don't

---

❓ How Long Will Herbs and Spices Last?

ANSWER: **Six months to five years, depending on type**

It may seem like a bargain to buy that two-pound container of oregano at the discount store. But it's a lousy deal if the stuff turns tasteless before you get a chance to use it. Keep the following guidelines in mind the next time that you consider bulk buying:

• Ground herbs, spices, rubs, and blends are generally good for six months to a year. Even those with salt don't hold up beyond a year.

• Whole seeds, beans, flowers, and leaves are good for one to three years.

• Barks, roots, and some tubers are good for up to five years.

Herb and Spice Jars

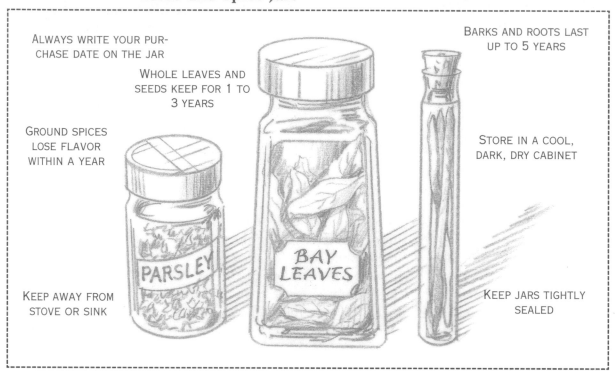

ALWAYS WRITE YOUR PUR-
CHASE DATE ON THE JAR

WHOLE LEAVES AND
SEEDS KEEP FOR 1 TO
3 YEARS

GROUND SPICES
LOSE FLAVOR
WITHIN A YEAR

KEEP AWAY FROM
STOVE OR SINK

BARKS AND ROOTS LAST
UP TO 5 YEARS

STORE IN A COOL,
DARK, DRY CABINET

KEEP JARS TIGHTLY
SEALED

PARSLEY

BAY
LEAVES

store them in an open rack on the wall. Exposure to light and heat will hurry the loss of flavor in these delicate seasonings.

Don't store spices near heat

It's tempting to line up your favorite herbs and spices over the stove, where they'll be handy for cooking. But this location speeds the drying process, causing them to lose flavor faster. Over the sink is also a bad storage spot—too much humidity.

Don't hang your herbs

Don't hang fresh herbs in bunches on the wall; bugs will get to them if the light doesn't do them in first.

Fresh ginger and chilies like room temperature

Fresh rhizomes, such as ginger and galangal, can be kept at room temperature for several weeks. The same goes for chilies and garlic.

Dry herbs in the microwave

A special dehydrator is great for drying fresh herbs, but if you don't have one, you can use the microwave. Set the microwave on half power, and turn it on in 10-second intervals until the herbs are dry.

Should you keep it?

How to know if that herb or spice is still good? First look at it. Is it still bright in color or has it faded? Are there any granules in it or appearance of bugs, weevils, or black spots? Black spots may be bug excrement. Has it gotten moldy or formed any foreign bumps, which may be fungus, bug nests, or such? You may have to pour it into a clear glass or dish to view the whole sample. If it passes that test, smell it. If it still smells like spices or herbs, it is still good. If it has no odor, then stir it up. Does this release the smell? If it has

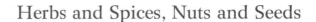
no smell, it won't have any taste either.

Get more flavor from dried herbs

Dried herbs may not be quite as savory as fresh ones. But often they are all you have on hand. And there are a couple of ways that you can spark up their flavor in no time. First, always crumble dried herbs between your hands before adding them to a dish. This will help to release more flavor during cooking. Second, before adding dried herbs to a sauce or salad

dressing, put them in hot water for a moment and then drain. They'll be greener as well as more flavorful.

Keep the joy in your almonds

If you use almonds on a regular basis in salads or for snacking, keep them in the refrigerator. They'll stay fresh for up to nine months.

If you buy almonds in bulk or don't plan to use your shelled almonds right away, freeze them; they'll keep for a year.

Almonds in their shells are best kept in a tightly sealed container in a cool, dry location. Inspect the shells for cracks and discard those.

Take advantage of Mother Nature's container

Nuts in their shells will keep in a bowl in your kitchen or dining room for up to a month. The nutshell should be free of cracks and mold, and the nuts should feel heavy. If a nut rattles inside its shell, it is likely dried out. To keep nuts in the shell for up to six months, refrigerate them in a tightly sealed container.

Refrigerate after opening

Shelled nuts in unopened cans or jars will last up to a year in your pantry. Once you open the container, though, they will begin to spoil. If you reseal the jar or can tightly, you can expect the nuts to last about a week on the shelf or up to six months in the refrigerator. Want them to last a year or more? Place the container in a freezer bag and freeze. Before freezing, check for moldy or discolored nuts and discard those.

---

new uses for Old Spices

When seasonings have lost too much taste to enjoy in cooking, you may still be able to enjoy their aroma, according to Mora Blackmarsh, herbalist and aromatherapist at Dragonmarsh, a California purveyor of bulk herbs. She suggests these uses for old herbs:

• Try boiling your old herbs in water on the stove or in a potpourri dish. Sometimes you can coax some scent out. Once you bring the stovetop mixture to a boil, turn down the heat to let it simmer, and the scent will permeate the air.

• Another technique is to burn old herbs and spices directly on an incense charcoal or on a dish. Or just toss them in your fireplace.

Pots, Pans, and Utensils

It's nice to have just one set of pots and pans and add to it over the years, rather than having to replace those that haven't held up. Here are a few simple methods of making your pots, pans, and utensils last.

Keep cast iron seasoned

Clean and reseason any pans showing rust or that make food stick. First heat the pan to a touchable temperature; then clean it thoroughly in hot water to remove food residue. Dry completely. Next coat the pan with grease or vegetable oil. Place the pan in a preheated 275° F (135° C) oven for 15 minutes. Pour out excess grease, and return to the oven for two hours.

☞ NEVER
scour cast iron

> Never use scouring pads or detergent on your cast-iron cookware. Instead, clean it with hot water and gentle scraping. Dry the cookware thoroughly and store it with lids off to prevent moisture from accumulating and causing rust.

Renew the gasket on your pressure cooker

Long before microwave ovens came on the scene, pressure cookers provided a way to reduce cooking times. Plus a pressure cooker will tenderize tough cuts of meats—something you can't do in a microwave. Not to mention that your mom's pressure cooker will still be steaming away after you've junked your next three or four microwave ovens. The only part of a pressure cooker that usually wears out is the gasket. If the gasket on yours is dried out or won't seal, try soaking it for 20 minutes in hot water, then rub it with vegetable oil. If it doesn't soften up, get a new gasket from the manufacturer or a cookware store.

Camp cookware is easy to care for

Your tin pots and utensils are an important camping companion. Here's some simple ways to make sure that they'll be around for a full lifetime of outdoor adventures:

• To prevent scratching your cookware, stir with a wooden spoon or a whittled stick.

• Be careful never to boil out liquid in your tinware pots. Overheating weakens the pot's integrity.

• Clean your tinware immediately after you finish cooking with it and wipe it dry with a soft cloth.

• If you don't plan to use your tinware vessel again soon, protect it with a light coat of mineral oil.

Copper care is simple

Keep your copper pots or copper-bottom pans in mint condition by following these simple guidelines:

• Don't use abrasives such as steel wool that will scratch the finish. Instead, soak immediately after cooking, and wash with a sponge or cloth. For tough jobs, leave the cookware to soak overnight.

• Avoid scratching your cookware by using only wooden, plastic, or nylon utensils when you are cooking.

• To avoid scorching, don't cook at the highest temperatures.

Brighten copper

Freshen up the copper with a paste made from cream of tartar and enough lemon juice to moisten. Rub the mixture on the copper, and let stand for five minutes. Wash in warm water and dry.

Don't machine-wash wood

Dishwashers are so convenient that it's always tempting to

throw everything in there. But put your wooden spoons and wood-handled utensils aside for hand washing. The heated drying cycle in your dishwasher robs wood of its natural oils. Dried-out wood utensils will crack and break, but those you hand-wash will reward you with many years of service.

The right oil is good for wood

Most wooden kitchen tools and bowls will benefit from a coat of oil when their surfaces seem dry and dull, but you have to use the right oil. Never use vegetable oil—it will become rancid and sticky. And never use furniture oils; they may include ingredients that are not safe for use with food. Look for products labeled "salad bowl oil" or "spoon oil." These contain mineral oil or sometimes a nut oil, such as walnut, combined with beeswax. Be aware that some wooden bowls and utensils

have a permanent surface finish that precludes oiling; check the cleaning directions that came with the item.

How to clean a wooden cutting board

Wipe the board with a clean, dry cloth after each use. To remove stuck foodstuffs, wipe vigorously with a hot, wet sponge or cloth; then towel off excess water, and dry upright in a dish rack.

Turn the board over

Trees suck water out of the ground through a network of tiny straws called cells. As a result, you can think of a cutting board as a pile of tiny straws glued together and laid on their side. When you chop on the board, you slice the top layer of cells. This means that a nicked-up side of a cutting board will suck up moisture from the food and even the air more readily than an undisturbed side. So to

get maximum life from your cutting board and to keep it flat and prevent cracks, be sure to use both sides.

Sand the fuzz away

If your wooden item has become a little fuzzy, it's because moisture has raised the grain. In this case, smooth the wood with medium-grit sandpaper followed by fine sandpaper before applying oil.

☞ DON'T
soak cutting boards

Never soak a wooden cutting board. Cracking and warping occur when wood repeatedly goes from a wet to dry state.

Keep it cool

Don't set hot pots and pans on a wooden cutting board. They'll leave burn marks and can warp the wood.

Kitchen Knives

Having a sharp, well-balanced knife for fast food preparation—and caring for it properly—can make the difference between the joy of cooking and kitchen frustration.

Skip the dishwasher

If your knives have wooden handles, you should never put them in the dishwasher or immerse the handles in a sink full of water. The process of wetting and drying wooden handles can make them crack. To clean your knives, simply wipe them off with a soft, damp, soapy cloth and then rinse them under running water. In fact, this is the best way to clean any kitchen knife, even ones with "dishwasher-proof" plastic handles; dishwasher jets can knock knives around, damaging their edges when they knock into other utensils. By washing knives separately, you also eliminate the possibility of cutting yourself while fishing around for sharp knives in a sink full of water.

Clean quickly

Some foods contain acids that can quickly start to stain even "stainless steel." To keep your knives in great shape, get in the habit of wiping them clean immediately after each use.

Keep 'em sharp

The edges on kitchen knives are different than the edges on other knives and cutting tools. A knife or chisel designed to cut wood, for example, is made of harder steel, and it relies on a straight, thin edge to keep it sharp. When the edge on these tools dulls, you rub them on a flat stone to remove steel to make the edge thin and sharp again. The edge of a kitchen knife blade is also thin, but it has saw teeth that are so small you'd need a microscope to see them. The teeth let the knife bite easily into soft foods, like a tomato. The knife becomes dull because these teeth get bent. So to sharpen, you want to use a sharpening steel to straighten the teeth, rather than remove them. Get in the habit of using the steel before or after each time you use the knife.

How to sharpen a knife

To use a sharpening steel, hold it vertically with the tip down on a solid surface. Place the knife blade against the steel at an angle of about 20 degrees. Start with the heel of the blade (the part of the cutting edge closest to the handle) against the steel. Pull the blade down and across toward you. Do this five or ten times, alternating sides of the blade. Eventually, using the steel will no longer sharpen the blade. This means it's time to have the knife professionally sharpened.

A sharp knife is a safe knife

A sharp knife gives you control as it glides through the food. A dull knife can slip, which can result in a nasty cut.

Whiten bone handles

Bone knife handles invariably yellow with age. In fact, some folks like this aged patina. If you don't, all you have to do to whiten them is occasionally wrap the handles in a piece of flannel moistened with hydrogen peroxide and water.

Preserve your knives with the right cutting surface

Your knives will dull quickly if you cut against hard surfaces, such as marble, metal, ceramic, or glass. So be sure to use a cutting board made of wood or plastic—softer materials the knife can cut into.

✦ BEST ADVICE ✦ **Kitchen Knives**

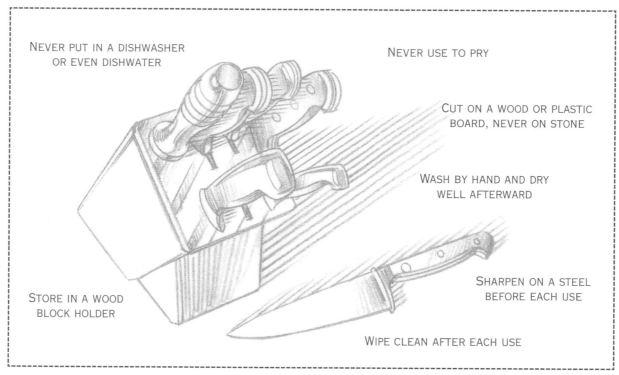

NEVER PUT IN A DISHWASHER
OR EVEN DISHWATER

NEVER USE TO PRY

CUT ON A WOOD OR PLASTIC
BOARD, NEVER ON STONE

WASH BY HAND AND DRY
WELL AFTERWARD

STORE IN A WOOD
BLOCK HOLDER

SHARPEN ON A STEEL
BEFORE EACH USE

WIPE CLEAN AFTER EACH USE

Cut peppers from the inside

The waxy exterior of bell peppers is harder on knives than the soft, fleshy interior. So when slicing peppers, cut them open and then slice them from the inside.

Store knives in a wooden block

Storing your kitchen knives in slotted wooden blocks keeps them safe from nicks in the blades that are sure to occur if you keep you knives in a drawer. It also keeps them handy and protects you from cuts that might occur if you accidentally grab a knife by the blade.

Dry knives thoroughly

To ward off rust, make sure your knife blades are completely dry before sliding them into the knife block. You'll also prevent mold from developing inside the wooden block slots.

Take special care with ceramic knives

Like most things in life, ceramic kitchen knives are a trade-off. These relatively new additions to the kitchen stay very sharp for a very long time. Food and food odors don't adhere to them, they don't rust, and they wipe clean with ease. On the downside, ceramic knives are brittle. Unlike a flexible, resilient steel knife, a ceramic knife cannot withstand pressure. Don't use it, for example, to bone a chicken. If you absentmindedly grab your ceramic knife to crush a piece of garlic with the side of the blade, you might snap the blade.

Don't pry with a knife

When you need to pry open a jar, it's tempting to grab that kitchen knife. Don't do it! Not only can you ruin the knife by bending and dulling the blade, you might end up with a deep cut in your hand.

Buy to Keep: A Chef's Knife

Sure, you can buy a dozen kitchen knives to do everything from slicing to paring to chopping. And if your budget is unlimited, it's fun to have a repertoire of knives to choose from. But if your money is limited, the smart approach is to invest in one top-quality chef's knife.

Length and shape	A knife with an 8-inch (20-cm) blade is long enough to slice through a large roast or quickly chop up a large onion, yet handy enough to let you deftly mince garlic. A good chef's knife has a curved blade so you can chop and mince with a quick rocking motion.
Handle	The part of a blade that joins it to the handle is called the tang. For strength and durability, look for a tang that goes completely through the handle and is attached with rivets through the side. In most full-tang knives, the handle is in two pieces, one attached to each side of the tang. The handle should be made of hardwood or good-quality plastic, and it should be smooth all around, with the rivets perfectly flush to the handle.
Blade	Get a blade made of high-carbon steel; it will stay sharp and be easy to clean. The best and most expensive models are forged. These knives have a thicker area between the knife and handle called a bolster. This extra steel makes the knife more balanced and easier to use when chopping. Knives can also be stamped from a sheet of high-carbon steel. This makes a fine knife, but stamping precludes a bolster. The most important thing is that the knife you choose feels comfortable and balanced in your hand—you might even prefer a knife without a bolster.

Silver and China

Caring for your fine china and silver items is delicate work but well worth the effort.

Keep silver under wraps

Wrap silver in plastic wrap or washed cotton, linen, or polyester to deter tarnish. You can also purchase specially designed bags or silver cloths to store your silver. Don't store in wool, felt, chamois, or newspaper, which can induce tarnish or, by contact, remove silver plating.

Never machine-wash silver-plated items

Don't put silver-plated utensils in the dishwasher. Detergents, high wash temperatures, and hot-air drying wear away the plating. Instead, hand-wash your plated silver and polish twice a year or so with a paste-style silver polish, sold in grocery stores and specialty houseware departments.

Cushion your china

If you don't use your fine china much and don't display it in a china closet, consider purchasing quilted bags and pouches designed to protect china. They keep your dishes dust-free and prevent chipping.

Spare the detergent

Antique hand-painted or metal-trimmed china should not be placed in the dishwasher, where harsh detergents and hot water may damage it. For a large set that you think may be suitable for the dishwasher, test by repeatedly washing one piece in the dishwasher over several weeks. Compare it to the rest of the set to see if it has faded.

Dishwasher safe

Whether you've inherited it from Great-grandma or intend to pass your own on to your progeny, you'll be pleased to know that some fine china dinnerware can safely go into the dishwasher. Just be sure to use the proper settings—"light wash" or "china." Stack the dishes carefully to avoid knocking during the wash cycle. Set the dry cycle for air-dry to avoid exposure to high heat.

Keep aluminum away from china

Black marks may appear on china or other white dishes if aluminum utensils, even foil baking dishes, rub against the china during the wash cycle. Be sure to load the dishwasher so no aluminum touches the china. If black marks do occur on your china, use a plastic scouring pad and a mildly abrasive cleaner to gently scrub them off.

Soak away tea stains

Make tea stains disappear from fine china cups by mixing up a solution of 2 tablespoons chlorine bleach in a quart of water. Soak the stained cup for just a minute or two; then rinse immediately and thoroughly.

Don't store crystal glasses upside down

Crystal glasses are fragile. Store them right side up. This way you won't put pressure on the lip of the glasses, possibly causing them to crack.

Hand-wash crystal

Never put crystal items in the dishwasher. They may crack or chip, and they will certainly fog from the heated water. Wash crystal items individually by hand in lukewarm soapy water with a mild soap. Rinse clear.

Watch your jewelry

Avoid wearing bracelets and rings when removing crystal from the cabinet. It's easy to crack the glass during a casual run-in with jewelry.

☛ DON'T
shine pewter

Gently wash pewter by hand and dry it. Don't try to rub it until it shines. Pewter is meant to have a dull patina. It shouldn't look like silver.

Tablecloths and Napkins

Think of fabric as a living, breathing medium—after all, the origin of most tableware is living cotton, flax, or perhaps silk. To keep these goods fresh and attractive, they need light and air and a gentle touch. Knowing how much of each is the secret to long life for your linens.

Store in view

If you have the space, use a drying rack or a quilt rack to store your attractive tablecloths. It keeps wrinkles to a minimum, making ironing easier and reducing the chances that you might scorch or burn a cherished cloth. This works nicely for vintage cloths or those whose patterns might brighten up your guest room. Try to keep them out of direct sunlight so that the colors won't fade. Check them frequently to make sure dust isn't collecting. Shake out dust and replace on racks.

Grandma says...

"To help your white table linens retain that crisp white look, dry them outdoors in the sun. The sunlight will bleach the fabric. Of course, you want to keep colored linens out of direct sunlight— or they'll fade."

°°°

Keep linens dust free

If you can't display them all, store your delicate linen and cotton tablecloths in tissue paper and lay them flat. This will protect the linens from sunlight, which can fade or discolor them, and will keep them dust-free.

Use the washer

Although many finer cloths recommend dry cleaning, you will find that other cloths and table linens do fine in the washing machine. In fact, cloths with linen fibers benefit by this treatment because the fibers become more luminous the more they are washed. Place the cloth in a mesh bag designed for fine washables, use a mild detergent, and wash on delicate setting. Hang to dry.

Wash in warm water

When washing white or lighter-colored linens, use warm, not hot, water to prevent running. Colored items should be washed in cool water. Linen is highly absorbent, so be sure to use enough water to disperse the soap.

Try this drying trick

Before hanging your linens to dry, you can remove excess water by laying the item along an absorbent towel and rolling tightly. The towel will sop up a lot of water, and your cloth will dry more quickly and with fewer wrinkles. Quicker drying time prevents mold from developing.

Keep it flexible

No matter which drying method you use, be sure to remove the linen from the line or the dryer while it is still damp. When dried thoroughly, linen becomes brittle and takes hours to recover its natural moisture and full flexibility.

Be kind to your linens with a prewash protocol

How you treat your fine table linens before you wash them is just as important as how you treat them during washing and drying. Here's a checklist of simple things to do to make your treasured linens last a lifetime:

• Always shake out any excess food or crumbs before washing.

• Check the inside of your machines. Look for objects that may have fallen from pockets and lodged in the washer, such as a paper clip or a coin, that could scratch or mar your linen.

• Wash tablecloths and napkins immediately after using them; don't wait until you have a full load. It's better to do a small

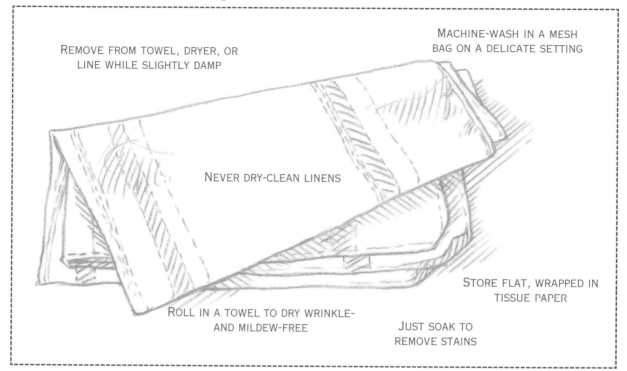

REMOVE FROM TOWEL, DRYER, OR
LINE WHILE SLIGHTLY DAMP

MACHINE-WASH IN A MESH
BAG ON A DELICATE SETTING

NEVER DRY-CLEAN LINENS

STORE FLAT, WRAPPED IN
TISSUE PAPER

ROLL IN A TOWEL TO DRY WRINKLE-
AND MILDEW-FREE

JUST SOAK TO
REMOVE STAINS

load with the napkins and tablecloths of one type. Plus, immediate washing may prevent stains from setting.

• Don't mix fabrics in the washer or dryer. Poly/cotton blends should not be mixed with straight polyester cloths. Cottons should go alone.

• Be sure to wash darks and lights separately to keep the lights from becoming dingy.

• For fine linens, use the most delicate settings on your washer and a low temperature or light setting on your dryer. Use a permanent-press cycle for poly/cotton blends.

• Use mild detergents; don't use any bleach.

• If you are concerned about using too much heat, halfway through the drying cycle, decrease the dryer temperature setting to FLUFF or AIR-DRY to avoid wrinkling.

☞ DON'T
dry–clean linen

If at all possible, clean heirloom linens and other delicate fabrics at home. Dry cleaning is not recommended, because the agitation, harsh chemicals, and heat used can damage them.

Try using the vacuum

To remove surface dirt and dust from your delicate antique linens, carefully vacuum the item on low suction. For extra-delicate items, place a piece of tulle or fiberglass screen over them for protection, and vacuum through the screening. Tulle, sold by the yard for making veils or tutus, is readily available in any fabric store.

Soak stains

Time is your best ally when it comes to removing stains from linen. Mix a gentle detergent with warm water, and let your linen soak in the solution for two to three days. It may take that long to remove the stain. You can let it sit inside the washing machine to soak. Change the water once it becomes dirty by removing the cloth and setting the washer to the spin cycle. If the cloth is very sturdy, you don't have to remove it.

For stubborn stains

If you encounter a particularly resistant stain on linen, try using a solution of lemon juice and salt, mixed to form a paste and applied to the stain. Once you've lifted a stain from a linen item, give the cloth a thorough rinsing to make sure you get all the detergent out.

Stir to distribute suds

When cleaning or removing a stain from a fine or antique linen in a tub or in the washer that you are using only as a vessel, stir the cloth in its soapy water with a wooden spoon to distribute the soap.

Towel-dry to remove excess water

Once you have finished soaking or washing your fine or antique linen, pat the cloth in a towel to remove excess water. Allow to dry on the towel. Don't let the cloth hang unevenly, or it will dry misshapen. If you can dry it outdoors, place it on a white cloth or bedsheet to reflect the sun, but be careful not to get grass stains on the cloth.

Wash antique linens with special care

If you've removed stains by any of the above methods, you already know that gentle handling is what it takes to keep your antique linens clean. Here's how to wash these precious linens without causing damage:

• Test each item to see if it's colorfast by blotting with a white cloth dipped into a mild cleaning product. Ivory Liquid and similar products that say they're gentle or suitable for hand washing are recommended.

• Once you determine that the soap solution you choose is suited to your cloth, gently immerse the linen into the liquid and carefully agitate it by hand. You can do this in the washing machine basin, but without turning the machine on. Or you can do it in a bucket or another type of basin or in a stoppered sink. Allow the cloth to sit in the suds for about 5 minutes.

• Drain the soapy water, and run clear water over the item, swishing it and rinsing to remove all soap residue. You may need to do this rinse process several times as you manipulate the cloth to remove all suds. If your water is hard, consider using distilled water for the final rinse. Hard water may leave a mineral residue on your linens. Distilled water has been processed to remove those minerals.

Clothing & Accessories

Clothes—General Cleaning and Storage Guidelines

Being smart about laundering and dry-cleaning your clothes will go a long way toward making them last a long time. It will save you time and unnecessary expense, too.

Get out of the laundry quickly

Doing the laundry can be the bane of our existence. Just when all your clothes are washed, dried, and put away, the hampers have filled up again. Does it ever end? No, but here are some tips that can quicken the washing process and help extend the life of your clothes.

• Carefully measure detergent. Too little detergent doesn't do the job, leaving lint on your clothes that should have washed away with the rinse cycle. Too much detergent won't all rinse out in the wash, leaving your clothes looking dingy. Remember that if you're using cold water for the wash, use a little extra detergent.

• Add 1/2 cup of vinegar to the rinse cycle of the wash load. When you pull these clothes out of the dryer, they will be lint-free. Vinegar also helps soften your clothes and helps them smell fresh. It's cheaper than commercial products, too.

• If you're dealing with particularly muddy clothes, blast them with a hose first to get out as much mud as you can. They'll be cleaner after you wash them, and the dirt you got rid of won't have transferred to other clothes during washing.

• If suds cover the walls of your washer drum after finishing a load, throw in a handful of salt to make the suds disappear before the next load. Extra suds can leave traces of soap on your clothes.

Faster drying with less wrinkles

• Speed the drying of a small laundry load. Throw a towel or two into the dryer. The towel will help absorb the extra water, resulting in drier clothes in less time.

• If your clothes are wrinkled from sitting in the dryer too long, place a damp towel in the machine with the load and run it five more minutes. The wrinkles will disappear.

Take care with delicate fabrics

• Let soap dissolve when cleaning delicate fabrics. Run the water first in the washer if you're using the gentle cycle setting or in the sink if you're washing by hand. Pour the soap in and let it dissolve for 15 minutes; then wash as usual.

• To get out the musty smell from delicates, mix 4 tablespoons of baking soda with 1 quart (1 liter) of cool water. Let the clothes soak for about an hour; then wash the item as you normally would.

• To speed-dry delicate clothes, place them on a dry towel and roll it up carefully to remove excess water. Then place on a drying rack, or if it's a light piece, hang up using plastic, not wire, hangers. With that extra effort, your delicates will dry faster.

Don't get taken to the cleaners

Sometimes we pay someone else to clean our clothes. But take care: Just because you're paying doesn't mean that it will be done right. Before you head out to the cleaners with that pile of clothes, take these ideas into account.

• Look at the label. Clothes with labels that say "dry clean only" should go to the dry cleaners. But if the label just says "dry clean," then test to see if you can hand-wash the item first. Dab a little water on an unseen part of the garment. If you see colors run, then off to the cleaners you go. If not, you can wash it by hand, saving money and the wear and tear on your garment caused by dry-cleaning chemicals.

• Keep sets of clothes together. Dry-clean both parts of a suit or both parts of a dress and matching jacket at the same time. If you don't, your pieces will end up becoming different colors, as one will fade a bit and the other will stay closer to the original color.

• Remove clothes from wire hangers. When you get your newly dry-cleaned garments home, take them off the wire hangers, which can rust and stain clothing. Replace them with plastic hangers. However, if your cleaner has stuffed the sleeves with paper, leave it there—it will keep the garment in shape until you wear it.

• Compare prices. In some areas it is illegal to charge more to dry-clean women's suit, pants, or jackets than to dry-clean the same articles of men's clothing.

Don't let a stain get set

Treat stained clothing quickly, especially items that need to be dry-cleaned. It's best to take the garment to the cleaners as soon as possible after it's been stained. When you bring in a stained outfit, make sure to point the stain out to your cleaners. Left untreated, it can become permanent. If you've successfully treated the stain at home, tell them how you did it so they can take steps to avoid making the stain reappear. Never iron a stained garment; heat will set the stain.

Prevent mildew on stored clothes

It's sad to pull a piece of clothing out of storage only to find you have to throw it away because it has been attacked by mildew. Here are some simple steps to take before storing clothing to make sure mildew doesn't strike.

• Make sure the clothes are dry—air-dry them thoroughly or iron them dry.

• Don't put clothes in plastic bags that can trap moisture.

• Pack the items loosely so that air can circulate around them. And on a cool, dry day open the drawer or closet to ventilate them.

• Don't use starch or fabric finish on items that you plan to store; mildew loves to feed on these.

• Put mothballs or crystals in drawers or closets to absorb moisture.

☞ NEVER
store clothes in the garage

It may be tempting to make more room in the closet by moving a box of out-of-season clothing to the garage or basement. But if you store clothes in a damp garage or basement, you are just asking for mildew.

Dresswear

Dressed up or dressed down, you want your suits, pants, dresses, and skirts to look good and provide years of long wear. Here's how to start.

Get a twofer

Often shoppers will buy two pairs of pants to go with a new jacket, but then wear only one pair, saving the other for when the knees wear out in the first. Instead, put both pair of pants in your rotation. That way, they'll wear evenly with the jacket.

Don't hang delicate pants

If you have a nice pair of silk, velvet, or satin pants, don't hang them up. Hangers can badly damage and crease such fabrics. Just fold them neatly and place them in a dresser drawer. Pants made of more durable fabrics are best hung from the cuffs, with the inseams together in a vise hanger.

ProTip

GIVE TWEED THE BRUSH OFF

If you want that tweed or wool jacket to look as good as the day you brought it home, don't dry-clean it too often. If it's dirty, grab a stiff nonwire brush to clean it up. Chemicals in professional dry cleaning can wear the fabric out faster.

Fix a wasted waistband

If your pants still look good, but the elastic waistband is all stretched out, consider a replacement. Get new elastic, measure it to fit around your waist, cut a little extra, just in case, then slip it into the pants casing for a new fit.

Eliminate deep creases

You've grabbed a forgotten pair of pants from the back of the closet. Ugh, the creases are deep and ugly. To remove the creases, try this pressing trick on each crease: Apply white vinegar to the crease with a sponge. Then iron with a warm—not hot— iron, drying the vinegar. The crease will go away.

Keep those offcuts

If you cut off a piece of fabric during your hemming job, keep the swatch. The material will come in handy when you need to repair holes and tears in the same garment.

Buy for comfort and long life

Here's some tips to make sure you leave the store with clothing that fits right and will give you years of comfortable wear.

• Buying a new jacket? When figuring out how well it fits, try different positions in the fitting room, such as grabbing at a seat belt, reaching for a dropped pencil, and sitting at the keyboard. Lining on a roomier jacket will survive these stress points.

• You grab the size you need in pants and head for the dressing room. But they're too tight in the waist. Grab another pair in the same size. Sometimes waist sizes can vary by as much as an inch.

• Say the pants fit fine in the waist, now what about the length? When trying on a new pair of pants, if they wrinkle upward, that means they are too short in the crotch area. If they wrinkle horizontally across your midsection, then they are too tight.

Save the wales

Don't throw your favorite corduroy pants in the dryer. Line-dry them to keep the wales from flattening. Never wring those pants for the same reason.

Iron 3–D fabrics from the inside

Fabrics in three dimensions, such as corduroy and embroidery appliqués, will keep their shape if you iron them from the inside. Direct heat will crush them.

◆ BEST ADVICE ◆ **Suits**

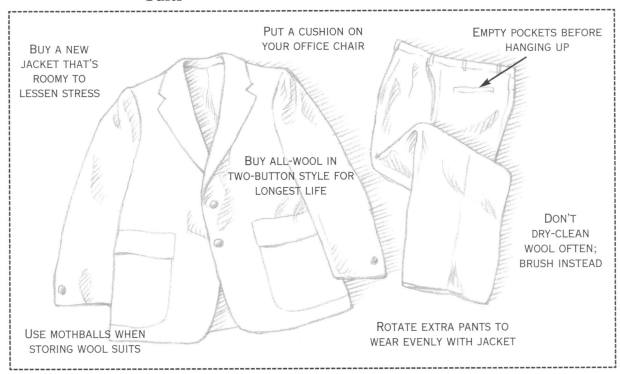

BUY A NEW JACKET THAT'S ROOMY TO LESSEN STRESS

PUT A CUSHION ON YOUR OFFICE CHAIR

EMPTY POCKETS BEFORE HANGING UP

BUY ALL-WOOL IN TWO-BUTTON STYLE FOR LONGEST LIFE

DON'T DRY-CLEAN WOOL OFTEN; BRUSH INSTEAD

USE MOTHBALLS WHEN STORING WOOL SUITS

ROTATE EXTRA PANTS TO WEAR EVENLY WITH JACKET

Keep your kick pleat complete

Your new skirt has a snazzy kick pleat in the back, but it threatens to rip apart after a few wears. Reinforce the top seam of the pleat so that it won't become a long slit the next time you wear the skirt.

Keep your whites white

Before you hang your favorite white dress, skirt, or other white garment to store it for the summer, cover it with dark paper, such as package wrapping. This will prevent yellowing. Plastic wrap from the dry cleaners won't offer the same protection.

Keep your belt in the loop

Don't lose that special belt that accessorizes your dress. Sew the belt to the belt loops of the dress, and you'll never have to worry about not being able to find that part of the dress again.

Check those pockets

Before hanging up suit jackets and outerwear, perform a thorough pocket check. Remove everything from the pockets; then smooth the pockets flat.

What a waist

There's nothing more annoying than waistbands that twist

new uses for Old Dresses

• Love the dress, but the style is outdated? Cut the dress in half and make the lower half into a skirt.

• A floor-length dress can be shortened to a more in-style length, too.

Buy to Keep: Suits

It is said that clothes make the man (or the woman). A way to make a good impression is with a good suit. And good quality suits can be expensive at the outset but will serve you better in the long term. They wear better, drape better, and retain their shape better.

Fabric	When selecting a fabric for your new suit purchase, wool will give you the best value. An all-wool suit should last about six years. A wool blend lasts only four years and a synthetic fabric, less than four years—plus it just doesn't look as good on as a wool suit does. Scrunch up the fabric of a suit you are considering purchasing. It should bounce back and not wrinkle at your touch.
Styling	Consider the style of the suit. While three- and four-button jackets are popular for men's suits, the classic look is for just two buttons on the front of the jacket. That style will never fade. Pants are also a consideration. Cuffed pants are considered more formal, as are pants with front pleats. Uncuffed pants and those with a flat front are considered informal. They should hang from your waist, not your hips. In addition, they should break near the tops of your shoes.
Fit	Figure out the fit. Shoulders of the jacket shouldn't be too square or slope too much. Make sure you can see your shirt collar over the jacket collar. Your shirtsleeve should peek out about 1/2 inch (12 mm) from the jacket sleeve.
For women	If you are a women, keep things basic when buying a suit. A simple black, blue, or tan suit can be dressed up or dressed down—or used with other pieces to create different looks. Buy suits a little larger. If you are between sizes, buy up. A larger size will look better than a tight-fitting one.

inside their casings. Avoid the problem by tacking the elastic at several points along the waistband casing to keep it in place and lying flat.

Make a quick hem

Fusible lining, which comes in rolls similar to wide transparent tape, can be ironed into place in a jiffy if the hem on your skirt or dress is coming loose. This is also a good method for keeping your hem in place while you adjust the skirt length. Measure where you want the new hem and pin it in place. Now use the fusible lining and iron the new hem. You can try on the skirt or dress again to make sure that it's where you want it. When it is, sew into place.

Protect your pants from shiny-seat syndrome

If your office chair is covered in plastic or leather, you may get a shiny seat on your pants. Avoid this wear by covering your chair with fabric or a seat cushion.

Grandma says...

"Moth larvae still hate the same stuff they always have. If you don't want the larvae feasting on your woolens, do what I always do: Store them for the winter with moth flakes, mothballs, or even bars of soap. Come spring, no holes."

Shirts and Blouses

You want your favorite shirts to look good even after years of wear—and they can with a little tender loving care.

Clip loose threads

You've just purchased a nice new dress shirt or silk blouse. Before you wear it, check all seams, hems, buttons, and buttonholes for loose threads. To avoid unraveling later, clip them off instead of pulling them.

Secure loose buttons

New shirts can also have loose buttons. Check each button on your new garment and add a few stitches if they are not sewed on properly. Doing this is especially important for buttons that have only two holes.

Sew on buttons with dental floss

If you know that the buttons on a garment are going to get a lot of wear and tear, resew them on with white dental floss, not thread. The buttons will hold a lot longer.

Polish the buttons

To quickly reinforce buttons, put a dab of clear nail polish on the threads. The nail polish will keep threads in place and prevent unraveling.

Cover your buttons

Button covers can give your old blouse a new look. Slip the cover over the button, snap into place, button, and go.

Lint be gone

Have pesky little lint balls invaded the buttonholes of your favorite shirt? Dampen a cotton ball and run it through. The lint balls will disappear.

Stop, stuff, and roll

Your blouse has a flattering soft-roll collar. Keep it that way by twisting some tissue paper and

◆ BEST ADVICE ◆ **Shirts**

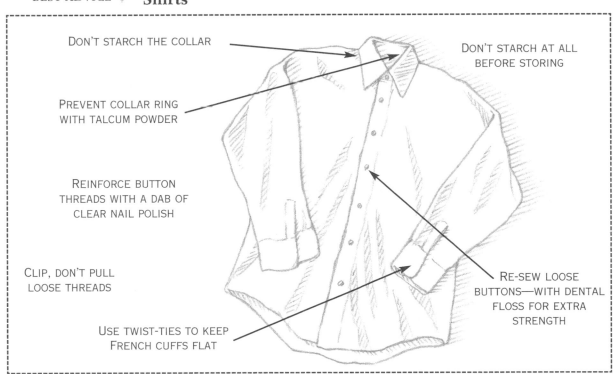

DON'T STARCH THE COLLAR

DON'T STARCH AT ALL BEFORE STORING

PREVENT COLLAR RING WITH TALCUM POWDER

REINFORCE BUTTON THREADS WITH A DAB OF CLEAR NAIL POLISH

CLIP, DON'T PULL LOOSE THREADS

USE TWIST-TIES TO KEEP FRENCH CUFFS FLAT

RE-SEW LOOSE BUTTONS—WITH DENTAL FLOSS FOR EXTRA STRENGTH

slipping it under the collar roll while the shirt is stored for its next wearing.

Link cuffs

If you wear shirts with French cuffs or other shirts that use cuff links, here's how to keep the cuffs from getting accidentally creased. After pressing a shirt, use a bag twist-tie to link the two sides of the cuffs. They'll stay nice and flat while waiting to be worn.

Prevent ring-around-the-collar

Remember that old detergent commercial that touted the horror of ring-around-the-collar? Well, you don't need any particular soap to get rid of those rings, because it's really very easy to prevent them in the first place. Just apply a little talcum powder or chalk to the collar of your shirt before you put it on. The powder will absorb sweat before it can cause rings.

You say you read this tip too late to prevent rings on some of your favorite shirts? No sweat. Get rid of the stains by applying a paste of baking soda and water. Scrub with a small brush, such as an old toothbrush; then launder as usual.

Skip the starch at the Chinese laundry

If you have your shirts cleaned professionally, they'll last longer if you don't starch the collars. At very least, don't include starch in the last laundering before putting your shirts away for the season. Starch is an organic material that attracts bugs that will feast on your garments while they are stored.

new uses for Old Shirts

Take that worn shirt off your back and put it to one of these new uses:

- Shorten a long-sleeved shirt. If your shirt has frayed cuffs but otherwise looks fine, cut off and hem the sleeves to make it a short-sleeved shirt. You'll get lots of extra wear out of it.

- Worn-out long-sleeved shirts make great painting smocks. On your next household project, don an old long-sleeved shirt. You won't have to worry about paint splatters and mud. And of course, old-shirt smocks are de rigueur for kids during creative painting or arts-and-craft time at home or school.

- Make a shirt into a backpack. Tie a knot in the bottom of the shirt and stuff items in through the collar part. Tie the sleeve ends together, and sling it over your shoulder. This is a good way to carry a small load of laundry to the Laundromat.

- Old shirts make great rags. They are particularly good for cleaning cobwebs and other dust from ceilings and corners. Just stick one on the end of a broomstick and start dusting. Rags from shirts also are good shoe polishers.

- Make napkins. Cut the backs of shirts into 12-inch (30-cm) squares of fabric. Hem each side, and you have a new set of dinner napkins.

- Cut off trims. Remove all buttons and embellishments from your shirt, and set it aside for your grandchildren, who will love all of the trinkets you have given them for arts-and-crafts projects.

Pamper your silk with the right hangers

Drop that metal hanger. When hanging up a silk blouse, use plastic or padded hangers. Metal hangers will leave small creases in your silk, and wooden ones may cause snags.

Casualwear

Dungarees, Levis, denims—we've all got them. Now here's how to take care of them and your other casual and sportswear.

Turn T-shirts inside out to wash

T-shirts with appliqués and other decorative touches should be turned inside out before washing. This will help preserve the embellishments and keep the T-shirt looking newer longer.

Zip it up

Remember to close zippers on your favorite jeans before placing them in the washing machine. This will help keep the zipper's teeth aligned and keep the jeans in good working order.

Delay bottom fray

There's nothing more annoying than a pair of comfortable jeans fraying at the bottoms. Prevent this at the start by ironing on strips of mending tape to the hems inside each pant leg. This will keep threads in place before they start to come undone.

Salt softens your jeans

If your new pair of jeans is too stiff and you don't want to wait to "break them in," throw a handful of salt into the wash with the detergent. The salt softens up the jeans so they won't be too uncomfortable during those first few wearings.

The knees go first

If you are especially hard on your jeans, do a little preventive maintenance. When you get them home from the store, reinforce the knees from the inside with an iron-on jeans patch. You'll be glad you did when your denim knees start to wear through.

Unstick a zipper

If you can't get the zipper up on your jeans, try some of these methods for lubricating it. Rub a pencil, a bar of soap, a bar of paraffin, or a candle along the length of the zipper. Any of them will get it running smoothly again.

Keep GOR-TEX waterproof

Keep that new GOR-TEX jogging suit in tip-top shape by rubbing the seams and areas such as elbows, shoulders, and underarms with GOR-TEX sealant, which is available in outdoor-equipment stores.

Buy to Keep: T-shirts

Though T-shirts are ubiquitous, you should still take care when purchasing this wardrobe basic.

Construction	Hold up the shirt and check the seams. Look at the bottom hems and the armholes. The T-shirt should have straight seams and should not twist to one side.
Size	T-shirts usually shrink when you wash them, so it's best to buy them one size larger. A larger T-shirt also won't stress at the seams when you're exercising, working in the yard, or puttering around the house. It'll last longer and be more comfortable to boot.
Fabric	Heavier-duty materials will outlast thinner ones and poly/cotton blends will last longer than all cotton. But on hot days, you may prefer the comfort of a lighter weight all-cotton T-shirt.

Buy to Keep: Swimsuits

Sure, you want to look great in your new swimsuit, but that's not the only criterion for choosing one. Here's how to choose the best swimsuit for the money:

Size and fit	Make sure the suit fits. You want a suit that will last in the pool while you swim or will be comfortable while you lounge around poolside reading. Try on your choice of swimsuit; then sit, lie, and make swimming movements to make sure it fits right. Also, for the most comfortable fit, chose a swimsuit that's a few sizes larger than your regular clothes size. Your body will look better in it.
Fabric	Examine the fabric. Longer-lasting swimsuits are made of nylon and lots of spandex. These suits are the best to withstand sun, salt, and chlorine. A new fabric now available, called Miratex, is receiving attention for its ability to stretch in four different directions. This enables the suit to act like a girdle, tightening your figure without forcing bulges of skin to other parts of your body. Examine the fabric of your choice suit. Expand the fabric, and make sure it retracts firmly.
Style	Try different styles of suits. For women, there are "tankinis," which look like a one-piece suit but have a tank-style top. Other women's swimsuits come with halter-style tops and shorts for the bottoms. Manufacturers and many mail-order catalogs will allow you to purchase a bottom in one size and a top in another for a more comfortable fit.
Color and patterns	Create illusions. Black swimsuits are slimming and do not draw attention to your stomach. If you are lean, choose patterned or bright-colored suits. If you have a small bust, choose a top with horizontal stripes. Busty women can wear light-colored suits.

If you are a shorter man, don't buy swim trunks that are longer than 20 inches (50 cm) in length. Also popular are "volley" shorts, which are shorter still and can draw attention from the stomach area and elongate the leg.

When laundering GOR-TEX, use powder detergent. Don't use liquid detergent, which will inhibit the fabric's ability to be waterproof. And never dry-clean it.

Banish the chlorine

To avoid chlorine damage, rinse your swimsuit as soon as you can after swimming in a pool. Follow this up by washing the swimsuit in the delicate cycle of the washing machine and letting it drip-dry. It's a good idea to follow this same procedure if you go swimming in salt water or spend time on a sandy beach.

Coats and Hats

Grab your coat and grab your hat. If you are careful in how your handle your outerwear, you can enjoy protection from the elements for a long time.

Keep your down jackets puffy

After several washings, your down jacket may not seem as warm as you remember it. You're not imagining things. Washing down jackets can compress the down inside, removing the air between the feathers that acts as insulation. Next time you wash your down jacket, put a sneaker in the dryer with it to keep the loft high. Or if you don't want to wait until then, fluff the jacket up by putting it and a sneaker in the dryer with the machine set on the air-fluff setting. Another way to help preserve a down jacket's loft is to hang it upside down while storing it.

Re-treat raincoats with repellent

After a long time, a raincoat may loose its water-repellency. Just treat your raincoat with a spray fabric water repellent, and it'll shed water like a duck for many years to come. You'll find water-repellent sprays in stores that sell outdoor equipment.

Treat leather jackets

An expensive leather jacket must be cared for properly because dust, dirt, even oil from your skin can make it look dull. First wipe off any dirt with a damp cloth. Then regularly apply commercial leather cleaners and conditioners to your coat to keep its luster. This is especially important if you live in a dry environment. Hang your jacket on a sturdy, preferably padded hanger to help it keep its shape. Store it in a cool, dry, well-ventilated place where it isn't exposed to direct sunlight. And don't cover it with plastic; it's a natural product that needs to breathe.

Give your fur some TLC

If you've waited years to get your fur coat, you'll want it to last for years more. Here are a few fur-care pointers:

• Avoid crushing the fur. Try not to sit down while wearing it. If you must, then brush up the crushed parts afterward.

• Don't use any oils or chemicals around your fur coat. Perfume, for instance, can damage it. For the same reason, avoid using mothballs.

• Protect the collar of your coat by wrapping a scarf around your neck. That way, no residue on your skin will rub off on your fur. Avoid other damage by never poking jewelry into your fur coat or wearing sharp necklaces and bracelets. Also, don't use a shoulder bag; it will rub off the fur.

• When storing your fur, don't wrap it in plastic, use a cloth bag instead. Keep some room around it in your closet to allow air to circulate. Hang it with a wide, sturdy hanger—not a wire one—to help keep its shape.

• If your coat gets wet, hang it up to dry away from light and heat. Professionally clean it only once every two years.

Hang-dry nylon outerwear

Nylon jackets, even if they are soaking wet, should be dried in a dark space. Light can damage nylon, so avoid direct light when you hang-dry your nylon jacket.

Reinforce nylon jackets

Some nylon jackets fasten with Velcro or, known by its generic name, gripper strips. Reinforce the fabric by stitching around the strips so that they will not tear off one day.

Sweaters and Other Knits

What could be more comforting on a cold morning than pulling on a warm, toasty sweater? Sweaters need a little TLC to help them last longer.

Tackle pills

There are several ways to remove pills and lint from a sweater. Lightly rub a pumice stone over the sweater to pull them off, or use a small pair of scissors or a razor to snip them off. Try wrapping your hand with masking tape or transparent tape with the sticky side out; then blot the sweater with your hand.

Grandma says...

"Don't give up on a favorite wool sweater if it has shrunk. There's a time-tested way to return it to its proper size: Boil it. Put it in a large pot with one part vinegar and two parts water. Boil for 25 minutes. Then take it out of the pot, remove excess water, reshape the sweater, and lay it flat to dry. Don't move it until it is completely dry."

Tackle snags

Snags, those pesky little threads that can appear on the outside of your sweater, can also be sent away. Stick a needle into the base of the snag. Then thread the needle with the unwanted snag. Pull the needle through the clothing, and the snag is gone. If your sweater is made of wool or cotton yarn, take a crochet hook, poke through the sweater, grab the loose yarn with the hook end, and weave it back into the body of the sweater or through to the inside.

Get your cotton sweaters back in shape

If a cotton sweater has lost its form in the wash, there are some steps you can take to bring back its original shape. Lay the sweater out on a towel or drying rack. Pull it back into shape, and let it dry in a well-ventilated area, away from sunlight. A cotton sweater will dry quickly if air circulates around it. If you need to dry the sweater a bit faster, you can place it, turned inside out, in the dryer. Run the dryer on the air-fluff setting for just 15 minutes, and then block the sweater as usual. Never hang a cotton sweater to dry on a hanger, because the weight from the water in the piece will stretch it out as it dries.

Allow for shrinkage

When purchasing a sweater, check the label to see if there is a note about shrinkage. If so, buy one size larger. Many knitted sweaters will shrink because yarns are stretched out in the knitting process.

Repair elbows

The elbows of sweaters can be restored several ways. Patch them with an oval of leather or suede to prevent further unraveling. Or reinforce the elbow by finding yarn the same color as the sweater. Turn the sweater inside out and weave lengths of yarn through the sweater's stitching.

Keep wristbands in shape

Wristbands of sweaters sometimes get stretched out. To avoid this problem, weave a long length of narrow elastic through the yarn strands of the wristbands on the undersides of the cuffs. This works on mittens as well. You can also get the cuffs wet in hot water, and then dry them with a hair dryer to get them to shrink up.

Say no to sweater hang-ups

Sweaters will loose their shape if you store them on hangers.

♦ BEST ADVICE ♦ **Sweaters**

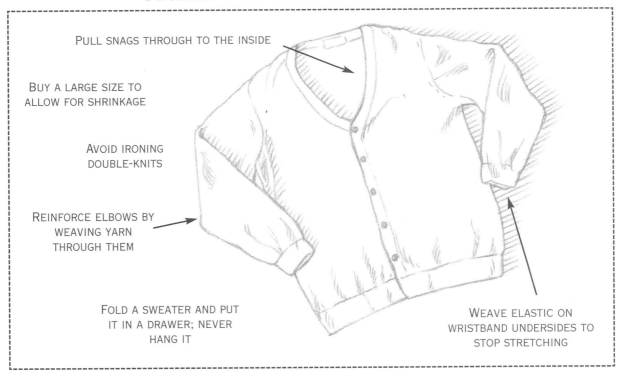

PULL SNAGS THROUGH TO THE INSIDE

BUY A LARGE SIZE TO
ALLOW FOR SHRINKAGE

AVOID IRONING
DOUBLE-KNITS

REINFORCE ELBOWS BY
WEAVING YARN
THROUGH THEM

FOLD A SWEATER AND PUT
IT IN A DRAWER; NEVER
HANG IT

WEAVE ELASTIC ON
WRISTBAND UNDERSIDES TO
STOP STRETCHING

Instead, fold them and place them in a drawer. If your only choice is to hang a sweater, fold it in half and hang it on a hanger that has cardboard over the crossbar. (Or make your own by splitting a paper towel tube lengthwise and placing it on the hanger.)

☞ **DON'T**
iron double-knits

Avoid ironing your double-knit sweaters—the heat will make the fabric shiny. If you must iron a double-knit sweater, cover it with a cloth first to protect it from direct heat.

Underwear, Socks, Sleepwear, and Hosiery

Your unmentionables deserve good care, too. Here's how to keep them in good shape.

Keep the elastic stretchy

Unfortunately, the elastic that keeps undergarments in place often wears out long before the fabric. Here are some tips to prolonging the life of the stretchy stuff:

• Rotate how often you wear your undergarments so that all get even use. If a pair gets buried deep in your drawer, the elastic will loose its stretchiness, rendering the undergarment useless.

• Avoid drying underwear and bras at high temperatures, which can also wear out elastic. Bras should be line-dried to keep them in proper shape.

• If the elastic straps on your bra are starting to loosen and fall off your shoulders, sew a piece of elastic across the straps in the back, about 6 inches (15 cm) above the bra's back strap, to hold the arm straps in place.

Minimize runs in nylons

Your nylon stockings and panty hose will last longer without runs if you soak them in alum before you wear them for the first time. Alum is a pickling spice that can be purchased in the spice aisle of your local supermarket. Powder your feet and put lotion on your hands before pulling on nylons. Another preventative measure is to place nylons in plastic bags and then store them in the dresser.

Don't toss nylons with runs

Although you can minimize runs, you can't prevent them altogether. But sometimes you can still use the nylons when runs happen.

• If the run is on the thigh, knee, or calf area—and doesn't stretch down to the ankle or heel—wear the nylons under pants for extra warmth.

• If you have a run in the right leg of one pair of panty hose and a run in the left leg of another pair, cut off the legs with the runs and put on both pairs of one-legged panty hose for a complete pair.

No more lost socks

Why is it so hard to find both socks in a pair at the same time? It's a universal problem. Here are a few tactics that you can use to keep track of them:

• When you're doing the laundry, pin pairs of socks together with safety pins.

Buy to Keep: Panty Hose

If you seem to go through a new pair of panty hose everyday, here are two tips on purchasing ones that will last you much longer.

Size	When purchasing panty hose, be sure to check the sizing chart on the back of the package. One brand's size B may be another brand's size A. If your weight is in one size and your height in another, go with the larger size.
Fabric	Choose opaque panty hose over sheer panty hose. Opaque pairs have more fibers in the fabric and therefore are more durable than sheers.

• Before tossing them in the wash, place all your socks in a zippered, mesh bag—the kind sold for hand washables.

• Buy several pairs of the same kind and color of socks. That way, if one gets lost, then the remaining sock can be paired up with another one like it.

Smooth feet mean long-lasting socks

Deter holes from forming in your socks by pumicing the rough spots on your feet. Getting rid of dead skin is good for your feet, too.

Keep your socks up

Dry socks on a low setting in the dryer so that the elastic stays flexible and your socks stay up on your legs.

Take pride in your pajamas

Buy pajamas a size too big to allow room for tossing and turning when you sleep. Choose pajamas with expandable waists so that you can breathe comfortably while sleeping. Wash pajamas in a pillowcase to preserve the flannel. Hang them to dry on plastic hangers to avoid pilling.

new uses for Old Panty Hose

A pair of panty hose may not have long life, but it can have a new life. But before you throw panty hose out, consider the many uses for this piece of clothing:

• Use as a polishing cloth for your shoes.

• In the garden, use panty hose to stake plants, store flower bulbs in the winter, or deter deer by stuffing panty hose with clippings of human hair and hanging them outside.

• Fill pillows, aging toys, or seat cushions that are losing their stuffing.

• Keep clothes tightly rolled in your suitcase while traveling, allowing you to pack more into your suitcase.

• Use rings cut from the legs as giant rubber bands to hold together blankets going into temporary storage, or newspapers going out to be recycled, or to keep plastic trash bags in place in the can.

• Store potpourri for homemade drawer sachets or store mothballs in your closets.

• Dry a sweater by threading the panty hose legs through the sleeves and hanging the sweater, using clothespins to attach the feet to the clothesline.

Shoes and Boots

Your boots were made for walking, and that's just what they'll continue to do as long as you give them a bit of regular maintenance.

Buy shoes late in the day

Shopping for shoes? Do it in the afternoon, when your feet have enlarged to their fullest size. Buying shoes in the morning can result in cramped toes when you wear the shoes later in the day. In the morning, our feet have not yet expanded to their maximum size. Also, remember that the glossy finish that is sprayed onto new shoes doesn't really protect them. So give those new shoes a baptismal polish as soon as you get them home.

True-Life ♦ *Long* Life

Paul Ellis of Sugarloaf, New York, sure as shootin' loves his cowboy boots. Why, he's got more 'n a dozen pairs. He's got boots made from exotic snakeskins, including python, boa constrictor, rattlesnake, and water moccasin.

"You can't wear those exotics too often," Ellis said. "The skin is too thin—more like cloth than leather. Except for the alligator. That skin is as durable as leather. The most durable of all, though, is bull hide."

Ellis, 54, grew up with horses and has been wearing cowboy boots all his life. "They're just the most comfortable," he said. "I can't wear anything else. I played tennis in them once."

Ellis's oldest wearable boots are 14 years old, and his bull-hide "working pair" is 12 years old. Ellis's formula for boot longevity? Before he wears a pair for the first time, he has them fitted with rubber soles. When the rubber wears out, he just replaces it. Besides protecting the boots, the rubber soles keep his feet dry should he step in a water puddle or, worse, the kind of puddle that occurs in horse barns. He cleans the boots with saddle soap, and then uses a leather conditioner such as Neats Foot Oil. Finally, he polishes them with a shoe polish that is one shade darker than the boots. "That seems to hold the real color better," he said. "Never use neutral polish."

Ellis's twin brother, Rick, is also addicted to cowboy boots. "He's got about a dozen pairs, too," Paul Ellis said. "He's got stingray, elephant, eel, and he told me he recently got a pair of African frog, though I haven't seen those yet."

Don't get down in the heel

If you notice the heels of your shoes are starting to wear down, get them reheeled as soon as you can. By preventing further damage to the shoe, reheeling makes the shoes last a lot longer, and the cost of reheeling is a fraction of the cost of buying another good pair of shoes. To save the backs of your shoes, use a shoehorn or soupspoon to put them on.

Keep shoes shapely

When you store leather shoes, put shoe trees in them. That way you won't pull them out of the closet to find ugly creases in the leather. Place the shoes in plastic bags to keep off dust.

Keep the shoebox

Another way to keep your shoes in good shape is to store them in their original boxes. This works great if you have lots of shoes in limited space because you can stack the boxes without crushing the shoes. Label the ends of the boxes so that you can find the pair you want quickly.

Erase scuff marks

Patent-leather shoes get scuffed easily. Fortunately, it's just as easy to remove the scuffs—just rub with a clean pencil eraser. Polish and wax leather shoes often to keep them shiny and scuff-free. If your shoes have

Women's Shoes

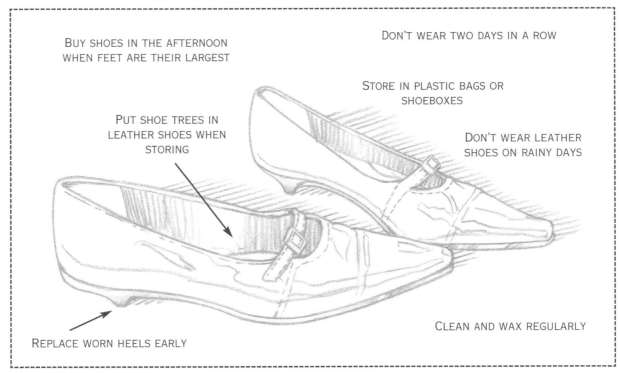

BUY SHOES IN THE AFTERNOON WHEN FEET ARE THEIR LARGEST

DON'T WEAR TWO DAYS IN A ROW

STORE IN PLASTIC BAGS OR SHOEBOXES

PUT SHOE TREES IN LEATHER SHOES WHEN STORING

DON'T WEAR LEATHER SHOES ON RAINY DAYS

REPLACE WORN HEELS EARLY

CLEAN AND WAX REGULARLY

dried out, apply castor oil to rejuvenate them.

Keep your leather shoes dry

It's best to leave your leather shoes at home when it's raining outside. Rain will cause the leather to shrink. If your leather shoes do get caught in the rain, stuff them with old nylons to soak up the wetness and help them retain their shape.

Keep your sneakers looking and smelling new

If you have to quickly clean your sneakers, try squirting them with some window cleaner. You have a little more time? Make a paste of baking soda and water, and apply it to the sneakers. Wipe it off and let it dry. Baking soda is also great for absorbing sneaker odor. Put some in a small square of cloth, twist the cloth, and insert it in the sneaker.

Clean your hiking boots

If you got your hiking boots muddy on your last trek, the most effective way to clean them is to let the mud dry and then brush it off with a sturdy brush. To maintain the finish, apply boot wax frequently and afterward warm the boots in the sun so the leather can absorb the wax. This will help hiking boots repel water.

Treat your tall leather boots with care

A good pair of leather boots is an investment. Here's how to keep your boots around long enough to become comfy old friends:

• Don't let your boot tops flop over in the closet. They'll develop an unsightly crease. Instead, store them over boot trees.

• Wax your boots often to keep them water repellent and looking new.

• If you get salt on your boots from walking on city sidewalks in the winter, wipe the salt away with a cloth soaked in vinegar.

Stain
chart

Nothing wears clothes out faster than dirt and stains. But every stain is different and requires a different approach for removal. Never rub a stain, which will break down the fibers of the fabric and can set it permanently. Always blot. Take a stained "dry-clean only" item to a dry cleaner.

Stain	What to Use	Method
Beer	*Vinegar*	Combine one part vinegar with two parts water. Soak garment, blot stain, then launder.
Blood	*Hydrogen peroxide, salt, ammonia, milk*	Small stain, dab peroxide on garment. Large stain, use 1 cup of water, add 1/2 teaspoon of salt. Let soak. Or splash some ammonia in a sink filled with cold water and soak garment. For milk, let garment soak in it before laundering.
Chocolate	*Ammonia*	Apply to stain and gently scrub.
Coffee with milk and sugar	*Soap and vinegar*	Flush garment with cold water. Mix 1 quart (1 liter) warm water, 1/2 teaspoon dishwashing soap, and 1 tablespoon vinegar. Blot the stain and let it sit in the solution for 15 minutes. Rinse again with cold water, blot area with rubbing alcohol.
	Meat tenderizer	Make a paste of the tenderizer with a bit of water and work it into the stain.
Fruit	*Water and vinegar*	Flush with water immediately, then blot with solution of one part water, one part white vinegar. Rinse again and air dry.
Fruit juice	*White vinegar*	Blot white vinegar immediately on stain. Let it sit for 15 minutes. Before laundering, rub some detergent on stain.
Grass	*Glycerin*	Pour or rub on stain. Let sit for an hour before washing.
Grease	*Baking soda, cornmeal, cornstarch*	Pour on stain, wait for it to cake up, then brush off to remove grease.

Stain	What to Use	Method
Ink	Hairspray	Spray should contain alcohol. Spray, about four inches away, on ink stain, placing a piece of fabric behind stain to prevent bleeding. Then wash.
	Petroleum jelly	Rub onto stain and leave for several days before wiping off and washing.
Lipstick	Hairspray	Spray on stain, pause, wipe off spray. Lipstick should come up with spray.
	Peanut butter	Rub onto stain then remove before it dries. Wash thoroughly with warm water and dish soap.
Pencil	Window cleaner	Scrub stain with diluted window cleaner applied to an old toothbrush.
Perspiration	Meat tenderizer	Dampen fabric, sprinkle on tenderizer, wash.
	Salt	Soak in 1 quart (1 liter) of water with a handful of salt added. Let soak for an hour before washing.
Rust	Lemon juice and water	Place equal parts on stain and leave it for a few minutes before washing. Stubborn rust stains can take straight lemon juice; then hold garment over a steaming teakettle.
	Salt and vinegar	Combine equal parts into a paste and apply to stain. After 30 minutes, launder.
Soda	Rubbing alcohol	Soak in cold water, blot with rubbing alcohol
Tea	Glycerin	Rub on stain, let sit for a few minutes. Wash as usual.
Wax	Vegetable oil	Work into wax stain, wipe off excess, wash as usual.
Wine	Seltzer water	Pour immediately on stain and blot.
	Salt	Remove garment, pour on salt to soak up stain. Rinse in cold water and soak for a half hour. Wash immediately.
Yellowing	Salt and baking soda	Brighten whites by boiling in 2 gallons (8 liters) of water with a cup each of salt and baking soda for an hour.

Accessories and Jewelry

Ties, scarves, belts, purses, hats, umbrellas, and jewelry: Some are practical; some are just for show. But all put the finishing touches on our fashion statement. Here's how to keep them looking great.

Selecting a tie

Here are some guidelines to keep in mind when you're out shopping for a tie:

• Look for ties with linings made of wool or several layers of silk. This crucial padding will make the knot look better when you tie it. The lining should extend the full the length of the tie.

• A good tie should be made of three pieces of fabric, not two pieces.

• When choosing which tie will go with what shirt and jacket, remember not to clash. A bold shirt should be paired with a more subdued tie. Limit patterns to two. Choose patterns for either your shirt, tie, or jacket, but not all three of them.

Avoid creases in your ties

Here are two ways to keep your ties from developing ugly creases that shorten their useful life:

• After wearing a silk tie, rub it across your thigh to take out any creases and remove lint. Never iron the edges of a silk tie, or it will lose its ability to tie.

• Folding ties for storage eventually causes creases that are hard to get out. They are best stored by hanging.

Resize a belt

If you have gained or lost a little lately, you don't have to go out shopping for a new leather belt. Just make adjustments in your current belt. To add a hole, make a mark where you want the new one, place an awl on the dot, and then hammer it through.

Polish the buckle

Belt buckles can stay shiny and bright if you coat them once in a while with clear nail polish. Store leather belts hanging on a hook, not curled up, which stretches the leather.

Store silk scarves in tubes

Nothing adds to an outfit more than a beautiful silk scarf. But how do you store a scarf when you're not using it? Gently roll up the scarf. Take an empty paper-towel cardboard tube, and insert the scarf. The next time you wear it, it will be free of creases.

Treat you gloves with care

A nice pair of leather gloves gets more comfortable with age as they stretch to fit your hands precisely. They'll last for many years with proper care. To clean and condition your gloves, use a leather-conditioning oil, saddle soap, or even the cream used for leather furniture. Do this regularly, as you would for leather shoes. If your gloves get wet, put them on and let them dry so they will preserve their shape.

Polish your purse

Polish your purses as regularly as you would polish leather shoes. If your purse is covered in soil or fingerprints, mix equal parts vinegar and water and wipe down the outer surface. When storing a purse ready for its next use, remember to stuff it with recycled plastic bags or tissue paper to keep creases away.

Revive an umbrella

Fabric that has freed itself from the ribs of an umbrella can be easily stretched and re-stitched to extend the life of the umbrella. Use dental floss if you want extrasturdy stitching that won't pull out.

Take care with your felt hat

A felt hat should last you for years if you give it extra attention. Here are some tips:

• To clean your felt hat, just brush it with a soft brush. If

Buy to Keep: Umbrellas

Why do some umbrellas fall apart so easily? Here's what to look for in an umbrella that will stick around for a while:

Tensile strength	When purchasing an umbrella, open it up and press on the ribs from the top. If the umbrella is sturdy, the ribs shouldn't move when pressure is applied.
Fabric	It's always better to choose an umbrella of synthetic fabrics, like nylon, because they repel water better than natural cloth, like cotton.
Mechanism	Open an umbrella up in the store several times. Look for an opening and a locking mechanism that are simple in design, open smoothly, and are sturdy.
Handle	The handle should fit comfortably in your hand. A handle that's too large will be difficult and uncomfortable to grasp in bad weather.

that doesn't do the trick, you can hold it briefly over a steaming teakettle, then brush again to remove soil. This will remove creases as well.

• Store your felt hat clean and in a hatbox to keep off dust. The best way to store it is upside down, stuffed with tissue paper or plastic bags, so that it won't lose its shape. It's also best to clean your hat before storing it.

• If you get caught in a shower or snow with your felt hat, let it dry naturally—don't use a heater or hair dryer.

• If you are adjusting your hat on your head, use the front and back brims. Don't touch the crown to avoid getting oils from your skin on this most visible part of your hat.

Water your straw hat

Panama or straw hats must be kept moist to retain their shape and durability. They can be sprayed occasionally with water (use a plant mister, for instance). When picking up your hat, grab it by the brim, not the crown, so that it won't crack there later. Finally, don't store it in the light, which will also cause damage.

Diamonds are forever

It's true that diamonds are among the hardest materials known to man and yours will last virtually forever. Still, you want to clean them properly. When grime, fingerprints, lotions, and cooking oils leave a film on your diamond jewelry, soak it for about half an hour in a solution of water with a couple

of squirts of liquid hand soak. Then, with a soft brush, such as an old toothbrush, scrub the jewelry clean; then rinse and dry it. Remove your diamond ring when working with harsh household chemicals.

Pearls are perishable

Unlike diamonds, pearls can deteriorate and must be handled carefully. Never use any jewelry-cleaning chemicals, harsh soaps, or even abrasive brushes or cloths to clean pearls. They can be wiped down with a soft cloth that is slightly wet with water. Let them dry before putting them away.

Shine up your gold and silver

Has your gold necklace lost its sparkle? Place it in a solution of a 1/2 cup of ammonia and 1 cup of water. Soak for 10 minutes, remove, and shine it up with an old toothbrush. Then dry. To shine your silver jewelry, first clean it with a mild detergent, and then use a tarnish remover.

Clean up your watchband

Between skin dander and human sweat, a metal watchband can get pretty disgusting. The best way to clean a watchband is to make a 50-50 mixture of vinegar and water, and scrub it on to the watchband with an old toothbrush. This works well for rings, too.

Get more joy from your jewelry

Here are some more tips that will help you get a lifetime of pleasure from your favorite jewelry:

• To help keep your jewelry clean, always apply your makeup, hair spray, and hand lotions before you put on your jewelry, not after.

• To restring a pendant that has fallen apart, just use a needle and thread.

• If you are experiencing an allergic reaction to a ring or bracelet, coat the surface that touches your skin with clear nail polish.

• Clean costume jewelry made of brass, pewter, and other metals with a liquid brass cleaner.

Care for your cameo

The delicate materials that cameos are made from—such as coral and seashell—need to be protected from dryness and dirt. Dryness especially can cause a cameo to crack or chip, and the key to keeping a cameo long-lasting is to wash and moisturize it a couple of times a year. First wash the cameo in warm water with a few drops of dishwashing liquid. Then dry it with a soft cloth, and apply a little bit of fine oil, such as olive oil, mineral oil, or baby oil, with a cotton ball. Let it sit overnight; then wipe off any oil

you can still see with a soft cloth. Store your cameo in a soft cloth or lined box away from heat and light.

Get the right shades

When purchasing sunglasses, look for the maximum level of sun protection. Try on the shades and look down. If they slide on your nose, they're too loose. Feel for a pinch behind your ears to see if they are too tight. Gray and smoke-colored lenses will give you the truest sense of colors around you (think traffic lights, for instance). Treat sunglasses as you would eyeglasses. Keep them in a case when not in use so they don't get scratched.

❋

Grandma says . . .

"To give your cameo a fresh and surprising scent, try this tip from times past: Instead of mineral or baby oil, moisturize the cameo with fragrant oil of wintergreen, available in drugstores."

ooo

Grooming & Health

table of contents

Toiletries and Cosmetics

Cosmetics have come a long way since ancient Egyptians first started putting heavily scented unguents into jars and Romans colored their fingernails with a mixture of sheep's blood and fat. While your toiletries and cosmetics may not last as long as the ones found in Egyptian tombs, these practical tips will help them last as long as possible.

Stretch shampoo and conditioner

Most of us tend to dump more shampoo or conditioner into our hands than we really need. To prevent this waste, just add water. A little water added to the bottles will makes the products last longer, and they'll continue to work just as well. Many shampoos now come with conditioner already added so you don't have to purchase them separately.

That versatile shampoo

Aside from cleaning hair, shampoo has many other uses that can save you money and help out in a pinch. Here are just a few of them:

• If you run out of shaving cream, shampoo makes an excellent substitute. Use it straight from the bottle, adding just enough water to work up a good lather.

• Use tears-free baby shampoo to remove eye makeup.

• Make a bubble bath using a gentle shampoo.

• Use your regular shampoo and a nailbrush to clean combs and hairbrushes. The nailbrush gets between the teeth of the comb and the bristles of the brush to help the shampoo rid them of dirt, lint, and skin oils.

Save soap slivers

Don't throw out your last sliver of bar soap when you open a new bar. Avoid waste by attaching the sliver to the new bar instead. First moisten both the sliver and the new bar. Rub the new bar until it lathers a bit and then stick the sliver on top. It will dry as one with the new bar. If you would rather not deface a brand-new soap bar, you can still put those slivers to good use by inserting them in a sponge or washcloth to soap yourself with while bathing or showering.

Extend your liquid soap

Liquid hand soap is more expensive than bar soap but you can cut the cost substantially by using a few simple techniques to make liquid soap last longer.

• When the dispenser is half empty, add enough water to fill it and shake gently to mix. The diluted soap will still do a good

---

❓ How Long Will Cosmetics Last?

ANSWER: Up to 2 years, often more

Most cosmetic and personal care products have a shelf life of up to two years once opened. If they are stored unopened in a cool, dry place, this can be extended by months or even a couple more years. You can save a bundle of money by waiting for your favorite products to go on sale and then buying enough to last for a year or two. Just remember to store all products—opened and unopened—in a cool, dry place. Of course every product is different, and there is no overall guideline regarding shelf life that will work for everything. Also keep in mind that liquids are generally shorter lived than solids. In other words, lipstick will last longer than a foundation or moisturizer.

job cleaning your hands…at half the cost.

• Once the dispenser is empty, refill it with a 50-50 mix of liquid soap and water.

• Try less expensive brands for refills or even inexpensive brands of shampoo that come in large containers. These can clean as well as expensive liquid soaps and can be mixed with water as well.

Rejuvenate nail polish

To keep nail polish from gumming up, store it in the refrigerator, where it will stay smooth and ready to apply. To make gummed-up polish smooth again, just uncap it and put it in a pan of simmering hot water for a few seconds. Be sure to remove the pan from the burner before putting the nail polish in the pan.

Get the last of the lipstick

Use a lipstick brush to get those last bits of lipstick out of the tube. To clean the brush, apply a small amount of mineral oil or petroleum jelly and wipe clean with a tissue.

Mix foundations

If you decide you don't like the shade of foundation you bought, don't throw it out. Keep it to mix with other shades. It will come in handy when your skin changes color over the different seasons of the year.

Use less makeup

Teenagers aren't the only ones who tend to use too much makeup. Virtually all of your cosmetic products will last longer if you remember that a little dab will do just fine. For example, remember to "dot your eyes" when you apply an eye-care cream in the morning after cleansing: a small dot on the fingertip will be more than enough for each eye. Then gently apply to fine, dry lines, and dab upward and inward under the eye area, making sure to avoid the eyelids.

☞ SAY NO
to play cosmetics

Never buy cheap toy cosmetics for young children. They often contain lead and other toxic and potentially harmful ingredients. Instead, buy inexpensive regular cosmetics made by well-known companies. Then have fun teaching your child how to use them.

Remove makeup with baby wipes

Baby your skin for an inexpensive, effective way to quickly remove makeup. Next time you're at the supermarket, head for the diaper aisle and pick up a package of baby wipes. They have just the right combination of moisture, cleanser, and soothing ingredients to get the job done quickly and gently.

INFO STATION

COSMETIC BUYING ADVICE

For unbiased reviews of cosmetic products, buying tips with cost-conscious consumers in mind, and links to other sources, check out this website.

> **Consumer Search**
http://www.consumersearch.com/ www/family/facial_moisturizers

Buy the right stuff to save money

Experts say that anyone who is serious about skin care must use a variety of items daily, including cleansers, toners, moisturizers, and eye-care products. Here are some long-range money-stretching ideas to consider when buying cosmetics:

• Buying each item individually is a costly proposition so look for products that do double or even triple duty. In other words, some cleansers have toning properties and some treatments also serve as moisturizers. To achieve the desired "anti-aging" effects, a moisturizer should also include a full-spectrum sunscreen that protects against ultraviolet A (UVA) as well as UVB rays.

• Products labeled "dermatologist tested" or "dermatologist approved" are not necessarily better than ones that do not carry such claims. There are no standards and these words may mean only that one or two dermatologists tested a product at the request of a manufacturer.

• You don't need to buy expensive, high-end brands. Many low-cost brands are just as effective. In fact, many are produced by the same parent companies as the expensive brands. Often the main difference is in the packaging. Beauty experts say there is little need to spend three or four times more for a department-store moisturizer when you can find a comparable product at your local supermarket or neighborhood drug store.

Combs and Hairbrushes

Your hair needs to be combed or brushed regularly to keep it healthy and well groomed. You'll want a comb or brush that is right for your specific hair-type and you'll want it to last. Here are a few pointers to ensure success.

Match comb to hair type

Make sure to buy the right comb for your hair type. If you don't, you risk damaging the comb as well as your hair and scalp. As a general rule, if you are of European descent your hair will fall into one of three broad categories: fine and thin, medium, or coarse and thick. Asian hair tends to be thicker and African hair tends to be coarser, although it can sometimes be fine or medium. Caucasian hair is oval, whereas Asian hair is rounder, and African hair is alternately thick and thin. This is what makes it curly as well as fragile and prone to breakage at the thin spots.

Protect a comb's teeth

To protect a comb, use it only on hair that is wet or on very fine hair where a brush might create a "flyaway" appearance. But do not use it on dry, thick hair—unless you believe that combs have a tooth fairy— because you are more likely to break off the teeth. Combs that do lose teeth should be discarded and replaced immediately.

Keep combs clean

Keeping your combs clean will help them stay in good repair. Remove hairs and wash them regularly in warm, soapy water. To remove the yucky build-up from the teeth of your comb between washings, press adhesive tape, masking tape, or transparent tape along the teeth, and lift it off. Then dip the comb in an alcohol or ammonia solution to sanitize it.

What kind of hairbrush?

With so many brushes available to choose from, how do you

Buy to Keep: Combs

A good comb can last many lifetimes, as comb collectors the world over well know. Hair-care experts offer the following tips for purchasing a comb:

Material	Avoid a cheap comb made of thin, brittle plastic. It won't be long before the teeth start breaking and you will have to buy a replacement. In the long run you will save money by investing in a better quality comb. These are often made from a synthetic tortoise-shell like material. Also stay away from combs made in two halves that have sharp edges and ridges where the halves are joined. These can damage your hair. Better quality combs are made from a single piece of material.
Type of teeth	Hand-made combs with "saw-cut" edges are preferable. The inside edges of the teeth have rough impressions that will collect dirt and dust and will also stimulate production of natural scalp oils as the comb is drawn through the hair. The teeth will appear shaped and polished, which will help them glide smoothly through the hair. Make sure the tips of a comb's teeth are rounded to avoid tearing the hair and scratching the scalp.

know which one is right for you? That depends on your personal preference, your hair type, what you want to use it for and the "look" you want to achieve.

• For most types of hair, a brush with stiff natural bristles and widely spaced tufts is best. The more space between the tufts, the better the hair will flow and the more thoroughly it will be brushed.

• If you have fine or thinning hair, look for a brush with soft bristles. Bristle tips should be uneven in height. This will provide more thorough penetration than level tips that will just skim the surface.

• Besides bristle, brush filaments are made of rubberized quills, nylon, and metal (for coarse hair). For everyday grooming and to help clean hair, experts say bristle is best. Quill brushes are best for blow-drying and styling.

Keep hairbrushes clean

Makers of top quality hairbrushes recommend you replace them after six months of use but you can extend that many times over by keeping your brushes clean and well maintained. Just follow this regimen at least once every two weeks: Wash brushes regularly.

• Before washing a hairbrush, use a comb to gently lift away trapped hairs, taking care not to scrape the back. If the brush has a rubber cushion base, block the air hole with a wooden matchstick.

• Wash the brush in warm, soapy water (never ammonia or harsh detergents). Submerge just the tufts, not the brush back or handle.

• Rinse thoroughly in cold water. Shake off excess water and wipe gently with a towel.

• Let brushes dry naturally in the open air (but not in direct sunlight), bristle-side down. Never dry brushes on a radiator or next to direct heat.

Vacuum your hair dryer

Take a look at the intake vent at the back of your handheld hair dryer. All that dust you see stuck in there is making the motor work harder to draw in air to blow on your hair. Press the tube of your vacuum cleaner—with no attachment—directly against the vent to suck out the dust. If the dust doesn't come right out, pluck it loose with a toothpick and vacuum again. Your dryer will last much longer if you keep the vent clean.

Toothbrushes and Toothpaste

Recent studies show that good tooth care is essential to preventing serious medical problems. Here are some tips to help you take care of your teeth and get the most out of your toothbrushes and toothpaste.

Refresh your toothbrush in the dishwasher

Get a clean, fresh toothbrush without buying a new one. If your old brush is still serviceable, try putting it in the dishwasher with the silverware. The high heat and detergent that kills bacteria on dishes and silverware will also work on the brush. If you have a "sanitize" setting on your dishwasher, make sure to use it when washing the toothbrush. This will also extend the life of the brush heads of electric toothbrushes. Try it with other personal hygiene items, such as nail brushes and sponges, too.

Ease up when you brush

Many people tend to brush their teeth too hard. Dentists say that putting too much pressure on your toothbrush when you clean your teeth can actually harm your gums. It also wears out the bristles on the toothbrush much faster. This is true of the brush-head attachments for electric toothbrushes as well. So if you want to replace your toothbrush a little less often than the every three months that dentists recommend, let up on the pressure that you apply to your toothbrush.

Fancy electric toothbrushes: Pros and cons

You don't need an expensive electric toothbrush to give your teeth a good cleaning. Many dental-health experts say that if you brush for two minutes at least twice a day, floss regularly, and make scheduled visits to the dentist, manual toothbrushes are just as effective as powered brushes that can cost 50 times more! Of course, most of us only brush for 30 seconds or so, and brushing for a full two minutes is just too taxing for a lot of people, especially older folks and those who have restricted use of their hands or arms. For many, a powered toothbrush is a necessity for proper care of their teeth and gums.

A good high-end model can sell for more than $100, but here are a few things experts say to consider before you buy:

• If you are buying a high-end brush, look for one that signals (beeps) or turns off automatically after two minutes. Some models beep after 30 seconds to remind you to switch to a different quadrant of the mouth.

• Look for a model with a built-in, rechargeable battery. A fully charged brush should have enough power for at least one week of brushing.

• Make sure the brush-head replacements are reasonably priced, because they normally need to be replaced every three months.

• If you tend to brush too hard with a manual toothbrush, consider a model that has a built-in sensor that stops the bristle movement when it senses you are applying too much pressure.

• The standard warranty for a high-end electric brush is two years, but many users report no problems after four or more years of service.

Grandma says . . .

"Why buy expensive toothpaste when you can easily make your own tooth powder that's just as good? Just shake together equal amounts of baking soda and salt in a small container. When you brush, just sprinkle a small amount on your wet toothbrush and brush as usual."

Should you buy an inexpensive electric toothbrush?

If the thought of spending $100 or so on an electric toothbrush gives you sticker shock, good inexpensive alternatives (from Crest, Colgate, and Braun Oral B, among others) are now available for about $10. And studies suggest that they clean almost as well as the pricey models. Here are some things to keep in mind:

• Like their high-priced cousins, low-priced brushes require replacement of brush heads about four times a year. And the low-end models run on either one or two nonrechargeable AA batteries that require changing about once a month. Battery cost can add up.

• There are no built-in signals or beeps with the no-frills bargain brushes, so you may wish to use a timer to ensure that you brush for a full two minutes.

• Inexpensive electric brushes won't last as long as expensive models—warranties, if any, are brief—but you would have to go through ten of them to equal the cost of a high-end one.

Waste no toothpaste

Before you start using a tube of toothpaste, put a round, split-style clothespin on the bottom. Then as you use the toothpaste, wind the tube around the clothespin. This will keep pushing the unused toothpaste toward the top of the tube and reduce the hassle of using your fingers to squeeze the tube when it is nearly empty.

Get the very last bit of toothpaste

Whether you use a clothespin or your fingers to squeeze the tube, there will still be enough toothpaste in it for two or three more brushings even when you can't force it out of the opening at the top. That's when it's time to perform a bit of minor surgery on your toothpaste tube. Just slice the tube open and pick up some of the remaining toothpaste inside on your brush. When you're done loading the toothbrush, close up the tube with a paper (or bulldog) clip.

---

new uses for Old Toothbrushes

When it *is* time to buy a new toothbrush, don't throw out the old one. That old brush may be retired from cleaning teeth, but it can still have an extended, productive life assisting with numerous household chores. Clean it in the dishwasher; then save it for any of the following uses:

• Clean artificial flowers and plants, combs, silverware, shower-door tracks, crevices between tiles, typewriter keys and computer keyboards, around faucets, and telephones.

• Clean a grater or garlic press before putting it in the dishwasher.

• Use with a stain-removing agent to remove stains on clothing.

• Remove clingy strands of silk from fresh corn ears.

• Oil and clean a waffle iron.

• Use to apply hair dye.

• Dip in soapy water to clean between appliance buttons and raised-letter nameplates.

Scales and Health-Care Monitors

Aside from bathroom scales, the most common home health-care devices are blood-pressure and blood-sugar monitors. Here are a few pointers to keep them in shape.

Don't overload your scale

To keep your bathroom scale from wearing out, don't exceed 80 percent of capacity. (This is a more effective safeguard than the recommended 90 percent limit made by most manufacturers.)

Weigh yourself less often

Weighing yourself once or twice every day could wear out a scale before its time. Experts recommend that you weigh yourself *once or twice a week*. To ensure accuracy, make sure the scale is on a hard, flat surface, and stand as still as possible. Always weigh yourself on the same scale and under the same conditions (i.e., naked, before breakfast in the morning).

Keep your blood-pressure monitor away from heat

If you have a home blood-pressure monitor, one way to extend its life is to keep the unit away from excess heat, which can cause the rubber tubing that goes between the cuff and the monitor to crack.

Check batteries on blood-sugar monitors

When you select a blood-sugar monitor, the batteries used are important. Some units use standard batteries, while others take less common (and often pricier) batteries that may be harder to find. Still others don't have replaceable batteries at all, so you have to buy a new meter when the batteries fail. These batteries will last for thousands of readings, but if you test frequently, the thousands can add up more quickly than you expect.

Blood-sugar test strips

The real cost of using a blood-sugar monitor is in the test strips, which cost from 50 cents to a dollar each. You can buy them in bulk and lower the cost per strip. But using strips past their expiration date can give you inaccurate readings. So always consider how often you use them before you buy bulk. If you end up having to throw out some unused strips because they've expired, it may be more cost-effective to buy them singly.

Buy to Keep: Scales

How much you spend on a scale should depend on how long you want it to remain accurate.

Spring mechanism	An inexpensive scale with a spring mechanism can decorate your bathroom for a decade or more, but it will not remain accurate for anywhere near that long, because the springs will ultimately stretch. Nor will a "digital lithium" scale necessarily be more accurate than an old-fashioned mechanical scale: It just has a fancier display.
Load-cell mechanism	The most accurate scales use a load-cell mechanism rather than springs to take the weight. If you have a health condition that requires a reliable and accurate measurement, consider buying a professional digital scale that uses load-cell technology. It will cost several times more than the others, but it will stay accurate much longer.

Razors and Electric Shavers

Many men—and women, too—spend the better part of a life-time in search of the elusive "perfect" shave. Some find it in a razor blade, others in an electric machine. Whatever your preference, your shaver will last longer and shave smoother if you heed the following advice.

Lubricate your blades

To make your razor blades last longer, store your razor with the blade submerged in a cup of mineral oil after each use. The oil will prevent oxidation that leads to nick-causing imperfections, and you'll enjoy close, smooth shaves for a lot longer before you need to replace the blade or disposable razor.

Make your shaving brush last

There are two surefire ways to prolong the life of your favorite shaving brush: Prevent mildew, and apply proper technique when using the brush.

• Mildew, present wherever there is moisture, is the major cause of bristle breakdown. To fight mildew, hang the brush with the handle up to allow moisture to drain away from the base of the knot that is covered by the handle. Also don't store the brush in a confined area, such as the medicine cabinet. To further discourage mildew, rinse the brush in a mild borax solution every three to four weeks.

• When using the brush, employ a gentle side-to-side stroking action, with only the tips of the brush coming into contact with your face. If the brush is used with pressure and a rotating motion, the bristles will twist and bend over time and will gradually break and come loose.

◆ BEST ADVICE ◆ **Electric Shavers**

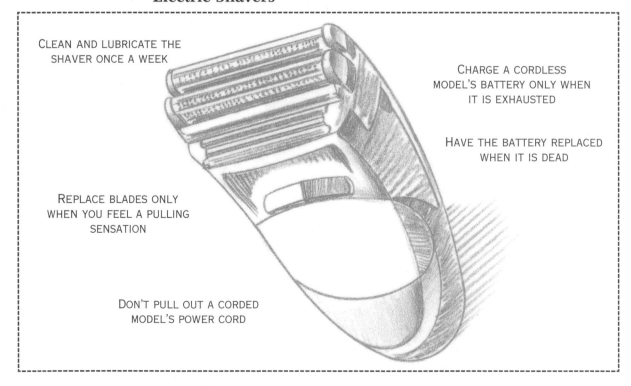

CLEAN AND LUBRICATE THE SHAVER ONCE A WEEK

CHARGE A CORDLESS MODEL'S BATTERY ONLY WHEN IT IS EXHAUSTED

HAVE THE BATTERY REPLACED WHEN IT IS DEAD

REPLACE BLADES ONLY WHEN YOU FEEL A PULLING SENSATION

DON'T PULL OUT A CORDED MODEL'S POWER CORD

Extending a cordless's battery life

The rechargeable battery in a cordless electric shaver lasts an average of five years before it needs to be replaced. To make your rechargeable shaver last longer, use it cordless exclusively and charge only when the battery is exhausted or when the shaver itself indicates that it needs to be recharged.

Replace your cordless's battery

Many people throw out their cordless electric shaver when the battery dies. In almost all instances (with the exception of very old models), it is far more economical to replace the battery in your existing shaver instead of buying a new shaver. If you replace the battery when it dies, your shaver might even last as long as cord-only models.

☞ DON'T
disconnect the cord

Don't routinely remove the plug from a cord-only electric shaver. Constant plugging and unplugging of the cord can damage the socket that the plug goes into, leading to electrical shorts.

Clean and oil to keep your shaver buzzing

Lubricate and clean your electric shaver regularly, as often as once a week. Follow the owner's manual for precise details on how to do this. If you don't clean shaved stubble from the shaver, it can eventually make its way into the housing, where it could clog up the mechanism or cause an electrical short. After cleaning, spray the shaving surface with lubricant and turn on the shaver for a few seconds to ensure distribution of the lubricant.

When to replace a shaver's blades

Some manufacturers suggest that you replace an electric shaver's blades every two years, but with proper maintenance they can last much longer, depending on your personal preference and the thickness of your beard. As a general rule, you should replace the blades if the razor starts to cause irritation and pulling or if it no longer shaves to your satisfaction.

Cut the cost of shaver cleaning

To save money, use alcohol and mineral oil to clean your shaver instead of the manufacturer's lubricants and cleansers—they work just as well.

INFO STATION

REVIEWS OF ELECTRIC SHAVERS

Helpful, comprehensive product reviews and price comparisons can be found at Consumer Search, while Electric Shaver Page and Electric Razor Rap are two great sources chock full of news, owner opinions, FAQs, and surveys.

> **Consumer Search**
www.consumersearch.com/www /family/mens_electric_shavers

> **Electric Shaver Page**
http://iavbbs.com/gflinn

> **Electric Razor Rap**
http://jimelliott.suddenlaunch2.com

Buy to Keep: Electric Shavers

A good electric shaver can easily last ten years. Here are five important factors to consider when buying.

Brand name	Stick with a known, quality brand name with fewer features rather than a lesser-known brand with lots of bells and whistles. All models of a specific brand line shave identically. The cost increases with added features, like a charging base with cleaning function or an LCD panel that provides data on charge status and maintenance. You'll get just as good a shave without them. Another great money-saving idea: Look for discontinued or refurbished models of your favorite shaver.
Motor speed	Look for a motor speed of 10,000 or faster (meaning the blades move back and forth 10,000 times per minute). Faster blades mean a closer shave and less irritation. Slower models cost less but take longer to use and do not do as good a job.
Trial period	Buy a shaver that has at least a 30-day (and preferably a 60-day) money-back guarantee. It takes about 30 days for your face to adjust to a new shaver, so an adequate initial adjustment period is essential before you can tell if the shaver is right for you.
Comfort factor	Make sure the shaver feels comfortable in your hand. It should not vibrate excessively or be annoyingly noisy.
Battery features	In a cordless rechargeable shaver, look for a quick-charge option and a long charge life so that you won't have to worry that it will quit before it finishes the job.
Corded models	If you're really intent on buying to keep a shaver as long as possible, get a corded-only model as your primary shaver—you won't have to worry about dying batteries. Rechargeable shavers are fine for travel, as are some cheaper shavers that use ordinary removable batteries.

Medicines and Vitamins

When we reach for the medicine bottle, we want to be sure the contents are potent and fresh—even if the expiration date on the bottle has passed. Here are some ways to ensure that your medicines and vitamins don't go bad before their time.

Don't put drugs in the medicine cabinet

To make your prescription and over-the-counter (OTC) medicines last longer and retain potency, store them in a dry area where they will stay at a steady room temperature. Avoid the bathroom—including the medicine cabinet—and any areas near the stove in the kitchen, where temperatures and humidity are likely to fluctuate. As always, remember to keep all medicine out of reach of children. Store all medicine in a locked cabinet or other secure location. Don't leave it on the counter or rely on childproof packaging!

Buy generic

When purchasing OTC medications, make sure that you look for the products by their generic names. There is no advantage to buying a brand name. Store brands contain the exact same amount of active drug and work just as well—often at a fraction of the cost. And always look for products with the most far-off expiration dates.

Remove the cotton plug

Although some people think leaving the cotton plug in the bottle will help keep aspirins or other OTC drugs or vitamins fresh longer, this is not so. Experts say it is a good idea to remove the cotton plug from the bottle for storage to reduce the chance of moisture getting inside.

Hardy aspirin

You can store aspirin in a metal pill box, if you want. Aspirin won't interact with metal. Aspirin will also not be negatively affected by freezing, light, or high altitudes.

Don't precut a lot of pills at once

Perhaps like lots of folks, you use a pill cutter at home to slice your pills in half to achieve the prescribed dose of medication. And while it's more convenient to cut a lot of pills all at once rather than bringing out the pill cutter for every dose, this is not a great idea. Cutting the pills causes the medicine in them to break down faster. Pharmacists recommend that you don't cut more than five days' worth of pills at one time. In general, it doesn't matter whether the pills are cut precisely in half, as long as the cumulative dose is the same over time. However, some medications may require more exact dosage, so it is best to ask your pharmacist or the prescribing doctor whether cutting the pills is advisable with your particular prescription.

☞ TOSS
old Tylenol

Do not use acetaminophen or products containing acetaminophen beyond their expiration date even if the bottles have been stored properly. Acetaminophen deteriorates more readily than aspirin and other analgesics like ibuprofen and naproxen. When acetaminophen breaks down, it can cause serious harm to the kidneys.

Expiration date leeway

Most prescription drugs gradually lose potency over time, but if they are properly stored in a dry and cool location, they may be safely used for weeks and even a few months after the expiration date on the package. The same is true of most over-the-counter products (with the notable exception of acetaminophen, see above).

Drug companies may not be eager to tell you how to extend the shelf life of their products, but they can offer some good advice about how best to keep and store them. Most have customer service departments that will be glad to answer questions about specific products. The two below let you send your question directly to the company online and provide prompt responses.

> Johnson & Johnson
www.jnj.com
Click on "Contact Us" and then on "Product Information" from the index.

> Bayer
www.bayer.com
Click on "Contact Us" then "Health Care" and then the appropriate category ("Prescription drugs," "Diagnostics," and so on).

Or in Canada, you can contact
> Canadian Pharmacists Association
www.pharmacists.ca

Sniff out old aspirin

If you have a bottle of aspirin that is past its expiration date, just use your nose to tell if the contents are still okay for use. Aspirin and aspirin-based products will take on a vinegarlike smell when they deteriorate. So sniff any "expired" bottles before using them, and if they smell vinegary, toss them out. If they still smell fine, chances are the contents will be only slightly less potent, if at all, than when you first brought the bottle home.

Get the most from your supplements

Many people don't get enough nutrients from their regular diet. For some, vitamin pills and other supplements can provide the nutrients that they are missing. Pregnant women and older adults have special nutritional needs that may require supplementation. If you are currently taking supplements, nutrition experts advise you keep the following tips in mind:

• Avoid megadoses. Choose multivitamin and mineral supplements that provide 100 percent of the recommended daily value rather than a product that contains 500 percent of one vitamin and 20 percent of another. (An exception is calcium; providing 100 percent of calcium in one pill would make it too big to swallow.) Most cases of nutrient toxicity are caused by megadose supplements.

• Beware of gimmicks. So-called natural vitamins cost a lot more than synthetics, but in most cases the synthetic is the equivalent of the natural. And don't be tempted by the addition of herbs, enzymes, or amino acids: The main thing they add is cost.

• Consult your doctor. You don't need a prescription for vitamins and supplements, but that doesn't mean they are without potentially serious side effects. High doses of vitamin A can cause liver problems or weaken bones in women. Liver problems have also been linked to high doses of vitamin B-3 (niacin). And vitamin E can interfere with blood-thinning medications.

Store vitamins and supplements safely

Keep all vitamins and supplements in a cool, dry place. Like medicines, they lose potency over time. As with medicine, avoid hot, humid locations, such as the bathroom and the kitchen near the stove, and keep them in a locked or secure location, out of sight and reach of children. Be especially careful with any iron-containing supplements: Iron overdose is a leading cause of poisoning deaths among children.

Eyeglasses

If you wear glasses, you know how frustrating it is when you scratch a lens, or a frame suddenly falls apart and you can't find the tiny screw. Here are a few ideas to keep your lenses scratch-free and your frames in one piece for as long as you need them.

Be careful how you wipe your lenses

Most eyeglasses made today use coated plastic lenses that are easily damaged and scratched if wiped with a paper tissue or towel. Keep the lenses scratch-free and damage-free by using a soft, dry, lint-free cloth to clean your glasses. A scrap of silk will work nicely, or you can buy a package of cloths from your optician for just a few dollars. Opticians will often be happy to give you a cloth free for the asking.

Take care what liquid you use, too

If you need to use a liquid to wash smudged plastic lenses, use a lens-cleaning solution, available from your optician or your local pharmacy. (Do not use window cleaner or other abrasive substances that can damage the protective coating on the lenses.)

A homemade solution for glass lenses only

If your eyeglasses have glass lenses, you don't need to buy a special lens-cleaning solution. You can use an inexpensive homemade solution instead: Just mix equal parts of white vinegar and water.

Keep screws tight

Don't let a loose screw or two lead to the untimely demise of your eyeglass frames. Next time you replace or tighten a screw, make sure it is twisted tight and then use a toothpick to apply a small drop of clear nail polish to the top of the screw. Take care not to get any of the polish on the lenses or frames, as it can damage the plastic. The nail polish will keep the screw from loosening again.

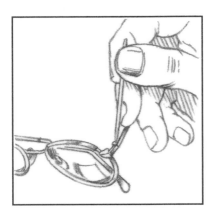

new uses for Eyeglasses

Don't throw away your old eyeglasses after you get new ones. Here are a few suggestions to give your old glasses a second lease on life:

- If your prescription is the same or has changed only slightly, you can turn your old glasses into a new pair of prescription sunglasses. Having the lenses coated and using the same frame will provide substantial savings over buying a brand-new pair.

- Keep your old glasses as a spare. If you misplace, lose, or break your new glasses, you will have the old pair to use in a pinch.

- Take out the lenses and use the frames as part of a Halloween costume, or save them with other props the kids might use when putting on a show.

- Donate the old glasses to a charity that provides free eyeglasses to the needy.

Eyeglasses

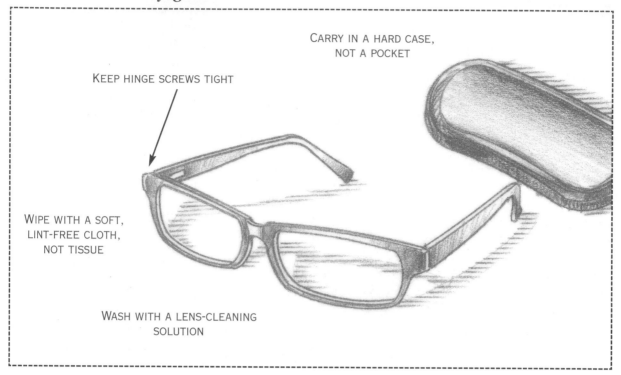

CARRY IN A HARD CASE,
NOT A POCKET

KEEP HINGE SCREWS TIGHT

WIPE WITH A SOFT,
LINT-FREE CLOTH,
NOT TISSUE

WASH WITH A LENS-CLEANING
SOLUTION

Bath Mats and Towels

There's something so comforting about a nice soft towel when we step out of the bath or shower. Here are some tips to keep yours in service for many years to come.

Fight bath-mat mildew with bleach

A vinyl mat is a useful addition to any bathtub or shower stall. But along with the comfort and stability it provides comes an added risk: mildew formation. Some manufacturers sell bath mats billed as "antibacterial" and "mildew resistant," but you don't have to spend the extra money to keep your mats mildew-free and fresh for years to come. Here's how:

• Use your regular all-purpose cleaner to clean the top of the mat, and periodically spray the bottom (where the mildew usually develops) with bleach. Leave the bleach on for five minutes before washing it off. In addition to getting rid of the mildew, the bleach will deodorize and sanitize the underside of the mat. Spraying once or twice a month should do the trick.

• To further reduce the risk of mildew, pick up the mat after you're finished bathing or showering and drape it over the side of the tub or the door to the shower stall. This will prevent water from collecting under the mat and creating a breeding ground for bacteria and mildew.

Stop colored towels from fading

Keep your brand-new colored towels from fading by adding a cup of salt to the water the first time you launder them. The salt will "set" the color and help the towels gleam brightly longer. When the color does start to fade, throw in some salt to perk up the color again. Adding salt will also give dark clothes a boost when they begin to fade.

Timing when to add detergent

Be sure not to let full-strength detergent come into direct contact with your colored towels, because that can cause colors to fade, too. Wait until the washer is filling with water and the detergent is dissolved before putting in the towels.

Predry towels

On humid days, don't let wet towels hang in the bathroom all day. To keep them fresh, toss them in the dryer for 10 minutes or so and then hang them up.

Reduce laundering time

You don't have to wash your terry-cloth bath towels after every use. The towels will last longer if you limit the amount of time they spend in the washer and dryer. Let them air-dry after several uses before laundering. (You'll want to wash them more often in humid weather, however.) They'll stay fresher between launderings if you add 1/4 cup of baking soda

---

new uses for Old Towels

Why throw out your old bath towels when you can still put them to good, money-saving use? Here are a few suggestions:

• Speed drying-time and save energy when drying big bulky items and jeans. Just add a clean, dry bath towel to the wet items in the clothes dryer and the load will dry faster.

• Cut up old towels and use them as rags for cleaning and polishing.

• Cut them into strips and use as sweatbands when working in the yard, running, or doing other sweaty activities.

• Keep them in the garage for drying the car after washing it.

with the detergent when washing. Rinse in cold water to save energy and money.

Give wet towels a shake

If you air-dry towels outdoors, give them a vigorous shake before hanging them on the clothesline; then shake them again before you fold them. This makes the towels soft and absorbent again by fluffing up the terry fibers.

How to judge fabric quality

When you buy bath towels, the quality of the fabric is even more important than the weight. Most towels are terry cloth, a cotton fabric with uncut surface loops. Less absorbent is velour, which has a soft, velvety feel that comes from cutting the loops.

The quality of cotton is based on the length of its "staples," or fiber. Longer staples are stronger, more durable and absorbent; the longer the loops, the more the towel should soften over time. For maximum absorbency, look for long, dense loops across the entire surface on both sides of a terry-cloth towel. The grade of cotton is also important in determining the "hand" (how it feels). Premium grades of cotton include:

• Egyptian cotton, grown in the Nile Valley, is known for its long staples, lush feel, and soft drape. (This is also true of Turkish cotton.) By industry standards, a towel can be labeled "Egyptian cotton" when it contains as little as 10 percent Egyptian cotton. Cheaper, low-quality cotton is often used to make up the balance, creating a coarser hand. For best quality, look for towels labeled "100 percent Egyptian cotton."

• Pima cotton is the strongest of the U.S.-grown cottons. It was first produced by combining Egyptian cotton with cotton grown by the Pima Indians in the Southwest. It is known for softness, long staple, and durability.

Don't use fabric softener on towels

Fabric softener added to the washer or dryer will coat your towels and interfere with their absorbency. Instead, try adding a cup of white vinegar to the final rinse cycle of your wash. It will act as a natural fabric softener, reduce static cling, and get rid of extra suds and soap deposits. Using vinegar instead of fabric softener will leave your towels soft and fresh and save you money, too.

Paper & Collectibles

chapter

5

Antiques and Collectibles—General Guidelines

Collectors of all stripes strive to keep their treasured works in top condition. Proper handling and storage are key.

Dust without feathers

Avoid using feather dusters to clean paintings, wood carvings, glassware, and other antiques. The feathers can catch in small crevices and result in breakage, or they can dislodge delicate pieces or fragments of paint. Use a soft paintbrush or cleaning cloth instead.

ProTip

TAPE UP YOUR BRUSH

If you use a soft-bristled paintbrush to dust off your valuables, put a couple of layers of masking tape around the brush's metal ferrule to avoid putting any accidental dents or scratches in your valuables while you are dusting.

Handle with care

Always handle your *objets d'art* with clean, dry hands—or wear clean cotton gloves if you're handling unbreakable items. Hands-on time should be kept to a minimum, however, because the oils and salts on your hands can cause tarnish on silver or damage lacquered and ceramic surfaces. To protect against dings and scratches, be sure to take off any jewelry (including your wristwatch) whenever inspecting your treasured objects.

Mount small items

Most people have seen Riker mounts used for displaying butterflies or gemstone collections, but they also offer an affordable and convenient way to preserve small collectible items, such as coins, arrowheads, campaign buttons, and rocks, in the home. Riker mounts are available in various sizes; most range in price from about $3 for a small 3x4-inch case to about $15 for a large 12x16 case. You can purchase them from most hobby and scientific-supply shops as well as many online vendors. Although they can provide good protection against moisture, glass-covered Riker

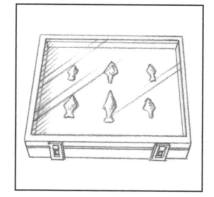

mounts do not filter out light and ultraviolet radiation, so be sure to keep your mounted collections out of the sun and away from bright light sources.

Condition is everything

Regardless of whether you collect comics or corn huskers, the monetary value of your collection will ultimately be determined by its overall condition. The single best step you can take toward protecting any collection is to provide proper storage conditions, which typically translates to avoiding spaces prone to excessive light, moisture, heat, or dust. In general, whatever is comfortable for you usually will be comfortable for your collection—although some items may do better at cooler temperatures. If you have items on display, make sure safeguards are in place against improper handling and indoor pollutants. Use sturdy cases or boxes to store delicate or perishable items, and be sure to keep them out of heavily trafficked areas.

Humidity is relative

Humid conditions generally won't have much impact on glass, ceramics, and other inorganic materials, but they can wreak havoc on most other collectibles. In addition to promoting mold and mildew growth, excessive moisture in the air can also create inviting conditions for insects and other pests. Protect your precious objects by keeping them in a stable environment with a relative humidity level between 45 and 50 percent. You may consider adding air-conditioning during the hot summer months, as well as a dehumidifier, if needed. If you live in a dry climate or require heat in the winter, you may need to use a humidifier to maintain an adequate moisture level.

Fight indoor pollution

Dust and light are the enemies of all precious possessions. Fortunately, you can significantly reduce the amount of dust around your home by regularly cleaning or replacing the filters in your heating and air-conditioning units. Keep exposure to sunlight to a minimum wherever valuable objects are stored. The sun's ultraviolet rays are particularly harmful to most valuable items—especially paintings, glassware, textiles, and paper items—and should be avoided at all costs. If valuables need to be kept in a bright room, use window shades or drapes to filter out as much light as possible. Damage caused by light is both cumulative and irreversible.

Other unseen dangers are posed by the presence of adhesives, wood products, wet paint, and other fume-producing chemicals—all of which should be banned from the spaces where collections are stored. Also, avoid keeping valuable objects near cooking areas or locations where flames may be in use.

Stay out of the woods

Wooden cabinets (and those made of oak, in particular) are not recommended for storing textiles, dolls, stamps, coins, or metal of any sort. Both unfinished and painted wood emit sulfuric and acidic vapors that can age paper, yellow fabric, or cause corrosion on metal. Instead, use polyethylene plastic containers, acid-free cardboard boxes, or metal storage cabinets, preferably with an enamel coating. If you must store your textiles or dolls in a wooden drawer or closet, wrap them in acid-free tissue paper or a sheet of prewashed, unbleached cotton muslin so that they never come in direct contact with the wood. Seal any wood surfaces with at least two coats of polyurethane varnish.

Make your move...with care

You can substantially lower the risks of accidentally damaging any of your prized possessions when moving them by always making any needed preparations—such as clearing away obstacles, closing window shades, removing sharp objects, and so on—to the room or workspace where you'll be placing the object *before* moving it.

Paper Documents

Paper is ubiquitous—and surprisingly durable. By following a few simple rules, you can make it possible for future generations to enjoy your cherished letters, prints, and news clippings.

Keep paper dark and dry

Most types of paper can tolerate cool temperatures fairly well, although they can get brittle with prolonged exposure to light and temperatures above 75° F (24° C). Dampness may be a far more serious risk to all paper products, however. Excessive moisture destroys fibers and sizing, and often results in the development of harmful mold and mildew. Ideally, paper should be kept away from light sources and stored at temperatures between 45° and 65° F (7° and 18° C), with a 60 percent relative humidity level (although levels between 30 and 70 percent are acceptable).

Flat is where it's at

Keep newspaper clippings, prints, and other works on paper lying flat in storage. This eliminates the need to fold and unfold them, which inevitably results in rips along the creases.

Use special plastic folders

For additional protection, store documents in polypropylene or polyester-film (Mylar) folders or envelopes. Polyester folders offer no added alkalinity, but they are clear and provide good support and protection for your documents. Be careful, though. They can produce an electrostatic charge that may damage certain types of media, including pastel, charcoal, and some pencil drawings.

Store newspapers on buffered mats

Put newspapers and other types of paper with a high-acid content on buffered mats or paper, which contain added calcium carbonate or magnesium carbonate for extra alkalinity. Buffered materials don't neutralize a paper's acidity, but they can slow down its rate of deterioration and prevent the acids from spreading to other documents. They will eventually lose their protective properties, however, and need to be replaced periodically.

Acid on the move

"Acid migration" may sound like something out of a bad science-fiction movie, but it's an actual term used to describe the transfer of the acidity from an acidic material to a neutral material, resulting in discoloration, brittleness, and other types of damage to both items. (Unfortunately, it doesn't work in reverse; you can't transfer an object's neutral properties to something that is acidic.) The term also underscores the importance of using acid-free papers and storage materials and why it's best to isolate highly acidic materials, such as newspaper clippings or telegrams, from photographs, drawings, and other documents in long-term storage.

Take care with buffered mats

Beware of using alkaline-buffered storage materials with watercolor paintings; the added alkalinity can damage some watercolor paints.

Keep handling to a minimum

It's no contest: Improper handling is to blame for the overwhelming majority of rips, creases, and stains on valuable paper documents and books. Obviously, the best way to prevent such mishaps is to handle collectible prints and books as infrequently as possible. If handling is required, it's a good idea to wear white editing gloves to prevent damage from the oils and salts on your hands (use extra care, however, because the gloves make it much easier for things to slip out of your hands). When you need to move prints or other documents around your house, try sliding a slightly larger piece of stiff paper or matting underneath it to use as a carrying board. Don't eat, drink, or smoke when handling paper, and make sure there are no pens and markers nearby.

Take a segregated approach to storage

Looking for an effective, space-efficient way to store your valuable prints and important documents? Pack them inside stackable, rigid storage boxes made of noncorrosive metal, polyethylene, polypropylene, or acid-free cardboard. To make it easier to locate specific items—and to limit unnecessary handling—label sheets of white, acid-free paper and place them between each document as dividers. Don't forget to label the outside of the boxes as well.

Get it framed

The best way to preserve old prints or precious documents is to have them professionally matted and framed. Be sure to request a frame with both starch-paste hinges and an acid-free mat for mounting. Also, make certain that the paper doesn't touch the frame's glass. If you intend to display the work in a sunny room, consider a frame with conservation glass or sheet acrylic (such as Plexiglas), either of which will reduce the document's exposure to the sun's harmful ultraviolet (UV) radiation. (Remember, light damage cannot be reversed.)

☞ DON'T
put plastic over drawings

> Avoid using Plexiglas or other plastics in frames that house pastel or charcoal drawings; plastic tends to build up static electricity, which can pull the powdery renderings right off the paper.

Make a reference copy

Although photocopying documents, or scanning them into your PC, requires you to briefly expose them to intense light, the process may be beneficial over the long haul. Because you have the copies to refer to, it will significantly reduce the amount of handling of the originals needed and will allow you to safely store the originals in the dark from that point on.

An easy way to protect youngsters' artwork

It's not an acid-free container or anything even approaching archival storage, but if you're looking for an easy, effective, and inexpensive way to save those precious drawings from your kids or grandkids, that empty cardboard tube from a used roll of paper towels could be just what you've been looking for. You can even put several rolled up (with the image facing out, of course) masterpieces in each tube. The tubes are easy to store and will provide adequate protection against most forms of damage for years to come. Don't forget to label the outside of your tubes, or each drawing, with the date and child's name before putting them into storage, though.

This method also works for certificates and other documents—although it's not recommended for long-term storage of important or valuable papers.

Preserve kids' art with hair spray

Make those masterpieces created by the youngsters in your family last much longer by gently spraying the surface of the drawings with hair spray. The same polymers that hold your hair in place also do a dandy job of keeping the chalk, pastel, charcoal, and paint particles on the paper. But be careful not to use a conditioning spray, because it may contain oils that will cause the colors to run.

Books

What is it about books that makes us want to surround ourselves with them? Is it the way they feel in our hands? Their smell? Or is it just the thought of all the wonderful places and times they can take us to? Whatever the reasons, here's how to make sure your beloved books are around for your grandchildren to enjoy.

Move books to the front of the shelf

Experts recommend that you position books at the front of bookshelves instead of pushing them to the rear, as is common practice in so many homes. By leaving some space behind your books, you're permitting air to circulate and inhibiting the growth of mildew and molds on the books.

Treat books right while reading

It's not that far-fetched to imagine that the best seller you're currently reading may become a precious family treasure in the years to come. Do your part to keep books in good condition while reading them by following a couple of simple steps:

• Instead of turning down page corners, use a bookmark—or, better yet, a long strip of acid-free paper.

• Don't forget to turn pages by the top corner; turning them from the bottom edge is a good way to cause accidental tears.

Remove grease stains from books

If someone has left greasy fingerprints on one of your cherished cloth books, you can usually remove the stains by rubbing over them with a piece of stale bread. Another method is to sprinkle some baking soda or cornstarch (or baby powder with cornstarch) over the marks and let it sit overnight. The following morning, remove the powder with a soft, clean camel hair or cosmetics brush and the stains should go along with it.

Everyday items pose paper hazards

They may seem innocent enough, but tape, glue, paper clips, staples, and other ordinary fasteners can cause irreversible damage to books or to valuable papers. Metallic fasteners like paper clips and binder clips can corrode and leave rust stains on paper. Even the ubiquitous Post-it notes can leave behind residue that may cause pages to become stuck together. Also avoid using rubber bands as bookmarks. A rubber band left in a book for a prolonged period can dry out and leave pages stuck together or badly stained.

Protect delicate books

Treasured family heirlooms, such as Bibles and scrapbooks, are difficult to enjoy without being handled. Yet it is the constant handling over the years that causes them to become worn and fragile. An excellent way to protect them, and to preserve them for the enjoyment of future generations, is to have a sturdy, custom-made box built to accommodate the dimensions of the book. The box—often called a phase box—should be made of acid-free barrier board or some other neutral material, though not wood or conventional cardboard (due to the presence of lignin and other acidic chemicals).

Books with dry, flaking leather covers can also be wrapped in acid-free paper or polyester jackets. This will slow down further disintegration, as well as prevent the leather flakes and dirt from soiling the inside pages or other books that might be nearby.

Beware of bookends

They may look nice, they may have been a gift from a dear friend or loved one, but decorative bookends aren't always kind

✦ BEST ADVICE ✦ **Books**

HOLD LARGE VOLUMES
WITH BOTH HANDS

AVOID LOW OR ROUGH
BOOKENDS

TURN THE PAGES BY THE
TOP CORNER

ARABIA

GRASP IT FIRMLY IN
THE MIDDLE TO TAKE
IT OFF THE SHELF

DON'T USE PAPER CLIPS
OR RUBBER BANDS AS
BOOKMARKS

STORE FAMILY BIBLES AND
SUCH IN SPECIAL BOXES

support for your books and don't have any sharp edges to cut book covers.

Watch out for mold

If you see active, moist-looking mold growing on your books or documents, don't attempt to remove it yourself. Instead, carefully enclose each moldy item in plastic and contact a restorer or conservator (see "Find a conservator," page 81). Mold spores are very difficult to remove completely, and they can be spread through the air to put other books and nearby works at risk. In addition, some forms of mold can cause acute respiratory problems in humans and their pets. Be sure to wipe the shelves with a mild bleach solution.

ProTip

**GET RID OF
MUSTY ODORS**

Librarians sometimes use charcoal to get rid of musty odors on old books, and you can, too. If you keep your books in a glass-enclosed bookcase, it may be trapping moisture inside that can provide a welcome environment for mold and mildew. You can eliminate any excess humidity and keep your books dry and mold-free by placing one or two charcoal briquettes or some deactivated charcoal in a small bowl inside. Be sure to replace it with fresh charcoal every two to three months.

to your books. Many don't support the full length of the books they lean against, which can leave books warped and worn. Other types of bookends have rough or uneven edges that can actually rip or tear book covers. If you have some empty space left on a shelf and want to keep your books standing upright and undamaged, a smooth block of wood covered with either leather or felt is the best way to go. If you decide to keep your bookends, make sure they provide adequate, top-to-bottom

Other ways to end musty smells

If you detect a musty smell from your books or papers in storage, but don't see any mold or mildew, try thoroughly drying both the objects and the storage area using fans or space heaters or opening windows for a few hours until the odor is gone. You can also eliminate musty odors from books and papers by sealing them in an enclosed chamber. Place a plastic garbage liner inside a clean garbage can. Pour in about 4 cups of odor-absorbing cat litter or baking soda. Then insert another liner over the first, and add the books or papers. Close the lid, and leave it in a cool, dry space until the odor dissipates. (It may take a few days.)

Give dust the brush off

Dust is not only unattractive; it can soil paper and book bindings. And it can also attract insects and promote mold growth. That's why it's so important to regularly dust your books—and all unframed pencil drawings, prints, and watercolors as well. Light strokes with a soft, clean shaving brush or artist's paintbrush usually work better than a cloth or feather duster (which often just spreads the dust from one object to another). Before you start dusting, however, carefully check your documents to make sure there are no loose or powdery materials on the surface that could be altered during cleaning. Pastel and charcoal drawings, for example, should never be dusted, as you could permanently damage them.

ProTip
IMPROVE A BOOK'S SHELF LIFE

According to librarians, who should know, the secret to removing a book from a shelf or bookcase without tearing it is to push the books on either side of it slightly inward, then gently grasp the book around its midsection and ease it free. Never pull out a book by it spine; you'll eventually damage the binding and cause it to rip. Also, be sure to use both hands when handling large, heavy tomes or encased volumes.

Take care if you vacuum books

You can also use a vacuum cleaner to remove dust from books, but if you do, place a piece of nylon stocking or cheesecloth over the end of the hose nozzle. This will prevent pieces of paper or binding from coming loose or being sucked into the vacuum cleaner.

The last name in protection

Many libraries and professional archivists around the world prefer to keep their most important documents, drawings, and individual books in what are known as Solander boxes. Invented by Swedish botanist Daniel Solander (1733-1782) while he was a librarian at the British Museum, these expensive boxes are lined throughout with acid-free paper and are virtually light- and dust-proof; they even offer good protection against fluctuations in humidity and temperature. Most are covered in cloth and constructed on a plywood frame. Solander boxes typically incorporate a *drop-front* design for prints and documents or a *drop-back* design (below) to accommodate a single book.

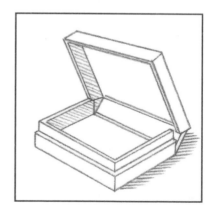

Jewelry and Precious Metals

Jewelry, silver, and other precious metals are part of the legacy we hand down. It takes just a little care and know-how to keep your precious pieces in pristine condition.

Polish your jewelry

Most modern jewelry can be safely cleaned using a mild soap-and-water solution and a soft-bristled brush or a soft cloth (even soft brushes can cause scratches on silver). Don't use hard water, though; it can cause discoloration or leave mineral deposits. Make sure to clean jewelry over a mat or a towel so that it will catch any stones that may come loose. Antique jewelry should never be cleaned with water. Rather, use a soft, dry paintbrush or chamois to remove dirt and dust. Heavily soiled jewelry should be professionally cleaned.

Keep claw settings away from water

Do not wet rings or other pieces of jewelry with claw settings. Claws are tiny prongs that hold a stone in place, and on pieces with claws, water can seep into small crevices and cause corrosion. Many antique jewelry pieces with claw settings also use adhesives to set the stones; immersing them in water can soften or disintegrate the glues, resulting in lost gemstones. Have loose stones reglued by a jeweler.

Condition a cameo

As shell cameos age, they can develop cracks or discoloration due to changes in the weather or too dry conditions. But you can keep your cameos in great shape by moisturizing them once or twice a year. Use a soft-bristled brush to gently scrub the cameo in warm water mixed with a bit of mild soap (such as Ivory liquid). Rinse immediately and thoroughly pat dry. Once the residual water has evaporated, apply some oil of wintergreen or mineral oil to the cameo using your finger, a soft cloth, or a cotton swab. Be sure to coat both the front and back surfaces. Let the oil soak in for several hours or overnight; then wipe off any excess.

Keep your mitts off the metal

Most metal artifacts should not be handled with bare hands. Salts and oils from your skin may etch into polished and uncoated metals and can even cause permanent damage. It's best to wear cotton gloves when handling any precious metal object or to grasp the object with a clean cloth. Lift objects from their center of gravity, and avoid lifting objects by limbs, handles, spouts, or other extended areas; metal joints can develop undetected weaknesses over time and may break off if stressed.

Remove wax from silver candlesticks

The safest way to remove dripped wax from your silver candlesticks is lay them down on soft, absorbent cloth or paper towels in a warm room for about an hour so. (If you're impatient, you can try using a hair blower.) Once the wax softens, use a blunt wooden stick to slowly peel away and chip off the wax. Repeat, if necessary; then buff with a silver polishing cloth. Never try to use a knife to slice off the wax; you're more likely to scratch the candlestick. And never, as is commonly advised, put silver candlesticks in the freezer to harden the wax. Some metals may have an adverse reaction to extremely cold temperature, especially if two metals were used to make the object (for example, silver over an iron core), and they contract at different rates when they get cold.

Don't get uptight over tarnish

Silver tarnishes as a reaction to sulfur gases that are naturally present in the air. They are primarily produced by decaying animal matter—although they are also released by many food-stuffs, paints, plastics, textiles, and other common household materials. Humid conditions also promote tarnishing.

Although it's unsightly—especially those dense black or purplish rings evident in its latter stages—tarnish itself does not pose a threat to silver artifacts. In fact, most damage to silver occurs during the polishing required to remove the tarnish. Overpolishing often results in a loss of detail definition over time. On silver-plated objects, frequent polishing can actually remove the plating, leaving dull areas of exposed base metal that can be mistaken for stubborn spots of tarnish.

It's easiest to remove tarnish in its beginning stages, when it appears as a yellowish or light brown staining. You can usually remove these early formations of tarnish by washing silver items in water mixed with some phosphate-free detergent. Avoid immersing the metal if possible; try rubbing it with a cloth moistened with the solution first. After washing, rinse gently; then dry and buff it with a soft, clean cloth or flannel.

Say "no" to latex

If you're looking for a common cause of tarnish around your home, look no further than the latex gloves you normally wear while washing your silverware.

Latex, which is also found in rubber bands and other elastics, contains enough sulfur to cause silver to tarnish. Remove all elastics from your silverware, and pick up a pair of nitrile gloves at your local drugstore or pharmaceutical-supply outlet instead (Request the gloves you would wear if you had a latex allergy.)

ProTip

HOW TO POLISH METAL

Many commercial metal polishes and silver dips are highly abrasive and may leave scratches on your fine silver. It's usually best to lightly polish silver pieces on a regular basis with a silver-polishing cloth, such as a Hagerty Glove or Birks Silver Polishing Cloth. Many museums polish most types of metal by making a runny paste of calcium carbonate (chalk), mixed with equal amounts of ethanol (denatured or ethyl alcohol) and distilled water. To use, rub the paste across the surface, using cotton rags, cotton balls, or cotton swabs to work a small area at a time. Then rinse the piece with distilled water to remove all residual polish. (You can accelerate drying by adding some ethanol to the rinse water or by giving the object a final wipe with the alcohol.)

Wrap up silver to fight tarnish

Keep tarnish at bay by wrapping silver jewelry, eating utensils,

coins, or artifacts in silver tarnish-inhibiting cloths, also known as Pacific Cloths or treated-silver cloth (available for about $20 per yard from better fabric stores). After wrapping, place your silver items in clear polyester (Mylar) or polyethylene bags. Silver kept wrapped and stored in this fashion requires a minimal amount of polishing and can be taken out and enjoyed as often as you like.

Protect the patina

The light green to dark brown patinas often seen on bronze arms and armor can be intentionally added with chemicals or can occur naturally over time. Although it's tempting to clean off the discoloration to "restore" the object, it's usually best left alone. You could wind up drastically altering the condition of the item—and significantly impacting its historical and monetary value.

Wax your irons

The best protective coating for your historical iron pieces is wax. It's easy to apply and can be often renewed without causing any harm to metal. Many museums use microcrystalline waxes (the wax of choice is Renaissance Wax), which will not yellow over time like many other types of wax. Apply the wax to your iron pieces with a clean cloth, and buff it out with a rag or bristle shoe brush.

Porcelain, Ceramics, and Glassware

Porcelain, ceramics, and glassware are durable but fragile stuff. If you handle and clean them carefully, they will last indefinitely.

Use both hands when handling glass

Most damage to glassware and ceramics is the result of improper handling. To prevent any mishaps, always use both hands when moving your pieces, and be sure to lift them from their strongest points. Never hold ceramic or glass objects by their handles or spouts—especially if the object has been previously repaired.

The safe way to display

The best and safest way to display delicate porcelain and glass pieces is in a solid cabinet in a quiet area of your home. It's also a good idea to cut pieces of felt or chamois to fit under the base of your breakable objects. It will keep them steadier and protect the furniture underneath.

Definitely not dishwasher-safe

There are ways to clean your old glassware items and ceramic bowls, but putting them in the dishwasher isn't one of them. Regardless of their condition, *never* place any antique bowls, plates, or dishes inside your dishwasher.

Clean cracked glassware carefully

Before cleaning any antique glassware, examine it for cracks or repairs. If you see any, don't immerse the glass in water. Instead, try cleaning it with a cloth slightly dampened with a mild soapy solution. Use a second cloth dampened with clean water to remove any excess soap, and then allow it to air-dry.

Hand wash undamaged glassware

If no cracks or repairs are spotted, you can wash the piece in warm water mixed with a bit of mild detergent. Rinse off the soap by gradually lowering the glass into cold water. Don't plunge it in the water, as the change in temperature can cause it to crack. Dry each piece by gently patting it with a chamois or towel. Don't forget to line the washbasin and drying area with clean cloths or mats to guard against accidental breakage. Also, never wash more than one piece of glassware at a time, and remember to use distilled or softened water if you have hard tap water.

Blow dust off porcelain

Instead of using a duster, brush, or cloth to wipe your delicate porcelain figurines, try using a can of compressed air to remove the surface dust. Make sure to lay the objects on a soft towel first or hold them as you're spraying them to prevent the force of the air from knocking them down. Cans of compressed air are available at photography-supply shops.

Clean ceramics gently

Never clean ceramics by immersing them in water. Porous, unglazed, or cracked ceramic pieces often develop stains after being soaked in water. Soaking can also cause old repairs to come loose. In addition, porous objects may absorb water that could result in future damage. Never try to clean antique ceramics with flaking gilding or paint; such items require professional maintenance.

Before cleaning, brush off any loose dust or dirt using a dry, soft-bristled paintbrush. Most glazed ceramics can be safely cleaned with a soft cloth or sponge dampened with some mild soapy water. Gently rinse off any excess soap, and let the piece air-dry on a clean towel. Commercial detergents and soaps can leave stains on unglazed ceramics, but you can use equal parts water and ethyl alcohol applied to a soft cloth instead.

Remove stains from porcelain

Do you spend more time looking at the marks and stains on your favorite porcelain pieces than you do admiring their beauty? Try removing the blemishes by applying cotton swabs or balls of cotton wool soaked in a solution of hydrogen peroxide mixed with a few drops of ammonia. Leave the cotton on top of stains for an hour or two, but don't let it dry out. (Use an eye-dropper to keep it moist.) Do not use this method on pieces with gilt or painted designs, however.

☛ **DON'T**
heat ceramics

Antique ceramic dishes or bowls should not be heated beyond room temperature. Higher temperatures can cause any existing stains to darken. Sudden changes in temperature of either extreme can also result in the formation of cracks in ceramics.

Paintings

If handled carefully and protected from sunlight and moisture, paintings will provide generations of viewing pleasure.

Support your paintings

Make sure that your paintings get the support they need:

• Always use weight-appropriate hooks when hanging paintings. Use two hooks per painting to help it hang straight.

• When hanging a particularly heavy painting, put an L-bracket or two under the lower edge to help support the weight and relieve some of the burden on the hooks.

Get a painting varnished

When purchasing a new painting, check to see if it has been varnished. If not, ask the artist or the gallery to varnish it for you. (Most will do so free of charge.) A coat of varnish will not only enhance the image, it will also protect the surface and reduce the likelihood of cracking.

How to clean a painting

Once the painting has been hung, clean it regularly with a soft-bristled brush or dry, soft cloth to prevent dust buildups that can foster mold growth or dry out the paint and cause cracking or peeling. Don't dust older paintings with loose, flaking paint, however; you may dislodge paint fragments. Seek a conservator's care for valuable paintings with loose paint.

Keep the spotlight off your paintings

Although indoor lighting contains much less UV radiation than direct sunlight does, the heat produced by bright spotlights on an overhead track and by lights that attach directly to the picture frame can cause cracking and irreversible damage to paintings. Picture-frame lights should be avoided altogether, because they produce uneven, excessive heat at the bottom or top of the frame that can adversely affect a painting's natural expansion and contraction.

If you do want to use overhead spotlights, try to keep them about 10 feet (3 meters) away from your paintings. You may also want to consider installing a dimmer to lessen the lights' impact on your artwork, and be sure to keep the room dark when it's unoccupied.

Watch the indoor conditions

Temperature and humidity levels in the rooms where paintings are displayed should be carefully monitored, and extreme fluctuations in either should be avoided. Keep room temperatures between 65° and 70° F (18° to 21° C) in the winter and 70° to 75° (21° to 24° C) in the summer, with relative humidity levels ranging between 40 and 55 percent.

ProTip

STORING DOS AND DON'TS

When you need to store paintings, always place framed and unframed works in separate groups; combining the two is begging for snags and tears. Paintings should be stored vertically in a closet or central area of the home (never in the basement or attic). Place unframed paintings face-to-face and back-to-back. It's also a good idea to loosely cover the paintings with a sheet or other lint-free cloth. Never wrap them tightly in plastic, because this can trap in moisture, resulting in warping or mold growth.

DON'T
touch paintings

Never touch the front or back surfaces of an oil painting; the oils and salts on your hands can cause cracks and other types of damage.

ALWAYS HANG ART SECURELY:
USE TWO HOOKS
AND SUPPORT THE BOTTOM

HAVE A NEW PAINTING VARNISHED

DUST WITH A
SOFT-BRISTLE BRUSH

NEVER TOUCH THE
CANVAS, FRONT OR BACK

KEEP AT ROOM TEMPERATURE

DON'T SPOTLIGHT OR
FRAME-LIGHT

DON'T PUT A PAINTING OVER THE FIREPLACE

Don't hang paintings over the mantel

It may seem like the most appropriate location in the house to hang your finest artwork, but the space over a fireplace is actually one of the worst places to display a painting. The wall temperature behind the chimney often varies wildly and can get quite hot and dry when the fireplace is in use, hastening the development of cracks and other damage in the painting. Moreover, soot from the fires can accumulate on your artwork, making it appear dark and dirty.

Handle unframed works with extra care

Some paintings are meant to be framed; others are not. Unframed paintings are more susceptible to surface damage, however, and require additional care in handling. Before moving or hanging an unframed painting, always wash and dry your hands to avoid leaving fingerprints and smudges along the edge of the painting. (Do not wear gloves, though, because the painting could slip out of your hands.)

Quilts and Textiles

Preserving quilts and textiles is mostly a matter of storing them properly and protecting them from insects and the sun.

Clean quilts before storing

Make a quilt or an old textile less appetizing to insects by taking the time to clean it before placing it in storage. Never dry-clean or wash antique fabrics, because either one can cause permanent damage. In fact, the only completely safe way to clean them is by vacuuming them. Use a portable handheld vacuum or a canister-type unit with a piece of nylon stocking or panty hose placed over the hose nozzle. (Keep it in place by wrapping the ends with a piece of masking tape.) Don't let the nozzle touch the material while vacuuming. Quilts should be taken out and vacuumed at least twice a year.

☞ NO plastic, please

Never store quilts or other textiles in airtight containers or plastic bags, which can trap in heat and moisture and result in mold and mildew growths. Some plastics also produce fumes that can hasten disintegration of antique textiles.

Care for quilts in use

If you have an old quilt that's still on active duty, be sure to minimize its exposure to bright lights—especially the rays of the sun. While making the bed, pay careful attention not to catch quilts on the bed frame or any sharp edges. Equally important, don't let fragile quilts hang over the edges of the bed. Gravity can further weaken the fibers, and eventually your quilt won't be able to support its own weight and may tear.

Keep textiles flat

It's best to lay textiles flat when storing them in order to provide even support across the entire fabric and to prevent fibers from breaking. Store textiles in acid-free or polyethylene boxes with lids or on a shelf. Line the box or shelf with a clean, unbleached muslin or acid-free tissue paper.

If folding is unavoidable, pad the creases by putting muslin, tissue paper, or polyester batting inside each fold. When folding heavy textiles like quilts, you can place the quilt over a well-washed cotton sheet and fold them together. Wrap the quilt and sheet in a second sheet for added protection. You can also keep quilts folded in white cotton pillowcases.

It's best not to stack delicate textiles, because it might harm the fibers. If you need to layer them, however, put the heaviest items on the bottom and separate each piece with a sheet or two of acid-free paper.

Fold quilts anew

If you store quilts on a quilt rack or keep them folded in storage, remove them every three to six months and refold them in a different way before returning them to storage; this will avoid creases and dirt lines. If you had a quilt folded in half, for example, refold it in thirds. Try to fold it as little as possible and keep the the undecorated underside of the quilt on the inside. Most wrinkles will occur on the inside of a fold.

Patch a quilt

Do you have a patch quilt in need of patching? Frayed, torn, and split patches can be covered with silk organza or crepeline (a fabric made especially for textile conservation repairs). Use a very fine needle and silk thread or the warp yarn from the silk organza to attach the fabric to the quilt over the damaged patch. Try to use as few stitches as you can, since each pass of the needle will leave a permanent hole in the quilt. Use seams as attachment points whenever possible;

they are usually the strongest parts of the quilt.

Crepeline sells for about $26 a yard and is available from conservation supply specialists, including Talas (212-219-0770 or http://talasonline.com) and Lacis (510-843-7290 or www.lacis.com).

Cushion a carpet

Any antique or high-quality carpet or rug that is still in use or displayed on a floor should rest on top of a well-made underlay. Good underpadding provides protection against insects and prolongs the life of a carpet or rug by cushioning the unevenness of the floor and the weight of furniture. Underlays should be 1/8 to 1/4 inch (3 to 6 mm) thick and large enough to extend to the edge of a carpet. Never fold or overlap an underlay. Also, don't use a self-adhesive underlay or ones that are made of foam rubber, vinyl, or recycled felt. They will need replacing much sooner than those made of better types of material.

BEWARE OF BUGS ON HANGING TAPESTRIES

Carpets and tapestries that are wall-mounted may be more susceptible to attack by moths and carpet beetles, because it's easier for the pests to get between the material and the lining on its back. Regular inspections and vacuuming will help discourage any infestations.

Toys and Dolls

Caring for your collection of antique dolls or toys is mostly a matter of knowing how to store and display them safely. Beyond that, they mostly want to be left alone.

Dust toys, but don't clean them

Got some venerably aged toys or dolls that are looking a bit dingy? Fight the urge to clean them. Dust them off regularly with a soft paintbrush, but don't go near them with commercial cleaning products or chemicals. And go very sparingly with water. Wetting a cracked item often causes additional damage when the water seeps inside. Never try to replace lost stuffing in an old doll or touch up damaged toys or chipped game pieces with paint. Not only can you make the problem worse, but even successful touch-up jobs often diminish a collectible toy's overall value.

Erase a stain

You can often use an ordinary gum eraser to remove pencil marks and other stains from painted wooden toys and ceramic doll faces. Rub spots with the eraser, but gently and not too fast—overcleaned, patchy surfaces can look even worse than a stain. Don't use an eraser on surfaces that have signs of flaking paint or cracking. It could make the damage *much* worse.

Keep Raggedy Ann and Teddy out of the tub

Although many antique dolls are wholly made of fabric, they can't stand up to a bath, much less the rigors of the modern washing machine. The same holds true for teddy bears and most other stuffed dolls and animals. Instead, use a vacuum cleaner with a soft attachment to keep your dolls and teddy bears looking fresh and dust-free.

Store toys in noncorrosive surroundings

When storing toys and dolls, wrap them in acid-free tissue paper or washed unbleached cotton muslin, and place them in acid-free cardboard or plastic boxes made from polyethylene or polypropylene. Don't tightly seal the boxes, however. It's best to provide fabrics with some circulating air, as well as to permit any acidic vapors from stuffing or plastics to diffuse into the air.

Display toys away from sunlight

Don't display toys or dolls on window ledges. Exposure to the sun's rays will hasten their deterioration and can damage dyes and fabrics. The best way to display antique toys and dolls is to place them inside a sturdy, glass-fronted cabinet. If you choose one made of wood, make sure it has been sealed with several coats of polyurethane varnish and line it with acid-free paper to control any damaging fumes. (Also, be sure to position it away from sunlight.)

Store wooden toys separately

It's a good idea to separate the wooden trains and similar toys made from wood from the other toys in your collection. They can have rough sides or edges that could snag or rip fabric and cause other types of damage. And as it ages, wood emits acidic fumes that can harm textiles and other materials.

Preserve your doll's old clothes

Those new duds may look great on that old doll, but whenever you purchase or make new outfits for your antique dolls, be sure to hold on to all the original clothing no matter how tattered it has become. Replacement clothing doesn't provide any of the historical information that the original garments do. These spanking new duds will lower the financial value of the doll if you ever decide you want to sell it.

Antique Dolls

NEVER USE CLEANING
PRODUCTS ON THE DOLL

DUST IT WITH A SOFT
PAINTBRUSH

KEEP DOLLS
AWAY FROM WOOD,
INCLUDING WOODEN TOYS

DON'T DISPLAY IT IN
DIRECT SUNLIGHT

DON'T SEAL IT IN
A STORAGE BOX

STORE THE DOLL IN AN
ACID-FREE BOX,
WRAPPED IN MUSLIN

USE WATER SPARINGLY,
IF AT ALL

Coins and Stamps

Ever popular collectibles, coins and stamps represent fascinating little bits of history. Here's how to keep your collection in tip top condition.

Store your coins safely

Coins exposed to the air are susceptible to tarnish and more serious damage. Fortunately, you have a wide range of choices when it comes to storing them—all readily available from local and online stores that cater to coin collectors:

• Many collectors prefer to simply keep their same-sized coins in clear styrene coin tubes.

• Another choice is flexible transparent holders called coin flips. Look for flips made of polyester or Mylar (avoid vinyl or PVC). Most flips are designed with two pockets— one for the coin and another that can be used to hold a piece of paper with information about the coin. They are available in a variety of sizes.

• You can also place coins in individual cardboard holders lined with Mylar, which are usually less expensive and easier to find than flips. Coins are positioned in the middle of the holder, on the Mylar window, and held in place when the cardboard is folded over. The holders are usually stapled on three sides to keep coins from slipping out. (Use a pair of pliers to flatten the staples against the card so that they can't scratch other coins.)

• Keep your oldest and most valuable coins in hard plastic holders. They are more expensive than other coin holders, but they offer good protection against scratches and other damage. You can get plastic holders for individual coins or for small sets of coins.

Hold coins by their edges

Always handle coins by their edges and, if possible, wear cotton or polyethylene (but not latex) gloves. Gloves protect the metal from corrosive oils and acids on our hands. This is particularly important with proof coins, which have a mirrorlike surface. Any mark on them can disfigure the coin and lessen its value.

Lay coins on cushioned surfaces

When it's necessary to set a coin down outside its holder, always place it on a clean, soft surface. A velvet pad is an ideal surface and can be an invaluable asset when you regularly need to handle valuable coins. A clean, soft cloth or a blank piece of paper is usually sufficient for less valuable items. Never drag coins across any hard surface, because you are likely to scratch or damage the raised areas.

Don't polish–clean old coins

You can use a gum eraser to shine up those pennies in your pocket before giving them to your children or grandchildren, but most numismatists advise against such intensive cleaning of rare or old coins. Certain kinds of light tarnishing, called toning, are considered part of a coin's value, and removing it can diminish its worth.

Gently wash a dirty coin

Removing surface dirt from a coin is about the only cleaning that should be done. To remove surface dirt, gently wash the coin using a mild liquid soap in lukewarm distilled water. (Don't use tap water; it contains chlorine, which can cause corrosion.) Rinse off any remaining soap with a cotton ball dipped in distilled water. After cleaning, use another cotton ball dipped in acetone to remove any grease that may remain on the surface. Use acetone—like all solvents—only in a well-ventilated area. Air-dry the coins on a paper towel.

Store stamps carefully

Most serious collectors keep their stamps in acid-free albums, available from local and online outlets that specialize in gear for stamps and similar collectibles. There are two main ways of holding individual stamps:

• Peelable stamp hinges, which have adhesive backing, are fine for mounting most used stamps in an album.

• For mint-condition and valuable uncirculated stamps, it's better to go with a stamp mount, a clear plastic sleeve with a gummed backing. Stamp mounts are specifically designed to preserve the original adhesive gum on the backs of your best stamps.

Steam apart stuck stamps

If your stamps become stuck to one another, you can usually peel them apart by briefly steaming them for several seconds. Be very careful not to rip them as you're separating them. If the adhesive still holds, repeat the steaming process.

Don't throw away old envelopes

Some antique stamps are more valuable with the original envelope and postmark intact. Be sure to consult a philatelic expert whenever you're in doubt about whether or not you should throw away the envelope.

HANDLE STAMPS WITH TONGS

Stamps are inherently fragile. Don't handle them with your bare fingers, and never use ordinary tweezers, which may pierce or otherwise damage the stamps. Instead, whenever you need to hold or move stamps, use stamp tongs. These specialized

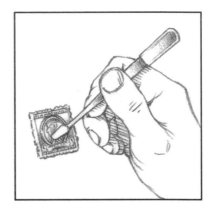

instruments—available from hobbyist-supply stores—are usually made of stainless steel and resemble large tweezers with dulled or flat blades at the ends. They protect the stamps from bending and limit the need to handle them with your fingers.

Comic Books and Trading Cards

Just picking up that old Superman comic or Mickey Mantle baseball card takes you right back to your childhood. Here's how to make sure you preserve the memories.

Keep old comics cool, dry, and in the dark

Prior to the 1980s, the vast majority of comic books were printed on inexpensive newsprint—the grade of paper used for daily newspapers. Newsprint is acidic and can be difficult to preserve. And environmental factors can dramatically accelerate the paper's aging process, so it's essential to store comics away from bright light (especially direct sunlight), high temperatures, and moisture. The ideal environment is between 50° and 70° F (10° and 21° C) with a relative humidity of about 50 percent.

Put comics in protective sleeves

Keeping comic books in Mylar or polypropylene sleeves—backed with acid-free backing boards—is the best way to slow down the yellowing of the paper and to protect the comics against damage from mishandling and moisture. Place each comic, cover facing out, into a sleeve followed by the backing board. (If you purchase a buffered backing board, make sure the buffered side is facing the comic.) Don't put any tape on the bag; you could accidentally tear the comic if it catches on the tape while you're removing it from the bag. Many collectors change bags and boards every two years or so to minimize the spread of acid. It's also advisable to store comics standing up inside specialized, acid-free "comic boxes." (To find box suppliers, just do an online search for "comic storage boxes.") Be sure to label the boxes to make it easier to locate comics by title, publisher, year, or volume.

Don't tape a torn comic

Of course, you would have taken better care of your comics when you were a kid if you knew how much money they'd be worth now. Still, it's the fact that so many folks didn't care for them (or even keep them) way back when that makes those comics so valuable today. Tempting though it may be, don't try to compensate for your past mistakes by trying to tape torn covers and pages in your comics now. It may look better to you, but it can make them less attractive to collectors if you ever want to sell them.

Protect trading cards in sleeves or cases

Baseball cards have long been popular among collectors. In recent years, however, they have been joined by hundreds of different types of sports and nonsports trading cards. And a number of methods of protecting the cards have been developed:

• The most common, and least expensive, form of card protection is the soft sleeve, a thin plastic pouch that envelops the card and protects it from scratches and overhandling.

• The next step up is the top-loader, a semirigid plastic cover that provides some added protection against bending and creases. (Many collectors prefer to place cards in soft sleeves, which are then housed inside top-loaders.)

• The Rolls-Royce of card holders is the screw-down or snap case, a hard-plastic casing that protects cards from most types of damage but is still clear and suitable for display. These are two-piece cases held together by small screws. They are considerably more expensive than either sleeves or top-loaders and are usually reserved for only the most valuable cards.

Store cards in binders or boxes

Storage systems for trading cards have evolved from the

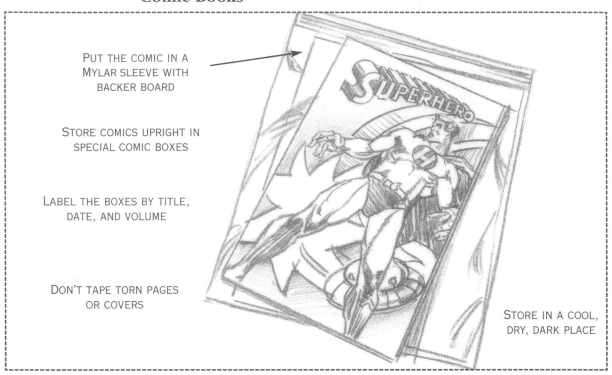

PUT THE COMIC IN A
MYLAR SLEEVE WITH
BACKER BOARD

STORE COMICS UPRIGHT IN
SPECIAL COMIC BOXES

LABEL THE BOXES BY TITLE,
DATE, AND VOLUME

DON'T TAPE TORN PAGES
OR COVERS

STORE IN A COOL,
DRY, DARK PLACE

shoe boxes of yesteryear (although they remain popular among fledgling card collectors) to various kinds of specialized binders and cartons. Today's trading-card collectors can choose from a range of options to house their collections:

• There are different-sized boxes, each type specifically designed to hold top-loaders or unprotected and sleeve-enclosed cards.

• Cards can also be placed in special protector sheets—which usually hold nine cards per page—that are designed to fit inside three-ring binders. Storing cards in binders is a more expensive option than boxes and arguably one that offers less overall protection. Still, binders make the cards more accessible and can be a good option for displaying favorite cards or parts of a collection.

What's that old comic worth?

Want to know exactly how valuable that stack of old comics is? Pick up the latest edition of *The Official Overstreet Comic Book Price Guide*. This authoritative source for comic book collectors and aficionados is published annually and provides comic book values according to their condition (mint, very fine, fine, very good, good, and so on). You can find the Overstreet guide at most bookstores or you can buy it online from one of the major book-selling websites, such as amazon.com or bn.com.

Audio Video Materials

Photographs, Negatives, and Slides

A picture is worth 1,000 words...or so they say. For most folks, however, family photos are far more precious than that. Keeping them in picture-perfect shape isn't always easy, but it's always worth the effort.

Keep photos cool and dry

Photographs are extremely susceptible to deteriorating from adverse environmental conditions. Here are some suggestions from experts for giving them comfortable, life-extending surroundings:

• Store black-and-white photos of any vintage in an interior closet or air-conditioned room with an average temperature of 68° F (20° C) and a relative humidity level between 30 and 40 percent. Relative humidity levels in excess of 60 percent will accelerate the deterioration of your pictures.

• For color photos, temperature—not relative humidity—is the key concern. Color photos stored at low temperatures—namely, 40° F (4° C) or below—will last much longer than photos stored at room temperature.

Test humidity with a hygrometer

Relative humidity measures the amount of water in the air; it is stated as a percentage of the total amount of moisture the air can hold at a given temperature—warm air holds more water than cool air. A relative humidity of 30 to 40 percent will keep black-and-white photos dry, but not so dry that they become brittle.

Relative humidity is measured with a tool called a hygrometer. Consumer models sell for as little as $20. But professional models give far more reliable results, although they are a lot more expensive, with prices ranging from $100 to $500. You can buy them at stores that carry professional test equipment. If you can't locate a supplier in your area, try an online vender such as Amazon at www.amazon.com, The Human Solution at www.thehumansolution.com, or Professional Equipment at www.professionalequipment.com.

Newspapers are bad news

Newsprint, the stuff your newspaper is printed on, degrades quickly, thanks to the high level of lignin and other acids present in the wood pulp used to make it. That's good news for the environment, but unfortunately, those acids can be transferred to nearby items, like important documents, photos, or negatives, causing them to deteriorate faster, too. So always store newspaper clippings in separate, sealed containers or in a different location inside your home.

Create lasting memories in black and white

No matter how well you care for your color photographs and negatives, their color will fade over time. Black-and-white photos, on the other hand, have been known to hold their detail for more than 100 years. So do future generations a favor: Shoot an occasional roll of black-and-white film to document your family get-togethers and other special moments.

Give negs and slides the "white glove" treatment

The natural oils in your fingers keep your skin healthy and pliable, but they're poison to photo negatives and the surfaces of 35 mm slides. And they're almost impossible to remove without leaving a scratch. Before you handle your negatives or move your slides around, slip on a pair of clean, cotton photo-editing gloves (available at most photo supply stores).

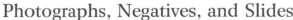

Photographs

STORE BLACK AND WHITE PHOTOS AT LOW HUMIDITY

USE ACID-FREE SPECIAL PHOTO MATERIALS FOR STORAGE

AVOID SELF-STICK PHOTO ALBUMS AND PVC PLASTIC LEAVES

ARCHIVE PHOTOS DIGITALLY ON A CD OR DVD FOR POSTERITY

DISPLAY A DUPLICATE; PRESERVE THE ORIGINAL

STORE YOUR COLOR PHOTOS AT LOW TEMPERATURES

KEEP PHOTOS AWAY FROM NEWSPAPER CLIPPINGS

Don't delay developing film

Once you've finished shooting a roll of 35 mm film, have it developed as soon as possible. Long delays, especially in warm, humid climates, can result in noticeable deterioration of your developed photos.

Make copies of displayed photos

It's natural to want to display your favorite photos in the sunniest spots around your home. Unfortunately, the sun's ultraviolet rays accelerate the aging of photographs. That's why it's a good idea to make a second print of any photo you decide to frame. For safekeeping, store the extra print—along with the negative—in an acid-free container in a cool, dark place (although not in the basement, where it may be too humid; or the attic, where it can get too hot).

Store your slides safely

Although a slide's mount makes it appear sturdier than a color print, the delicate film inside the housing actually leaves it more prone to the ravages of time, the environment, and mishandling. Even the occasional ride through a projector will hasten color fading. All of which makes proper storage essential for extending the life of your 35 mm slides. While most slide carousels are made of stable, heat-resistant plastic, they are not suited for long-term storage. Instead, use metal or metal-reinforced slide storage boxes (such as those made by Logan and other manufacturers) or archival-quality slide sleeves, which fit comfortably in a three-ring binder. Consider making duplicates of your best slides or transferring them to a digital medium, for archival purposes.

Archive your photos digitally

Transferring your photo collection to CDs or DVDs is a great way to preserve the past. If you have a personal computer, all you need is a flatbed scanner. (Many models sell for under $100.) You'll be able to make copies and prints of your photos while keeping the originals safely tucked away. Plus, you can purchase inexpensive software that will let you digitally enhance old photos that may be faded or damaged. You won't have to worry about the images on the disks fading or deteriorating, and the disks themselves are much more durable than photographic materials, although they still need to properly stored and handled (see page 116). You can also find companies that will transfer your photos, negatives, and slides to disk for you; expect to pay about $1.50 per image.

Don't get stuck on photo albums

You may believe those self-stick or "magnetic" photo albums will keep your pictures in pristine condition for years to come. In fact, they all use highly acidic glues that can discolor or degrade your pictures over time. What's more, the glue itself may dry out after several years, making it impossible to remove the photos from the pages. Likewise, the polyvinyl chloride (PVC) contained in many plastics, including the coverings of self-adhesive albums and many picture sleeves, produce vapors

that are extremely damaging to photos. Be particularly suspicious of photo albums that have a strong "new car" smell. That indicates the presence of vinyl, which should be avoided at all costs. Instead, look for albums with page coverings made of polyester (or Mylar), polyethylene, or polypropylene.

ProTip

PUT UNUSED FILM IN THE FRIDGE

An expired roll of film can produce less vibrant colors and other image flaws. If you don't expect to use a roll of 35 mm film before the "use by" date on its package, pop it in your refrigerator. This trick is a favorite of many professional photographers, who buy film in bulk and store it in a refrigerator or freezer until they're ready to use it. The cold, consistent temperature slows down the aging process by at least several months.

Remove the film from the fridge a few hours before you plan to load it into your camera. This will let it warm up to room temperature and keep built-up condensation from damaging your camera.

Store photos in acid-free containers

Don't keep your prints, negatives, or slides in plastic, cardboard, or wooden containers—including wooden cabinets and dresser drawers; they all release gases that are harmful to photographic materials. You can

find much safer choices at most art- or photo-supply stores:

• The best place to store your photos is in an airtight metal container sold for that purpose, preferably one with an enamel finish.

• Second best: House your photo collection in boxes, bins, and albums that are labeled acid-free or archival quality. If you need to wrap or separate photos, use acid-free tissue paper.

Leave old albums alone

Think twice before transferring photographs from an old, paper-paged photo album. The antique paper probably isn't harming the photographs, whereas removing them can cause serious damage. Many times, old family albums also contain useful information about people, places, and events. The best way to preserve an old photo album is to layer each page with a sheet of acid-free tissue or photographic conservation paper.

Carry on your film in airports

With today's increased airport security, your checked baggage is almost certain to be x-rayed. While the X-ray scanners used for carry-on baggage won't harm photographic film under 800 ISO, the scanners used for checked luggage employ much higher levels of radiation and will damage any film (or disposable cameras) packed inside. Keep all your film—both exposed and unexposed—in your carry-on bags. If you are worried that even the carry-on scanner may harm your film, a Federal Aviation regulation allows travelers within the United States to request a non-X-ray inspection of photosensitive products. However, depending on the length of the line behind you, you may have a difficult time finding a compliant baggage inspector.

Always label, but do it carefully

Even if you have a...well, photographic memory, make it a habit to label your photos and slides (if for no other reason than to document them for your descendants). Here are some pointers:

• When labeling photographic prints, use a piece of acid-free paper with notations written in a water-based ink and attach it using an acid-free glue or tape.

• You can also use an acid-free pen or a soft-lead pencil to write on the backsides of prints, but be sure to press very lightly so the writing doesn't dent the paper or damage the emulsion on the front. Put acid-free tissue between stacked prints to prevent pencil lead from rubbing off on another print.

• When it comes to labeling slide mounts, you have a bit more leeway, but be careful not use a ballpoint pen or any other ink that can run or smudge.

• Try to provide as much information about the image as possible. (Keep the "5 W's" — who, what, when, where, and why—in mind.) But even a little information is better than none.

Avoid sticky situations

Don't use white glue, transparent tape, or rubber cement on or near your photos. Almost all commercial adhesives contain acid levels that will eventually damage your pictures. If you need to attach a photo in an album, opt for an acid-free glue, glue stick, or tape sold by photo-supply stores (popular brands include Elmer's, Helmar, Pioneer, and Scotch).

Think positive about negatives

Treat photo negatives with the utmost care and respect. Never remove negatives from their sleeves. If your photo-developer doesn't put negatives in sleeves, buy some at a photo-supply store to keep them safe. Then store the sleeved negatives in acid-free containers for additional safekeeping. Also try to keep your negatives and photos in separate locations in your home; in the event of a disaster at either location, you'll still be able to make copies.

Videos and Movies

Whether your home movies are on old Super 8 film reels or more recent 8 mm videocassettes, a bit of care today will keep the action rolling for years to come.

Don't rewind videotapes

Although most of us have been trained by our local video stores to rewind tapes when we're finished watching them, videotape manufacturers recommend forwarding videos to the end of the reel when storing them. This protects the beginning of the tape when it's inserted and removed from the VCR. Rewinding tapes just before viewing them also ensures that they are loaded properly into the VCR and that the proper tension is maintained throughout the reel.

Dampness equals destruction

Exposure to high humidity, in particular, causes magnetic tape to degrade. Excessive ambient moisture can result in fungus growth and, in some cases, "sticky shed" syndrome—a condition that occurs when a tape soaks up excess moisture from the air and actually sheds its coat of magnetic oxide when played back. Sticky shed syndrome can happen to both audiotape and videotape and is extremely damaging to the tapes themselves as well as to your playback equipment.

Keep tapes cool, too

Regularly watched videos can be stored safely at room temperature, but infrequently viewed tapes will last longer in a cooler environment, about 55° F (13° C), but no lower than 35° F (2° C). When you want to watch a tape that's been in cold storage, let it acclimate to room temperature for at least 24 hours before playing it to minimize the risks of forming condensation inside your VCR. Either way, a relative humidity level of approximately 45 percent is ideal; most tape damage occurs at levels above 65 percent.

Don't mingle with magnets

The images on your home videos are created by the arrangement of tiny iron particles on a magnetic tape. But the same force that created your precious home videos can just as easily destroy them. Always place your home videos *away* from all magnetic sources— including stereo loudspeakers, TV sets, musical amplifiers, and anything with an electrical motor. A magnet placed even a foot (30 cm) away can cause unrecoverable damage. This applies to prerecorded video too.

Practice the three-year stretch

Proper storage is essential to preserving your home videos, but so is some periodic exercise. Although they don't exactly get flabby, tapes left sitting idle on the shelf for years on end can develop problems. In particular, when a video tape is tightly wound, the polyurethane binder on the tape can get stuck to the adjacent layers and tear off the oxide particles from the base when it's inserted into a VCR and played. That's why experts recommend rewinding and fast-forwarding your tapes at least once every three years.

Remove the record tab

You can easily prevent someone from taping over your treasured videos by breaking off the little black tab on the backs of your videocassettes. If, for some reason, you decide you want to record on a cassette that has the tab removed, simply place a piece of transparent tape over the gap left by the missing tab.

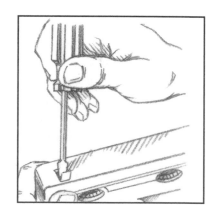

Use the right case for cassettes

The cardboard sleeves that videocassettes come packaged in offer little protection for your valuable tapes, and those translucent plastic cases used by many video rental stores are no better. In fact, such containers are sometimes made of materials that deteriorate over time and may even damage the cassette itself. A far better way to go is with a polypropylene storage case, which is inexpensive and reusable and can provide additional protection against natural disasters like floods. You can buy polypropylene cases from many of the dealers listed in Online Archival Supplies on page 105.

Keep them upright

Don't stack your videotapes on top of one another; it leaves them prone to warping and other types of damage. Rather, stand them upright with the full reel on the bottom.

Check your VCR before inserting a tape

Malfunctioning hardware is the leading cause of videotape damage. If you're uncertain about whether a VCR is working or not, conduct a "test run" with a tape you don't value. If the tape plays, rewinds, and ejects without any signs of damage, the VCR is probably safe to use. If you observe any problems while testing, or if the tape shows signs of fraying after it's ejected, reconsider using the machine. Periodic maintenance of your VCR is essential to keeping it in good working order. For tips see page 222.

Make a backup plan

Once a home movie or video is destroyed, it's gone for good. Having duplicates made of your favorite home videos or films by a professional transfer service is a relatively inexpensive insurance policy against losing priceless memories forever.

• For VHS duplication, prices can vary greatly depending on where you live, but you can expect to pay about $25 for a 1-or 2-hour videotape-to-VHS duplication to approximately $180 for 1,000 feet of 8 mm or 16 mm film transferred to VHS.

• You can also transfer your videos and films to DVD, which is a much more stable format than tape and one that won't lose its quality over time. In that case, add another $30 to $50 to the total for transferring a film or video to DVD.

• Whatever method of duplication you use, make two copies if possible. Keep the original and one of your dupes as your archival backups. Don't circulate them, and store them in a location in your home that's separate from your viewing copies.

 Pro Tip

INSPECT VIDEOCASSETTES

Unlike audiocassettes, videocassettes hide the magnetic tape behind a protective door that moves up automatically when the cassette is inserted into a VCR. While this goes a long way toward keeping out dirt and other contaminants, it does

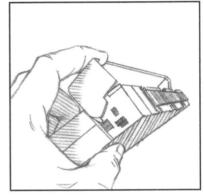

make it slightly more challenging to inspect your videos for damage. In order to view the tape, locate the small door latch on the side of the cassette. Press the latch, and lift up the door. Be careful not to touch the tape with your fingers. Natural skin oils are destructive to tape and can attract and hold dust and dirt to the tape's surface. The tape should appear smooth and wrinkle-free; any fraying or tears along the edges indicates damage that could be harmful to your VCR. (It may also be caused by misalignment inside your VCR.) Never insert a damaged tape into your VCR.

It's a wrap

Your films should be kept on reels only if you view them frequently (but be sure to replace any bent, warped, or broken reels). For long-term storage, films should be wound ends-out onto plastic cores in even, tight rolls with the ends secured with archival tape. Be sure to wind the film well; loose rolls can cause cinching, tears, and other damage. Store film rolls in non-corrosive metal cans or in acid-free plastic film boxes. You can purchase cores, reels, and boxes at photo-supply shops. Stack film cans horizontally to prevent warping.

Beware of flammable films

Although 35 mm nitrocellulose (also known as cellulose nitrate or nitrate) film has not been manufactured for more than 50 years, it may still be found in some collections. Nitrate film requires professional maintenance and storage, and should not be stored in your home. It can be a serious fire hazard and has even been known to self-ignite.

☛ DON'T
seal film cans

Do not seal cans or boxes containing film with tape; it will trap moisture inside that can promote the growth of molds or mildew on the film.

Smell for sour film

Before putting your rolls of 16 mm or 8 mm film into storage—and periodically thereafter—give each a good whiff. If any smell like vinegar, it's a sure sign that it's time to get it transferred to a different format as soon as possible; the film is starting to decompose.

Although the process can be slowed down by cold storage, it cannot be stopped (and affected rolls should be stored separately. This condition is known as "vinegar syndrome," and it occurs when the acetate content of cellulose acetate film starts to turn to acetic acid—the same chemical in vinegar.

Keep films the cool way

In general, the colder and drier your films are kept, the longer they'll last. It's best to store black-and-white film in an area with an average temperature of 50° F (10° C) or lower, and a relative humidity of 30 to 50 percent. Color film, like color photos, does best in lower temperatures and lower humidity. The best results will be seen at temperatures of 32° F (0° C) or lower, with a relative humidity of 20 to 30 percent.

Follow the leader

Attaching 2 or 3 feet (65 to 95 cm) of white leader film at the beginning and end of your films is a good way to protect them against damage during lace-up and projection.

Clean up those dirty movies

You can remove dust or fingerprints from your films by gently wiping them down with a clean flannel or soft cotton batiste cloth. Frequently refold the cloth to avoid transferring the dust back to the film.

Vinyl Records

They are the soundtracks of our youth—and some may even be worth a pretty penny as well. So take care of old records. At the very least, they contain great music and great memories.

Think vertical when storing records

If you think the term "a stack of records" is to be taken literally, think again. Stacking is the absolute worst way to stow your vinyl albums—and it's even worse for 78 phonograph records, which were cut on hard shellac. In addition to being unsightly, stacking is a surefire way to cause distortion in the grooves, warping, and other serious problems. The only proper way to store records is to keep them standing upright on shelves, preferably not at floor level because they collect dust much faster there.

Use strong shelves for records

Bear in mind that that LPs weigh approximately 35 to 45 pounds per square foot—78s weigh even more—so it's *absolutely crucial* to use sturdy shelving material, such as steel or oak, that won't sag or bend. For extensive collections, it's also advisable to place full-length vertical dividers every 4 to 6 inches (100 to 150 mm) for additional support. Don't use half- or partial-length dividers, which may cause the albums to warp. You can keep smaller record collections in a sturdy cabinet or in sealed boxes to keep the records away from dust and light.

Keep records away from heat

Although vinyl and shellac records can be safely stored at room temperature, they are extremely vulnerable to heat and should never be placed in close proximity to heat sources such as heating-duct vents or radiators. Also avoid putting records near bright lights or in the path of direct sunlight, due to the potential of built-up heat and damage caused by ultraviolet radiation, which will fade, discolor, and dry out record jackets.

Keep records dry

Water is another potential hazard to old records. Even small amounts of dampness can cause mold to grow on record sleeves and covers—and eventually, on the records themselves. Lastly, never keep your records where they could be exposed to smoke or cooking grease; both act as magnets for dust and mold on the records and can disfigure album covers.

Don't get in the grooves

All LPs, 45s, and 78s need to be handled properly in order to prevent contamination and other types of damage. Putting your hands on the record's grooved surface will leave behind oils or sweat that, in turn, can attract dust or promote mold growth. When removing an LP or 78, tilt the sleeve so that the record's edge slips into the inside of your thumb and lets you place your middle or ring finger on the center hole. (You can place your thumb in the center hole of a 45, however.) Hold records with both hands, fingers along the edges, when positioning them on the turntable.

Replace old sleeves

Although those old paper record sleeves can often evoke a sense of nostalgia with their images of ancient albums and promotional offers from bygone eras, they are usually not made of acid-free paper and will eventually disintegrate. The resulting dust will invariably wind up in the grooves of your records, where it could impair playback or cause other problems. A more preferable, though clearly less sentimental, choice is the use of antistatic, polyethylene or HDPE (high-density polyethylene) inner

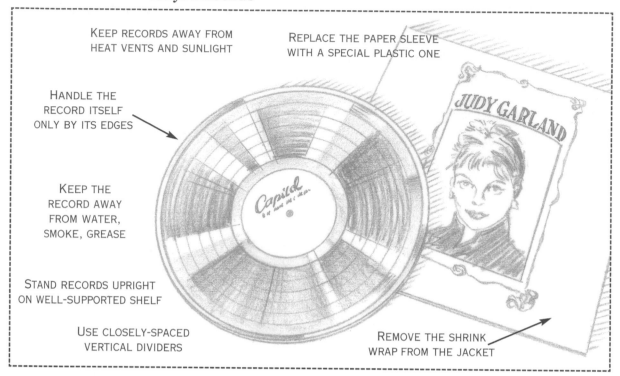

KEEP RECORDS AWAY FROM
HEAT VENTS AND SUNLIGHT

REPLACE THE PAPER SLEEVE
WITH A SPECIAL PLASTIC ONE

HANDLE THE
RECORD ITSELF
ONLY BY ITS EDGES

KEEP THE
RECORD AWAY
FROM WATER,
SMOKE, GREASE

STAND RECORDS UPRIGHT
ON WELL-SUPPORTED SHELF

USE CLOSELY-SPACED
VERTICAL DIVIDERS

REMOVE THE SHRINK
WRAP FROM THE JACKET

sleeves; prices start at about $12 for 100. You can also replace them with plain-white acid-free paper sleeves, but steer clear of any sleeves made of polyvinyl chloride (PVC); they emit gases that can adversely react with vinyl records. For sleeve suppliers, check the sources in "Online archival supplies," page 105.

☞ NO
alcohol on 78s

> Alcohol should never be used to clean 78-rpm phonograph records; it will dissolve the shellac base.

Take off the shrink wrap
Be sure to remove all plastic shrink wrap from the outside of your LPs. The wrap will continue to shrink over time and will eventually warp the record inside. If you want to protect your album covers, a far better solution is a protective outer sleeve made of clear polyethylene or acid-free paper.

How to clean your records
Cleaning your records not only ensures you the best possible playback; it's also an essential step for keeping your records playable in the years to come. (Some experts even recommend a second cleaning *after* playback

to prepare the record for "dust-free storage," although this is probably most effective when a new inner sleeve is used as well.)

To clean a record, first place it on a dry bath towel. Then take a soft, lint-free cloth and gently move it in a spiral motion on the record, going in the direction of the grooves. Start in the center of the record and work your way out to the edge. A camel-hair paintbrush can also be used to remove any visible dust particles.

Another way to clean vinyls
If your vinyl records (either LPs or 45s) need a more thorough cleaning, try using a cloth that's

been slightly dampened with a "water-based" solution of up to 20 percent isopropyl alcohol—one part isopropyl alcohol to four parts water (preferably distilled water). Pat the record dry with a clean chamois leather or soft-cotton cloth when done.

No more broken records

When it's time to return a record to its jacket, make sure the opening of the sleeve is facing up (as opposed to facing *out*, which may have been the preferred positioning during your teenage years to expedite removing the record from the

cover) so it's flush against the top of the album cover. This will prevent albums from accidentally sliding out of their jackets and crashing to the floor when you go to play them.

Clean 78s with care

Use a clean cloth saturated with a mixture of lukewarm water and a bit of mild detergent (such as Ivory soap flakes or Johnson & Johnson Baby Bath). Let the solution run through the grooves to wash out any dirt, dust, or iron particles from player needles that may be trapped between them. Then give the record a final cleansing under slow running cool tap water, and gently pat it dry with a soft towel. Allow the record to thoroughly air-dry overnight before playing it or putting it back into your collection; sandwiching a damp 78 among dry records can result in mold growth that could lead to disintegration.

Dust off your turntable mat

Why go through all the trouble of cleaning off your records only to be undermined by a dusty turntable mat? Be sure to wipe down the mat in your record player with a dry, lint-free cloth each time you get ready to play a freshly cleaned album. Some turntables use felt mats, which are considerably more challenging to clean. They should be vacuumed off, if possible, but never wetted.

Straighten out a warped 78

Do you have an unplayable, warped 78 record? You may want to try straightening it out by placing it between two pieces of tempered glass to form a "shellac sandwich." Place the sandwiched record in your oven under low heat—or start at around 85° F (30° C) and gradually increase it, but do not go above 150° F (65° C)—for 12 to 25 minutes. Allow the record to cool for 30 minutes before removing it from the glass. If it's a hot, sunny day, you can try placing the sandwich outside for 10 minutes to 1 hour (depending on the temperature), with frequent checking. This method can also be used to straighten out unplayable, warped vinyl LPs and 45s, although it is notoriously difficult to remove the warp in a vinyl record. *Caution:* This procedure is not without significant risks; it's quite possible to inadvertently destroy the record in the process. It should

---

❓ How Long Will Records & Audio Tapes Last?

ANSWER: **From 15 years to 40 or more**

Vinyl LPs and shellac records (78s) last longer in storage than magnetic tapes, but repeated playing wears them out faster. Some tapes in library archives have remained playable after 40 to 50 years, but more typically, tapes begin to deteriorate after 15 years or so. Many phonograph cylinders, early hard-rubber records, and 78s, meanwhile, are still playable after more than 100 years—though all show some signs of aging. Vinyl records manufactured after 1960 are generally better made than their predecessors, however, and many have lasted more than 40 years without significant sound degradation.

WHERE TO
BUY CARE SUPPLIES

If your local electronics store doesn't stock the supplies you need for maintaining your record collection, you should be able to find the desired items from the online and mail-order vendors listed below. Sleeve City and Bags Unlimited specialize in inner and outer sleeves for records. The others carry a range of phonograph supplies and accessories, including turntables.

> Bags Unlimited
www.bagsunlimited.com

> The Disc Doctor
                1-314-205-1388
discdoc.com

> KAB
            1- 908-754-1479
www.kabusa.com

> Music Direct
            1-800-449-8333
www.amusicdirect.com

> Needle Doctor
            1-800-229-0644
www.needledoctor.com

> Sleeve City
            1-866-380-4168
www.sleevetown.com

only be attempted as a last resort on records that are otherwise unplayable.

Clean covers with care

It's usually best to leave blemishes on album jackets undisturbed—especially if they're collectible albums or have matte covers, which are damaged by most cleaning efforts. Glossy or laminated covers are easier to clean, but there's still a risk of damaging them. If you still feel compelled to perform cosmetic surgery on your album covers, here are some recommended approaches to removing common marks and stains. Be careful, though, and don't forget to remove the record and place it in a secure area before you begin.

• Dirt and dust can usually be removed from glossy covers with a slightly damp towel or a tiny bit of mild furniture polish for some added shine.

• Remove stickers, labels, or tape by heating them with a hair dryer, and then carefully peeling them off. (Any leftover adhesive will usually come off with a little citrus-based cleaner or lighter fluid.)

• Use a small amount of hairspray on a soft cloth to eliminate pen or ink marks on glossy covers.

• To get rid of permanent marker, try drawing over it with a dry-erase marker, and then wiping it off with a soft, dry cloth.

• To remove pencil marks and other types of nonink blemishes, lightly use a soft rubber pencil eraser. Or even better, use a less abrasive kneaded eraser, available from any art-supply store.

Never wet the inside labels

Record labels are even trickier to clean than album jackets. Even a small amount of water applied to a label will cause most labels to blister (which will diminish the value of a collectible album), while a single slip of your hand across the record's surface can leave a serious scratch. If you need to clean a dirty label, stick with an acceptable dry method, such as a sable brush or some gentle buffing with a soft towel or a strip of corduroy. A kneaded eraser, sold at art supply stores, is also effective for removing dirt and stains without dampening.

Audiocassettes and Tapes

When it comes to your audiotape, a few good habits make all the difference between an early demise and decades of enjoyment.

Keep tapes in shape

Here are some guidelines for keeping your taped music around longer:

• Like records, open-reel tapes and cassettes should be stored vertically upright. Stacking or laying them flat on hard surfaces for an extended period causes the tape to become slack and makes tape edges prone to damage.

• Keep tapes in a clean, dark, and dry environment. (A 45 percent relative humidity is ideal.) Moisture and sunlight are especially detrimental to all tape formats and need to be avoided at all costs.

• Tape can tolerate temperatures ranging between 35° F and 70° F (7° C and 21° C), but major fluctuations in temperature should be kept to a minimum.

• Bear in mind that audiotape is a magnetic medium, so be sure to keep tapes at least 3 inches (7.5 cm) away from all magnetic sources, including stereo speakers, television sets, and even headphones. This is also true for video tapes and floppy discs you use on your computer.

How to store open–reel tapes

With open-reel, 1/4-inch (6.4-mm) audiotape, place about 2 feet (65 cm) of white leader tape at both ends and wind it onto a take-up reel before storing. Secure the loose end with a piece of archival tape to keep it from unspooling. Acid-free boxes are preferable for long-term storage, although most original tape boxes are usually acceptable as long as any plastic or paper has been removed.

Care for cassettes

Store audiocassettes in clean, plastic cases—the ones they come in arc fine as long as the center hubs are intact. Always forward your tapes to the end of "Side One" before putting them into storage. This is an important maintenance tip for all tape formats (including home videos), because it requires you to rewind the tape before playing it, an exercise that relieves any tape stress or stickiness that may develop through inactivity. If you haven't played a tape for several months, rewind it two or three times before playing or copying it.

Clean your tape player

The best way to ensure the longevity of your tape collection has little to do with the tapes themselves and everything to do with the condition of the equipment you play them on. More tapes are destroyed due to malfunctioning hardware than anything else. That's why you should always make sure that your tape deck or player is working properly before you insert or spool up an important tape.

Although you can't see it, every tape loses a bit of its microscopic particles with each pass through your tape deck—and the older the tape, the more particles it sheds. Those particles, as well as everyday dust and debris, accumulate on the recording and playback heads and other tape-transport mechanisms inside the unit. If they are not removed, they will ultimately impair the deck's operation, resulting in garbled or diminished sound or, worse, mangled or "eaten" tapes. So don't forget to clean your tape-playing equipment on a regular basis, at least after every 25 hours of playing time. For cassette player maintenance, see page 231.

Avoid no–name tapes

"Bargain-brand" tapes may be inexpensive, but they're usually anything but a bargain. Besides having inferior sound quality and less reliable construction

Audiocassettes

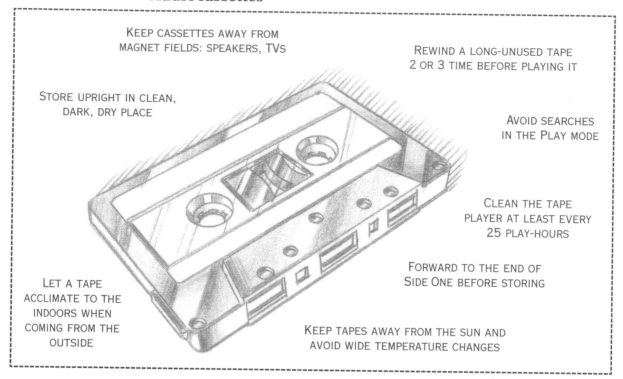

KEEP CASSETTES AWAY FROM
MAGNET FIELDS: SPEAKERS, TVS

REWIND A LONG-UNUSED TAPE
2 OR 3 TIME BEFORE PLAYING IT

STORE UPRIGHT IN CLEAN,
DARK, DRY PLACE

AVOID SEARCHES
IN THE PLAY MODE

CLEAN THE TAPE
PLAYER AT LEAST EVERY
25 PLAY-HOURS

FORWARD TO THE END OF
SIDE ONE BEFORE STORING

LET A TAPE
ACCLIMATE TO THE
INDOORS WHEN
COMING FROM THE
OUTSIDE

KEEP TAPES AWAY FROM THE SUN AND
AVOID WIDE TEMPERATURE CHANGES

than their brand-name counterparts, some Brand X tapes can actually ruin tape decks and players—clogging up machine heads and rollers because of excessive flaking of loose oxide particles, the result of shoddy manufacturing processes. So don't be pennywise and pound foolish: Always stick with well-known tape brands for your home recordings.

Don't rush the playback

When moving tape from a cold and dry or warm and damp environment to room temperature, always let it sit for at least two hours before you put it in your tape deck or player. This lets the tape acclimate to its new surroundings and minimizes the risk of it forming condensation, which could damage both the tape and the tape player.

Minimize wear and tear

Although audiocassettes can stand up to the rigors of the road, there are some precautions worth taking whenever you are using your favorite tapes:

• Don't leave the cassettes on your dashboard to bake for hours in the sun in the middle of summer. Even in spring and fall, considerable heat can build up.

• Don't subject the cassettes to strenuous workouts inside your tape player with constant stopping, starting, forwarding, or rewinding. And keep those "music searches"—in which the tape is kept in contact with the deck's play head while it's forwarding or rewinding—to an absolute bare minimum.

• Never leave your tapes partially played. Rather, fast-forward or rewind them to the end of a side, and be sure to remove them from the player to avoid potential creases in the tape from the play-back mechanism or putting unnecessary stress on the tape deck.

When recording for posterity

If you are taping something that you really want to preserve, it pays to take extraspecial measures:

• Record on only one side of the tape to prevent print-through (a problem seen in some older tapes in which the sound on one layer is imprinted onto the next).

• Avoid using cassettes with a total recording time longer than 90 minutes—60-minute tapes are actually preferable. The longer tapes are typically thinner and less durable.

• Use cassettes that are screwed together rather than welded; it allows the tape to be disassembled and possibly repaired if it is ever damaged.

Don't forget to dub

Even with expert care, records and tapes will continue to degrade with repeated playing. In fact, most cassettes wear out after 200 playback/record cycles. That's why it's a good idea to make copies of your originals and use the duplicates for everyday use.

• The most desirable format to copy to is compact disc, which maintains its pristine digital sound quality regardless of the number of times you play it. And the easiest way to transfer records and tapes to CDs is to use a CD recorder attached to your stereo system; prices for these devices range between $200 and $300. The only problem: You must use special audio CD blanks, which cost more than the regular CD blanks sold for computers.

• You can also use a computer's recordable CD or DVD drive to make CD copies of your records or tapes, although it's a more complicated endeavor. Check with a computer store about what items you'll need to connect your particular computer to your stereo.

• If you don't have access to a CD recorder, cassette copies should certainly suffice. You'll need a dual-well dubbing deck to make duplicates of your cassettes, however.

Buy to Keep: Cassette Tapes

It often pays to go the extra mile when recording those special performances for posterity. This is especially true of the type of tape you select when you buy audiocassettes.

Tape quality	High-bias or metal tapes may cost more than normal-bias formulations, but they are usually better made and yield better sound quality with a higher dynamic range and a lower noise level. *Note:* First make sure your recording hardware has the proper settings to accommodate these types of tape.

CDs and DVDs

They may not last forever, but CDs and DVDs are today's best bets for long-term storage of your digital documents and images—as well as your music and videos.

Watch your CD wallets

Those slim, zippered CD wallets certainly make it easy to transport your CDs from one place to another, but they should never be used for long-term or archival storage. Many wallets provide adequate cushioning behind the discs, but your CDs are still prone to scratches (typically as a result of frequent trips in and out of the sleeve) and other hazards.

Handle DVDs with care

Although the error-correction encoding for DVDs is almost ten times more thorough than that used for audio CDs, DVDs are still more susceptible to damage by scratches and mishandling than CDs. That's because DVDs cram a lot more information into a comparable amount of space (up to 4.7GB per side compared with 700MB in a CD—that's more than six times as much). With that in mind, you may want to handle your DVDs a bit more carefully than your CDs.

• Never touch the disc's flat surface; rather, always hold it with one finger in the center hole and the other fingers around the outside edge.

• When removing a DVD from its case, always be sure to press the button on the center hub and push downward on it; never remove a DVD from its package simply by prying up the outer edge of the disc.

Keep CDs off the dashboard

If you keep a CD wallet in your car, never, *ever,* leave it on the dashboard or front seat in hot climates or during the summer months. The plastic sleeves of some poorly made wallets have been known to melt and adhere to CDs after several hours of exposure to the hot sun.

Don't buy blanks in bulk

Unless, of course, you intend to burn a lot of discs in a relatively short period of time. That's because the organic dye used to record the data on the disc will eventually spoil if it is not used. Although CD-R and DVD-R manufacturers claim blank, unused discs have a five-year

---

? How Long Will CDs and DVDs Last?

ANSWER: **From 20 to 200 years or more**

CDs and DVDs may not be indestructible, as we were led to believe at the time of the compact disc's introduction in 1983, but they are far more durable than records, tapes, or magnetic media, such as floppy disks and hard drives. In fact, a recent study conducted by the National Institute of Standards and Testing has determined that some of today's 5.25-inch optical discs could last 200 years or more.

Of course, that long life is contingent upon maintaining ideal storage conditions with a minimum of handling. To those ends, the NIST recommends storing discs in their jewel cases upright (rather than stacked) in a cool, dry environment—between 39° F and 67° F (4° C and 19° C) with a 20 to 50 percent relative humidity. Prolonged exposure to heat or direct sunlight can be particularly damaging to most discs.

The NIST also found that not all optical media is created equally. Commercially available audio CDs, CD-ROMs, and DVD movies have a life expectancy of only 20 years or more, while recordable CDs (CD-R) and DVDs (DVD-R, DVD+R) are expected to last 100 to 200 years or longer. But this doesn't apply to CD-RWs; see "Don't back up on rewriteable CDs," page 118.

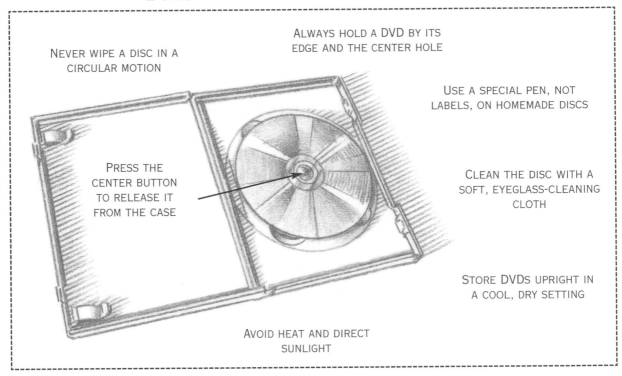

NEVER WIPE A DISC IN A CIRCULAR MOTION

ALWAYS HOLD A DVD BY ITS EDGE AND THE CENTER HOLE

USE A SPECIAL PEN, NOT LABELS, ON HOMEMADE DISCS

PRESS THE CENTER BUTTON TO RELEASE IT FROM THE CASE

CLEAN THE DISC WITH A SOFT, EYEGLASS-CLEANING CLOTH

STORE DVDs UPRIGHT IN A COOL, DRY SETTING

AVOID HEAT AND DIRECT SUNLIGHT

shelf life, that claim has not been verified by independent testing, and you won't find any expiration dates on the packaging. All things considered, it's best to buy new discs on an as-needed basis, rather than purchasing a large quantity to use over several years.

Keep your discs clean

CDs and DVDs need to be kept free of dust and fingerprints, which can cause tracking errors by blocking the path of the laser that reads the discs. Cleaning is just a matter of wiping your discs with a damp nonabrasive cloth—the cloths designed to clean eyeglasses are

ideal. You should never use harsh chemicals or cleaning agents. You can, however, use a water-based lens cleaner or mild detergent, if needed.

Gently wipe the disc by moving the cloth in a curved line from the inside hole to the outer edge. Don't wipe in a circular

motion; you can make the disc unreadable if you accidentally scratch it while wiping around the disc's circumference.

Repair a scratched disc

Do you have a scratched CD or DVD that's headed for the trash? Before you toss it, try fixing it with some Brasso metal polish (which sells for under $6 for 8 ounces in the U.S. and under $4 for 142 ml in Canada). The idea is to use the polish to smooth out the scratch so the player's laser can read the data; you don't necessarily have to make the scratches disappear. Use a soft cloth to rub a couple of drops of Brasso into the disc until the scratch is almost gone. Scratches are best handled by rubbing along the direction of the scratch, while scuff marks should be polished in a radial motion. Let the Brasso dry on the surface; then use a fresh soft cloth to rub it off, using a radial motion.

You can use other products in a similar fashion to smooth out the scratches on your discs. Nongel white toothpaste and car wax are two popular choices. There are also many commercial disc-repair kits and devices available, some of which—such as the Alera 240121 DVD/CD Disc Repair-Plus Kit (about $27) and the Skipdoctor CD Repair Kit (about $23)—can be very effective. They are sold by audio-equipment retailers.

Of course, if a scratch is deep enough to damage a disc's data layer, it can't be repaired no matter what you do. (The same is true for any scratches on the disc's label side, which back onto the disc's reflective layer.) Still, any attempts to salvage a scratched disc are always worth the effort—not to mention the money and time you'll save when you're successful.

Don't back up on rewriteable CDs

A rewriteable CD (CD-RW) should never be used for archival purposes. Although they're designed specifically for data backups, CD-RWs are fundamentally different from CD-Rs: They have an aluminum reflective layer, and record data on a phase-changing metal-alloy film rather than an organic dye. CD-RWs are less stable, more sensitive to heat damage, and have a much shorter lifespan than CD-Rs (typically 25 years or less, depending on how many times they're recorded on).

Buy to Keep: Recordable CDs

When archiving important data, such as digital photos and videos, original music or irreplaceable files, you want a recordable CD (CD-R) that will last as long as possible. The type of reflective metal layer and the type of recordable dye layer that the CD has are the most important considerations.

Reflective layer   A gold reflective layer is the way to go. Gold is chemically inert and won't oxidize over time, a possible risk for CD-R media with silver reflective layers. Consequently, gold discs are believed to offer better longevity than silver discs, although they usually sell for roughly the same price. You can purchase blank gold CD-Rs from many vendors; brands include Apogee, HHB, Imation, MAM, Mitsui, and Verbatim.

Dye layer   The disc's dye layer, where the data is actually preserved, is equally important. The leading choice is phthalocyanine, a clear or light-green dye that offers the best resistance to light and heat; it is used almost exclusively with gold discs. Azo dye, which has a deep blue color, is a close second. Cyanine, which has a light blue tint, is the most common and least expensive dye and is the one most susceptible to damage by sunlight and UV radiation. You can usually tell what type of dye is used by examining the underside of the disc—that is, the side that faces down in your player or PC disc drive. Note that the color you see will be affected by material used for the disc's reflective layer. (For example, a gold reflective layer with a blue dye will appear green in color.)

Stick to longhand labeling

The need to label your home-recorded CD-Rs and DVD-Rs is obvious; how else will you identify them? Although there's no shortage of labeling kits on the market, you may want to think twice before using any of them. The problem is that the adhesives used for virtually all of the labels included in these kits can harm the data stored on your discs or offset the discs' balance when they're played, which can damage computer drives and CD and DVD players. Until true archival-quality labels for optical discs arrive, it's best to simply write the information in the printed area of the disc with a nonsolvent-based felt-tip pen—such as TDK's CD Mark or Maxell's DiscWriter pens, both of which come in packages of four for about $6. Never use a ballpoint pen, pencil, or other types of permanent markers, as they're likely to destroy the disc or the data.

Save as data instead of music

There are a number of digital audio formats in use these days, although MP3, WAV, and MID (MIDI) are probably the best known of the bunch. Audio CDs, meanwhile, have their own formatting (although they use WAV files) that allow them to work with all CD players—including models that predate the arrival of CD burners.

When storing music files onto a CD-R or recordable DVD for archival purposes, experts recommend recording them as WAV files rather than as CD Audio files. You won't be able to play the discs on most home or portable CD players, but you'll be getting some added insurance on the integrity of your music in return. When a scratch or other flaw causes a loss of data on an audio CD, it's typically heard as a loud click or pop as the CD is played. All computer data files (including WAV files), however, have an extra level of error correction that provides additional protection against data loss with fewer audible artifacts. Besides, you can always burn an audio CD using your archived WAV files at some later time.

Use slower speeds for archival audio recording

If you decide to use the CD Audio format when making archival copies of your digital music, it's a good idea to record the discs at a slow speed, preferably 4x. Decreasing the recording speed ensures a more exact burn with better laser response. Higher speeds are fine for recording data, where significant error correction is inserted during the burn and implemented during the readback. But when the lack of error correction in the CD Audio format is combined with irregularities in the quality of the blank media and inaccuracies of the laser during recording, the end result can be inferior-sounding discs. A slow speed makes sure you're getting the best-possible recording.

new uses for Old CDs

Although CDs and DVDs can last as long as 200 years, many often meet an early demise through mishandling or accidents. The good news is that there are lots of inventive ways to recycle your retired discs. Here are ten suggestions:

- Buy an inexpensive clock mechanism from a hobby shop or electronics store, and turn the disc into a novelty clock.

- Create a decorative hanging sun reflector.

- Hang them on fruit trees to scare away birds and deer.

- Position them outside your house as sidewalk or driveway reflectors.

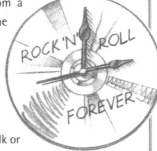

Recreation & Pastimes

Golf, Tennis, and Other Individual-Sports Gear

Give your individual-sports equipment a little TLC, and it'll pay you back with years of enjoyment and healthy living.

Create simple storage for sporting gear

Place a sturdy, empty wine or liquor carton (the kind with the built-in dividers) in your den, playroom, or garage for safe and convenient storage of tennis rackets, hockey sticks, balls, fishing poles, and other items. You can easily decorate the boxes to match the room's decor.

Clean your golf clubs

Clean clubfaces using a soft-bristled toothbrush (or a similar soft brush) and warm, soapy water. Be sure to towel-dry the clubface and shaft immediately after cleaning. Wipe down steel shafts with a damp cloth; never use abrasives, as they can leave scratches. While you're cleaning, check the shafts for dents, rust, pits, or any structural abnormalities. You can also use mild soap and water on a soft cloth to clean graphite club shafts.

Swingin' in the rain

Be sure to clean and dry your clubs after playing a round in the rain or on a wet course. Wet clubs stored in your golf bag are almost certain to emerge with rust spots.

Cover those clubheads

Use covers for clubheads—especially woods—to keep them clean and to prevent scratches and chipping. Also use long-neck head covers to protect the finish of your graphite shafts, which are easily scratched.

Get a handle on golf grips

You can prolong the life of your golf grips by regularly cleaning them with a bit of water and mild dishwashing soap. Clean buffed grips (including tour velvet and cord grips) with a soft abrasive pad or bristle brush. Trade in the brush for a soft washcloth when cleaning nonbrushed grips (tour-wrap style). Be sure to rinse grips well with luke-warm water and thoroughly towel-dry them after washing.

Mark your golf balls

If you and your golf buddies like the same brand of golf balls, you can always be sure who got on the green first by marking your balls with a dot of bright nail polish. This color-coded approach can also make it easy to identify golf tees, batting gloves, and other items that don't have enough room to fit your name.

About tennis racket strings

All tennis rackets should be restrung at least twice a year. A good rule to follow is to restring your racket about as many times in a year as you play in a week. If you don't break strings often, try using a thinner (17- to 18-gauge) string. Thinner strings provide greater resilience and better spin control.

Keep your tennis racket cool, but not too cool

Tennis rackets don't do well in extreme temperatures at either end of the thermometer. High temperatures can cause racquets to lose tension. A two-hour exposure to temperatures of 115° F (46° C) or higher, for example, can cause synthetic strings to lose 7 pounds (3.2 kg) of tension or more. This damage is irreversible; the racket doesn't regain that tension once it's cooled off. So don't leave your racquet in the car trunk in the summer where temperatures can exceed 130° F

> ### ❓ How Long Will Tennis Racket Strings Last?
>
> **ANSWER: 30 to 70 hours of playing time**
>
> Nylon strings will typically give you about 30 to 40 hours of playing time, while natural gut strings provide almost twice as much, about 60 to 70 hours. That's assuming, of course, that you don't break a string first.

(54° C). Likewise, cold temperatures can cause your strings to lose resilience and create "dead zones" that can weaken your swing. Cold temperatures also make strings brittle and more likely to break.

Touch up an old wooden tennis racket

If you have an old wooden tennis racket with a few dings in it, lightly sand out the damage using fine-grit sandpaper followed by a few coats of polyurethane varnish. Make sure you apply the varnish with an artist's brush or equally small-headed brush. Varnish can dissolve some types of string. Or do the varnishing just before you have the racket restrung.

Clean a bowling ball

Regardless of whether you bowl strikes or gutter balls, it's important to wipe down your bowling ball—with a soft cloth and a bit of rubbing alcohol or Windex—after each game to remove any dirt or debris that may be picked up while playing. Many serious bowlers additionally maintain their balls' surface by applying Neo-Tac's Liquid Nitro—about $7 for a 6-ounce (360-ml) bottle— every week or so. Each bottle lasts several months.

Recondition a bowling ball

Most bowling balls—particularly reactive resin models—will lose some ability to "react" with the pins over time due to the resettling of the oils inside them. Here are some guidelines for reconditioning a bowling ball:

❶ Place the ball in a large bucket or basin and soak it—with the holes pointing down—in 1 to 2 gallons (4 to 8 liters) of the hottest tap water your sink can muster mixed with 2 ounces (60 ml) of Dawn dishwashing detergent or 4 ounces (120 ml) of an environmentally friendly cleaner—both have excellent degreasing properties. If the water isn't really hot, heat it on the stove, but don't boil it. After a while, you may notice oil "bleeding" out of the ball; this is to be expected.

❷ After half an hour or after the water cools, pour it out. Then rinse the ball in warm water, pat it dry with a hand towel, and let it sit (again, with the holes down, but with some wadded-up paper towel in each one) on top of the towel for several hours.

❸ To complete the job, wipe the surface of the ball with some isopropyl alcohol, and let it dry before bagging it up for your next game.

Tighten up loose skates

Many types of ice skates and old-style roller skates (except those used for activities such as speed skating and ice hockey) use screws to fasten the blade supports to the boot's leather sole. It's a good idea to always inspect these screws before using the skates, and tighten them if necessary. If the threads wear out and you can't tighten a screw, try squeezing a bit of epoxy into the hole before reinserting the screw. Let the glue harden completely before hitting the rink.

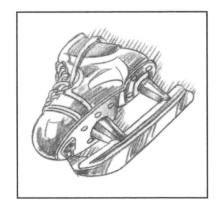

Baseball Gear

Ah, the smell and feel of an old mitt that fits the hand like a second skin. The crack of a favorite bat. New stuff can never replace your favorite old baseball gear, so you'll want to keep it in tip-top shape.

How to soften a stiff mitt

There are nearly as many opinions about the "right" lubricant to use to break in a baseball mitt as there are rules in the game. Traditionalists opt for Neats Foot Oil (available at most shoe stores), linseed oil, or a specialized glove oil (such as Rawling's Glovolium II). Others maintain that petroleum jelly, WD-40, and even bath oil are just as effective, if not better. Still, the method for breaking in a glove is more or less the same in all cases.

1. Spread some of the lubricant of your choice all around the glove using a soft cloth; then rub a bit more into the pocket of the glove and under each finger.

2. Place a baseball in the pocket and fold the mitt sideways. Keep it tied up with a belt, an Ace bandage, or some heavy-duty rubber bands. Let it sit for one or two days; then open the mitt and wipe off any excess oil with a clean cloth.

3. As soon as you get a chance, use the mitt for about 15 minutes (50 to 70 throws) to help it contour to the shape of your hand.

Love the glove

Once your baseball glove is broken in, you can keep it around a lot longer if you follow these few simple rules:

- Don't leave it in the trunk or on the seat of your car—or anywhere else where it can be exposed to excessive heat or light (either of which will eventually dry out and crack the leather). That also means you shouldn't dry a wet glove on a hot stove or radiator; use a soft absorbent towel instead.

- Don't over-oil your glove; twice per season should be fine.

- Keep the laces tight, and store it with a ball in the pocket when it's not in use.

Baby that wood bat

Metal bats may be all the rage, but wood will never lose its appeal among baseball purists. Here are a few ways to keep those wooden bats swinging:

- Wipe down bats with alcohol after each game or practice session to remove any buildups of dirt or pine tar.

- Try to avoid getting bats damp or wet. When a bat does get wet, dry it off as soon as possible with a soft cloth and rub in a little linseed oil.

- Periodically condition your bats by rubbing them against another wooden bat. Use hard strokes for about five minutes until surface looks smooth and even.

- Store bats vertically in a dry place, with the handle up.

True-Life ◆ *Long* Life

Steve Rath of Bayside, New York, confesses he was never much of a ballplayer. Still, he says, his two children view his 35-year-old baseball mitt as a treasured family heirloom. "It's in amazing shape," he says. "It even has that original leather smell." Rath notes that the Manchester S-161 shortstop glove wasn't considered state-of-the-art gear in its day, nor could he recall ever oiling the "prime grain steer hide." Rather, he attributes its longevity to a comfortable retirement inside a closet after his Little League days. "It hasn't seen much sunlight in the last thirty years or so," he adds with a chuckle.

✦ BEST ADVICE ✦ **Baseball Mitts**

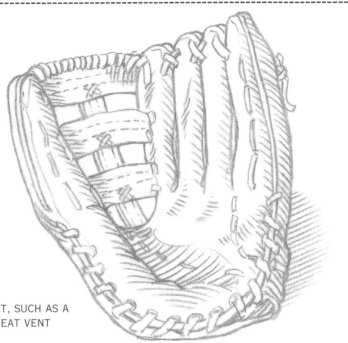

KEEP OUT OF BRIGHT
SUNLIGHT WHEN NOT IN USE

LACE TIGHTLY AND STORE
WITH A BALL IN POCKET

OIL ONLY ABOUT TWICE
A SEASON

KEEP AWAY FROM HEAT, SUCH AS A
CAR TRUNK OR A HEAT VENT

Buy to Keep: Baseball Bats

When buying a baseball bat, you have a choice of metal or wood. Here is how they stack up. It's important to choose one that's easy to swing with good control and speed.

Metal bats	Many Little Leaguers and adult players choose aluminum or composite-metal bats over traditional wooden ones these days. Aluminum bats have some clear advantages: They are noticeably lighter and are capable of hitting balls farther and with less vibration (which can sting hitters' hands) than their wooden counterparts. Moreover, although they can be dented, aluminum bats won't split or chip, as is known to happen with wood.
Wood bats	Despite metal bats' advantages, many players still prefer a wooden bat. The first wooden bats were almost exclusively made out of hickory, although most are now made of white ash and maple. When shopping for a wooden bat, pick one with a wide grain on its surface; such bats tend to be more resistant to chipping and splintering.

Clean up your ball game

Get dirt and stains off your baseballs by soaking them in 1 cup of water and 1/4 cup of ammonia (turn the ball as needed in the solution). Rinse with cold water and dry. Works for basketballs, footballs, golf balls, soccer balls, and volleyballs as well.

Bicycles and Exercise Equipment

A well-maintained bike can make whizzing down the road seem almost effortless. It just takes a few minutes at frequent intervals. And keeping treadmills and other exercise equipment in shape brings the joy of outdoor aerobics indoors.

Maintain proper tire pressure

Always inflate bicycle tires to the recommended air pressure (as noted on the tire's sidewall). Some tires can handle an inflation range. When inflating these types of tires, consider the rider's weight, as well as any loads that may be carried. Higher pressure gives better performance on pavement and other hard surfaces, while lower pressure works better for off-road rides. Gas station air hoses may inflate a bicycle tire too rapidly and often give inaccurate tire-pressure readings, which can result in a blowout. Whenever possible, use a manual hand- or foot-operated pump with an accurate gauge. It's also a good idea to pack a good air-pressure gauge whenever you go out for a ride; choose one that can read up to 120 psi (pounds per square inch).

Check your brakes

It's a good idea to regularly inspect your brakes before you go for a ride. Squeeze each brake lever toward the handlebar to make sure the brake moves freely and stops the bike.

If the brake lever reaches the handlebar, it needs to be tightened. Now, check out the brake pads: They should be about 1/16 to 1/8 inch (1 to 2 mm) away from the rim when the brakes are not applied—if you can stick a matchbook cover between the rim and brake, your brakes are properly adjusted.

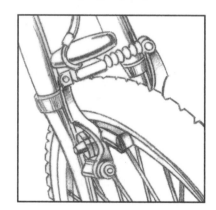

Preserve your bike chain

Want to extend the life of your bicycle chain? Lay off the oil. Yep, you heard that right. Machine oil does a fine job lubricating bike chains, but it also attracts dirt and debris that could wind up damaging them. Instead, use a dry chain lubricant. It will keep your chain running smoothly without sucking up the dirt. You can buy dry lubricants at most bike shops.

Powder a new inner tube

Getting a flat tire on your bike is never enjoyable, but it's a lot worse when you aren't equipped to fix it. Always pack a couple of spare inner tubes when you go for a long ride—and don't forget some talcum powder, too. A light dusting of talc around the inside of the tire will make it easier to fit the inner tube and get you back on the road that much faster.

Never play with plugs

Make sure that the electrical cords of all your electronic workout gear are free of tangles and unencumbered by weighty objects. If possible, avoid plugging more than one piece of equipment into each outlet. Even more important, try to keep your electronic fitness gear, such as treadmills and muscle-stimulation devices, on a separate circuit breaker in your home whenever possible (if not, be sure the circuit has an otherwise light load). The last thing you want is for the machine to lose power in the middle of your workout.

Dust off your treadmill

Accumulated dirt and grime often result in an early demise for treadmill belts. You can easily avoid this problem, however, and maximize your machine's longevity, simply by giving it a thorough dusting each week.

Also, be sure to keep the machine's deck (the two metal strips on both sides of the belt) dry and dust-free. You can clean it with a damp rag, but be sure to dry it off immediately afterward. Don't wax the deck (unless the manufacturer advises it); pretreated decks may react to the wax and result in a sticky surface.

Get in the grooves of your ski machine

Many ski-type and aerobic-walking machines are kept in motion by a drag strap wound around a flywheel (typically located between the foot grips). Remove the strap a few times a year, and clean out the grit that accumulates in the grooves around the rim of the flywheel. A little rubbing alcohol applied to a rag or towel will do the job. This will extend the life of the strap and keep it moving smoothly.

Finish with a rubdown

It's great to work up a good sweat when you work out, but never leave your perspiration behind on your exercise equipment (especially on metal parts, where it can cause rusting). Always use a soft, dry towel to wipe down stationary bikes, weights, treadmills, rowing machines, ski machines, benches, and other gear when you're done with your workout. You might also want to place plastic drip mats under your exercise equipment to prevent perspiration drips from staining carpeted and hardwood floors.

Get more mileage from running shoes

Running shoes are impermanent by nature, but you can still get your money's worth from them by exercising a little care. Don't keep shoes in cold environments (such as an unheated porch) during winter or in direct sunlight during summer. Also, never wear your running shoes for anything other than running, and be sure to thoroughly dry them off when they get wet by placing them near a heat source (though don't put them in a clothes dryer).

Picking shoes for the long run

The most durable running shoes have polyurethane midsoles and carbon-rubber outsoles. The trade-off is that these shoes tend to be heavier than other varieties and usually don't offer maximum cushioning.

☞ DON'T
put sneakers in the dryer

It's tempting to dry soaked running shoes by tossing them in the dryer. But don't; the heat shortens the life of the shoes' leather and plastic components.

Camping and Fishing Gear

The right equipment in good condition is essential for an experience that is both safe and enjoyable in your activities in the great outdoors.

Repairs in the wild

If there's one thing you should never leave home without when you head into the great outdoors, it's a roll of duct tape. Quite simply, nothing is better when you need a fast, effective, and waterproof patch for a tent, an inflatable raft, a backpack, a shoe—you name it—or for repairing any number of cracked or broken items. For the strongest patches, put duct tape on both sides of a hole.

A lighter lantern

A clean lantern is a brighter lantern. Clean off that black soot on your lantern's glass globe with a soft cloth dipped in 1/2 cup of ammonia mixed with 1 gallon (4 liters) of water—or just use a commercial glass cleaner that contains ammonia.

Don't store a wet tent

Did it rain on your last camping trip? Don't pack away a wet tent; it's likely to be covered with mold and mildew the next time you take it out of storage. Instead, hang the tent up to air-dry in a shaded spot when you get home. Once all the moisture has evaporated, roll up the tent with the poles and other parts tucked inside to prevent them from falling out if the bag is jostled.

Clean a tent

Most tents and backpacks can go for quite a while without needing a cleaning, but when it's time scrub them down, don't use any harsh detergents or household or industrial cleaners—they could remove protective coatings from the material. Instead, wipe down your dirty tents, backpacks, sleeping bags, and other outdoor fabrics with a sponge dipped in warm water and a bit of Woolite or some other mild soap. Hose off any excess soap; then hang them up to air-dry.

Fluff up sleeping bags and air mattresses

Keep your sleeping bags and air mattresses loosely stuffed in a porous sack or an old pillowcase. Leaving a sleeping bag tightly balled up in storage can bunch up or break the fibers in the filling material, which makes for lumpy bedding that's uncomfortable to sleep on. For optimum care, store your air mattresses flat with the valves left open.

Wax down a rod

Apply a thin coat of wax to your fishing rod (as well as to the reel seat and guides) once or twice a year. This will go a long way toward protecting your rod against harmful scratches, and it'll make it a lot easier to clean after a fishing trip. You can use either furniture polish or car wax, but avoid heavily scented products—you don't want to risk getting it on your line, where it may repel some fish.

☞ NO
hooks on guides

Never hang fishing hooks on your guides. The barbs can leave scratches on guides and even pull them off.

Test your rod's guides with panty hose

Any fishing buff worth his or her salt knows how important it is to inspect a rod's line and roller guides to make sure that they're tight and free of any rough spots.

• Test the guides for roughness by pulling a strip of old panty hose through each one. If it hits a snag, the guide may need to be replaced, although you can try to smooth it by gently filing it.

• Also check the wrapping around each guide's base; if it needs to be reglued, use a two-part epoxy. Don't use

✦ BEST ADVICE ✦ **Fishing Rods**

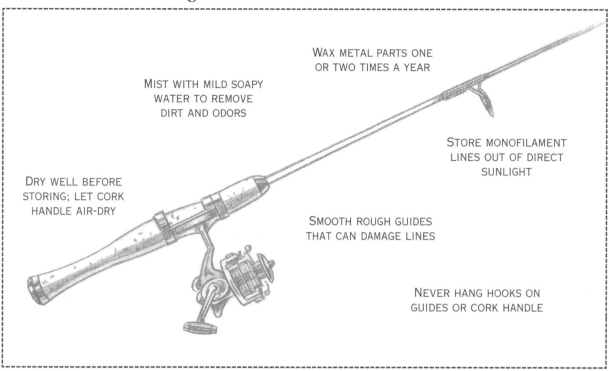

MIST WITH MILD SOAPY
WATER TO REMOVE
DIRT AND ODORS

WAX METAL PARTS ONE
OR TWO TIMES A YEAR

STORE MONOFILAMENT
LINES OUT OF DIRECT
SUNLIGHT

DRY WELL BEFORE
STORING; LET CORK
HANDLE AIR-DRY

SMOOTH ROUGH GUIDES
THAT CAN DAMAGE LINES

NEVER HANG HOOKS ON
GUIDES OR CORK HANDLE

fast-setting glue, such as Krazy Glue; it can make rods brittle and can cause cracking.

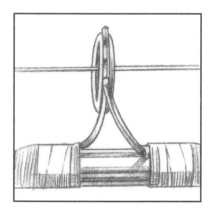

Don't pop the cork

Lightweight, durable, and eminently graspable, a cork handle remains a popular feature on many fishing rods. Cork doesn't require much care, either. Just be sure to let it air-dry after every fishing trip to prevent mildew. You can also give handles an occasional cleaning with some mild soapy water on a damp cloth. Don't use chemicals or solvents, which can disintegrate the cork. Also don't anchor hooks in the cork. The holes will trap dirt and oils.

Keep fish on the line

How well you treat your fishing line will ultimately determine if you land the catch of the day or bemoan the one that got away. Monofilament is the most delicate type of fishing line and needs to be replaced every year (or two at the most). This popular type of fishing line can be damaged by prolonged exposure to direct sunlight and should be stored a cool, dry area.

Cleaning your gear

Rinse off your lines, reels, and lures with a gentle mist of mild soapy water to remove dirt and odors after fishing, especially if you were fishing in saltwater. Don't use a high-pressure spray on reels, because it can push salt and other debris into the inner components, where it can cause corrosion. Make sure all your fishing gear is thoroughly dry before putting it away.

Musical Instruments—Storing and Transporting

With the proper care, a musical instrument can be a companion for life—one that can always carry a tune! How you store and transport it are particularly important.

Keep instruments out of car trunks

No matter how hot or cold it is outdoors, it's bound to be hotter or colder inside the trunk of your car. Extreme cold makes wood brittle and affects the tuning of many instruments. Extreme heat can ruin varnish and can destroy joints by softening the glues that hold instruments together.

Keeping an instrument in the trunk of your car also puts it at risk of being stolen or damaged in even a relatively minor collision. In fact, 95 percent of all instrument thefts involve popped trunks, which is why most insurance companies won't cover theft or damage to an instrument in an unattended car. So don't even think about locking that trusted friend in the trunk. Put your instrument in the backseat instead—and take it with you when you get out.

Follow the warm-up act

All musical instruments need to be protected from extreme temperature changes when traveling from place to place. If you don't have a padded or protective hard case, wrap the instrument in a blanket or a thick towel. When an instrument is moved from a cold to warm environment, don't open it immediately upon arriving at your destination. Keep it in its case or wrapped up at room temperature for at least two hours to give it time to acclimate to its new surroundings. (If it feels cold to the touch when you open it, give it more time.)

Drop the gig bag

Gig bags may look cool, and these popular padded fabric carriers can make it much easier to transport your instrument across town. However, they offer little in the way of real protection and shouldn't be depended on for long-term storage. Hard-shell cases may not look as good, but they're much better for instruments—and hold up better to the rigors of the road.

Don't overstuff cases

Although it often seems like there's room to spare inside your music case, that doesn't mean it's okay to fill it up with books or accessories. Small, loose items can bounce around inside the case and damage the instrument. And placing books or sheet music underneath your instrument can put unwanted stress on the instrument when the case is closed. A bit of breathing space inside your case will never hurt a musical instrument, but overcrowding it definitely will.

Never check instruments with your luggage

It may seem obvious, but it's amazing how often this simple rule goes unheeded. The fact is an airplane's baggage compartment is no place for a musical instrument. In addition to the cold, crowded conditions of most baggage areas, there's the ever-present risk of mishandling (those "Fragile" or "Handle With Care" stickers notwithstanding). Remember—if you can't carry it on, don't take it with you.

Keep instruments in their cases

Always keep an instrument *lying down flat* in a protective, hard-shell case or a padded bag when it's not in use. Not only is this the best way to prevent damage resulting from accidental bumps and falls or curious fingers, it also offers some protection from environmental dangers, such as excessive moisture (in humid climates, always keep a packet of silica gel inside your case as well), dryness, or damaging fumes.

Tend to battered cases

Sooner or later, all well-traveled cases show some bruises from their journeys. But a banged-up case is not only aesthetically displeasing; it could also put an instrument at risk. An unbalanced case can tip over and damage the instrument inside, while an exposed wooden frame may invite insects and other pests. If you have an antique case, you may want to have it professionally refurbished, although finding a qualified repair shop may be difficult in some locations and the job itself is usually quite expensive. Otherwise, consider replacing the case if it's badly damaged—especially if the handle is broken. You can also use duct tape to patch up minor splits and gashes. It may not be pretty, but it will usually stay put and prevent the damage from getting worse.

Winterize wooden instruments

Winter can be a hazardous time for musical instruments. When the heat comes on in your home, the air gets much dryer, and that can spell big problems for all wooden acoustic instruments—including pianos, guitars, clarinets, flutes, and violins. Wood shrinks without adequate moisture, and instruments—violins, in particular—have been known to crack when kept at relative humidity levels of 30 percent or less. Ideally, wooden instruments should be stored in an environment with a relative humidity level between 45 and 55 percent.

Many musicians take additional measures to protect their instruments in winter by using simple humidifiers called Dampits. Also known as green snakes, these devices typically resemble a length of garden hose covered with lots of small holes

(although they come in other shapes as well). All Dampits have spongelike material inside. They need to be soaked in water for 20 seconds each day—twice daily if the outside temperature is below 0° F (-18° C)—squeezed out, wiped free of any drips, and then placed inside the instrument to provide adequate moisture.

 Pro Tip

MAKE YOUR OWN DAMPIT

Although most Dampits sell for under $15, you can make your own for even less. Start by recycling a small travel-size plastic shampoo bottle or travel soap dish. Then heat a nail over a stove or open flame until it glows—hold it with pliers so you don't burn yourself—and use it to punch a dozen or so holes in the container. Cut a sponge to fit inside the bottle, and place it inside (cut into pieces, if necessary). Attach a 14-inch (36-cm) length of string to the bottle so that you can retrieve it from inside your instrument, and you're all set. Unfortunately, this type of Dampit is only good for guitars or other instruments with sound holes large enough to accommodate the width of the bottle.

Pianos

A little care for the case and the keys—it doesn't take much to keep the ivories tinkling.

Never treat a piano like a table

Your piano is a beautiful piece of furniture, but it should never be mistaken for a table or bookcase. Don't even consider placing a live plant on top. If the weight doesn't damage the wood or the finish, the water that eventually spills on it will—not to mention what it can do to the strings and metal parts if it seeps inside. Likewise, banish all candles, drinks, and ashtrays.

Polish your piano

Always use a compatible polish to keep up your piano's finish. It's best to seek out recommendations from the piano's manufacturer or a piano specialist in your area, though you can usually get by with pure lemon oil or a high-quality furniture polish. Typically, you should polish a piano twice a month to keep it clean and free of dust, but *never, ever* polish the keys or the bench top. Polishing the keys will make them sticky and dull-looking, while polish on a bench top will eventually combine with the varnish on the wood and body perspiration to form an adhesive-like substance that will stick to players' seats and ultimately destroy the wood.

Practice safety in the sun

It's a good idea to keep your piano out of direct sunlight. The light can bleach the wood and leave an uneven finish. Sunlight will also darken plastic key tops. Ivory keys, however, require periodic exposure to sunlight in order to maintain their whiteness.

Clean your piano keys

Use a damp cloth with a little nonabrasive cleaner added to wipe down your piano keys after each session to avoid stickiness and dulling. Don't forget to dry them off afterward.

Homemade piano-key brighteners

Even if your old piano still sounds great, those ugly, yellowed keys can hit a sour note. Try some of these tried-and-true methods to put the white back in your ivory or plastic keys:

• Mix up a solution of 1/4 cup of baking soda in 1 quart of warm water. Apply to each key with a dampened cloth. (You may want to wedge some pieces of cardboard or paper towels between the keys to avoid drips.) Then wipe with a cloth dampened with plain water, and use a clean cloth to buff-dry.

• Try cleaning them with a bit of toothpaste and a toothbrush; then wipe them down with a damp cloth and buff-dry.

• Cut a lemon in half, dip it in a bit of salt, and rub it over the surface of the keys. Once they have dried, polish the keys with a damp cloth and buff-dry.

• Use some plain yogurt. Just put a small dab on a clean, soft cloth, rub it on the keys, and then wipe it off.

Support the lyre on a grand piano

One of the most fragile parts of any grand piano is the lyre, the contraption that hangs down below the piano and contains the pedals. To prevent the lyre from breaking from excessive foot pressure, slide a phone book or a like-sized catalog between the pedal box and the floor. Make sure the fit is tight so that when you push on the pedals, the weight isn't on the lyre.

Guitars and Other Stringed Instruments

Just because you call it your ax doesn't mean you can treat your guitar like one. And whether it's a guitar or a violin, treat your stringed instrument right and it will only sound better as the decades pass.

Do the cleaning rag

Don't forget to wipe down the neck and body of a guitar or any other stringed instrument with a soft, dry cloth, flannel, or towel after each time you play it. A few rubs is all it takes to remove sweat and oils that build up on the fret board and shorten the life of the strings, as well as fingerprints that can mar the finish of your instrument. Regular, fast cleanups are far more beneficial for your instrument than a once-a-year, top-to-bottom polishing.

 Pro Tip

FEED YOUR FRET BOARD

Most guitar fret boards are made of unfinished wood and need to be conditioned every six months or so. Take off the strings and gently clean the fingerboard and frets with 0000 ultrafine steel wool. Use a soft-bristled toothbrush to sweep off the dust and steel wool filings left after cleaning. Finish the job by applying a small amount of mineral, lemon, or almond oil on a clean cloth along the length of the fingerboard and polishing with a soft, dry cloth.

Polishing your guitar

When it's time to polish your guitar, don't automatically reach for the furniture polish—many contain oils that can build up on a guitar's finish and make it dull over time. The best procedure for polishing varies from model to model; consult the guitar's manufacturer or an experienced guitar technician in your area about the best cleaning procedure for your guitar.

Don't play with dirty strings

How often you change the strings on your guitar is largely a matter of personal preference, although a fresh set of strings will always sound great. Generally speaking, the time to change guitar strings is when they start to lose tonal quality. That should be at least twice a year if you play your guitar regularly. When changing strings, you can maintain your guitar's setup by changing one string at a time, but you'll need to remove all your strings if you want to clean the fret board.

Check your neck

Chances are, the neck of your electric or acoustic guitar will need an adjustment at some point. This is most evident if you notice the intonation is off or if it takes more pressure than usual to push down the strings. You can easily tell if the neck of your guitar is warped by removing the strings and laying a yardstick on its edge across the length of the neck. It should lie evenly across the frets. If not, the neck needs an adjustment. You can get it adjusted at most stores that sell guitars.

Smooth out scratchy guitar sounds

If the knobs of your electric guitar start producing unwanted noise when you turn them, it's probably due to accumulations of dust and dirt in the potentiometers. Clean them out twice a year by removing the knobs and spraying a bit of WD-40 directly into each pot. Then replace the knob, and thoroughly work in the lubricant by turning the knob back and forth several times. Unplug the guitar and amplifier before cleaning.

Replace a missing amplifier knob

Do you have an old instrument amplifier that's missing a knob or two? If you can't find replacements or keep forgetting to look, you can at least stop guessing about your amp's settings by making your own replacement knobs. Start by cutting off a 3/4-inch (19-mm) piece from a wine cork. (You need a real cork, not one of those plastic stoppers they put in some wine bottles these days.) Then carefully insert a

sharp knife twice into one end of the cork so that it forms an X. Now with a permanent marker, draw a straight line on the other side of the cork from the center to the edge. Turn the potentiometer all the way down to its lowest setting, and gently work the cut-side of the cork (with the line in the appropriate position) over the pot. Viola! You're back in business.

Loosen up strings for storage

If you don't plan to play your guitar or other stringed instrument for a few months or more, loosen or remove the strings before packing it up. This will keep the body, bridge, and neck from warping or

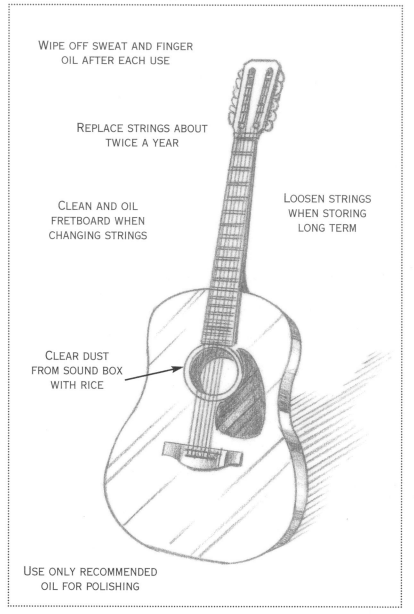

✦ BEST ADVICE ✦ **Guitars**

WIPE OFF SWEAT AND FINGER OIL AFTER EACH USE

REPLACE STRINGS ABOUT TWICE A YEAR

CLEAN AND OIL FRETBOARD WHEN CHANGING STRINGS

LOOSEN STRINGS WHEN STORING LONG TERM

CLEAR DUST FROM SOUND BOX WITH RICE

USE ONLY RECOMMENDED OIL FOR POLISHING

breaking from the constant tension of the strings.

Use rice to get dust out of the sound box

While you're changing strings of your acoustic guitar or other stringed instrument, don't forget to clean the dust out of the instrument's body. Simply pour about 1/2 cup of uncooked rice into the sound hole, give it a few shakes, then dump out the rice (and the dust).

Brush off rosin dust

Use a soft, clean cloth or paint-brush to remove the rosin dust from your cello, violin, or viola after each time you play it. If you leave rosin dust on the instrument, it will eventually harden and become increasingly difficult to remove.

Watch those pegs

The pegs of any stringed instrument should turn freely without slipping or rubbing against the sides of the pegbox. When pegs start to slip, they need to be refitted. A dry environment can cause pegs to shrink and slip, while excessive humidity can make them swell up and stick. Never force a peg into the pegbox if it slips or gets stuck; you could break it or damage the pegbox. If a string becomes pinched against the side of the pegbox, have it professionally repaired as soon as possible; continued friction on it can break the string or crack the pegbox.

Pencil in your strings

Use a soft pencil to apply a small amount of graphite to the bridge and notches on the top nut of your violin. It will enable the strings to slide more easily, and they'll last longer, too.

Take a bow

Taking good care of your bow is crucial for getting the best tone from your violin, viola, or cello.

Here are some essential tips for proper "bow etiquette."

• Never touch the bow hair; your skin's natural oils will counteract the gripping effect of the rosin.

• Always loosen the bow after playing by giving it three or four good turns. Leaving constant tension on the bow hair will not only stretch the hair but eventually will weaken or warp the bow as well.

• Replace the leather grip on the bow if it becomes worn. If you ignore it too long, it could damage the wood underneath the grip, which will affect the bow's tonality.

• Don't apply machine oil to a sticking bow screw; rub it with a candle instead.

• When tightening the hair on a new bow, leave just enough space to insert your pinky between the bow and the hair (slightly more for a cello). You can experiment with different tensions to find the best tone for you, but be careful not to overtighten the hair.

❓ How Long Will Violin and Cello Strings Last?

ANSWER: 3 to 6 months for violins, but 18 years for cellos

Violin strings should be replaced once every 3 months if you play daily or up to 6 months if you don't. The thicker strings on cellos and basses don't need to be changed as often; once every 18 years or so should be fine. When changing the strings on your violin, be sure to change them one at a time to keep the bridge in place.

Brass and Woodwinds

Cleaning your brass or woodwind isn't just a matter of longevity for your instrument. It's a matter of personal hygiene as well.

No polish, please

Never use metal polish or commercial cleaners on lacquered, brushed silver, or silver-plated instruments—such as trumpets, saxophones, or flutes; it could destroy the lacquer or cause corrosion in the exposed metal parts. Instead, thoroughly wipe the instrument down with a clean cloth (or a silver cloth for silver-plated instruments) after you play it. Sweat and moisture from your fingers can be acidic and can eventually mar the instrument or wear out the keys if they're not removed.

Bathe your brass once a month

All brass instruments should be flushed out at least once a month with a bit of mild detergent in lukewarm water. (Don't use hot water; it could damage the lacquer.) Work the valves (or trombone slide) with the water in the instrument; then rinse with cold water and dry thoroughly. Be sure to oil the valves or grease the slide before putting the instrument away.

Use a brush to clean tubing

Every three months or so, use a flexible instrument brush to clean slides and tubing before giving the instrument its bath. Make sure you use the right brush for the job: a flexible brass instrument brush to clean out the tubing, a valve cleaning brush to clean out the valve casing, and a mouthpiece brush to clean the mouthpiece. Using the wrong brush can damage these fragile parts. The brushes are available online, as well as from stores that sell musical instruments.

Remove leftover moisture

When you've finished playing your French horn, trumpet, or tuba, loosen the valve caps by giving them half a turn. This allows any leftover moisture to seep out and avoids trapping it inside the instrument, where it can promote bacteria growth or corrode the screw threads.

Cleaning clarinets and flutes

If you play a clarinet or flute, always clean the bore of your instrument after playing it—give it several run-throughs with a pull-through or a cleaning rod. When cleaning a flute, uncouple it at the joints. After cleaning a clarinet, thoroughly dry its sockets and tenons. These simple steps not only keep instruments in good working condition but also fight the growth of harmful bacteria and molds.

Clean out your mouthpiece

A dirty mouthpiece can become a breeding ground for germs and bacteria that can harm you and affect your instrument's tone. Use a mouthpiece brush and warm water to remove grime and food debris. You can clean a larger mouthpiece by pulling a twisted-up handkerchief or similar cloth through it.

Furniture & Furnishings

Wooden Furniture

Wood is the favored material of furniture makers because of its natural warmth and beauty and because it's easy to shape and finish. They also love it because it can last for generations, as long as you care for it properly.

Wax and polish: Know the difference

Paste wax and liquid furniture polish both help protect wood furniture finishes by reducing friction so that things will tend to slide across the finish instead of digging in. And they both add shine to dull surfaces. The significant difference is that liquid polish evaporates—some formulations hang around for a few days, others only an hour. And until the polish actually evaporates, you'll be able to smear it with your finger.

Paste wax contains a solvent that evaporates, but the wax remains to provide long-term protection and shine without smearing. On the other hand, polish does a much better job of removing dirt and dust, plus most polishes have a nice scent. So if you want maximum long-term protection—especially for a surface that will have things moved around on it—reach for the paste wax. If easy cleaning is your top priority, choose polish.

Wax doesn't build up

Don't you believe any of that advertising guff about "waxy buildup." Paste waxes contain a solvent—otherwise the wax would be as hard as a candle instead of as soft as paste. When you apply more paste wax, the solvent dissolves the wax that is already there, making a new mixture. When you buff the new finish after the solvent evaporates, you'll remove the lion's share of the wax and dirt, leaving behind a shiny, thin coat of wax—no thicker than the old coat.

✻
Grandma says . . .

"Dust and dirt can scratch the finish on fine furniture, so dust regularly with a dry, soft cloth. Use an artist's brush to clean intricately carved areas. For stubborn dirt, use a slightly dampened, soft cloth."

∘∘∘

Protect and clean

Some furniture polishes contain a little wax, which will be left behind to protect the surface after the polish evaporates. But you won't get as much protection as from a good hand-rubbed coat of paste wax. A better compromise between protection and cleaning is to polish a paste-wax surface. Like paste wax, polish contains solvents. So if you use furniture polish on a waxed surface, the polish will dissolve the wax and you'll take some of the wax off the surface as you wipe. This won't harm the furniture—just be aware that you'll have to wax more often or just switch to polish.

Make wax last

A good paste wax job can last for a few years, depending on how much you use the surface. To make the wax job last as long as possible, clean it with nothing more than a damp cloth.

Go for two coats of wax

The best way to apply paste wax is to put some in the middle of a piece of cotton cloth. The warmth of your hand will melt the wax, and just enough will seep through the cloth as you wipe it over the surface. Wait for the waxy surface to become dull, indicating that most of the solvent has evaporated. Then buff with a fresh, soft cloth, turning it frequently. A second coat is a good idea—you won't be building up the wax surface, just filling in any tiny spots you missed with the first coat.

Your furniture doesn't crave oil

Advertising has perpetuated the myth that all furniture wood contains natural oils that need to be replaced by furniture polish. Save the oil for your car. The pores of properly finished wood are sealed with finish. While many furniture polishes seem oily because they contain oily petroleum distillates, these distillates don't soak into the wood. They protect only the finished surface—until they evaporate, that is.

Keep away from heat sources and moisture

Most wood furniture is held together by tight-fitting joints where two parts have been glued together. The joints are very strong, but two things can undo them: heat and moisture. The former shrinks the wood and thereby loosens the joint. The joints of a wooden chair placed near a heat register or radiator, for example, may loosen and eventually fail due to shrinkage. Moisture, on the other hand, can cause joint failure by softening the water-based glues typically used with wood furniture.

Keep wood furniture out of sunlight

Light—especially direct sunlight, but indoor lighting, too—is your furniture finish's worst enemy. The ultraviolet rays break down the finish. Waxes and polishes do nothing to stop this deterioration—anything you can see through won't block light. Fortunately, this is a slow process, but it's worth slowing further if you have valuable pieces that you want to hand down in fine shape. Here are some tips:

• Keep the pieces out of direct sunlight by keeping drapes closed and keeping the furniture away from windows.

• Turn off lights when you are not using the room.

• Keep pieces covered when you can—use tablecloths and throw a sheet over the furniture when you go on vacation.

☞ **DON'T**
cover with plastic

Never cover your tables with plastic pads for long periods. The plastic might stick to the finish.

Keep it cool

You can think of oxidation as the price we pay for the air we breathe. Almost every material combines with oxygen in the air and turns into its oxide. That's what makes metal rust and furniture finishes turn dark and eventually start to crack. Heat accelerates oxidation. So while you can't stop oxidation, you can slow it down by taking those antiques out of the hot attic and making sure furniture is not too close to radiators or heating vents.

Watch the humidity level

Central heating makes your life comfortable, but it can be hell for your solid-wood furniture. Here's why: Cold air can't hold moisture as warm air can, so cold winter air is naturally dry. Your heating system warms dry air, increasing the air's ability to suck up moisture. And where will that moisture come from? Unless you provide another source in the form of a humidifier, the moisture will come from your skin, your nasal passages, and your furniture. This causes your nose to become irritated, your skin to itch, and your wood furniture to shrink, loosening its joinery and sometimes causing wood to split. Hot summer air can hold lots of moisture, and unless you live in a very arid region, your wooden furniture will absorb moisture from the air, causing it to expand. This is why drawers stick and table leaves warp. The summer solution is to use an air conditioner, which will cool the air and make it give up its moisture before it's absorbed by your furniture.

Eliminate the guesswork

If you own collectable antique furniture articles and want to preserve them, invest in an inexpensive hygrometer. Use it, along with humidifiers or dehumidifiers, to keep the relative humidity in your home between 40 and 60 percent.

Remove candle wax

Oh, darn! Candle wax dripped on your beautiful table. Don't worry; it's pretty easy to remove. First scrape away as much of the wax as you can with your finger, a plastic kitchen scraper, or a stiff piece of cardboard. Sometimes it helps to stiffen the wax and loosen its grip by placing a bag of ice cubes on top of it. If the weather is cold and dry and the table is small enough, you might even leave it outside for an hour or so to stiffen the wax. Once you get the bulk of the wax off, remove any residue with a cloth moistened with mineral spirits or cream furniture wax. After removing all traces of the wax, repolish the entire table with furniture wax or polish.

Buy to Keep: Furniture

Whether new or antique, it takes excellent materials and superb craftsmanship to create furniture that you'll be proud to hand down to your children. Here are a few pointers on differentiating between great furniture; good, serviceable furniture; and junk.

Type of wood	Most fine furniture, whether antique or new, is made of hardwoods, such as cherry, walnut, maple, oak, teak, or of mahogany. However, some of the most valued antique furniture is made of old-growth pine. Cut from tall, old trees, this was a strong, durable wood with a beautiful grain. Sadly, the old-growth pine is mostly gone. Plenty of serviceable furniture is built from new-growth pine, but it doesn't come close to the beauty and strength of old-growth furniture.
	Excellent, extremely durable furniture can be made from plywood. "Cabinet-grade" plywood is available with fine hardwood top veneers. This material is strong and won't expand and contract like solid wood. As a result, panels won't crack, and joinery is not likely to loosen due to humidity changes.
	Low-grade furniture, especially kitchen cabinets, is often made of veneered particleboard. This furniture can look great, but particleboard is weaker than plywood or solid wood and doesn't hold fasteners as well. If it gets soaked, it can turn into something that resembles oatmeal.
Construction	Check the joinery. The best solid wood furniture relies on precisely made interlocking joints to hold it together—for example, drawers that are dovetailed together rather than nailed or screwed. Narrow dovetails of varied spacing and width are the hallmark of a handmade piece. But regularly spaced and sized machine-made dovetails are just as strong. Other signs of quality furniture include mortise-and-tenon or doweled joints and wooden corner blocks that have been glued and screwed in place.
Wood finish	Check the finish. There should be finish on all surfaces. If the bottom of a tabletop, for example, is not finished, that surface will absorb more moisture than the finished top. This could cause the top to cup, split, or warp. Run your hands over all the surfaces of the piece, and make sure everything is smooth to the touch.

Bag your furniture bugs

Insects, such as powder post beetles, can infest wood and leather furniture, as well as furniture filled with horsehair. Their larvae can cause damage by burrowing into wood parts and creating tunnels. If you find material that looks like fine sawdust under your furniture, chances are you have an active infestation—not simply damage from one long ago. Place the affected piece in a plastic bag and contact an extermination company that can fumigate the article. Be especially careful of infestation on pieces that you've had in storage in a garage or basement; check them well before bringing them into the house.

Remove water rings

No matter how quick you are on the draw when it comes to whipping out those coasters, sooner or later somebody is going to put a drink down on your gorgeous coffee table and leave a white water ring. The rings are caused by water condensation on the bottom of the glass that penetrates the finish. Here are three ways to remove the moisture from the finish. Each way is increasingly more difficult and invasive, so try them in the order given.

❶ Put some furniture polish, petroleum jelly, or mayonnaise on the damage and let it remain overnight. All of these

◆ BEST ADVICE ◆ **Wooden Furniture**

KEEP AWAY FROM HEAT (E.G., RADIATORS) AND MOISTURE (FLOWERPOTS)

GIVE SURFACE TWO COATS OF PASTE WAX; AVOID USING FURNITURE OIL OR POLISH

DUST REGULARLY WITH A SOFT CLOTH; DAMPEN CLOTH SLIGHTLY TO REMOVE DIRT

NEVER COVER WITH PLASTIC

REMOVE, POLISH, AND RELACQUER BRASS HARDWARE

WAX DRAWER RUNNERS TO REDUCE WEAR

MOVE PIECE BY LIFTING, NOT DRAGGING

substances are oily. If you are lucky, the damage will be superficial and the oil will replace the water in the finish, causing the ring to disappear.

❷ If the ring persists, try using alcohol—denatured is best, but any alcohol will do. You have to do this very carefully—especially if the finish is shellac, which is dissolved by alcohol. Too much contact with alcohol can also damage lacquer and water-base finishes. So start by dampening a cloth very slightly with alcohol and wiping it across the watermark. If you make some progress but the ring remains, make sure the alcohol isn't making the finish sticky or soft; then add a little more alcohol to the cloth, and wipe gently again. Don't rub hard—you want the alcohol to evaporate as you wipe, so it doesn't have a chance to damage the finish.

❸ The last resort is to try rubbing with an extremely fine abrasive. If you have some automotive compound around, that might work. Or try mixing some rottenstone or pumice (which is coarser) with mineral oil or furniture polish. If you still have a ring, try 0000 steel wool, which is coarser still. The problem with using abrasives is that they scratch the surface. The scratches left by fine abrasives are so tiny that you'll see them only as a dulling of the area you rubbed. The solution is to use increasingly finer abrasives until you bring the sheen of the affected area up to the sheen of the rest of the surface. Alternately, you can even out the sheen by rubbing the entire surface with fine abrasive to dull it very slightly.

Keep it level

If your floor is uneven or out of level, it could be putting undue strain on your furniture's joinery, consigning it to an early demise. This is especially true for furniture that carries a heavy load, such as bookcases and china cabinets. If you can rock the piece, that's bad news right there. Otherwise use a spirit level to make sure the piece isn't tilted. If it is, a shim under one side or under one or two legs should level it out and put the load back where it belongs.

Reglue veneers

For centuries, furniture makers have applied thin veneers of beautifully figured wood to cover more pedestrian woods used to construct their pieces. With proper care, good wood veneer is as durable as solid wood. However, sometimes over the years, the glue used to attach the veneer will fail, causing an edge to lift or a bubble to form.

• Lifted edges are easy to fix. Use a sharp, thin knife blade—a utility knife works well—to scrape old glue from under the lifted area. Use a toothpick to slide yellow carpenter's glue between the veneer and the wood surface. Cut a piece of plywood a little larger than the repair area. Place waxed paper over the area, and then place the plywood over the waxed paper. Clamp the veneer with C- or bar clamps, and leave overnight. If your clamps don't have rubber pads, be sure to

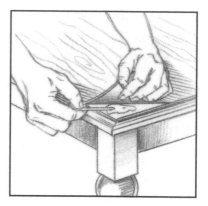

protect the bottom of the surface by putting wood scraps between the clamp and the surface. Use a wet sponge to remove glue squeeze-out as soon as you are done clamping.

• Bubbles are usually easy to fix, too. If the furniture piece is old, the veneer was probably applied with animal-hide glue, which can be softened and reactivated with heat. Set a clothes iron to medium heat. Place a damp cloth on the bubble, and then press the hot iron onto the cloth, removing it after a few seconds. Press again until the veneer sticks flat. Then remove the cloth, and press the iron directly onto the wood for

2 seconds. Any longer may damage the finish.

• If the bubble doesn't start to stick down after three or four brief applications of heat, you'll need to glue it. Use a sharp knife to split the bubble along the grain; then use a frozen popsicle stick to slide yellow carpenter's glue under the veneer. Press down on the repair with a veneer roller or wallpaper seam roller; then remove glue squeeze-out with a wet sponge. Place waxed paper over the bubble, and clamp the repair down using wood scraps between the clamp and the surfaces. If you can't reach the repair with clamps, use a heavy weight, such as a book or brick, instead.

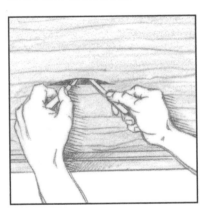

Never have furniture dip-stripped

If you have old furniture with multiple layers of paint and you want to return it to its former glory, it's possible to strip off the paint with a chemical stripper and refinish the bared wood. To preserve the joinery,

the safest way to do this is by hand rather than sending it out to be dip-stripped. Apply the stripper according to the manufacturer's recommendation, and scrape or rub off the old finish. Remove residue with lacquer thinner (outside or in a well-ventilated room) instead of water in order to preserve the glue in the joints.

No time for this messy and time-consuming task? Find a commercial furniture stripper that does cold-tank dipping, and ask for the residue to be removed with lacquer thinner. Avoid commercial strippers that use hot-tank dipping—lye heated to 120°F (49°C)—unless you are having old doors or stair balustrades stripped.

For antique furniture of value, avoid stripping altogether. Simply clean the piece with a damp, soft cloth. The aged finish and the patina that come with years of use are often beautiful and should be maintained. Removing them will also significantly reduce the value of your piece.

Don't forget the hardware

When polishing brass hardware on furniture, such as hinges, handles, and knobs, protect the surrounding finish with masking tape or remove the hardware altogether to polish it. Otherwise the polish may mar the furniture finish. Avoid polishes

that contain ammonia, because they can promote corrosion. Instead, choose a polish with a mild abrasive, such as Brasso. Wax regularly to forestall your next polishing session.

ProTip

HANDLE WITH CARE WHEN MOVING

Most of the damage to old furniture happens when it has to be moved. Often it's because of a bump against a doorjamb or because it gets jammed while carrying it down a stairway. Take extra care when moving valuable pieces by ensuring there is a clear path to wherever you are carrying the furniture. Remove doors if necessary to give you extra inches. Remove parts, such as drawers, shelves, and marble tops, and/or disassemble the furniture before moving it. If the doors can't be removed, bind them closed with straps or soft cord. Be sure to have adequate help. Furniture should be lifted and moved—not dragged, because this can put undue stress on its legs. Lift tables by the apron not the top, and lift chairs by the rails, not by the seat. Carry and store marble vanity tops vertically, not horizontally.

Keep it shining

Brass hardware is usually coated with lacquer to keep it bright. Eventually, however, the lacquer wears off, and the hardware will begin to tarnish. Then you're faced with the ongoing chore of polishing if you like a bright finish. To save yourself some work and to keep the hardware looking new, reapply the lacquer finish. First remove the hardware, and use acetone to remove any remaining lacquer. Then reapply several coats of lacquer from a spray can.

Resecure chair joints

Nothing will accelerate the demise of a wooden chair, such as a kitchen chair or rocking chair, more quickly than using it when it has loose joinery. A chair is designed to carry its load to the floor, but if the verticals wobble, it may soon drop its load—not carry it! Take a wobbly chair out of service until you can disassemble the loose stretchers. A rubber mallet helps

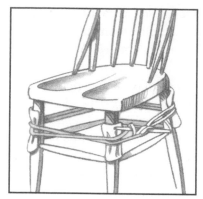

here. (Don't take secure joints apart.) First scrape the old glue from the joint with a sharp craft knife. Use a 50-50 solution of warm water and vinegar to remove any remaining glue and let dry. Test-fit the joints. If one is loose, glue a small strip of cotton to build up the tenon/dowel end of the offending part. Finally, reassemble with yellow carpenter's glue.

Wipe up squeezed-out glue immediately. To secure the joints while the glue dries, use clamps fashioned from loops of cord and twisted with a pencil or dowel until tight.

Straighten lopsided case furniture

The usual cause for cabinets and bookcases going out of square is that the backboard has become detached or was removed. The backboard is usually made of thin plywood or hardboard. Reattach it (or a new one) to the back of the cabinet at the sides, top, and bottom with brads or small screws. This is often all that needs to be done to add many years of useful life to treasured cabinets and bookcases.

Wicker and Caning

Light and surprisingly strong, wicker furniture adds a note of casual elegance to any room. But wicker and caning are natural materials that need a little special care.

Keep your wicker in top shape

A variety of vines, grasses, and plant can be woven into the furniture we call wicker. The four most commonly used materials are rattan, reed, willow, and bamboo. Here's how to keep your wicker from wearing out too fast.

• Regularly vacuum your wicker using a soft brush attachment—it is the gentlest way to clean wicker. You can use a new, dry paintbrush to sweep stubborn dirt, fuzz, or animal hair out of crevices. You can also carefully use an ice pick, awl, or tweezers to pry or pull stuck bits out.

• Wipe up any spills with a clean cloth dampened with a light detergent or Murphy Oil Soap in water.

• Reed wicker can be cleaned outdoors by using a spray hose and light detergent. Rinse the furniture well, and dry it completely before using it again. But be careful, because water can lift the finish.

Dealing with mildew

If you notice mildew growing on your wicker furniture, clean it with a 50-50 solution of bleach in water. Vacuum it first with a soft-bristle brush. Use a sponge to wash the wicker with the bleach solution, rinse well, then let it dry thoroughly in the shade, preferably on a warm, windy day. Remember—don't use the furniture until it is completely dry. To prevent more mildew, use a dehumidifier in the area or move the wicker piece to a drier place.

Don't soak paper fiber

At the turn of the 20th century, an embargo was placed on the importation of rattan reed from Asia. Since rattan was the most popular material used to make wicker furniture at the time, the embargo sparked the invention of paper fiber rush. This material, essentially long, twisted strands of chemically treated paper, was very popular for making wicker furniture through the 1930s and was also used instead of cattail rush or bulrush to weave the seats of wooden chairs. Overall, paper fiber is very durable, and you can wash it with a sponge. But since it *is* paper, you should never immerse it in water or soak it with a hose. If it becomes saturated, it can disintegrate.

Preserve wicker with finish or paint

If your wicker is in good shape but looking dingy, you can make it look like new with a clear finish. First vacuum the wicker, and then wash it with detergent and water. Let it dry thoroughly—for at least a day. Now you can apply any clear finish. Polyurethane is durable and easy to apply, but you can also use varnish, shellac, or lacquer. Flat finishes are the most natural-looking, but glossier finishes are more durable and easier to clean.

You can also paint wicker—again, semigloss or gloss paint is most durable. An eggshell-gloss paint is fine, too, but flat paint will be tough to clean. The most economical approach is to brush on interior wall paint, but cans of spray paint make it much easier to get an even coat while reaching all the crannies.

Get the sag out of caning

To fix a sagging cane seat, provided the material isn't broken, wet the seat thoroughly from underneath with a sponge. The underside is more porous than the top and will absorb better. Then let the caning dry in the sun. The cane should shrink back into shape. *Note:* Don't do this with paper-fiber caning.

Pro Tip
MAKE YOUR WICKER COMFORTABLE

The same humidity level that keeps you comfortable in your home will contribute to long life for your wicker, says Cathryn Peters, a Minnesota wicker restoration expert who runs The Wicker Woman, a wicker repair, seat weaving, and basket business. If the air is too dry, the wicker can start to creak and crackle. If it is too humid, mold and mildew can form, not only on your wicker but also in other areas of your home. If necessary, use a humidifier in dry weather and a dehumidifier in humid weather. In dry weather, it may also help to wipe your wicker with a damp sponge.

To add life to the seats of your wicker, Peters also recommends using padded chair-seat cushions. This is especially helpful for woven reed wicker and paper fiber seats and also for any cane seat that is more than 14 inches (36 cm) in diameter.

KEEP ROOM HUMIDITY MODERATE YEAR ROUND

VACUUM REGULARLY WITH SOFT BRUSH ATTACHMENT

NEVER GET WICKER MADE OF PAPER FIBER SOAKING WET

REMOVE ANY MILDEW WITH A BLEACH SOLUTION

USE MILD DETERGENT ON RAG TO REMOVE STAINS AND SPILLS

USE PADDED SEAT CUSHIONS TO REDUCE WEAR

RENEW TIRED WICKER WITH A CLEAR VARNISH FINISH; OR PAINT IT

LIGHTLY HOSE DOWN REED WICKER TO CLEAN IT THOROUGHLY

Care for your caning

Used on antique and contemporary chairs, footstools, and other small furniture pieces, caning is made of woven bamboo or reeds. Historically, it was often intended to support cushions, which also helped protect it. Cushioning is still a good idea. Here's how to keep your caning in good shape:

• To clean caning, use the brush attachment of a vacuum cleaner regularly to suck out lose dirt, or dust it with a soft brush, such as a paintbrush. To wash dirtier caning, use a little mild detergent in water applied with a sponge, cloth, or medium-stiff brush. Rinse with clear water, and towel. Don't use harsh detergents or cleaners.

• To prevent stains on caning, clean up any spills promptly with a wet cloth or soap and water. A stain may be impossible to remove. If you do get a stain, your best bet is to follow the lead of many old-timers and paint the cane.

Upholstered Furniture

If you purchase good-quality pieces and you manage to protect them from abuse, kids, and pets, they will serve you for decades—or, in the case of leather furniture, a lifetime. Here are a few tips to keep your upholstered pieces looking their best.

Rotate and fluff cushions

To keep sofas and upholstered chairs looking showroom new, rotate and turn the cushions each time you vacuum. Turn and fluff down cushions every time you use your sofa to prevent the down from settling and flattening.

What are the best springs?

Good-quality chairs and sofas are made with the same quality materials as they have been constructed with for decades. Eight-way, hand-tied coil springs are the strongest and most durable according to industry experts. The "eight-way" descriptor refers to how the coils are tied to one another in eight ways (for example, side to side, diagonally, and row to row). Zigzag springs are not as durable, but are acceptable for some applications, such as where internal mechanisms do not allow enough space for the use of coils. Such is the case with a fold-out bed. Webbing supports the springs of your chair or sofa. Jute or polyester webbing are preferred over nylon.

What makes a frame durable?

If you want to know if a frame will last or not, look for well-glued joints secured with double dowels or those that interlock with mortises-and-tenons, dovetails, or grooves known as dadoes. Major joints should be reinforced with corner blocks (a triangular wooden block glued and screwed to the inside of a corner to provide rigidity). Simple butt joints that are secured with screws or nails will not hold up to the wear and tear most furniture pieces must endure. On furniture with curves and contours, look for pieces with curved wood frames. This sounds obvious, but many curved pieces get their shape from padding and cushioning—not from the actual frame—and will not hold their shape for long.

What's the best fabric?

The rule of thumb when it comes to judging the strength and durability of upholstery fabric is, The tighter the weave, the longer the wear. Hold fabric to a strong light. The less light that shines through, the tighter the weave. Cotton and cotton-polyester blends are suitable fabrics, as well as many other synthetics (all of which are much improved over older versions of these fabrics). Another tip: Highly textured fabrics are subject to pulling, snagging, and tearing; flat weaves are not and will generally wear better.

Long-lasting fillings

Down is the preferred filling for softness, but other fillings can last at least as long, including down combined with other fibers, fluffy polyester, high-resilience polyurethane foams, and hair blends (mostly hog and cattle) for firm cushioning.

Stain treatment

Fabric on upholstered pieces should be treated to resist staining. You'll get optimal stain resistance from a factory-applied fabric treatment. Dealer-applied treatments are second best, and sprays you apply yourself are third—although much better than none at all. If you have a slipcover made, you can also have it treated to repel stains.

Disguise a scorch

Burn mark on your favorite chair? Cross your fingers and don't despair! If the burn didn't completely penetrate the fabric, you might be able to disguise the burn. Wet a paper towel with plain water and dab it on the burn. Be careful not to rub, or you'll damage the fibers further. Blot with a dry paper towel. If that doesn't take most of the charred spot out, put a drop of mild liquid laundry detergent on a wet paper towel and blot the spot. Follow up by blotting with a wet paper towel to remove the detergent and then with a dry paper towel to absorb the char stain.

For more serious charring or burn holes, there's not much you can do beyond patching the fabric, which probably won't be pretty. Take the furniture to a restorer to discuss whether or not it would be cost-effective to recover the piece.

Don't overclean leather

When it comes to caring for leather chairs and sofas, more is less. Regular cleaning requires nothing more than dusting. Don't use saddle soap on leather furniture—save it for your boots. Likewise, don't use oils, abrasives, varnish, straight ammonia, or ammonia diluted in water. Here is a cleaning regimen that will keep most leather furniture looking great for decades. Because leather coatings vary, it best to read the cleaning instructions that came with your furniture before cleaning. If you didn't keep the instructions, you may be able to get them from the manufacturer or the retailer.

• When a piece is new, treat it with a leather conditioner/preservative to protect it and keep it supple.

• The most important thing you can do for leather furniture is to dust it weekly. This keeps the pores from getting clogged with dust particles. Just wipe with a soft cloth.

• About four times a year, thoroughly clean leather furniture with a leather cleaner. Concentrate especially on wear areas, such as seats, arms, and backs. After cleaning, reapply a conditioner/preservative.

• Note that uncoated leathers readily absorb liquids and should not be cleaned with anything more than dusting or a damp cloth. Just dusting is better. Some stains just can't be removed from uncoated leather. You can try using an art gum-eraser to remove ordinary dirt.

Blot spills on leather quickly

Coated leather will initially repel most liquids, but then it will gradually begin to absorb the liquid. So if you use a clean, absorbent cloth or sponge to immediately blot up a spill, you'll usually have no trouble picking up the liquid without leaving a trace. If necessary, you can use a couple of drops of liquid hand soap in lukewarm water to help soak up the liquid. The good news is that even if

the liquid has had a chance to soak in, it will dissipate in time, just as human skin will absorb and eventually diffuse stains.

Keep leather cleaner on hand

If your leather should get stained with ink, grease, wax, urine, blood, or gum, you'll need to use a professional leather cleaning product to remove it. Follow the instructions that come with the product. It's smart to have the cleaner on hand because the sooner you attack the stain, the better chance you have of thoroughly removing it.

Keep leather away from heat and sunlight

Place your leather furniture at least 2 feet (60 cm) away from any direct heat source, such as a radiator, hot-air vent, or fireplace. Too much dry heat will cause leather to dry out and crack. Also, keep your leather furniture out of direct sunlight that will gradually fade the leather, as it will any dyed furnishing. Sunlight can also cause leather to crack.

Keep leather furniture out of traffic

Try to position your leather pieces so that people won't brush by them as they walk through the room. Repeated rubbing at one spot can cause marks that you can't remove.

Buy to Keep: Leather Upholstery

If you are looking for durable furniture upholstery covering, you just can't beat leather. It can last four or five times as long as any fabric, and if you take care of it, it gets more supple and comfortable with age.

Type of leather	Most leather upholstery is made with top-grain leather, so-called because it comes from the outer surface of the hide. The leather is usually coated with polyurethane or other coating to protect it from absorbing stains. Top-grain leather comes in two grades. "Full-grain leather" is considered the most attractive and requires no buffing or sanding before coating. Of course, full grain is the most expensive. The other grade is called "corrected-grain leather." This is leather that has been buffed or sanded to remove unsightly scratches. It is just as durable as full-grain leather.
	One more type of leather you should know about is called split grain. Hides are thick enough to split into several layers. Tanning the inner layers results in a stiffer, less durable leather than top grain. Split-grain leather is sometimes used for the backs and bottoms of leather furniture—surfaces that won't be seen and get little wear.
Dying and coating	Leather that is sold as "aniline" or "full aniline" has been dyed with aniline but not coated. This can be a little confusing because coated leather can be dyed with aniline before it is coated. Uncoated leathers are very soft and luxurious but not resistant to dirt and stains. Often uncoated leathers are buffed to create a very fine nap. Leathers sold as nubuck or suede have been treated this way.

Window Coverings

Blinds, shades, curtains, and drapes are a big part of any decorating budget. Ironically, though, they are often neglected once they're installed. And windows are harsh environments for most materials. To avoid having to begin all over again with new window treatments, take these simple precautions.

Dust to keep wood blinds looking new

As with other wood furnishings, dust wood blinds regularly to prevent them from becoming grimy and dingy-looking. Use a soft, clean, chemically treated dust cloth or dusting mitt. Lower the blind to its full length, close the slats almost completely, and dust. Then pivot the slats so they almost close in the opposite direction. By not fully closing the slats in either position, you'll be able to dust where the slats overlap. Alternately, vacuum wood blinds with the soft brush attachment of your vacuum cleaner, using the same sequence.

Clean with a soft damp cloth

If there is a filmy buildup on your wood blinds, dusting isn't going to do the trick. Instead, clean the slats by wiping them with a soft, damp rag and mild detergent or liquid dishwashing soap. Use the same method as described above. Wipe off excess water with a sponge, but do not rinse or towel-dry the slats. This can disrupt the anti-static treatment placed on the slat by some manufacturers. Disrupting it will cause the blind slats to soil quicker. For the same reason, do not rinse your wood blinds in a bathtub.

Clean shades in place

Shades usually only need to be dusted—a feather duster works well—or vacuumed with the brush attachment to keep them looking fresh and new. For local soiling, spot-clean as necessary, using a soft rag or sponge, mild detergent, and warm water. In the rare event that the entire shade needs cleaning, many types can be immersed in a tub of warm water. (Check your shade manufacturer's recommendations.) Wash carefully with a soft rag or sponge, and rinse in clean water. Then close the shade, and drain excess water before reinstalling it and allowing it to dry while open.

Clean drapes regularly

Follow the manufacturer's recommendations for cleaning drapes and sheers. Some can be hand-washed with a mild detergent in warm water. Others may require dry cleaning. When reinstalling still-wet sheers, place plastic sheeting and towels on the floor under the panes to absorb any drips.

Protect your drapes

If you've invested in good-quality drapes, you'll want to protect them. Here are some steps to prevent fibers from giving out before their time:

• Avoid unnecessary exposure to full sun. It can weaken hem threads and woven fibers and cause colors to fade. Use drapery lining or solar window tinting-film, or put shades or blinds behind the drapes to reduce exposure to sunlight.

• If your home is subject to big swings in relative humidity, use a humidifier or dehumidifier to help prevent shrinkage or stretching, especially in the case of loosely woven fabrics.

• Take care to prevent window condensation from staining your drapes. The best defense is insulated windows that form little or no condensation. Barring that, however, make sure the drapes and drape liners do not come into contact with the windows.

• Vacuum your drapes every few months with the soft brush attachment. Launder or have drapes dry-cleaned every few years, depending on the recommended cleaning method.

◆ BEST ADVICE ◆ **Drapes**

FIXING BROKEN BLINDS OR SHADES

Don't toss that broken blind or shade. Most window coverings can be repaired for much less than it would cost to buy new ones. Check the yellow pages or click on Google to find a repair shop near you. Many will restring Venetian blinds, retape mini blinds, and repair vertical blinds. If you're a do-it-yourselfer, several online companies sell repair kits. They provide complete instructions for restringing blinds and shades, including guidance on helping you select the correct string size. The website below has a comprehensive line of kits and sells everything from tools to tassels.

> **Fix My Blinds**
www.fixmyblinds.com

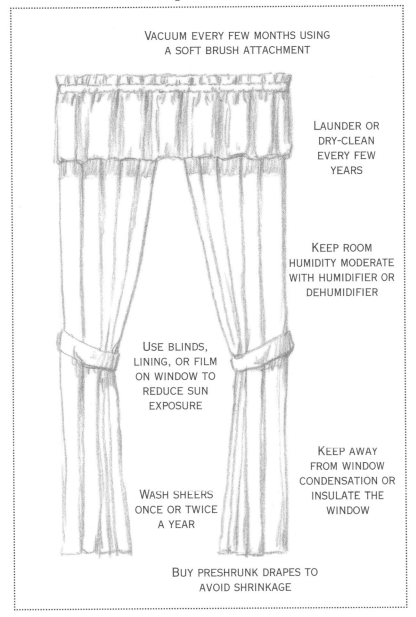

VACUUM EVERY FEW MONTHS USING A SOFT BRUSH ATTACHMENT

LAUNDER OR DRY-CLEAN EVERY FEW YEARS

KEEP ROOM HUMIDITY MODERATE WITH HUMIDIFIER OR DEHUMIDIFIER

USE BLINDS, LINING, OR FILM ON WINDOW TO REDUCE SUN EXPOSURE

KEEP AWAY FROM WINDOW CONDENSATION OR INSULATE THE WINDOW

WASH SHEERS ONCE OR TWICE A YEAR

BUY PRESHRUNK DRAPES TO AVOID SHRINKAGE

Lengthen short drapes

You should always buy preshrunk drapes, but if your drapes shrink significantly after cleaning, you can usually lengthen them by simply letting down the hems.

Install blinds correctly

With wide blinds, don't neglect to install the bracket that supports the center of the header. Without it the header will bow, hurting its operation and causing it to wear out sooner.

Rugs

Rugs are easier to maintain than carpeting because they can be lifted off the floor for cleaning. As a consequence, rugs are often a longer-lasting investment—and one that you can take with you when you move. Here are some steps you can take to ensure many years of enjoyment.

Remove shoes to preserve expensive rugs

It's the combination of dirt and sand that collects in the fibers of a rug, combined with the pressure of foot traffic, that causes a rug to wear. A sure way to maintain an expensive rug is to have a shoes-off policy in your home. Many different cultures do it—and so do many families in North America. Keep a collection of soft-soled slippers at the door for guests. Not only will this reduce the buildup of abrasive dirt particles, it will also keep hard-soled shoes from grinding away your rug.

Use a rug pad

Rubber rug pads will help reduce rug wear and prevent slippage on hard surfaces as well. The cushioning makes it tough for abrasive dirt particles to do their damage.

Have rugs cleaned regularly

Experts recommend having your rug cleaned by a professional at least once every two or three years. A good cleaning will remove the destructive residue from spills and pet accidents that build up over the years. More important, it will remove abrasive dirt particles that collect on the backing and between the fibers—up to 9 pounds (4 kg) of them in a 9 x 12 (275 x 365-cm) rug, according to the Carpet and Rug Institute. Look for a rug-cleaning service that has a beater. This is a machine that beats the rug with straps in order to remove grit prior to washing the rug.

Vacuum or shake rugs frequently

Vacuum your rug twice a week to keep it free of abrasive dirt particles—especially if it's in a high-traffic area like an entryway. If the rug is light enough, you can shake it outside or drape it over a deck railing and beat it with a tennis racket.

Remove rug stains

Many a rug is consigned to the attic or dumpster due to stains, not wear, but many stains can be removed with commonly available household chemicals. Tough jobs, such as removing chewing gum and car grease, require nasty solvents, such as dry-cleaning fluid. Most stains, however, can be removed with a sponge dipped in a detergent solution of 1 teaspoon of mild detergent (such as those used for lingerie), 1 teaspoon of white vinegar, and 1 quart (1 liter) of warm water. This works on most types of rug fiber for spots caused by watercolors, washable inks, urine, tobacco, tea, mustard, milk, ice cream, gravy, and fruit juices—if you act quickly. Remove spots as soon as you notice them.

If the detergent solution fails to remove a spot, check the Carpet Stain Removal chart on page 253 to select a cleaning method. The same cleaners recommended for carpets can be used effectively on rugs. Test the cleaner on a small, inconspicuous area first, before trying to remove the stain. If the cleaner removes rug dyes along with the spot, stop and try one of the other recommended spot removers. In all cases, carefully follow the manufacturer's directions.

Caring for handmade rugs

Hand-woven rugs made from natural fibers are prone to wear easily. Protect them with a foam pad; it will not transfer

♦ BEST ADVICE ♦ **Rugs**

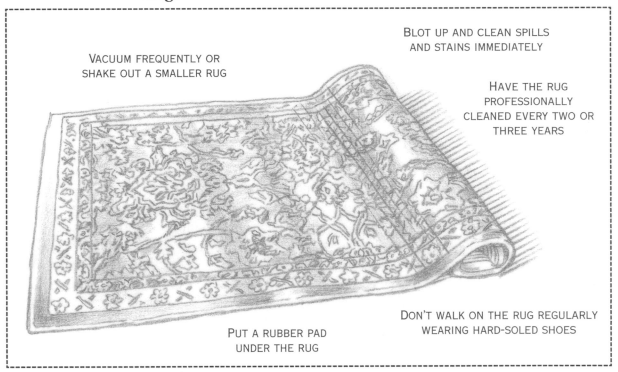

VACUUM FREQUENTLY OR
SHAKE OUT A SMALLER RUG

BLOT UP AND CLEAN SPILLS
AND STAINS IMMEDIATELY

HAVE THE RUG
PROFESSIONALLY
CLEANED EVERY TWO OR
THREE YEARS

DON'T WALK ON THE RUG REGULARLY
WEARING HARD-SOLED SHOES

PUT A RUBBER PAD
UNDER THE RUG

colors and may act as a moisture barrier. Flip rugs with reversible designs periodically to promote even wear and to help diminish the effect of fading. Also turn rugs you hang on the wall over regularly to offset the effects of sunlight.

Be especially careful with rugs made of plant-based materials—sisal, hemp, jute, and seagrass. They are easily damaged by too much moisture. They will not stand up to shampooing or steam cleaning. And use as little liquid as possible when treating stains. Wool, on the other hand, is naturally resistant to stains and dirt.

Rug storage

Before storing an Oriental or other valuable rug, make sure that it's clean and dry. Then roll it up and wrap it in brown paper. Store the rug in a dark, well-ventilated place where the temperature stays between 40° and 60°F (4° and 16°C). If you don't have such a space in your house, it's best to put the rug in professional storage.

Clocks

Clocks are for telling time, but more importantly, they are beautiful objects that can add serenity to any room. Treat them with respect, and they will continue to grace your home for many years.

Maintain humidity and temperature levels

Clocks are even more susceptible than fine furniture and paintings to big variations in temperature and humidity. Finishes can become alligatored and brittle. Painted metal clock faces and metal clock cases can corrode. Insects, such as powder post beetles, may feel welcome.

In winter, aim for 70°F (21°C) and a relative humidity of 35 to 50 percent. In summer, 70° to 75°F (21° to 24°C) and a relative humidity between 40 and 60 percent is ideal. Of course, this is not always possible, but you can avoid big swings in temperature and relative humidity, and always keep fine clocks away from heat sources, including heat vents, space heaters, fireplaces, and direct sunlight.

Move with care

As with other types of furniture, clocks are most likely to be damaged during transport. For large clocks, clear the path through which you'll be moving the clock. Remove jewelry, belt buckles, and the like prior to moving. Disassemble doors and, in the case of weight-driven clocks, wait until they run down so you can remove the weights and the pendulum. If you don't plan to remove the pendulum, pad it with foam to hold it in place. Always grasp the clock from secure points, not from weak appendages or from moldings.

Avoid overwinding

You will damage the mechanics of your clock by overwinding. Avoid this by developing a regular routine for when and how much you need to rewind.

Hang with a screw

When hanging a clock that generates vibrations, such as a cuckoo clock, use a screw driven at a 45-degree angle, rather than a nail. This will prevent the clock from working its way off the wall.

Mothballs keep bugs out

When they open the back of a large old wooden clock, many clock owners are shocked to find that a bunch of bugs have made their home inside. There's a simple solution: Put a few mothballs inside the back of your clock to prevent insect infestations.

Have your clock checked by a pro

Have a professional inspect your clock every five years, so he or she can check for worn parts and weakened springs.

Clean your clock

Clean wooden parts of your clock regularly with a soft, damp cotton cloth. Avoid commercial cleaners with silicone. Apply a furniture wax to protect the finish once or twice a year. For metal parts with lacquer coatings, clean with mineral spirits and then rewax. For metal that is slightly corroded, clean carefully with a fine-grit metal polish, remove residue with acetone, and apply a coat of wax.

Beds, Mattresses, and Bedding

Beds can last for generations if properly cared for. Mattresses have a far shorter life—typically around ten years—but a few simple procedures can add years to their lives and improve your sleep comfort as well. With bedding, long life is mainly a matter of buying quality and laundering correctly.

Watch for wobble

If your bed begins to creak and wobble, don't ignore it. Most beds are assembled with knock-down hardware, so you can probably fix the wobble simply by tightening the hardware. If you leave the hardware loose it may eventually strip out of the wood, creating the need for a much more involved repair.

Don't mismatch mattress to box spring

Never use a new mattress with an old box spring. Mattress-and-box-spring sets are designed to work in unison (the springs align), which adds life to your mattress and ensures maximum comfort. In fact, experts claim that using a mattress with a mis-matched box spring can reduce its life by 50 percent. It may also void the mattress warranty.

☞ DON'T
carry mattresses by the handles

The cloth handles found on many mattresses are not made for carrying. Use them only to rotate or reposition the mattress on the box spring.

Rotate your mattress

Most people tend to sleep in the same spot on their mattress every night. This can lead to uneven wear on the coil springs that provide support. To minimize this wear and to maximize comfort, manufacturers recommend that you turn your mattress every two weeks in the first three months after purchase. After that, turn it every two months. To turn a mattress, rotate it head to foot and then flip it over. Further disperse wear patterns by rotating only or flipping only on occasion.

Keep your mattress comfy

If you rotate your mattress and observe the following mattress maintenance tips, you should expect seven to ten years of restful sleep from a good coil-spring mattress:

• Use a high-quality, washable mattress pad to keep your mattress free from stains.

• Use a bed frame to keep your mattress from sagging in the center. King- or queen-size sets should have a center support to prevent bowing or breakage.

• Clean stains with mild detergent or soap and a clean cotton cloth dampened with cold water. Don't use volatile chemical removers, as they can degrade the mattress fabric and underlying materials.

• Don't allow your children (or adults!) to jump on your bed. Roughhousing can damage your mattress.

Launder sheets so they last

Make your sheets and duvet covers last longer by washing them in cool or warm water on the gentle cycle. Reduce the recommended detergent by half and avoid bleaches, because they break down the fabric fiber. Be careful not to let your sheets tumble in the dryer after they are dry, because this wears fibers as well. For flannel sheets with deep colors, add 1 cup of white vinegar to the wash water. This will help set the dyes.

Buy sheets that wear well

When shopping for sheets, begin by buying the right size. Many of today's mattresses are quite deep. Standard-sized sheets simply won't fit, and if you try to stretch a contoured sheet that's too small over a deep or nonstandard-sized mattress, you'll risk overstretching the elastic or actually tearing the sheet seams. Here are other features to look for when you shop for long-lasting sheets:

- The thread count tells you how many threads are woven into each square inch. Sheets with high thread counts are stronger and more durable than sheets with low counts. They are smoother and nicer to the touch as well. Avoid sheets with thread counts less than 175.

- Linen sheets, spun from flax, cost more and require extra care, but they can last for twenty years. Egyptian cotton has a relatively long fiber, making it stronger and long-lasting. Read the fine print, though, to be sure that the sheet is actually made from this fiber. Some manufacturers will mention Egyptian fiber in the large print but use only a small percentage of it in the manufacture of their product. Pima and Supima qualified cottons, from the U.S. South-west and West Coast, are also long-lasting fibers.

- The weave can affect the ability of sheets to survive many cycles of wash and wear. Sateen (four threads over and one under) weaves, for example, are lustrous and smooth, but not as durable as pinpoint (one over and one under) weaves.

Buy extras

If you find a pattern you like, buy extra pillowcases and an extra bottom sheet because these will wear out faster than the top sheet.

Wash blankets with care

Wash blankets in cool water with like colors and mild detergent. Hang to dry. Avoid machine drying of most types of blankets to prevent shrinkage and pilling.

Cover your comforter

Duvet covers are a great way of adding years of life to your comforter for the simple reason that they keep the costly comforter clean and reduce the number of times you need to wash it. Wash duvet covers often with half the recommended laundry detergent using cool or warm water. Wash the comforter itself only a couple of times a year. Dry on a gentle heat until nearly dry, and then hang to ensure complete drying. You may need to bring your comforter to a commercial laundry because they are often too large for a home washing machine. Cover you pillows with protective cases, too.

Buy to Keep: Mattresses

Mattress quality is difficult to judge in the showroom, so do your product research before you visit one. Here are some basic guidelines. As a general rule, it's best to buy the highest-quality set you can afford.

Foam cushioning	High-quality latex foam cushioning is longer lasting (loses resiliency slower) than polyurethane foam cushioning.
Springs and thickness	Extrathick mattresses require extralong coil springs—not simply short springs that have been stretched. Otherwise your mattress will lose resiliency quickly. Compare spring samples before you buy. Often the number of springs in a mattress is an indication of quality, but not always. Nor is thick mattress padding an indicator of durability.
Mattress size	If you sleep with a partner, opt for a king- or queen-size set to allow each sleeper extra space and so weight is not concentrated in the center of the mattress, where it can cause wear to the coil springs.

Kitchen Cabinets

Kitchen cabinets are subjected to moisture, grime, and frequent use. So they need more attention than other furniture to keep them looking and working great.

Keep those cabinets clean

Cooking grease, food spills, moisture, daily loading, and unloading—it all takes its toll on your kitchen cabinets. Grime builds up fastest around the handles of doors and drawers that are constantly opened by sticky hands. Frequent cleaning is key to keeping your kitchen cabinets in good condition— greasy soil comes off more easily if it isn't allowed to build up. Here's the program:

• If your cabinets are painted wood, metal, laminated plastic, or wood-grain vinyl, you can clean them with a solution of detergent and warm water. Rinse with a cloth or sponge dampened in clean water. Then dry with a cloth or paper towel to prevent streaking. Most all-purpose household cleaners can also be used—read the label to be sure it can be used on your cabinets' surfaces. Test inside a door to be sure it will not harm the finish.

• Natural-wood-finish cabinets can be cleaned with a variety of commercial products, usually sprays, made for this purpose. Read the label to make sure the product can be used on finished wood and follow the directions exactly. These cleaners are solvent based, so be sure you have adequate ventilation, and make sure there is no spark or flame or pilot light burning in the kitchen. Dispose of the cleaning cloths in a tightly sealed container, again not near a spark or flame. Virtually all modern, commercially made wood cabinets have finishes that are impervious to these cleaners. But check by trying the cleaner inside a door, just to be sure. Old or homemade cabinets might have a more delicate furniture finish that could be dissolved by solvent cleaners.

Mineral spirits cuts the stubborn grime

If there is a heavy buildup of grease and grime on your natural-wood-finish cabinets, commercial cleaners may not get them clean. In this case, you can try straight mineral spirits— again, be sure to test a small inside area to make sure the mineral spirits doesn't dissolve the finish. Dampen a cloth with the mineral spirits, and rub the cabinets vigorously. Refold the cloth because it picks up dirt, and store the dirty cloths in a sealed container for disposal. And again, be sure you have plenty of ventilation from open windows and that there are no flames or sparks nearby. In fact, it's a good idea to remove the drawers and doors and work on them outside if you can.

Bring back the shine with wax

Normally, there's no need to wax the finish on modern kitchen cabinets. But a heavy cleaning can leave the surface dull. If this happens, apply a paste wax and buff it off as described on the label. The wax should give your cabinets a like-new luster and will offer some resistance to future grime.

☛ DON'T
scour your cabinets

> Never use scouring powder or other abrasives on your cabinets—you'll scratch the surface, dulling the finish and making the cabinets harder to clean next time. For painted or plastic surfaces, use spray-on, all-purpose household cleaner and elbow grease to remove most stubborn grime; rinse well.

Give cabinets a facelift

Most kitchen cabinets start to look worn, dingy, and dated long before the doors and drawers wear out. There's no need to replace the cabinets to

Buy to Keep: Kitchen Cabinets

If you are in the market for new kitchen cabinets, you'll find that prices and quality vary enormously. In general, the prices reflect the quality, although the price for similar-quality cabinets can vary from dealer to dealer and there are diminishing returns at the upper end of the scale.

Material and assembly	A kitchen cabinet is essentially a box made of plywood or particleboard. Plywood is stronger and more expensive, but durable cabinets can be made of particleboard, too. More important than the material is the way the cabinets are assembled. The cheapest cabinets are constructed of 3/8-inch (9.5-mm) particleboard assembled with hot-melt glue and staples. Cabinets of 3/4-inch-thick (19-mm) particleboard assembled with dowels or special particleboard joint connectors can approach the durability of plywood, as long as they are kept dry. Particleboard turns to mush when it gets wet, and of course, that is a big consideration—particularly for the sink cabinet, where plumbing connections might leak, and for shelves where glasses and dishes are put away wet. For this reason, high-quality particleboard cabinets are often coated with Melamine or vinyl—plastics that resist water. Cheap particleboard cabinets have a very thin, paperlike coating that offers almost no protection from water. Whereas strong plywood cabinets can be constructed with wood screws and glue, screws don't hold well in particleboard. That's why dowels or special connectors are needed for strong particleboard construction.
Facing	Next you need to choose how the box will be faced. Here the choices are wide and varied, from flat, easy-to-clean plastic laminate to beautiful and expensive natural cherrywood. Your choice of facing materials is more a matter of aesthetics and budget than one of durability.
Workmanship	Run your fingertips over the door and drawer fronts to make sure that they are smooth. Sight along the surface to make sure there are no drips, tiny bubbles, or sanding marks. Look inside. Make sure all the joints are tight and the shelves look sturdy. Check that the doors open and close smoothly and fit perfectly.
Drawers	Make sure all the drawers operate smoothly without much side-to-side play. The best drawers have "full-extension" hardware that allows the drawer to pull all the way out, so you have access to the back. Drawers with enclosed ball-bearing hardware on both sides are superior to those that have one track underneath. Take out a drawer, and check the construction. Plywood or solid wood drawers should have an interlocking joint between the sides and front. In particleboard, this joint should be made with dowels or connectors. This joint takes the impact when the drawer is closed—if you see a butt joint held together with glue and nails, it's only a matter of time before the drawer fronts will break off. Make sure the bottom is rigid—these drawers will need to support a lot of weight.

give your kitchen a new look. For about 30 percent the cost of new cabinets, you can buy a do-it-yourself kit that contains everything you need to resurface the cabinets with 1/8-inch-thick (3-mm) veneers and replace the doors, drawer fronts, and hardware. The kits are surprisingly easy to install—you don't need special tools, and you certainly don't need to be a carpenter. But it's still plenty of work, so you might want to consider having the work done professionally.

Home centers can order a kit to fit your kitchen or arrange for professional installation.

New life for old drawers

In many old kitchen cabinets, as well as other types of furniture, the drawers simply ride on wooden glides at the bottom or sides. After many years of use, these glides wear due to friction, and the drawers may no longer operate smoothly or seat properly. You can make them work like new by placing one or two smooth-headed

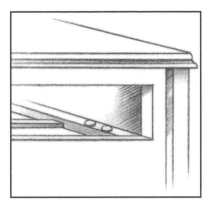

thumbtacks or upholstery tacks on the glide. It's also a good idea to rub candle wax on all wood-to-wood contact points as a lubricant.

Metal Furniture

Because metal is tough stuff, it gets used to make a lot of outdoor furniture. It holds up great with a little care. Metal can be crafted into pieces that are elegant enough for indoors, too. Indoor metal has an easier life but still needs a bit of attention.

Clean your indoor metal

Indoor metal furniture is usually made of chrome, wrought iron, or steel—either painted or stainless. It's easy to keep clean. Just wipe it regularly with a damp cloth, or use a vacuum with the brush attachment. If the metal gets dirty, you can wash it. Squirt a little liquid dishwashing soap into warm water. Dip in a sponge or cloth, wring it out, and use it to scrub off the dirt. Wipe dry with a cloth or paper towel to avoid water spots.

Most metal furniture can also be cleaned with metal-cleaner polish—check the product label to make sure it is intended for the type of metal you are cleaning. Also check the label on the furniture—some metal finishes should not be cleaned with commercial cleaners. If there's no label, try cleaning a small, inconspicuous area first. A coat of regular paste furniture wax also can offer extra protection to most indoor metal furniture, but again, check the label or try a small area first because some metal finishes shouldn't be waxed.

Protect aluminum from pollutants

Aluminum does not rust, and that has made it the most popular metal for outdoor furniture. However aluminum is susceptible to air pollutants that stick to the surface in the form of a fine grit that will not easily wipe away. Cleaning strategy depends on the condition of the aluminum:

• If the aluminum is only slightly discolored, mix up some soap and water and add a mild household acid—vinegar, lemon juice, or cream of tartar. Wash with a sponge, and rinse with clear water. Clean your aluminum this way, as needed, during the season and before you put it away for the season. If you keep on top of this chore, your aluminum will need no other care. If you like, however, you can apply a coat of auto wax or a silicon spray. This will provide some protection against corrosion and pitting, so you won't have to wash your aluminum furniture as often.

• If the aluminum is very dirty, the mild soap and acid mixture might not do the job. In this case, you can try any of the commercial cleaners sold to clean aluminum surfaces on boats and cars.

• If the aluminum has become pitted, you'll need to polish it with a soap-filled steel-wool pot cleaner. If you do this, be sure to thoroughly rinse and dry the furniture. Any steel particles left behind will quickly cause the aluminum to corrode.

Be gentle with colored aluminum

Two different processes are used to color aluminum: If the surface is shiny and the color seems to be in, rather than on, the aluminum, the piece has been color-anodized—a process in which the surface is hardened and dyed. If it looks textured or spray-painted, it has been powder-coated—a process in which colorful polyester powders are applied and then baked on. Powder-coating is more common for outdoor furniture. Both processes make aluminum more durable and resistant to pollution. Both should be cleaned only with a mild detergent (such as liquid dishwashing soap) and water.

Clean shore furniture more often

Salt spray, human perspiration, and suntan oils can all attack the powder-coating on metal furniture. If your powder-coated furniture is subjected to these things, clean it at least twice a month with liquid dishwashing soap and water.

Iron needs attention

Iron furniture can easily last a century. Unpainted iron furniture left outdoors will develop a patina of harmless, fine rust. If you like this look, just clean your iron furniture several times each season with warm, soapy water. Then dry it thoroughly. Clean painted iron furniture the same way, and then, for added protection, use paste wax on smooth surfaces and apply mineral oil or baby oil to textured surfaces. Oil springs and moving parts at the beginning of each season.

If your iron furniture is painted, touch up scratches or chips immediately, or rust will work its way under the paint and spread the damage. First lightly scuff up the area with fine steel wool; then apply several thin coats of paint. If you are using spray paint, use short, light strokes.

Solid metal outlasts hollow

If you want a piece of iron furniture that will last, look for pieces made with solid metal rather than hollow tubing. The best pieces have parts that are welded together, not bolted. If you are buying aluminum furniture with vinyl straps or webbing, make sure the vinyl has been processed with mildew inhibitors and ultraviolet stabilizers. Armrests or any other wood pieces should be thoroughly coated on all sides with a smooth coat of finish.

Protect glass furniture

Glass is tough stuff. Except for breakage, you need to wipe a glass table top only with a soft rag and mild cleaner, such as Windex. Help avoid breakage by keeping glass tables out of traffic zones. Soft plastic corner protectors will also help preserve the glass from chips and cracks due to bumping the table. During parties, it may be wise to cover low glass-topped coffee tables with a tablecloth to make them easier to see and less of a tripping hazard.

☛ DON'T
scratch outdoor steel

Good-quality modern outdoor steel furniture is powder-coated, in the same process used for aluminum. As with aluminum, powder-coated finishes should never been cleaned with any kind of abrasive. If you scratch the surface, the steel beneath may begin to rust. Clean with a mild detergent (such as liquid dishwashing soap) and water.

Outdoor Furniture

UV light, moisture, intense heat and cold all conspire to shorten the lives of outdoor furniture. With a little extra care, however, you won't have to find yourself, open wallet in hand, at the nearest leisure-living outlet every few years.

Put outdoor pieces in a shed

To keep your outdoor furniture pieces looking great year after year, be sure to store them indoors at season's end. If you don't want to lug them all to the basement and don't have a shed, there are many inexpensive vinyl storage containers available at home centers. Some come in the shape of lockers and can be placed on the deck. Others look like small sheds.

Cover chairs and tables

For better-quality outdoor furniture items, opt for vinyl patio furniture covers. Made to fit common furniture and grill sizes, these covers are waterproof and treated against UV. Look for covers that are at least 7 mil thick. In addition to keeping expensive furniture looking good, the covers are worth the effort because they reduce the need to clean pollen, dust, and bird droppings off your furniture.

Add life to canvas

Canvas, usually made from tightly woven, heavy cotton thread, will last many years if you take a little care with it. Avoid leaving it out in the rain. If it does get wet, allow it to dry thoroughly in the sun. Remove mildew by scrubbing with a stiff brush and detergent. Rinse afterward and dry thoroughly. Treat both cotton and synthetic canvas with a silicone-based water repellant for maximum protection. It's available from boating supply companies under brand names such as Aqua-Tite.

Renew patio umbrellas

Give your patio umbrella a little maintenance when you take it out in the spring. It will reward you by looking great and lasting longer. Wash the cover with mild soap, a soft-bristle-brush, and cold water. If the frame is metal, spritz the joints with spray lubricant. If it is wood, renew the shine with paste wax.

Use a towel over vinyl

Furniture with vinyl straps is popular for poolside use because the vinyl is waterproof. The problem is, those vinyl straps are porous. If the pores become clogged with body oil or suntan lotion, they become an ideal environment for mildew and fungi. The straps soon become stained and nearly impossible to clean. The solution is simple. If you are wearing a bathing suit, place a towel on the vinyl before you sit down. You'll prolong the life of the chairs by years.

Buy light-colored straps

When choosing a color for vinyl-strap furniture, remember that the darker the color, the hotter it will get and the sooner the color will fade. So stick with white and pastel strapping.

Paint resin furniture

After a few seasons, plastic resin furniture gets discolored and dingy, and the stains can be very difficult to remove. You can, however, make it look brand-new with spray paint designed specifically to bond with plastic furniture. Follow the manufacturer's directions to prepare the resin surfaces for the paint.

Grandpa says. . .

"Don't have room to store your picnic table and benches indoors during winter? Just tuck the benches under the table. Put a few wood blocks on top of the table to let the air circulate and cover everything with a tarp or sheet of plastic. You'll extend their life by years. Be sure you anchor your tarp to keep it from blowing away."

Holiday Decorations

You can't put a dollar value on your family's treasured holiday ornaments. Ensure many years of holiday service by following a few simple guidelines.

Store ornaments at room temperature

Ornaments will last longer if you store them inside your home in a closet, as opposed to the basement or garage, where they may be destroyed by mildew. Attics are okay for storing glass ornaments.

Protect fragile ornaments

Avoid breakage by storing ornaments in their original packages or by wrapping in acid-free white tissue paper several times. Put the repackaged or wrapped ornaments in a sturdy box or plastic storage bin to help prevent them from being accidentally crushed. Do not stack heavy ornaments on top of light ones. Store ornaments made from natural materials, such as dough or pine cones, separately. Wrap in tissue paper, and put in airtight containers or in plastic bags with zip-type closures.

Save ribbon and wrappings in a bin

Careless storage of wrapping materials will mean they'll be too crushed and wrinkled to use when you need them. Store them in a large, sturdy plastic container so you won't have to buy new. Store reusable gift bags, folded flat, in a large shopping bag.

Keep lights and garlands tangle-free

Wrap garlands and ornamental tree lights around a sturdy piece of cardboard to keep them tangle-free and out of harm's way.

☛ DON'T
wrap ornaments in newspaper

> Never use newspaper to wrap your holiday ornaments. The ink may transfer to the ornaments and ruin them. Stick to tissue paper.

Wrap wreaths for reuse

Ornamental wreaths, such as those made from dried flowers and herbs, can be used for years. Just wrap each one in tissue paper, and place it in a cardboard box. Do not stack other wreaths or ornaments on top.

Hang lights with care

Avoid damaging ornamental lights and creating a potential fire hazard by never puncturing the insulation on the light string with tacks, staples, nails, or sharp hooks. Do not install lights near gas or electric heaters, fireplaces, or other heat sources. Avoid overloading wiring by connecting more than the recommended number of light sets together (usually three).

Dealing with a blown holiday light fuse

Sometimes a light string will blow its on-board fuse (usually located in the plug). If this is due to an overload (such as connecting more than the recommended number of light sets together in a continuous run), you can replace the fuse and continue to use the lights. If the overload is due to a short, however, discard the string.

Longer-lasting cut Christmas trees

The best way to ensure a fresh-cut tree on Christmas eve is to cut a live tree several days before the holiday. Cut down the tree so you are left with as much of the trunk as possible. Once home, cut 1 inch (25 mm) off the bottom, place the tree in a bucket of water, and store it in a cool place, such as the garage. Refill the bucket as necessary. When you are ready to decorate the tree, cut the trunk to suit your tree stand and to ensure adequate water absorption. Then replenish the reservoir in the tree stand as required.

Furniture & Furnishings

Small Appliances

chapter

9

table of contents

Small Appliances—General Guidelines

From toasting our bread to ironing our clothes, these special-ized helpers make life better in lots of little ways. Most need just a little attention to keep them whirring and humming along year after year.

Know the scoop on extension cords

When it comes to appliances, its best not to use extension cords at all. It's just one more connection that can come loose and cause power surges that can damage your appliance. But if you must use an exten-sion cord, make sure that it is heavy-duty enough for the job. If you try to suck more than the recommended amount of juice through a cord, you'll strain the motor on the appliance and create a fire hazard because the cord can get hot enough to melt its insulation.

Here's what you need to know: The higher the cord's gauge number, the fewer amperes it can handle. Most appliances are labeled with how many amps they draw. Be sure to use a cord that can handle more than the amount listed.

• A lightweight 16-gauge lamp extension cord can handle no more than 10 amps.

• A medium 14-gauge exten-sion cord can handle up to 15 amps.

• A heavy-duty 12-gauge cord can handle up to 20 amps.

The same rule applies if you replace an appliance's power cord, but keep in mind that heat-producing appliances, such as irons, toasters, hair dryers, and space heaters, require cords with special heat-resistant insu-lation. Never use extension cords with these appliances.

Be circuit savvy

Most modern kitchens have sev-eral electrical circuits in order to let you use the blender while the microwave is cooking. But that doesn't help if you plug both appliances into the same circuit. So be aware of which outlets are on which circuits so you can spread out the electrical demand. Short on circuits? Well then, you'll have to wait until microwave popcorn is ready before blending the daiquiris.

Don't wrap cords

When electricity travels through a wire, it creates heat. The cords on your appliances need to be kept loose while in use to let the heat dissipate. This is especially important for appliances that heat up and draw a lot of amps, such as toasters, space heaters, and hair dryers. If you tightly coil or wrap an appliance cord, the heat may build up while the appliance is in use, potentially melting the cord's insulation. This may even cause a fire. Also, tightly wrapping an electrical cord could cause an internal break in the wire.

Checking a detachable cord

If your appliance has a detach-able cord and works intermittently, the plug that goes into the appliance might also be faulty. Check to see if the plug has screws that can be removed to open up the plug. If it does, open it up and see if tightening the connec-tions inside helps. If this plug is faulty, you'll need to order a replacement cord from the manufacturer. As a general rule, even though a cord is detachable, it is best not to detach it. Plugging it in and pulling it out a lot wears out the plug and the socket.

Repair a control knob

If the shaft breaks on a control knob—whether for a small appliance, like a toaster, or a large appliance, like a washing machine—installing a new one is as easy as slipping it into place. The problem is usually finding a replacement that

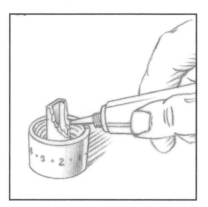

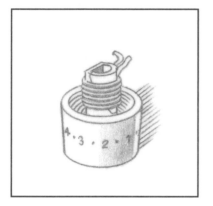

matches. Fortunately, it's easy to fix a control knob if the break is clean and you have the broken-off piece. Put epoxy glue on the break, and fit the pieces together. Then wrap the shaft tightly with nylon thread. Finally, coat the thread with epoxy—the thread will reinforce the repair. *Note:* Often the shaft fits into a hole in the appliance's case. Make sure the thread won't interfere with re-inserting the shaft.

Before You Call the Repair Guy . . .

If your appliance works intermittently, there's a good chance it just needs a new plug. A plug is cheap and takes only minutes to replace—it's just a matter of screwing two wires into place. The important thing is to make sure you get the right plug for your appliance. It's a good idea to remove the old plug so that you can take it to a hardware store or home center to find a replacement. If the plug is too light-gauge for your appliance, the cord won't fit through the hole in the cord's cover. So when you cut the old plug off, take an inch or so of cord with it. That way, you can make sure the plug is correct before you buy it. Also, if you have a hard time getting the wire to fit around the plug's screws, or find it difficult to close the plug, that's a sure sign the plug is too light-duty for the job.

1 Lamps and many low-amperage appliances use flat cords. You can purchase quick-connect versions of flat-cord plugs. These plugs have little spikes that piece the insulation and dig into the wire to make a connection, and they require no tools to install. Just snip off the old plug, and slip the new plug cover over the cord. Spread the prongs on the plug core, insert the cord, then squeeze the prongs to drive the spikes into the cord. Next slip the cover in place, and it is ready to plug in.

2 Appliances that draw more amperage, such as irons, sometimes have round cords. On these screw-on plugs, tie the cord into an Underwriters knot, as shown, to ensure that pulling on the cord won't loosen the connections.

Lamps

Lamps are simple devices, and that means it's almost always easy to bring them back to life.

Save a lamp in minutes

When a lamp flickers or stops working completely, you can usually solve the problem in a matter of minutes.

1 Check the bulb by trying it in another lamp. If the bulb is good, unplug the lamp and use a small piece of fine sandpaper to rub the contact strip inside the socket until it is shiny.

2 Lamp still doesn't work? It's probably the plug. If the wire is connected to the plug with screws, try tightening them. If that doesn't work— or if you have a clip-on plug or molded-on plug—get a new clip-on plug at a hardware store or home center and attach it, as described, in Before You Call the Repair Guy box on the previous page.

3 Hmmm, still no light? Must be the socket—another easy job. Unplug the lamp. Pull off the socket's outer shell, and remove the cardboard insulating sleeve. Maybe you'll get lucky and discover that one of the wires has come loose. Put it back around the screw—make

sure the end of the wire is at the right side of the screw. If you discover tight connections, pick up a new socket at a home center or hardware store. Make sure the amp and volt ratings are the same as the old socket. Lamp cord has two parts: One half is ridged or marked. Attach this wire to the silver screw terminal. Attach the other wire to the brass screw.

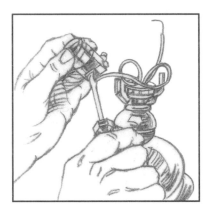

4 If it still doesn't work, the problem is with the cord, which may be frayed or pinched and shorted. If you are at all adventurous, it is not difficult to replace the cord on a regular lamp with one socket. Buy a length of new cord—or even better, a replacement cord with a

molded-on plug. Then remove the socket and plug on the old cord, and attach the new cord to the plug end of the old cord—twisting metal wires together and taping them smooth. And then pull out the old cord to pull in the new one. If you feel any resistance, look for a hook holding the old cord in the base of the lamp.

Remove a broken lightbulb

You're changing a lightbulb in the nightstand lamp, and it breaks off in your hand. So now the glass is off, but the stem and base are still inside. Unplug the lamp. Cut a potato width-wise, and place it over the broken bulb. Twist, and the rest of the lightbulb should come out easily.

Long-lived, energy-saving bulbs

Compact fluorescent bulbs cost more than regular incandescent bulbs, but they use much less electricity to put out the same amount of light and last up to 10 times as long, so they are cheaper in the long run. Fluorescent bulbs always list the equivalent regular-bulb wattage, making it easy to get the right one. The only drawback is that the light that compact fluorescents give out tends to be cooler—that is, bluer—than regular bulbs.

Toasters and Toaster Ovens

Can you imagine breakfast without the "boing!" of the toaster? These clever little devices need a little occasional maintenance to keep them popping.

A crummy toaster is no fun

Turn bread into toast, and you are bound to get crumbs. If your toaster is full of crumbs, it won't work properly and may even start to smoke. So, to keep your toaster popping along, clean out the crumbs about once a week, depending on how often you use it. Fortunately, most toaster makers provide an easy way to empty the crumbs. Some toasters have slide-out crumb trays; others have hinged doors on the bottom that let you empty the crumbs. No matter what kind of toaster you have or what sort of mechanism it has for crumb removal, always unplug the toaster before cleaning it.

For those stubborn crumbs

To get at hard-to-reach crumbs clinging to the toaster's innards, use a new, dry toothbrush or an old, clean paintbrush. Again, be sure the toaster is unplugged. Loosen crumbs with the brush, and then dump them out. Turn the toaster upside down and shake. Do it gently, being careful not to damage the heating elements. If you still can't get all the crumbs out, try disintegrating them with heat. Run the toaster empty on the hottest setting two or three times.

Give your toaster a wipe

Use a damp cloth to wipe around your toaster's control knobs. Add a dash of vinegar or a squirt of dishwashing liquid to the cleaning water for more cleaning power. For stainless steel toasters, polish with stainless steel polish, available at supermarkets and home-improvement centers.

Dissolve melted plastic

Did a plastic bread wrapper melt all over your chrome toaster or toaster oven? Dab a little acetone or nail polish remover (which is mostly acetone) on the melted mess; then buff with a soft cloth. But be very careful not to get any acetone on a plastic part, because the solvent could eat it.

☞ DON'T
line with foil

It's a tempting way to avoid a chore, but lining the crumb tray with aluminum foil is a bad idea. Aluminum deflects heat, so the oven won't work properly. It might even cause a fire.

Get the gunk out of your toaster oven

Toaster ovens typically need more thorough cleaning than toasters, since many people do more than just toast bread in their toaster ovens. They make drippy cheese toast, heat-oozing fruit pies, and even broil small grease-spattering hens. All that gunk can make your oven burn out prematurely, and more seriously, it could cause a fire. Here's how to keep your toaster oven looking and working like new:

• Clean the toaster oven soon after a messy cooking session. Let the oven cool, and unplug it. Then remove any cooking trays or racks, and wash them in hot, soapy water. Wipe the inside of the oven with a damp cloth. If you're lucky, your oven has a nonstick interior surface, and baked-on food will come right off. Carefully lift the heating element (if possible) and clean under it.

• Every week or two, depending on how often you use the oven, empty the crumb tray, which in most toaster ovens is removable; then wash it. Most trays are thin aluminum and may not be dishwasher safe. Check your owner's manual. If you are unsure, hand-wash the tray in warm, soapy water. Some ovens also have a trapdoor on the bottom to let you remove crumbs that fall past

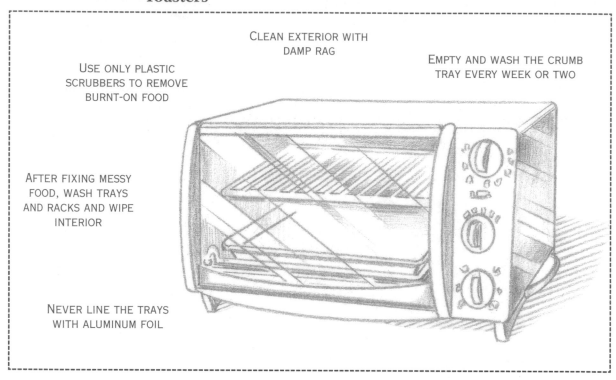

USE ONLY PLASTIC
SCRUBBERS TO REMOVE
BURNT-ON FOOD

CLEAN EXTERIOR WITH
DAMP RAG

EMPTY AND WASH THE CRUMB
TRAY EVERY WEEK OR TWO

AFTER FIXING MESSY
FOOD, WASH TRAYS
AND RACKS AND WIPE
INTERIOR

NEVER LINE THE TRAYS
WITH ALUMINUM FOIL

the tray. Be sure to unplug the unit before opening this door.

Removing burned-on deposits

To remove stuck-on food in your toaster oven, try a moist plastic or nylon scrubber. Never use anything abrasive, such as steel wool. You'll scratch the smooth surface, which will make the food stick worse next time. If the plastic scrubber fails, put a small bowl of full-strength ammonia inside the unplugged oven with the door

closed. Leave it overnight, and then remove the ammonia. The fumes will loosen the food. Wipe the inside again, and let the oven air out before using.

Buff the outside of your toaster oven

To keep the outside of your toaster oven clean, just wipe it regularly with a damp cloth. Add a splash of vinegar or a squirt of dishwashing liquid to the wash water for added cleaning power. The control buttons may pull off to make cleaning

the control panel easier. Check your owner's manual.

Restore the view through a toaster-oven door

If the inside of the glass door on your toaster oven is caked with stubborn, burned-on cooking residue that obscures your view of the food, here's how to get it off: First spray the glass with oven cleaner and let it sit for at least half an hour. Wipe off the oven cleaner with paper towels, and then clean to a sparkle with glass cleaner.

Food Processors and Blenders

These whirring wonders take a lot of the elbow grease out of kitchen work. Here's how to keep them working smoothly.

Process in small batches

To avoid straining the motor on your food processor, add food to it in small quantities. Cut the food into manageable chunks, and always use the pusher to guide food into the feed tube. Let gravity do most of the work. Don't fill the bowl with more than the amount recommended in your owner's manual—usually about half-full.

Clean food processor parts separately

It purees, minces, mixes, kneads, and blends. The multi-talented food processor requires an equally multifaceted approach when it comes to cleaning it. That is, it should be cleaned part by part. Cleaning it properly after each meal preparation will extend its life.

• Remove the bowl and lid from the processor, and knock off the bulk of the food stuck on them using the sprayer on your sink—with the water pressure as high as possible. For really tough cleaning jobs, consider using the outdoor garden hose; it'll have the same effect as a high-powered restaurant sprayer.

• Once you've gotten the tough stuff off, you can put the bowl and lid in the dishwasher—many people do—but they'll last longer if you hand-wash them in hot soapy water. This protects them from harsher dishwasher detergent, which can make the plastic brittle and prone to breakage.

• Wash the blades in hot, soapy water and then dry with a cloth. Never wash the blades in the dishwasher, where they could bend or be dulled—or be burned if they touch a heating element. And be careful handling the blades—they are extremely sharp.

• To clean the base unit of your food processor, which contains the motor, unplug it and wipe it with a damp cloth. Never immerse the base unit in water or use a really wet sponge on it, and don't clean it with coarse or caustic products.

Watch out for the spring

On some models, the plastic bowl has a safety spring located at the point where the bowl attaches to the base unit. It's difficult to get this spring dry after washing the bowl, so after you've dried the bowl with a cloth, let it air-dry before reassembling the processor. Otherwise the spring may rust.

Use your blender's "self-clean" feature

To clean your blender, fill it about half-full with hot water and add a few drops of dish-washing liquid. Put the lid on, and hit the BLEND button. After about 10 seconds, empty the blender, give it a quick rinse, then fill it halfway with clean water. Run it for another 10 seconds, empty it out, then run it empty for 10 seconds to dry the blades.

Keep the blender blade spinning freely

Sediments can collect and harden at the bottom of the blender, preventing the blade from spinning easily. This puts a strain on the motor that shortens the blender's life. So carefully clean the blade assembly with warm, soapy water after each use to prevent sediment buildup.

☞ DON'T
process hard items

Don't use your food processor or food chopper to process especially hard foods, such as ice, coffee beans, and raw grains, which can damage the blades—or really sticky ones, such as dried fruits, that may clog it up and strain the motor.

Coffeemakers and Coffee Grinders

Ah, that morning cuppa joe. Here's how to make sure it will always be fresh and delicious.

Preserve the carafe

There are a number of ways you can inadvertently crack your coffeemaker's glass carafe—all of which are easily avoidable:

- Don't wash a hot carafe. Let it cool before bringing it into contact with cold or even warm water.

- Never heat an empty carafe.

- Don't try to reheat cold coffee by placing the carafe on the stove or in the microwave.

- Never place a hot carafe in the refrigerator or freezer.

Wash the carafe and coffee basket

Thoroughly clean the carafe, basket, and any other removable parts from your coffeemaker after each use to remove any leftover oils or coffee residue that can diminish the flavor of your next pot of coffee. Wash all the pieces in hot, sudsy water, and even better, let them soak for 20 minutes or so. Rinse well, and let dry.

Clean a drip coffeemaker

If your coffee consistently comes out weak or bitter, chances are your coffeemaker needs cleaning. Start by filling the decanter with 2 cups of white vinegar and 1 cup of water. Place a filter in the machine, and pour the solution into the coffeemaker's water chamber. Turn on the coffeemaker, and let it run through a full brew cycle. Remove the filter, and replace with a new one. Then wash out the machine by running clean water through it for two full cycles. (Don't forget to replace the filter for the second brew.) Ideally, you should clean your coffeemaker about every 4 weeks if you use it every day, but you can go as long as 80 brew cycles if you have soft water, or 40 cycles if you have hard water.

If you have hard water

To get rid of mineral or scale buildups that often come from using hard water, periodically run a solution of equal parts white vinegar and water through the coffeemaker to dissolve it. You may have to repeat the process a few times if the buildup is especially heavy. Thoroughly rinse out the water chamber; then brew up a couple of pots of plain cold water to remove any traces of vinegar that could affect your coffee's taste.

Exercise caution with power cords

For your own safety, as well as the well-being of your coffeemaker, keep the power cord away from hot surfaces—in particular, the coffeemaker's warming plate when the carafe is removed. Also avoid hanging cords off the edge of a table or shelf. Always keep all power cords out of the reach of young children.

Read the fine print first

Check the base plate or back panel of your coffeemaker for a warning against owner servicing. If you find a warning of this type, do not attempt to repair the unit yourself without checking with the manufacturer first—it may void your warranty if it is still in effect. Some companies will even provide replacement parts to consumers despite the warning. Replacement parts for some older units, however, may be hard to come by.

Put the drip back in your coffeemaker

When that trickle of water from the top of your coffeemaker stops flowing or comes out in spurts, it's probably due to a clogged spreader plate—the coffeemaker's spout, so to speak. Turn the coffeemaker upside down, and use a toothpick to clean out the holes in the plate. If that doesn't work, you may be able to order a replacement plate from the manufacturer. The same trick

works for unclogging the holes in the metal baskets used by electric percolators.

Choose the right grind

Different types of coffeemakers require different grinds of coffee to brew the perfect cup of java. Most drip-type coffeemakers, for instance, need a medium grind, while many percolators and French-press-type coffeemakers take a coarse grind. If you don't know which grind works best in your particular coffeemaker, check with the manufacturer. In addition to providing you with a better cup of joe, using the appropriate grind will help prevent basket overflows and other messy mishaps.

It's all in the water

Regardless of what type of coffeemaker you have, always start each brew with a potful of cold water. Warm water has a higher mineral content that will affect the taste of your coffee and hasten the formation of mineral deposits inside your coffeemaker.

☞ DON'T
heat an empty percolator

> Never plug in an empty percolator. Heating up a dry pot can burn out the heating element and cause other damage.

Perk up a percolator

Keep each batch of your perked coffee tasting as fresh as the first by regularly cleaning your electric percolator.

• Wash the pot after each use with hot, soapy water, rinse thoroughly with cold water, and let dry.

• Periodically remove any mineral deposits by filling the pot with water plus 2 tablespoons of cream of tartar. Run the pot through a complete percolating cycle, then follow the cleaning procedure described above.

• If your percolator is made of stainless steel or chrome (but not aluminum), you can also clean it by mixing 2 teaspoons of baking soda and 8 cups of

---

INFO STATION

COFFEEMAKER REPLACEMENT PARTS

Can't find a replacement part for your coffeemaker or espresso machine at your local appliance store? Maybe you'll find what you're looking for online. Here are three prominent appliance-parts suppliers. Each supports several major brands: Culinary Parts carries Braun, Cuisinart, KitchenAid, Melitta, and Proctor Silex. At Mar-Beck you'll find Bunn, Farberware (percolator), Hamilton Beach, and KitchenAid. Nelson has Braun, Delonghi, Krups, and Mr. Coffee. And if you want a Canadian source, ShaverSpot carries Braun and Cuisinart. They all carry parts for many other types of appliances as well.

> **Culinary Parts**
www.culinaryparts.com
1-866-727-8435

> **Mar-Beck Appliance Parts**
www.marbeck.com
1-800-959-5656

> **Nelson Appliance**
www.nelsonappliance.com
1-866-635-1928

> **ShaverSpot**
www.shaverspot.ca
1-604-688-2941

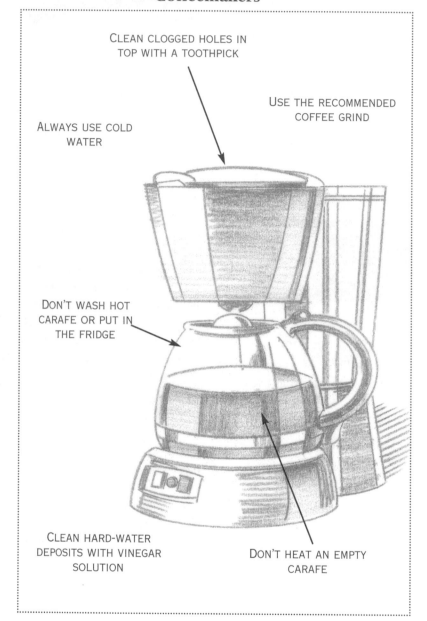

◆ BEST ADVICE ◆ **Coffeemakers**

CLEAN CLOGGED HOLES IN TOP WITH A TOOTHPICK

USE THE RECOMMENDED COFFEE GRIND

ALWAYS USE COLD WATER

DON'T WASH HOT CARAFE OR PUT IN THE FRIDGE

CLEAN HARD-WATER DEPOSITS WITH VINEGAR SOLUTION

DON'T HEAT AN EMPTY CARAFE

water and percolating it for one complete cycle.

• If you have hard water, skip the baking soda and use equal parts water and white vinegar instead. Clean the outside of the percolator with a damp cloth; never use steel wool or abrasive cleaners on it.

Get a handle on that percolator

Is your percolator leaking around its handle? Many manufacturers attach percolator handles with one or two bolts that are run through the body of the pot. You can usually stop those leaks by using a wrench to remove the nuts inside the pot and replacing the gaskets underneath each one.

Keep the espresso flowing

Here's how to get more years of reliable service from your espresso machine:

• Rinse or wash the filter basket parts after each use. Wipe the other surfaces with a damp cloth or sponge. Never immerse the unit in water.

• Remove the milk film from the frother before the milk can harden. To clean the frother, allow steam to escape into a water-filled frothing pitcher for a few seconds, then wipe the tube and the frother itself with a damp cloth.

• To prolong the gasket's life, remove the filter basket and loosen the tank cap when the espresso maker is not in use.

• For the best taste, always use the proper espresso coffee grind—about the texture of table salt. If the grind is too coarse, the brew will be thin and weak. If it is too fine, it will taste bitter or burned.

• If you have hard water, remove mineral deposits from the inner channels using this technique: Remove the filter screen from the hot-water dispenser head. Then fill the tank with equal parts distilled water and white vinegar and brew, collecting the solution in the brew pot. Repeat two or three times with distilled water to flush the system out and remove the vinegar taste.

Give coffee grinders the brush off

The spinning blades and baskets used by all electric coffee grinders need to be cleaned after every use. First, unplug the grinder, and wipe out the bowl with a soft cloth. Next, brush it out using an old toothbrush, a pastry brush, or a small (and clean) stiff-bristled paintbrush. You don't have to scrub it to perfection, just enough to shine up the stainless steel parts inside the grinder so that tomorrow's batch of beans isn't sullied by the stale grounds left over from yesterday's java. Wash the grinder's plastic lid with a sponge using warm, soapy water. Rinse well and dry with a soft cloth. Never immerse the body of a grinder in water; it's a surefire way to break it for good.

Grind in short bursts

Using your grinder for more than 30 seconds at a time, or more than a minute in any 5-minute period, can result in an overheated motor, which will drastically shorten its lifespan. Since most grinders have a single-speed switch, it's best to process beans using pulse action. That is, press and release the switch so it goes on and off every few seconds.

Replace a dull blade

Although grinder blades can't be resharpened, they are not difficult to replace. Before you chuck your old grinder in the trash, see if you can find a replacement blade for your model; it's often a lot cheaper than purchasing a whole new unit.

Warm beans are better for grinding

Lots of coffee lovers keep their beans fresh by storing them in the freezer. If you're one of them, be sure to take the beans out of the freezer and allow them to come to room temperature before grinding them. They will break up much more evenly and place less stress on the motor.

☞ **NO**
running on empty

Never run an electric coffee grinder when the bowl is empty. The lack of weight on the blades may cause them to spin too fast and damage the motor.

Clothing Irons

Keep your iron clean, and it will reward you with crisp clothes for decades.

Use the right water in your iron

Your mom may have routinely used distilled water in her steam iron. Many manufacturers recommended this to prevent minerals from clogging the iron. But be sure to check your owner's manual because most newer models are designed to use tap water—the minerals actually help the steaming process.

Steam-clean your iron regularly

If you haven't cleaned your steam iron for a while, you may find that the water or steam looks rusty. This is actually burned lint, which can stain your clothes. So it's important to clean your steam chamber and vents every couple of months. Here are the steps for steam-cleaning your iron. The steam will remove lint, dirt, dust, and mineral deposits that have built up in the steam vents.

❶ Unplug the iron; then fill it with the recommended distilled or tap water.

❷ Plug in the iron, and depending on your model, either set the iron to its cleaning-mode function or to the steaming feature.

❸ Hold the steaming iron over the sink, with the soleplate facing down, until the steam stops. (Or place the iron facedown on a heatproof cooking rack while it steams.)

❹ Unplug the iron, and leave it in the sink (or on the rack) for another half-hour to fully dry.

❺ Finish by wiping the iron with a dry cloth.

Vinegar dissolves the tough deposits

If the steam-cleaning technique described above doesn't remove the mineral deposits from the steam chamber, try using vinegar if your manufacturer's instructions allow it. Pour white vinegar into the steam chamber, and steam it through the vents. Rinse out the vinegar, and refill the chamber with water. Let the water steam through the iron to remove all the vinegar. Repeat if necessary. If you're not careful about removing the vinegar, it may stain your clothes the next time you use the iron. The acidic nature of vinegar may also etch and damage the interior of your iron if left inside the steam chamber. Besides, you don't want to walk around in clothes that smell like a salad.

Treat nonstick soleplates with care

Some iron soleplates are coated with Teflon or a metallic non-stick coating to make it easier to clean off melted fibers. Usually, a wooden spatula is all you need to scrape the fibers off. The trade-off is that these surfaces

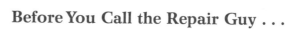

Before You Call the Repair Guy . . .

If your iron heats but doesn't steam properly, chances are the vents in the soleplate are clogged. Poke the vents gently with a straightened paper clip or a pipe cleaner. Tip the iron so debris won't fall into the vents. If the clogs are stubborn, the vents might be easier to clean if you heat the iron first, but don't touch the soleplate until it is sufficiently cooled.

If your iron has a spray nozzle and it is not working properly, chances are that it has become clogged. Clean it with a very fine sewing needle. Work carefully and don't push the needle forcefully into the nozzle hole—you might break off the needle, plugging the hole, or you might enlarge the opening, causing a leak.

are more easily scratched—
even a baking soda paste can
etch them. If a spatula doesn't
do the trick, you can rub a
nylon scouring pad on the soleplate. Make sure the soleplate is
cool when you do—or the
scouring pad may melt, making
a worse mess than the one you
started with.

Remove mystery material

If you don't know what's stuck
on the soleplate of your iron
and the mark doesn't liquefy
when you heat the iron to its
highest temperature, try using
one of the hot-iron cleaners
available at fabric shops and
hardware stores.

If the stain still remains on an
aluminum or chrome soleplate,
make a paste of baking soda
and water to the consistency of
toothpaste. Rub it on a cool
iron with a soft cloth, then wipe
it off with another damp cloth.
Don't use this method on a
Teflon or metallic nonstick soleplate. For these surfaces, see the
next hint.

Remove melted synthetic fibers

It's a double-whammy that's
bound to happen sooner or
later. You'll heat that nylon or
polyester garment to the melting point and wind up with a
scorched garment and synthetic
fibers stuck to your iron's soleplate. There's nothing you can
do to save the garment, but

✦ BEST ADVICE ✦ **Steam Irons**

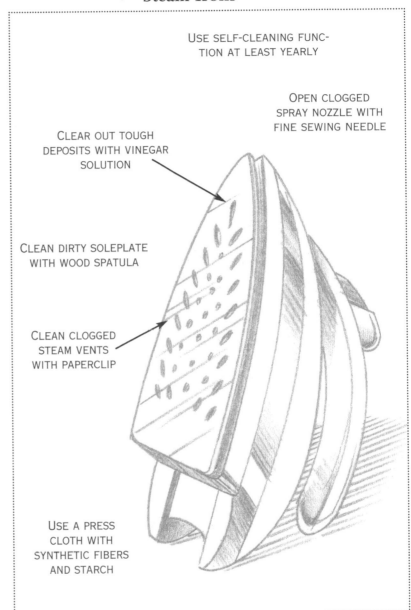

USE SELF-CLEANING FUNC-
TION AT LEAST YEARLY

OPEN CLOGGED
SPRAY NOZZLE WITH
FINE SEWING NEEDLE

CLEAR OUT TOUGH
DEPOSITS WITH VINEGAR
SOLUTION

CLEAN DIRTY SOLEPLATE
WITH WOOD SPATULA

CLEAN CLOGGED
STEAM VENTS
WITH PAPERCLIP

USE A PRESS
CLOTH WITH
SYNTHETIC FIBERS
AND STARCH

there's plenty you can do to get
the gunk off your iron.

❶ Heat the iron until the fibers
liquefy.

❷ Scrape off the fibers. On
nonstick and aluminum or
chrome soleplates, use a

wooden spatula, or a tongue
depressor; never scrape with
plastic, metal, or anything
abrasive.

❸ Run the iron over a scrap of
terry cloth to remove
remaining fibers.

Vacuum Cleaners

With a little care, your vacuum will suck the dirt from your house for many years to come.

Clean out the beater bar

The floor attachment on most vacuums employs a beater bar—a curving strip of brushes mounted on a roller. Over time, these brushes are likely to become ensnared with hair, string, or threads, which diminishes their ability to remove dirt and lint from your floors. But you can easily break "the ties that bind" with a utility knife or seam ripper—either of which will make short order of any tangles or knots. Always unplug the vacuum before cleaning the beater bar.

Repair a vacuum hose

Did you just suck up a sock, dog toy, or other object that is now firmly lodged in your vacuum hose? It doesn't have to spell the end of your vacuum. You can often remove an obstruction by sliding a garden hose or broom handle through the hose. Or you can try a straightened-out wire coat hanger or any other length of wire. If your machine permits, you can also try reversing the airflow, so that the machine blows out through the hose. Sometimes a lodged item will come out more easily if it does it the same way it came in. If none of these works, simply cut the hose, retrieve the obstacle and repair the rip in the hose with duct tape. You can also use duct tape to repair a damaged bag on an upright vacuum.

The same principle holds true for those holes left in your vacuum hose after your dog mistakes it for a chew toy. In this case, repair the holes with electrical tape by stretching the tape tightly across the hose as you wrap it. The electrical tape should thoroughly seal the hose.

Dump the dust

To keep your vacuum running at peak performance, always change or empty the dust bag when it's about three-quarters full. If you allow it to fill more than that, the decreased room in the bag reduces suction and puts a strain on the motor that will cause it to wear out sooner.

Care for a cordless vacuum

Those cute cordless vacuums may not be much use when it comes to cleaning deep shag carpets, but they're great for small jobs and quick cleanups on hard surfaces. To keep your compact vac in top working order, be sure to shake out dust and dirt from the filter after each use. Periodically, you should also wash cloth filters in warm, soapy water. Let the filter air-dry thoroughly before putting it back in the vacuum.

Replace a worn belt

One of the most common problems with an upright carpet-sweeper-type vacuum or a powered carpet-sweeping attachment for a canister vacuum is that the beater bar—the roller with brushes—will suddenly stop rotating. The cause is almost always that the belt that turns the bar is broken or jammed. This is a relatively simple repair, and one that can spare you a handsome bill from the repair shop. Many vacuums come with instructions or diagrams for replacing belts (although you typically need to start by removing the screws that hold the cover over the sweeper section). Many hardware and appliance stores stock belts for commonly used vacuum models; they are typically sold in a package of two for about $4.

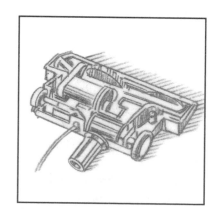

Sewing Machines

A sewing machine is a symphony of precisely moving parts. If you keep these parts well oiled and lint-free, your sewing machine can last a lifetime.

Keep it covered

Dust that settles on your sewing machine can work its way into the moving parts, turning the lubricating oil into gunk. So keep your machine in the case if it has one, or closed into the cabinet if you have a cabinet model. Otherwise, use a plastic cover that you can purchase for a few dollars at a fabric store.

Don't forget the pedal

Residing, as it does, on the floor, your machine's foot pedal is subjected to more dust and dirt than the machine itself. Keep it clean when not in use by slipping it into a plastic bag and tying the bag around the cord with a twist tie.

Pull the plug

Before you do any cleaning or lubrication work on your sewing machine, make sure that it is unplugged.

Give lint the brush off

Sewing involves piercing fabric with lots of little holes. This process produces a surprising amount of lint that can gunk up the works, shortening the life of your machine. So keep a small lint brush on your

INFO STATION

A THOROUGH SERVICING FOR YOUR MACHINE

If your sewing machine is giving you problems, a more thorough cleaning may be all that is needed to get it humming smoothly again. This involves some disassembly of the machine. You can take the machine to a shop, where they will clean it and replace any parts that might be worn. Or you could do it yourself. This doesn't take special skill; you just need to be organized and keep track of the parts you remove. If you are thinking about the do-it-yourself route, check out this website run by the New Mexico State University College of Agriculture and Home Economics. Here you will find an excellent guide to sewing-machine maintenance complete with photographs illustrating the steps involved. You can download the guide as a PDF file.

> New Mexico State University College of Agriculture and Home Economics
http://cahe.nmsu.edu/pubs/_c/c-102.html

new uses for Thread Spools

Remember the fun you could have as a kid with a bunch of empty wooden thread spools? Pry your kids away from the boob tube and see if you can use those memories to wake up the imaginations of a new generation, even if most spools are now made from polystyrene foam. For three- to five-year-olds, use nontoxic paints to paint spools in bright colors. (Older kids might enjoy painting the spools for their younger sibs.) The little ones will enjoy stacking the spools or stringing them together to make necklaces. Or break out the finger paint, and let them experiment with the paint patterns they can make by stamping or rolling the spools. *Caution:* Don't give the spools to kids under three who could choke on a small spool.

sewing table—one may have come with your machine. A small paintbrush will work, too. Get in the habit of brushing off all easily accessible, movable parts each time you use the machine. These parts include the take-up lever and thread guides, the presser foot and needle bar, and the bobbin case and needle-plate areas.

Clean the exterior

If the surfaces and covers on your sewing machine become dusty or dirty, clean them with a damp, soft cloth and mild soapy solution.

Tweeze or blow the stubborn stuff

You may find at times that there are little bits of thread or lint that your brush can't pull out of your sewing machine. But don't give up. You can usually pluck the stuff out with a pair of tweezers. A blast of compressed air from a can does a great job, too. You can even try blowing the lint out with a hair dryer on a cool setting.

Or floss your machine

Another way to banish the fuzzies from your sewing machine is to slide the edges of a thin piece of muslin between the tension disks (those metal pieces the tread passes through). Make sure that the presser foot is in the up position to slacken the tension springs. If you don't have any muslin, gently slide a credit card between the disks to loosen dust and dirt caught between them.

Use the right lube in the right spots

Every sewing machine has its own set of lubrication points, sometimes as many as 30 of them! Check your owner's manual to find the lubrication points. About once a year, depending on how often you sew, put one or two drops of sewing machine oil onto each indicated spot or hole.

☞ **DON'T**
use just any oil

Use only the oil sold especially for sewing machines to lubricate your machine. Other commonly available lubricants, such as WD-40 or 3-IN-ONE oil, tend to dry too fast and eventually may cause your machine to seize and stop.

Humidifiers, Dehumidifiers, and Fans

Maintaining the right level of moisture in your home's air helps ease skin and nasal irritations and can prevent dry-house problems, such as shrinking wood joints. Moving the air with fans can reduce or replace the need for air conditioners that are much more costly to run. Here's how to keep these valuable appliances working efficiently.

Keep humidifier reservoirs clean

Many portable humidifiers work by slowly rotating a sponge through a water reservoir, then past a fan that blows air through the sponge, where it picks up moisture on its way back into the room. Sometimes the sponge is on a drum; sometimes it is in the form of a belt. In either case, it is very important to keep the reservoir water clean not only to keep the humidifier working properly but also for your health: Dirty sponges can spew bacteria, mold, fungi, and mineral dust into the air. Here's the routine:

• Mold starts to grow in only 48 hours, so empty and clean the reservoir daily. First turn off the unit; then empty the reservoir. Wash it out with hot, soapy water, using a brush or other scrubber to remove mineral deposits or film. Rinse well with running water, taking care that no water gets into the motor. Wipe all surfaces dry with a clean cloth before refilling the reservoir.

• Every three days, clean your humidifier more thoroughly. Begin as you would the daily cleaning. After rinsing, wipe the reservoir with white vinegar (diluted with water if you wish) to break up mineral deposits. Wipe off the mineral deposits, rinse again, wipe dry, and refill the reservoir.

Keep an eye on the filter

Some evaporative humidifiers use a disposable filter instead of permanent sponges—thus avoiding the buildup of bacteria and other nasties that are tough to chase out of a permanent sponge. If you have a unit like this, keep the reservoir clean, as described above. Check the filter every three days. If it is gray, replace it.

Ultrasound humidifiers need frequent cleaning

This type of humidifier uses a high-frequency sound waves to create a mist. As with evaporative humidifiers, the reservoir on ultrasound models can spew bacteria and other unhealthy stuff into your air if you don't clean it regularly. Wash out the reservoir with white vinegar each time you fill it. The nebulizer—the vibrator—itself can often get clogged, so be sure to clean it at least once a week.

Use vinegar to clean the boiling chamber

The safest type of humidifier boils water and mixes the steam with air to cool it, creating a warm mist. The heat distills minerals and kills microbes. In this type of humidifier, mineral deposits tend to build up in the boiling chamber. When they do, clean the chamber with a soft brush and a mixture of equals parts vinegar and water.

Distilled water is best

Most humidifiers are designed to work with either tap water or distilled water—check your owner's manual. However, in most cases your unit will last longer and cleaning will be easier if you use distilled water because it doesn't contain minerals that quickly build up in the reservoir.

Keeping a dehumidifier working

A dehumidifier is essentially a scaled-down air conditioner that doesn't cool. Just like an

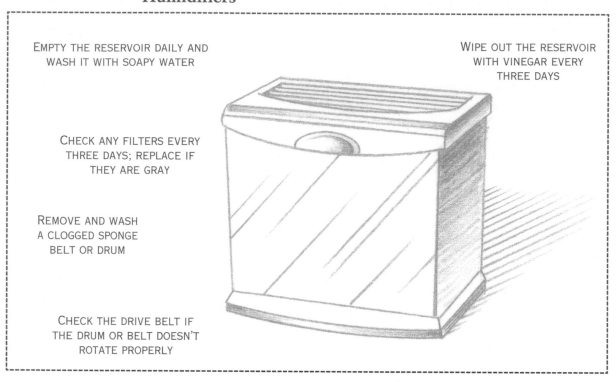

EMPTY THE RESERVOIR DAILY AND WASH IT WITH SOAPY WATER

WIPE OUT THE RESERVOIR WITH VINEGAR EVERY THREE DAYS

CHECK ANY FILTERS EVERY THREE DAYS; REPLACE IF THEY ARE GRAY

REMOVE AND WASH A CLOGGED SPONGE BELT OR DRUM

CHECK THE DRIVE BELT IF THE DRUM OR BELT DOESN'T ROTATE PROPERLY

air conditioner, the dehumidifier uses a fan to draw air over cold evaporator coils. Water condenses out of the cooled air and is collected in a container (instead of dripping outside as a window air conditioner does). Unlike an air conditioner's condenser, which expels warm air outdoors, the dehumidifier returns the warm air to the room. But like an air conditioner, your dehumidifier will work most efficiently and last the longest if you keep the filters and condenser fins clean. Here's how:

• Every day, empty the water container; do it more often on humid days when water collects

quickly. Don't let water stagnate in the container.

• Once a month, clean the container with a sponge and mild detergent, and let it dry completely. At least once a month, wash the filter in warm, soapy water. (Replace the filter if it starts to disintegrate.)

• Every 6 to 12 months, clean the evaporator coils, with your vacuum's brush attachment. Be careful not to damage the fins. Remove grime or mildew with a mild household cleaner and an old toothbrush, or use an auto degreaser that's safe for use on aluminum. Spray with water to rinse off all the degreaser.

• Each season, oil the fan motor—if the motor requires lubrication. To tell if it does, check your owner's manual, or look for oil ports in the motor. Oil as recommended; a fan motor typically requires only one or two drops of SAE 20 oil in each port.

Get your noisy fan in line

If your older fan with metal blades has become excessively noisy, the problem may be that the blades are out of alignment. To check, unplug the fan, and remove the screws that hold the front grille in place. The fan-blade hub is usually just friction-fitted onto the motor shaft or held in place with a simple clip. Remove the hub and place it on a flat surface. Each blade should touch the surface. If any blade is more than 1/4 inch (6 mm) from the surface, bend it into alignment or replace the hub assembly.

Lube for long life

At least once a year, lubricate your fan's motor shaft. Do this more often if your fan is used continually for long periods. But note that if the motor on your fan is sealed—you can't find any oil ports—it doesn't need to be lubricated.

Clean your exhaust fans

Is that exhaust fan in your kitchen, bathroom, basement, or attic nearing exhaustion? Here's how you can tell: Hold a tissue up to the grille with the fan running. If the tissue stays tight against the grille, it's working well. If the tissue flaps against the grille, the airflow is uneven and your fan probably needs cleaning. Attic and basement exhaust fans only require cleaning about once a year, but bathroom and kitchen fans need to be cleaned every six months. Here's how to clean an exhaust fan:

• Unplug the fan or shut off the circuit breaker, and remove the grille. Soak the grille in warm water with a bit of dishwashing detergent. Use an old

toothbrush to work off any stuck-on grime. Rinse and dry. For a kitchen exhaust fan, also wash out the filter.

• Some fans also let you remove the fan and motor for cleaning by unscrewing the mounting bracket and unplugging the cord. If you can't remove the fan, use a vacuum with a nozzle attachment to remove the greasy dust on the blades, motor, and inside housing; then wipe them with a damp cloth.

• Don't forget about fans in kitchen-range hoods. Many recirculate the air rather than vent it outside, and employ charcoal filters inside that should be replaced about every six months.

Degrease grates, fans, and grilles

Even in the cleanest homes, air-conditioner grilles, heating grates, and fan blades can eventually develop a layer of dust and grease. In addition to being an eyesore—and even unhealthy for some folks— such accumulations can significantly reduce the airflow from the device. Clean off the grime by wiping the fan blades and air grates with some full-strength white vinegar. Use a recycled toothbrush to work the vinegar into the tight spaces on air-conditioner grilles and exhaust fans. You can also use general household

cleaner, such as Fantastik. But be sure to wipe it off thoroughly with a damp rag.

Dust off ceiling fans

Give the blades in your ceiling fan a gentle rubdown once a week with a lamb's-wool duster to prevent dust buildups. You can also clean them once a month with some general household cleaner, but avoid using water—it can cause wood blades to swell.

Wax ceiling-fan blades

A good way to help keep dust off your wooden ceiling-fan blades is to take them off and coat them with paste car wax. You can use liquid car wax, but use it sparingly; too much may cause discoloration of the blades or damage the protective coating on the wood. Once the wax dries, simply buff off and reinstall the blades. This is also a good time to remove the light globes and wash them as well. Make sure to shut off the power to the fan's circuit at the service panel while you're removing the blades, or at least put a piece of tape over the switch so no one accidentally turns on the fan during removal or reinstallation.

Stop a wobbly ceiling fan

Beyond being annoying, a wobbly ceiling fan will wear out its bearings sooner. If your fan wobbles, take these steps:

• Clean the blades. Although it's not likely, accumulated dirt can throw the blades out of balance.

• Check to see if loose screws or uneven weighting in the fan's blade mounts are the cause of the wobbling. First check that the screws in the blade mounts are all tightly fastened. Then try reversing the position of adjacent blades, and test the fan at various speeds to see if that diminishes or eliminates the wobble.

• If the wobbling continues, contact the fan's manufacturer to see if the company provides a special balancing kit for your model fan, (If they do, some will even send you one for free.) You can also purchase balancing kits at many hardware outlets. Or you can do it yourself (see next hint).

How to balance fan blades

To balance wobbly ceiling-fan blades yourself, start by using some masking tape to temporarily secure 3/8-inch (10-mm) flat washers partway down the top part of a blade. Apply the washers to one blade at a time or in adjacent pairs, each time running the fan at several speeds to determine which blades require balancing. You can then permanently fasten the washers through the screws on the blade mounts, or if there is not adequate give, use some 2-inch (5-cm)-wide Scotch mailing tape to hold each washer in place on top of the blade.

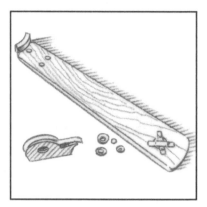

Large Appliances

Refrigerators and Freezers

Most appliances have a pretty easy life—you use them for an hour or two, and then they have the rest of the day off. Not so the faithful fridge, which we expect to be on duty 24–7. Here's how to keep yours humming into the next decade.

Check the door gaskets

When it comes to your refrigerator, it is an open-and-shut case: Your refrigerator is the case, and your family probably opens and shuts it at least a dozen times a day. All that use is eventually going to cause the door gaskets to lose their resilience, and when that happens, the precious air that you spent hard-earned dollars to make cold will steadily leak out. This means your refrigerator will have to work harder to cool more air. The harder the fridge works, the shorter its life.

Check both the gasket around the freezer door and the one around the main door. Put a 150-watt floodlight on a thin, flat extension cord in the refrigerator or freezer compartment. Check one edge at a time. Point the bulb toward the suspect edge with the cord coming out of the opposite edge. With the light on, the door shut, and the kitchen lights off, check for light seeping through the edge. If any light is leaking out, the gasket is worn and should be replaced. Check with your local appliance store to see if they have the right gasket for your particular model in stock; if they don't, they can special-order it.

How to replace a gasket

There are three ways your gasket might be attached: On older models, screws go through the gasket into a retaining strip. You'll have to remove the screws to remove the gasket. On some newer models, the gasket fits around the retaining strip, and you'll only need to loosen the screws to remove the gasket (A). On other new models, the strip has a groove down the center, and the gasket has a lip that fits in the groove. In this case, you don't have to loosen the screws, just pull the old one out and push the new one in (B).

The screws that hold the retaining strip in place also secure the inside door panel, keeping the door rigid. To prevent warping the door, you don't want to remove or loosen all the screws at once. You do want to empty the door compartments before loosening any screws.

Before installing the gasket, you want to warm it to remove any kinks and get it nice and pliable. You can either soak it in hot water or throw in it your clothes dryer on medium heat for 10 minutes. To make the replacement, first loosen or remove the retaining strip screws along the top of the door and pull out the top section of the old gasket. Slip the top section of the new gasket in place and tighten the screws. Work your way around the door, removing and replacing one side of the gasket at a time.

Caulk a cracked gasket

If an inspection of the gasket around your refrigerator door reveals just a small crack in a gasket that is otherwise serviceable, you can usually fill the

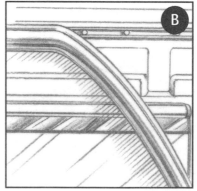

crack with a little silicone caulk. Roll the gasket back, and fill the crack with a tiny bit of the caulk—don't use so much that it squeezes out all over the place.

Keep it on the level

Like most appliances, a refrigerator's motor and other parts are designed to work best when the machine is level. In addition to putting life-shortening strain on the mechanical parts, an out-of-level refrigerator can cause the doors to sag—or, if tilted forward, not close properly. Sagging doors don't seal properly, and expensive cold air will leak out, even if the gasket is fine. Place a carpenter's level on

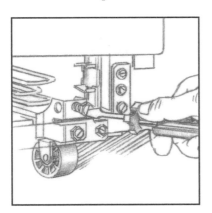

top of the fridge, and check it from side to side and from back to front. Inspect the legs or casters to be sure all are firmly on the floor. If one is not on the floor, or the refrigerator is not level, adjust the legs until the unit is level in all directions. Here's how:

Take off the grille at the bottom of the fridge—it's usually held

on by clips and pops off when you pull up on the bottom edge. If the legs are threaded, simply change the height by turning the legs with a wrench. More likely, the unit has casters. In this case, turn the leveling screw clockwise to raise, or counterclockwise to lower, until the unit is level. Prop the corner of the unit on a piece of 2x4 to take the weight off the leg or caster while you are making adjustments. Check for level

after adjusting. Before you pop the grille back on, take the opportunity to vacuum the condenser coils.

Fix a sagging door

If, after making sure that your refrigerator is level, the door still sags, it's easy to fix. First remove the hinge cover, if any, from the hinge at the top of the door. Use a nut driver or screwdriver to loosen the hinge screws. (If the unit has a

True-Life ✦ Long Life

Accented in shiny, curvy chrome, it exudes the exuberance and optimism of 1950s America. Not only does it look cool, it actually still keeps stuff cool. In fact, it keeps a few things downright frozen. It is Sarge Russell's 1957 General Electric refrigerator, and he wouldn't trade it for any fridge made today. It even has a chrome pedal that pops the door open if your hands are full.

"It reminds me of a '57 Chevy," Russell of Frenchtown, New Jersey, said of the fridge he acquired along with another old fridge in 1979. He paid 50 bucks for the pair.

Russell attributes the '57s longevity to good design and manufacture more than to any special maintenance. "At one point, I replaced a thermostatic switch," he said with a casual shrug.

He points out that old fridges had much thicker, more heavily insulated walls than today's models. Moreover, modern frost-free refrigerators actually have heat coils to keep the freezer compartment frost-free. This means modern fridge motors have to come on more often to keep stuff cold, so they wear out quicker and cost more to operate. Russell has to defrost his fridge about twice a year. He empties it out and pulls a plug that lets melted ice from the freezer drain into the meat drawer.

A few years back, Russell decided to treat his fridge to a makeover. He sent it to an auto-body shop, where it got a new coat of glossy white paint and new chrome. Now it looks like it was just wheeled out of the showroom—a GE showroom that is, not Chevrolet.

separate freezer door, you may have to open or remove the top door to adjust the lower one.) Reposition the door, and hold it firmly in place while you tighten the hinge screws.

 ProTip

KEEP IT COOL

If you are designing a kitchen layout, plan to keep the refrigerator out of direct sunlight and away from items that generate heat such as the stove, a hot-air vent, or a radiator. The fridge's compressor won't have to turn on as often, and that will not only make your refrigerator last longer, but it will also lower your electric bill. If your current fridge does receive direct sunlight, draw the shade over the window during the hours when the sun is hitting it.

Fix a warped door

If your refrigerator door isn't sealing because it is warped, you usually don't need a new door. Here's the easy fix that works most of the time: First empty the door compartments. Then pull back the door gasket so you can loosen all the retaining screws. (On some models you'll have to remove the gasket to get at the screws.) Grab the outer door panel at the top and side, and twist it opposite the warp to flatten the door. Have a helper tighten the retainer screws while you hold the door in this position.

Refrigerators

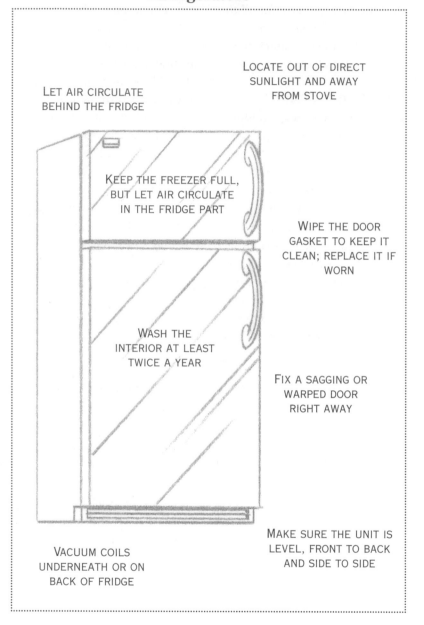

LET AIR CIRCULATE BEHIND THE FRIDGE

LOCATE OUT OF DIRECT SUNLIGHT AND AWAY FROM STOVE

KEEP THE FREEZER FULL, BUT LET AIR CIRCULATE IN THE FRIDGE PART

WIPE THE DOOR GASKET TO KEEP IT CLEAN; REPLACE IT IF WORN

WASH THE INTERIOR AT LEAST TWICE A YEAR

FIX A SAGGING OR WARPED DOOR RIGHT AWAY

MAKE SURE THE UNIT IS LEVEL, FRONT TO BACK AND SIDE TO SIDE

VACUUM COILS UNDERNEATH OR ON BACK OF FRIDGE

Vacuum the condenser coils

The condenser under or behind your refrigerator gives off heat. Dirt and dust on the condenser coils act like insulation, inhibiting dissipation of that heat. Reduce the strain on your refrigerator's condenser by vacuuming the coils monthly—more often if you have pets that shed.

• On frost-free models, the condenser coils are under the fridge. To reach them, unplug the refrigerator and pop off the grille at the bottom by pulling up. Put the crevice tool on your vacuum cleaner, and push the tool as far under the unit as you can. Be careful not to bend the condenser tubing or coil fins.

• On models that you have to defrost, the coils are on the back of the fridge. Just pull the unit away from the wall slightly to vacuum them.

Give the condenser coils breathing room

Keep your fridge a few inches away from the wall so heat from the condenser coils will have plenty of room to vent away.

Is there water under your fridge?

If puddles form on the floor underneath your refrigerator, the cause could be a clogged drain tube, which you can fix, as described in Before You Call the Repair Guy, at right. But first make sure the cause isn't something even simpler—a misaligned drain pan or drain tube that isn't going into the drain pan.

Keep a full freezer

It takes more energy to keep air at freezing temperatures than it does to keep solid items frozen. So you'll prolong the life of your freezer and reduce your energy bills if you keep the freezer packed. On the other

---

Before You Call the Repair Guy . . .

Are there mysterious puddles of water inside your refrigerator? It almost certainly has a clogged drain tube. Here's what's going on: When air in the freezer compartment is cooled by the condenser, it gives up water. This water drains through a tube that runs down the back of the fridge, where it drips into a pan under the unit and evaporates. Sometimes the drain gets clogged—usually with algae spores—and this causes the water to back up and drip into the refrigerator compartment. Here's what to do about it:

❶ Pull the refrigerator away from the wall. You'll find the tube stuck into a hole in the back of the unit, sometimes secured with a clip.

❷ Remove the tube, take it over to the sink, and flush it out with a bulb baster. Using a small funnel, pour a teaspoon of ammonia or bleach into the tube to inhibit algae-spore growth.

❸ Replace the tube, making sure the bottom end is resting in the drain pan.

---

hand, it's most efficient to leave room for air to circulate in the refrigerator compartment.

Do a temperature check

To keep your fridge and freezer humming along at maximum efficiency, it's a good idea to take their temperature occasionally. Let a glass of water cool near the center of the refrigerator compartment for 24 hours. Then put a refrigerator-freezer thermometer (sold at houseware stores) in the water for a few minutes. Look for a reading between 34° F and 40° F (1° C to 4° C). In the freezer, insert the thermometer between two frozen food packages. Look for a reading between 0° F and 4° F

(-17° C to -8° C). If necessary, adjust the temperature setting and repeat the test.

Keep your fridge clean

Wash the compartments, drawers, and shelves of your refrigerator twice a year with a solution of baking soda and water. Also clean the drain pan with warm, soapy water. Wipe the door gaskets every couple of months. Be sure to clean up spills promptly.

Test the door light switch

If the light inside your refrigerator doesn't shut off when you close the door, the heat of the bulb will keep the motor running overtime and will cause poor refrigeration. The switch

When purchasing a new refrigerator, it's important to get one with the right capacity for your family. If it's too small, you'll be constantly struggling to stuff items in. If it's too big, you'll spend too much when you buy it, and you'll keep paying too much with every monthly electric bill. Check this chart to determine how big your fridge should be:

Family size	Refrigerator compartment	Freezer compartment	Total
1 person	10 cu ft	4 cu ft	14 cu ft
2	12	4	16
3	14	4	18
4–5	16	6	22
6–8	16	10	26
9–10	17	10	27

has a button or a lever that's depressed by the door when it closes. You can check by pushing it in by hand. If the light stays on when you press the switch, unplug the refrigerator, gently pry out the switch with a

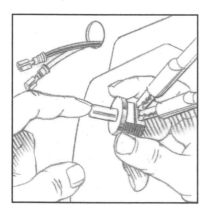

screwdriver, and disconnect the wires. Attach the clip and probe of a continuity tester to the switch terminals. If the switch is working properly, the tester should light when the button is out and go off when it's pushed in. Replace a faulty switch with a duplicate from the manufacturer or an appliance store. A continuity tester—which usually looks like a screwdriver with a cord coming out of the top of the handle—is really a small flashlight that lights up when its probe and the clip on its cord are connected to complete a circuit.

Also check the fan switch

In some frost-free models, there is a second door switch that turns on the evaporator fan when the door is closed. If this switch fails, air can't circulate and frost builds up in the freezer. When you press down this switch, the fan should go on. (With the compressor and fan running, you should be able to feel a draft in the freezer air duct.) If the fan doesn't go on, test the switch. If it's working properly, the tester should light when you press the button and go out when you release it.

Dishwashers

Wondering how you ever got along without your dishwasher? You don't really want to know. Follow these tips to make sure your memory doesn't get an unpleasant jog.

Jump-start the hot water

Do you notice that it takes a moment or two for your kitchen-sink water to get hot? If so, run the hot water from the sink faucet until it is hot before turning on the dishwasher. This way, the water will be hot when it enters your dishwasher, and it will clean your dishes more effectively.

Fix chipped racks pronto

If the plastic coating on your dishwasher racks is chipped, the damage will spread as water works its way under the coating and causes the rack to rust. As soon as you notice a chip, go to your hardware store or home center and pick up a can of Plasti Dip, a synthetic-rubber coating. Just brush the stuff on the damaged area.

Use a net to catch small items

If you find that small items are slipping out of the dishwasher's silverware basket and jamming the spray arm, place a piece of nylon netting at the bottom of the basket.

Keep your racks rolling

Dishwasher rack jammed? The rollers may be sticking. Turn them by hand to loosen them. If they are worn and no longer round, replace them. Some can be removed by taking out screws; most simply pull off. If a rack sticks because it is bent, replace it. You can get replacement rollers and racks from appliance dealers who carry your machine's brand.

Give your dishwasher the vinegar treatment

Back when your grandmother *was* the dishwasher, she knew that vinegar is one of the best household cleaners. Now you can apply this age-old cleaner to your newfangled automatic dishwasher. Every six months, pour a cup of distilled white vinegar in the unit, and run the regular wash cycle. The vinegar will dissolve soap residue and minerals that have collected throughout the dishwasher.

Should you get a stainless steel tub?

When purchasing a dishwasher, one of the most obvious upgrades is to go with a stainless steel tub instead of a plastic one. But this is a false economy. Yes, stainless steel will outlive plastic. But it's irrelevant because a plastic tub will also outlive your dishwasher. The sole advantage of stainless steel is that it won't stain as a plastic tub might.

Before You Call the Repair Guy . . .

If your dishes are still dirty after running the dishwasher, follow these steps:

1. Check that the spray arm can turn freely—perhaps a small spoon or fork slipped down and jammed it.

2. Check to see if the spray-arm holes are clogged. Just remove the racks, unscrew the hubcap holding the arm, and lift it off. Use a stiff wire to open the holes fully. Rinse the arm well under running water.

3. While you have the spray arm off, take a gander at the filter screen that's located right underneath the arm on the floor of the machine. If it is clogged, remove any clips that secure it. Hold the screen under running water and scrub it with a stiff brush.

Washers and Dryers

Provide this hardworking appliance duo with a little regular maintenance, and they'll happily keep your clothes clean and dry for decades.

Keep the top clean

When a laundry product spills on the top of your washer or dryer, wipe it up right away. The finish on your machines is tough, but some surfaces, control knobs, and other plastic parts can be damaged by bleach, ammonia, and solvents.

Level your washer

If your washing machine is slightly out of level, you may not notice it. But the basket will be out of balance, putting a strain on the bearings and the motor that will shorten the life of the machine. Not only that, if the front of the washer is higher than the back, the basket won't drain all the way, leaving a pool of water that can cause rust spots and holes. If the machine is badly out of level, you will hear the basket banging around during the wash cycle—your machine is quickly beating itself to death.

1. Using a carpenter's level, check first to see if the washer is level side to side at the back. It usually is, because the back legs are self-leveling. If not, tip the washer forward, and then let it down again to allow the back legs to readjust themselves.

2. Now check for level from front to back on one side. If it isn't level, use an adjustable wrench to raise or lower the threaded front foot on that side.

3. Check the other side the same way, and adjust the foot if necessary.

4. Finally, check across the front. If you made the other adjustments correctly, the washer should be level across the front. If it isn't, recheck the back and sides.

Shut off the water

It's a good idea to get in the habit of turning off the water-supply spigots to your washer when not in use—especially if you are going away for more than a day. You'll relieve pressure on the hoses and the inlet valves, prolonging their life. You'll also eliminate the possibility of a flood if one of the hoses should burst.

Winterize your washer

Do you have a washing machine in your summer cottage or do you fly south for the winter? If you don't winterize the washer before you leave, water in the inlet valve and pump can freeze and expand, cracking the valve and pump bodies. Here's how to protect your washer:

True-Life ✦ *Long* Life

When they moved into their home in 1999, Jack and Sue Katz of Whitestone, NY, sensed they would soon be buying a new washer. "The one left by the previous owners was pretty old," Jack said. "And it wasn't in great shape, either. Two of the three wash-selection buttons were missing." But Jack didn't realize just how old the washer was until his parents came for their first visit. "My mom recognized it immediately as the same Maytag she used when I was a kid," he said. "The one she got in 1962." The Katzes were even more surprised when they were able to squeeze another three years of use out of their 40-year-old washer before it gave up the ghost. "We had to spin the basket by hand to get it started for the last few months," Jack says. "Knowing how sturdy the machine was, I didn't want to find out how much longer it could have gone on like that."

---

1. Turn off the hot- and cold-water-supply valve, and use pliers to loosen the hoses from the inlet ports on the machine.

2. Set the washer controls to FILL and WARM WASH, and turn the washer on for about 10 seconds.

3. Pour 1/2 gallon (2 liters) of nontoxic antifreeze—propylene glycol—into the washer.

4. Turn the timer control to DRAIN and SPIN and let the washer run for another 10 seconds. Your washer is now ready to brave the winter cold.

When you return, reconnect the water-supply hoses. Pour in 1 cup of liquid clothes detergent, and run the washer through a complete cycle before you wash any clothes.

Prevent mineral buildup

Minerals in your water can collect in your washer's hoses, inlet valves, and pump, especially if you have hard water. These minerals restrict water flow and increase friction, which can shorten the life of your washer. To prevent the buildup, fill the basket with cold water and add 1 cup of vinegar. Then put your washer through a complete cycle. Do this every three months or so, more often if your water is hard and/or you use the washer more than the typical family of four.

✦ BEST ADVICE ✦ **Washing Machines**

CLEAR OUT HARD-WATER DEPOSITS WITH VINEGAR

WIPE UP ANY LAUNDRY-PRODUCT SPILLS ON TOP RIGHT AWAY

CLEAN THE INLET SCREENS IF THE WATER INTAKE IS WEAK

WINTERIZE AN EXPOSED UNIT WITH ANTIFREEZE

TURN OFF WATER SPIGOTS WHEN GOING AWAY ON A TRIP

MAKE SURE THAT THE UNIT IS LEVEL, FRONT TO BACK AND SIDE TO SIDE

Flush new water lines

You've just moved into a brand-new house—shiny floors, sparkling walls, new plumbing. All you need to do is move the washer and dryer into the laundry, hook them up, and you are ready to go, right? Wrong! New plumbing usually contains some dirt and solder flux, stuff that can send your washer's inlet valves to an early grave. So whether all the plumbing is new, or you just added hot and cold lines for the washer, you need to flush the lines before hooking up the washer. It's easy: Attach the hose to the hot-water line and hold the other end of the hose in the drain standpipe or sink. Turn on the hot water, and let it run for a few minutes. Do the same for the cold water.

Go easy on the dial

Never spin the timer dial on your washer while the machine is running. This sends erratic electrical surges to the timer switches, and before long, you'll be replacing the timer, an expensive proposition. To give the timer a long and happy life, turn the dial slowly and only clockwise, and only when the washer is off.

And go easy on the detergent

Using extra laundry detergent definitely will not get your clothes cleaner. But it might make the repair guy richer. Too much detergent will cause the wash water to spill over the washer tub ring and get into the drive motor. This could cause the motor to burn out. In addition, the filler in the soap can push clothes over the top of the basket, where agitation will pull them down into the washer's outer tub. From there, it's an easy trip to the water pump. If

Before You Call the Repair Guy . . .

You turn on your washing machine, and instead of the sound of rushing water, you hear a low hum or maybe you hear nothing at all. Or perhaps your machine stops midwash. Don't pick up the phone yet! There are a few simple things you can check first.

If there is no water flowing into the washer:

1. Are the hot- and cold-water-supply spigots on? Sounds like a dumb question, but it happens. Also, if it's below freezing outdoors, make sure you don't have a frozen water-supply pipe.

2. Check for a clogged inlet screen. There is one inside each of the machine's two water-inlet ports. Turn off the hot and cold water; then use pliers to unscrew the water-supply hoses from the inlet ports. Use a small screwdriver to carefully pry the screens from the ports. Rinse the screens under a faucet. Replace them, reattach hoses, and try your machine.

If the washer goes silent midcycle:

1. Your washer may have a built-in safety mechanism that shuts down power during a spin cycle if an off-balance load is detected. Try lifting the lid all the way open—you should hear a loud click as the mechanism resets. Rearrange the load, and close the lid. The washer should continue.

2. No click when you open the lid? Make sure the washer's plug is secure in the receptacle. Then check for a tripped circuit breaker.

3. Check the switch lever. It is part of the device that turns the machine off when you lift the lid. When you close the lid, a finger, called a strike, goes through a hole and pushes down a little metal or plastic lever that turns the switch on and lets the washer run. If the lever is metal, it might just be bent down a little so that the strike can't depress it fully. If so, all you have to do is bend it back up.

the repairman finds a sock in your pump, now you know how it got there.

Give dryer exhaust the path of least resistance

When it comes to your dryer exhaust pipe, think short and smooth. That means, first of all, use smooth metal duct pipe, not a flexible accordion plastic ones. Ideally, you want the duct to go straight out of the dryer to the outdoors. But if that isn't possible, design a pipe run that is as short as possible, with no more than two elbows. Lint can collect in elbows, and those flexible plastic pipes are virtual lint traps, especially when they are long and curled up behind the dryer. When lint clogs up the exhaust, the dryer can't circulate the hot air properly, so the machine must work harder and longer to dry each load. This makes the dryer more costly to run and shortens its life.

Keep exhaust vent clear

Lint will eventually build up in your exhaust vent pipe, even if it is a short, straight run. So to keep your dryer working efficiently, make it a habit once a year to clean out the vent duct:

❶ Unplug the dryer and remove the duct. Shake out any built-up lint. If necessary, run a wadded stick on a cloth through the duct. When replacing the duct, make sure to reseal the joints with fresh duct tape.

❷ Outdoors, clean the damper and its hinge by inserting a length of straightened coat hanger into the vent hood.

Don't vent your dryer indoors

It may seem like a good idea to vent your dryer into the house in the wintertime. Why not capture that moist, warm air? The biggest reason is that that air contains lots of lint that you do not want to breathe. In addition, the air is *too* moist and can cause condensation on your windows.

Remember the lint catcher

Make it a habit: Before you turn on the dryer for each load, empty the lint catcher. Your machine will work more efficiently, which means it will last longer and use less energy. Plus, you will be eliminating a fire hazard.

Check for door leaks

Occasionally move a piece of tissue paper over door's edge while the dryer is running; if the paper is drawn in, the seal need to be replaced. (A damp door is also a sign of a bad seal.) You can get a seal for your model of dryer from an appliance-parts store. Usually you can just pull or pry off the old seal, remove any old adhesive with mineral spirits, and attach the new seal with the special heat-resistant adhesive, which is usually sold with the seal.

ProTip

FIX APPLIANCE SCRATCHES

An occasional scratch on your appliances is inevitable. But that doesn't mean it has to be permanent. Go to the appliance dealer, and pick up some appliance touch-up paint in a color to match yours. It comes in a small bottle with an applicator brush, just like nail polish. Use the applicator brush to dab on just enough paint to cover the blemish. Follow the directions carefully. Fill a deep nick in layers, letting each dry before adding the next. After your touch-up dries, smooth it with fine auto-finish rubbing compound.

Water Heaters

A water heater is a simple device with simple maintenance needs that can extend its life by a decade.

Flush sediment from water heater

The hot-water heater is easy to ignore as it quietly works away in the basement or laundry room. That is, until one winter morning when nothing but ice water shoots out of the shower-head. You can delay that day by many years simply by draining out the sediment that collect at the bottom of the tank. Just stick a bucket under the drain-cock that you'll find near the bottom of the heater. Open the draincock, and let the water run until it is clear.

Check the pressure-relief valve

The pressure-relief valve sticks out of the side of your water heater. It should have a pipe attached to it that leads to within a few inches of the floor. The purpose of the valve is to release water if too much pressure builds up in the water heater. Test it every six months by pressing on the lever. If no water comes out, call a repairman.

Testing for hard water

Water is described as "hard" when it contains large amounts of minerals—specifically calcium and magnesium. This is not a health hazard—in fact, it may even be beneficial, since we need these minerals in our diets. However, hard water is hard on appliances. It builds up inside pipes and can shorten the life of your water heater and the pumps inside your dishwasher and clothes washer. It also reduces the performance of soap and detergent. If you have municipal water, the supplier should be able to tell you how hard it is. If you suspect your well water is hard, do this test: Add 10 drops of dishwashing liquid to a large glass of water, about two-thirds full. Cover and shake. If there is a big foamy head of suds, the water is soft. If the head is thin and flat, you have hard water. Whether you have municipal or well water, if it is hard, consider having a water softener installed on your water supply.

Before You Call the Repair Guy . . .

Is brown water coming out of your hot-water tap? If the cold water is running clear, you don't need a plumber. You just need to give your water heater a thorough flush. Here's how:

1 There are two water pipes sticking out of the top of the heater—the hot-water outlet pipe will feel hot. Note which one it is. If the heater is electric, turn off the power at the breaker box. If the unit is gas, turn off the gas shut-off valve. Open a nearby hot-water faucet, and let it run until the water is no longer hot. (This is so that cool water will drain out of the water heater—if you have a drain hose rated for hot water, such as an old washing-machine hot-water hose, you don't need to run the hot-water faucet.)

2 Follow the cold-water inlet pipe sticking out of the heater until you find the cold-water inlet valve, which is usually, but not always, just on top of the heater. Close this valve. Open a nearby hot-water faucet again.

3 Now attach your garden hose or a hot-water hose to the water heater's draincock, and let all the water drain out of the unit into a suitable drain. Close the draincock and the hot-water faucet. Open the cold-water inlet valve. When the unit is full, open the draincock and let it run until the water is clear. Restart the unit as described in your owner's manual or on the front panel. Your hot-water faucets will now run clear.

Stoves and Ovens

Stoves have simple working parts, and, with occasional repair and regular cleaning, yours should keep on serving you and your family for decades.

Prevent boil-overs

When cooking, use pots and pans that are deep enough to prevent boil-overs and splattering. Minimizing spillage will minimize cleanup work and help prolong the life of your stove.

Clean spills quickly

Cooking spills are inevitable. The good news is you can whisk away virtually any spill with a damp sponge or paper towel if you get it while it is still wet and the stove is still warm. So get in the habit of wiping down your stovetop after every use—your stove will gleam like new for decades, and you'll save yourself plenty of scrubbing.

Use elbow grease, not abrasives

Of course, human nature will prevail, and once in a while, you won't wipe up stovetop spills right away. If a spill has had a chance to dry out and cook for a while, use a sponge along with a solution of dishwashing liquid and warm water or a 50-50 solution of vinegar and warm water. The longer you wait, the more elbow grease you'll need to invest. An all-purpose cleaner such as Fantastik is fine to use,

but whatever you do, don't give in to the temptation to grab that can of abrasive powder—you'll create tiny scratches in the surface. The next spill will grip the scratches and be even harder to remove.

☞ DON'T
use the stovetop as a counter

Don't get in the habit of using the stovetop as a place to get pots, pans, and other kitchen stuff out of the way. Sure as taxes, you'll eventually scratch or even chip the top. Scratched surfaces are harder to clean, and it's all downhill from there!

Clean the stove parts regularly

In addition to an after-use wipe-down, periodically give your stove parts a more extensive cleaning. Wash the burner drip plates and other removable accessories (but not electric burner coils) either by hand in the sink or by running them with your next dishwasher load (if the owner's manual for your stove says they are dishwasher safe). Carefully remove control-panel knobs (usually by pulling

straight out) and clean around the knobs' bases. Wash the knobs in hot, soapy water, rinse, and dry before replacing them.

Clean under the hood

If your stove doesn't have a sealed cooktop, food and grease will fall down under the burners. It's easy to forget about this out-of-view debris, and any mice in the house are hoping you do. The grease is also a fire hazard. So remember to lift the cooktop (like lifting the hood of a car on many models) to clean beneath it. Follow the owner's manual instructions for lifting the top without damaging it. Then clean the grease buildup with a sponge and warm, soapy water or a 50-50 solution of vinegar and warm water. Rinse with clean water and a sponge.

Clean that grimy oven window

Oven windows tend to become so dirty we can't even tell what is in there, let alone whether it is done cooking. And when you think about it, a dirty window actually reduces the efficiency of your stove because you keep opening the door to check the food. To clean the window, rub it with a damp cloth dipped in baking soda. If stuff is really baked on, wipe the window with ammonia, let it stand for 30 minutes, then scrape it off a plastic ice scraper. Don't use a metal tool.

Electric Cooking Ranges

WIPE OFF THE STOVETOP AFTER EACH MEAL

NEVER SCOUR THE ENAMEL WITH ABRASIVES

AVOID BOIL-OVERS AND WIPE UP SPILLS RIGHT AWAY

BURN ANY SPILLS OFF THE BURNER COILS

LIFT AND CLEAN UNDER THE STOVETOP REGULARLY

NEVER REST FOOD ON OVEN DOOR

WIPE UP SPILLS IN A CONTINUOUS-CLEAN OVEN; DON'T RUB THE SURFACE

DON'T USE THE STOVETOP OR OVEN FOR POT STORAGE

Burn the coils clean

Heating coils on top of an electric range usually don't need washing. Instead, turn them on HIGH to burn off spills. If a spill is massive, wipe up as much as possible after the coil has cooled and then burn off the rest.

Replace burner pans with originals

Those shiny chrome pans under your burners are not there just to look good. They also reflect the heat upward, increasing the efficiency of your stove. When they get grimy and stained, they don't reflect the heat. Shine them up by rubbing with a paste made from vinegar and cream of tartar. If the pans have become too stained to clean, don't replace them with those thin, universal aluminum ones sold at the grocery store. Those don't last, and they quickly become hard to clean. And don't cover old pans with aluminum foil—you run the risk of causing an electrical short. Instead, replace burner pans with original equipment, which you can buy at an appliance store. They look better longer and will be cheaper in the long run.

Fix enamel chips

If the enamel on your stove gets chipped, touch it up with a porcelain enamel repair kit that you can buy at your appliance store. The paint comes in small jars with a brush in the lid like nail polish. Be smart, and do it before the damaged spot becomes rusty. If the chip is deep, apply the touch-up paint in two or three layers, letting each layer dry thoroughly before applying the next.

Look for a blue flame

If the gas flame on your stovetop burners is blue, they are working at top efficiency. If the flame is yellow, the burners are working inefficiently, and they should be adjusted by a service technician.

Send burner grate stains down the drain

If the burner grates on your gas stove get supergreasy, mix a can of sink-clog crystals such as Drano into a bucket of water. Wear rubber gloves when dealing with the crystals, and carefully place your grates in the bucket—you don't want to splash this caustic brew onto your skin. Let the grates soak overnight, and they'll look like new in the morning.

Extend the life of your continuous-clean oven

The key to keeping your continuous-clean oven looking great for many years is to be sure to clean up major oven spills promptly before they form a glaze that prevents the interior from burning off more minor spills. When you have a major spill, follow these steps:

1 Blot up as much of the spill as you can with paper towel. Do this while the oven is still warm and the spill is soft. Don't rub—any paper particles can clog the rough surface.

2 When the oven is completely cool, spray it with an all-purpose cleaner. Work the cleaner in with a nylon-bristle brush or net pad, let stand for about 30 minutes, then scrub with the brush.

Before You Call the Repair Guy . . .

If a cooktop heating coil on your range has burned out:

1 It's usually a very easy job to replace a cooktop heating coil. On many ranges, you can simply pivot up the coil and pull it out of its connection, much as you would pull a plug out of a wall socket. On other ranges, the wires are secured to the coil with a couple of screws that you'll need to remove. (Be sure to unplug the stove before you work on it.)

2 Get a replacement coil at an appliance store—take the old one and the stove model number with you; if necessary, you can order one from the manufacturer (check the website). There is one kind of coil that is tricky to replace: If you have the kind of coils that turn up to make them easy to clean under, the connections are probably soldered. For soldered coils, it's best to call for service.

If your electric oven is not heating properly:

1 The heating element on an electric oven is also easy to replace—it's just held in place with screws. (Again, remember to unplug the stove.) Remove the screws holding the elements to the back of the oven, and gently pull the element out a few inches. Now just unscrew the two wires connected to the element.

2 Test the element with a length of lamp cord attached to a plug. Attach the two lamp-cord wires to the two terminals on the element, and plug in the lamp cord. Make sure the element is on a surface that can't be burned, and be careful not to touch the element.

3 If the element is no good, it won't heat up; you should get a replacement at an appliance-parts supplier. If the element is good, it will get warm, but not red-hot, within a few minutes. If it does, however, that means that your stove has another problem that's causing the oven not to heat properly and it's time to call a service person.

3 Rinse thoroughly with cold water by squeezing a wet sponge over the area. Then wipe up the excess with a paper towel or a sponge.

Go easy on the oven door

Ease that oven door shut. If you slam it, you may spring the hinge or throw the thermostat out of whack. And whatever you do, don't rest that turkey or casserole on the open oven door—using the door as a shelf is another way to damage the hinge.

Give your racks a bath

Stop! Before you start giving your arms a workout scrubbing oven racks, give the racks a bath. Lay old towels in the tub to protect it from scratching and put the racks on the towels. Then mix 1/4 cup of white vinegar with 1/4 cup of dishwashing detergent and pour it in the tub. Fill the tub with enough hot water to cover the racks, and let it sit for an hour. Meanwhile, relax. When you return, just rinse and dry the racks. Rinse and wipe out the tub right away so the grease from the racks doesn't get a chance to adhere.

Scrape with plastic

When food splatters on the heating element of your gas oven, grab the plastic ice scraper from your car to scrape it off. A metal scraper is likely to damage the element.

Don't lay foil on the racks

Don't try to keep your oven clean by laying aluminum foil on the bottom or on the racks. Air needs to circulate freely through the oven in order for food to cook efficiently. Also, the foil reflects heat, which can throw off the thermostat.

Go with glass ovenware

If you use glass or enamel pans in your oven instead of metal, you can turn down the oven by 45 degrees F (25 degrees C) and cook just as quickly.

Buy to Keep: Ovens

When purchasing a new gas or electric oven, you'll have to choose between manual clean, continuous clean, or self-cleaning. Here are the pros and cons:

Manual-clean oven	If your top priority is durability at the lowest price, choose an oven that you have to clean manually. There's less to go wrong than with the other types, so you'll save money on repair bills over the years, too.
Self-cleaning oven	If you would rather save elbow grease than money, spring for a self-cleaning oven. These ovens use a cycle of very high heat to incinerate food residue off the walls. They are the most expensive type to buy and repair, but you might consider it money well spent when you contemplate crawling into a manual-clean oven on a regular basis.
Continuous-clean oven	Continuous-clean ovens are the least durable. They have a rough-textured surface that resists stains and contains a catalyst that causes most food to burn off at normal baking temperatures. But not all the food burns off, and the residue eventually causes a hard glaze that destroys the self-cleaning feature. Adding to the problem, abrasives or spray-on oven cleaners can destroy the continuous-cleaning feature, so you'll be stuck with a dirty-looking oven interior.

Microwave Ovens

Microwave ovens have become essential to our busy lives. Here are some tips to get years of trouble-free use from yours.

Give your microwave room to breath

Your microwave needs to vent the heat it generates when you use it. If you own a countertop model, the most important thing you can do to make it last is be sure that the vents have a few inches of clearance. When you set up a new microwave, be sure to check the owner's manual to find out where the vents are and exactly how much clearance they need.

It may pay to replace a broken microwave

Most parts of a microwave oven are not user-serviceable. If you haven't priced microwave ovens lately, make sure that you do before you pay someone to fix yours. With prices starting at around $40, it's usually smarter to buy a new one than to fix one that's got several years of use under its belt.

Keep hidden metal out of the microwave

Everybody knows that you shouldn't put metal in the microwave. If you do, you'll get a great mini-lightening display as you damage the magnetron tube that shoots the microwaves. Still, if we're not careful, little pieces of metal can sneak in. For example, if you like to warm your maple syrup bottle in the microwave, remember to remove not only the metal cap, but the metal taper-proof ring that remains when you take the cap off. And remember not to use metal twist ties in the microwave.

Keep your microwave clean

One reason you love your microwave, of course, is that it cooks so quickly. The other reason is it is so much easier to clean than a conventional oven. So clean it regularly to remove odors and keep it looking and working its best. Here's how:

• Food splatters inside your microwave are easiest to clean before they have a chance to dry. In this case, simply wipe down the interior with a sponge or paper towel dipped in a mixture of dishwashing liquid and water. Then rinse with clean water. Use the same method to wash removable trays or turntables in the sink.

• If food has had a chance to dry out in the microwave, put 2 or 3 cups of water in a bowl and heat it on high power for three to five minutes. The resulting steam will soften the dried food. Then just wipe down the interior with a sponge or soft cloth.

• To get rid of odors in your microwave, wipe down the interior with a solution of 1 cup of warm water and 1 tablespoon of baking soda. Rinse with warm water. Or combine 1 cup of water with 1/2 cup of lemon juice in a measuring cup or bowl and heat it on high for three to five minutes. Let it stand in the microwave for 5 to 10 minutes before removing.

• To remove stains from the microwave's ceramic floor or turntable, make a paste of baking soda and water and apply it to the stain. Let it sit until the stain disappears; then wipe it off, and rinse with a wet sponge or cloth.

Get a handle on your microwave

Some microwave ovens—particularly those models designed for installation over cooking ranges—don't use a push lever to open their doors. Instead, the door uses a plastic handle to pull it open and push it closed. Over time, the plastic bolts inside the handle can wear out and cause it to break off at one or both ends. The microwave itself probably still works fine; you just can't open it. Worse still are the exorbitant prices some manufacturers charge for replacement parts. (One company charges $67 for a new handle.) If your old handle is still in one piece, however, you may be able to call it back for active duty. Here's how:

❶ Open the door. If both ends of the handle have broken off, you may be able to gently pry the door open using a wrench or screwdriver. Use some medium-grade sandpaper to lightly scuff up the detached end(s) of the handle. Try to remove the bolts if they are still intact to make sure they won't get in the way when you stick the handle to the door.

❷ Clean the handle with a cloth moistened with some general household cleaner, such as Fantastik, wipe it dry, then mix up and apply some clear two-part epoxy to the detached end(s). Put a small amount on the corresponding surfaces on the door as well.

❸ Press the handle in place. Use a damp cotton cloth to wipe away any big drips before the glue sets, but don't worry if a little epoxy squeezes out and remains on the outside of the joint—it will form a stronger bond between the door and the

❓ How Long Will A Microwave Oven Last?

ANSWER: **Four to ten years**

As microwave oven prices drop, so do their life expectancies. It's not unusual for newer models to simply stop working after four or five years of heavy family use. But sometimes microwave ovens hang on for a gradual death. If your microwave is more than ten years old, you may be noticing that food is still frozen in the middle after cooking for the time recommended on the box. Here's a test: For a 600- to 1,000-watt oven, place an 8-ounce (240-ml) cup of water in the microwave on high power for three minutes. If it doesn't reach a rolling boil in that time, it's time for a new unit. A microwave that's given more than a decade of service is not worth repairing.

handle. Hold the handle in place for a couple of minutes; then place a rubber band around both the handle and the door to keep things in place. Leave it alone for at least 24 hours.

Use the smallest container possible

A microwave oven works by agitating the water molecules in food. Since the container itself—whether plastic, glass, or ceramic—doesn't contain water molecules, the microwaves don't heat it. The container gets hot because the heat from the food is transferred to it. The bigger the container, the more heat it will suck out of the food and the longer the food will take to get hot. The appliance

will cook quicker and last longer if you always use the smallest container that will hold the food.

Don't overload circuits

You pop something into the toaster while the microwave is running. When you push down the toaster handle, you notice the microwave's noise becomes lower in pitch. Or the lights dim when you turn on the microwave. These are both signs that you are overloading an electrical circuit. This taxes the microwave and shortens its life. It's best to give your microwave its own circuit. Or failing that, don't run other big energy-users such as toasters, toaster ovens, or electric griddles at the same time as the microwave.

Home-Office Gear

Home-Office Equipment—
General Guidelines

The fact is, today's home-office equipment is doomed to a much shorter life than those manual typewriters that easily survived decades of hunting and pecking. Still, the stuff isn't cheap, and a little maintenance can mean several extra years of service.

Cover up equipment when it's not in use

You might think the compact designs of today's printers, fax machines, scanners, and other home-office gear provide adequate protection against dust and other household pollutants, but you'd be wrong. The open paper trays found on most inkjets, for instance, offer an easy way in for dirt and even small objects like paper clips and staples. To keep your home-office gear in top working condition, use dust covers to keep them clean between jobs.

Buy a can of compressed air

Nothing beats a can of nonflammable compressed air for blasting dust out of tight spaces inside computers, keyboards, and other home-office and home-entertainment equipment. Buying a can, and maybe a spare, is a wise investment. But remember to employ compressed air effectively; you'll need to use the strawlike plastic wand that comes with it to direct the air precisely. So do

yourself a favor: As soon as you bring home a can of compressed air, attach the plastic wand to the side of the can with masking tape. This is a good habit for all sprays packaged with wands, including those cans of WD-40 and electrical contact cleaner in your workshop.

☞ DON'T
vacuum electronic gear

Never use a regular plug-in vacuum cleaner or hair dryer to clean off computers, printers, monitors, and other home-office equipment. When powered by your home's electrical system, such appliances can generate enough static electricity to cause serious damage to your electronic gear. Use a can of compressed air, a soft brush, or a battery-powered vacuum instead.

Tidy up the home office

All your home-office equipment will work better if it's kept clean and dust-free. Before you start cleaning, however,

check to see that all the devices have been unplugged. (If they're hooked up to a power strip, you can simply disconnect the power strip—after all the devices have been shut off.) First use a can of compressed air to blow off any loose dirt that's been waiting to get inside your gear. You may want to skip over the printer, though; a blast of air there may actually spread dust to the insides, which would be counterproductive. Next lightly dampen a clean cloth with some Fantastik or other household cleaner, or with a solution of equal parts water and white vinegar, and start wiping. Never use a spray bottle to spray the cleaner directly onto the equipment; you don't want to get the wires and circuit boards inside wet. You'll also want to keep a dozen or so cotton balls on hand for getting to the dirt buildups in tight spaces, like the grooves or indentations around power buttons and vents.

Don't leave the plug in

Step Number One whenever you're cleaning or repairing any electrical device is to detach its power cord or remove the plug from the wall socket or power strip. Overlooking this simple step can result in serious injury or electrocution—to say nothing of causing serious damage to the device.

WEAR AN ANTISTATIC WRIST STRAP

When poking around inside your computer case or other electrical gear, wear an antistatic wrist strap. It will keep you grounded at all times so that you can't transfer static electricity to the equipment you are working on. The chances that you are carrying a static electrical charge increase greatly in dry environments (indoors in winter, for example) and when you have carpeting underfoot

or are wearing synthetic fabrics. A small bit of static electricity won't harm you, but it's enough to fry delicate electronic circuitry. You can get an antistatic wrist strap at Radio Shack and other electronic-parts supply stores. The strap has a wire with a clip on it coming off the wrist strap. A good way to ground the wire is to loosen the screw on an electrical receptacle cover and attach the clip to it. If you don't have an antistatic wrist strip, at the very minimum, touch a metal object before you touch the inside of a computer or other equipment.

Use a surge protector

Although especially important if you live in thunderstorm-prone areas, surge protectors are a wise investment for all users of computers and other home-office equipment regardless of locale. Connecting a PC or other equipment to a surge protector will shield it from damage that can occur from excess voltage due to lightning strikes or faulty wiring. Depending on the strength of the surge, potential damage on a computer runs the gamut from losing any unsaved data to a fried motherboard that makes the computer worthless. Other plugged-in equipment can be similarly damaged. The best surge protectors provide jacks for Ethernet, coaxial, and phone lines to guard against potentially damaging fluctuations in power that may also arrive over the data lines running into your computer, fax, or phone.

Don't mistake an ordinary power strip for a surge protector. Unless a power strip has a label that says it contains a built-in surge protector, it is merely a fancy extension cord that may include a switch that turns your gear on and off; it won't offer any protection from power spikes.

Use the ON/OFF switch

Although you may use a surge protector or power strip to accommodate the various electrical plugs from your home-office equipment, you shouldn't use it to turn off your gear. Some products perform essential power-down routines that can be performed only by using the unit's dedicated ON/OFF switch. (Many printers, for example, use a capping mechanism to cover the print heads between uses, a feature that is implemented only when the unit is properly shut down.)

Get rid of scuff marks

How can you get those dark scuff marks off your computer case, fax machine, or other piece of equipment in your home office? Try using a pencil's rubber eraser. It will literally "rub out" most stains. Go ahead and try it!

Replace the legs on a case

Has your desktop computer or other piece of home-office equipment lost its "legs"—those four small rubber feet that invariably fall off from moving your equipment around? Put your gear back on an even footing, and minimize noise and vibrations that can affect the life of the equipment, by cutting small pieces from a bathtub appliqué and applying them to the corners of the case where the feet used to be. You may need to cut a few to the identical size and stack them to attain the right height.

Computers

From shopping to bill-paying to games and e-mail, who would have thought computers would become such an integral part of our lives? Here's how to keep yours working quickly and reliably.

Have broadband? Get a firewall

If you use a DSL or cable modem to connect to the Internet, you have what is known as an always-on connection—that is, your online connection does not shut down when you close your Web browser. To protect your computer and your personal information from hacker and virus attacks, it's essential to use a hardware or software firewall.

• Hardware firewalls are built into network routers and are typically used to share a broadband connection among several PCs in the home; most routers sell for between $50 and $90.

• If you have a single computer in your household with an always-on Internet connection, you may opt for a software firewall. There are many excellent programs selling for less than $50—including Norton Personal Firewall (www.symantec.com), Sygate Personal Firewall Pro (www.sygate.com), and ZoneAlarm Pro (www.zonelabs.com). You'll also find some surprisingly good basic firewall programs

available online for downloading as "freeware" or "shareware." You'll find a good list of these firewall downloads at Tucows (www.tucows.com).

Don't switch off an operating PC

Never use the power switch to turn off your system while it's still running; always let your Windows or Apple operating system shut down your computer. (If you're still using Windows 95 or an even older version of Windows, also wait for the operating system to tell you it's safe before powering down your PC.) Shutting off the power before the operating system shuts down places a strain on the hard drive and can ultimately result in data loss or a hard-drive failure. Of course, your system may occasionally "lock up" or "freeze," which effectively disables the power-down feature. At such times, follow the suggestions below.

What to do when your PC freezes

Although it happens less and less often with newer operating systems, all computers at one

time or another will "freeze" — that is, they just stop working and become completely unresponsive to mouse or keyboard commands, with an unchanging image fixed on the monitor screen. When that happens to you, here's what to do:

• If a program freezes in Windows, try restarting your system by simultaneously pressing the CONTROL + ALT + DELETE keys a couple of times. If this doesn't work, use the RESET button (it's usually a smaller button found alongside the POWER button) or the power switch. The chances of damaging your system's hard drive after a crash are much less, since the hard drive typically stops running once a PC locks up.

• If a program freezes on your Apple, you can usually get things going again by using the "Force Quit" function found under the Apple icon on your tool bar or activated by simultaneously pressing the COMMAND + OPTION + ESCAPE keys. If the whole system is frozen, hold down the POWER button until the system shuts off.

Blackout protection

If you are worried about power outages causing you to lose data, purchase an uninterruptible power supply (UPS). This is a battery backup system that automatically turns on when the power goes off, giving you time to save your work and shut down your equipment. Of course, you don't have to do this if you use a laptop and you recharge its battery regularly, since the laptop will switch automatically to battery power if it loses line power.

 Pro Tip

TRANSCEND THE HARDWARE

Computer technician David Stout of Middletown, New York, travels around helping small businesses keep their computers running smoothly. Stout likes to tell his clients that they need to "transcend the hardware." What he means is that all their data should exist independently of their computers so it will be safe even if the computers are destroyed. For businesses that have only one computer, he recommends backing up onto an external hard drive with more capacity than their computer's on-board hard drive. Starting at less than $100, such drives are cheap insurance, and they can be programmed to automatically back up all your data once every day so that you don't even have to think about it.

Be sure to back up

One of the more painful lessons that most computer users learn is the need to backup important files onto removable media. Sadly, we all too often only see the value of backing up our essential data after it has been lost in a hard drive failure or system crash. The fact that backing up is a simple process that usually takes a minute or two only adds to that pain. You don't need to copy all the files on your system, just the ones you can't afford to lose. Be sure to back up immediately after you save your data—do not put it off for another time!

There are fewer excuses than ever not to copy your files these days, because there's a wealth of removable and easily portable mediums to choose from: recordable and rewriteable CDs and DVDs, removable USB (keychain or flash) drives, even most digital music players can be used to store data files. Although many computer manufacturers are phasing out floppy and Zip disks on new PC systems, you can still use them for your personal backups as well. (Just remember you'll need those drives if you purchase a new system.)

Give PCs an annual blowout

Although "no user-serviceable parts" labels have conditioned us not to poke around inside electronic appliances, this warning doesn't apply to desktop computers. Opening a computer case is usually a simple matter of loosening one or two screws and sliding off a side panel. This is to make it easy to remove damaged parts and upgrade components. But even

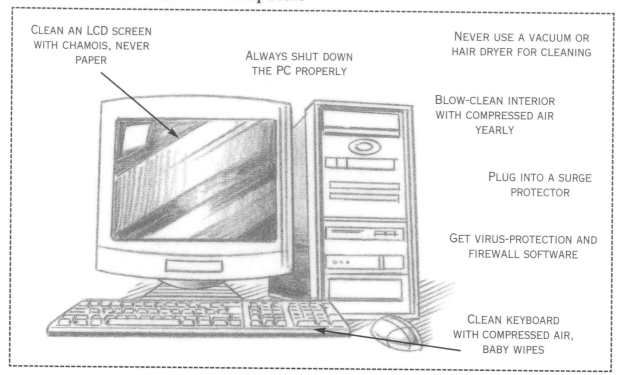

CLEAN AN LCD SCREEN WITH CHAMOIS, NEVER PAPER

ALWAYS SHUT DOWN THE PC PROPERLY

NEVER USE A VACUUM OR HAIR DRYER FOR CLEANING

BLOW-CLEAN INTERIOR WITH COMPRESSED AIR YEARLY

PLUG INTO A SURGE PROTECTOR

GET VIRUS-PROTECTION AND FIREWALL SOFTWARE

CLEAN KEYBOARD WITH COMPRESSED AIR, BABY WIPES

if you have no intention of swapping out your hard drive or adding a video card or more system memory (see tip at right for more about this), you should still open up your computer case at least once a year to clean out the dust and dirt that have accumulated inside—material that might affect your system's performance and shorten the life of your PC.

❶ Disconnect all the cords going into the PC—the power cord, the cords going the monitor, printer, and other peripherals. Then place the unit on some spread-out newspapers, and remove the side panel.

❷ Get a can of nonflammable, compressed air and attach the strawlike plastic wand that comes with the can to the nozzle. Keeping the wand at least 4 inches (10 cm) away from the components, give the interior of the case a thorough going-over to get out all the dust. If you don't have a can of compressed air, you can use a soft, clean paintbrush to remove the dust—be sure to brush gently, however, and be extra careful around the wires.

❸ Replace the side panel, reattach the power cord and cables, and you're good for another year!

Add more memory

One of the simplest and least expensive ways to boost the performance of your PC is to add more memory (commonly called RAM)—especially if you're running Windows XP. In fact, you should have at least 256MB of RAM for Windows XP to run efficiently. You also need more RAM if you use your computer for memory-intensive tasks, such as editing photos, music, or video. The good news is that prices for memory chips have continually dropped over the last few years. The bad news is that there are many different varieties of memory to choose from, and you have to use the right type for your computer. Before you run out to the store, check with your computer's manufacturer to make sure you are buying the right type of memory. If that's not possible, open the side panel on the computer and remove one of the memory cards (known as a DIMM) from your PC by pushing down the locks on either side of the card and then lifting it up in a side-to-side motion. Bring the card to your local computer shop; they should be able to identify it. Also, make sure you have a vacant memory

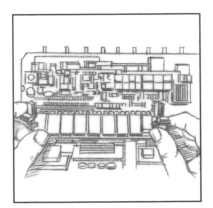

slot on your PC's motherboard to accommodate the additional memory (or replace an existing card in your system by purchasing a new card with at least double the amount of memory on it).

Update your computer's drivers

You've probably never loaded a device driver onto your Windows PC; most new systems come with the drivers preinstalled. Yet these sets of software instructions are vital for keeping all the various components in your PC running smoothly and problem-free. Oftentimes, however, equipment manufacturers regard drivers as works-in-progress and will update the software several times for better operation and to correct mistakes in earlier versions. To keep your PC running at top performance, it's a good idea to check online for any

driver updates every six months or so—particularly for graphics cards, printers, and CD and DVD drives. If your system is still under warranty, the system manufacturer should be able to provide you with any driver updates on its website. If your system warranty's expired, however, you don't have to scour the Internet in search of the latest drivers for your equipment. Simply head over to the Driver Guide (driverguide.com). Membership to the site is free, and it offers a massive, searchable archive of more than 100,000 driver files.

Silence a noisy PC

Has your desktop PC become as noisy as a jet taxiing down a runway? The rise in decibels may be caused by dust and dirt clogging up one or more of the cooling fans inside. To quiet your system—and help it run cooler and more efficiently and last longer—you'll need to venture inside the case and use a can of compressed air to blow away the stuff that's gumming up the works.

❶ Disconnect the computer's power cord and the cords going to the monitor and other peripherals; then remove the case's side panel. (You'll probably want to place the computer on top of some newspapers, as you're likely to be making a mess.)

❷ Look on the back of the case, and locate the cooling fan for the power supply by the vents in the case. For safety, don't open up the power supply, but use the can of compressed air to clean the fan as thoroughly as possible.

❸ Use the compressed air to clean out any other fans used inside the case, including those on top of the central processing unit and the graphics processor; you may need to remove these components to get to the fans. Be sure to clean out any other dust and debris you see inside the case before reattaching the side panel.

Remove a stuck CD or DVD

Although improper placement of a CD or DVD on the motorized tray is the leading cause of stuck disks, crooked labels and flawed disks can also result in jams. If a disk gets trapped inside your CD or DVD drive, don't panic; there's a simple way to get it out without breaking the tray.

❶ Locate the emergency tray release on the front of the drive. It's a small hole that's usually positioned toward the middle of the faceplate.

❷ Straighten a paper clip and gently slide it into the hole as far as it will go. This will trigger the tray's eject mechanism, and you should be able to remove the disk. If this doesn't work, you may need to have the drive professionally serviced or buy a new one.

Patch a broken CD tray button

If you regularly use your CD or DVD drive to run programs, access backup files, listen to music, or watch videos, you should know that all that opening and closing of the drive tray can take a heavy toll on the tray button: Many simply give out over time and become detached or lodged inside the drive. But you don't have to buy a whole new drive if the button goes. Simply rip off about half the cover of a matchbook, and fold it over a few times lengthwise. Then bend it in half and cover it with a small piece of masking tape. Carefully position it over the tray switch (which is housed inside the slot that was previously occupied by the button). Insert the folded matchbook cover so that about 1/8 inch (3 mm) of the cardboard protrudes from the body of the drive. Press it a few times to test the drive; the tray should open and close with each push. Once you've made sure it works, cover over your new "button" with one or two pieces of masking tape. It may last even longer than the original!

Monitors, Keyboards, and Printers

Your computer can't perform its job without these basic input and output accessories, so it's essential to keep them functioning smoothly. In fact, with just a little care, most will outlast the computer they came with.

Get the dirt off a dirty tube display

No one enjoys looking at a dirty monitor. Unfortunately, the electrical charge inside a monitor acts like a magnet for dirt, dust, and, yes, those mysterious fingerprints that seem to appear out of nowhere. Cleaning monitors that employ a cathode-ray tube (CRT)—the type with TV-like picture tubes—is a relatively easy task, though. Just pour or spray a small amount of a general household cleaner (such as Fantastik) onto a clean cloth or paper towel and wipe. Avoid cleaners containing ammonia, however, as they may leave unsightly streaks.

🖝 DON'T
spray cleaner on the screen

Never spray household cleaner directly on the screen of a tube computer monitor. The concentrated cleaner might harm any protective coating on the screen or seep under the casing. Always spray a small amount of the cleaner on a cloth before wiping the screen.

Wipe down an LCD flat-panel screen

Use a soft chamois—never a tissue or paper towel!—to clean the liquid crystal display (LCD) screens on flat-panel computer monitors. This also applies to laptop screens. Use a back-and-forth, *not* a circular, motion. Never apply any cleaning product without first checking with the display or system manufacturer. Commercial cleaners may damage the LCD, void the warranty, or both. If tougher measures are needed (and the owner's manual recommends it), try lightly moistening a lint-free cloth with equal parts rubbing alcohol and water. Use the same back-and-forth motion to clean; then gently wipe with a dry, soft cloth.

Deep-clean a PC keyboard

Periodically disconnecting your computer keyboard and shaking it out is a good way to get rid of the dust and debris that gathers under and between the keys. But that's only half the job. A can of compressed air can also come in quite handy to blow away the bits of food, pet hair, and other flotsam that typically get trapped under the keys. Once you've removed all the loose material, use a baby wipe or lint-free cloth dampened with some alcohol to remove the dirt, dried spills, and unspecified gunk that builds up on the keys themselves.

Save a failing keyboard

Are some of the keys on your computer keyboard responding intermittently or not at all? Before you go out and buy a new one, see if you can salvage it. Start by disconnecting and cleaning the keyboard as described above. If that doesn't do the trick, you can usually pop off the offending keys with a small screwdriver. Clean the little button at the key position with a cotton ball dipped in alcohol, and clean the key itself the same way. Pop the key back in place. The key still doesn't work? Oh well, keyboards are pretty inexpensive these days.

Keep that mouse moving

Is your computer mouse becoming less responsive? It probably just needs a good cleaning. If the mouse has a removable tracking ball, use some alcohol or a 50-50 solution of water and vinegar to clean the accumulated gook and grime from the ball chamber.

❶ Disconnect the mouse from the computer, and remove

the ball from the mouse's underside by twisting off the plastic holder over it.

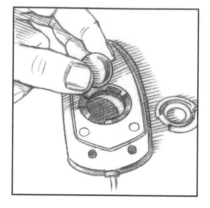

2 Use a cloth dampened with the vinegar-water solution to wipe off the ball and to remove dirt and fingerprints from the mouse itself.

3 Use a moistened cotton ball to clean out the gunk and debris from inside the ball chamber. If you are using the vinegar-water solution, let the chamber dry for a couple of hours before reinserting the ball.

Clean off printer paper rollers

You can minimize paper jams and botched print jobs by occasionally cleaning the paper rollers inside your inkjet or laser printer. Clean plastic rollers with cotton swabs dipped in denatured alcohol. For rubber rollers, use latex paint remover—the Goof Off brand is particularly well suited for this task—that can be purchased from most hardware stores. It

smells awful, but it works wonders when it comes to reviving rubber rollers. Be sure to have plenty of ventilation when you use it. Avoid getting the remover on plastic parts, however. And

be careful not to touch the printing mechanism with your fingers—you can wind up getting ink all over your freshly cleaned rollers!

Before You Call the Repair Guy . . .

You're working at your desktop computer when the spreadsheet on your monitor suddenly starts changing colors. Other times, onscreen images take on a heavy blue or green hue. Even stranger, you discover by accident (or released frustration) that you can often solve the problem by stamping your foot on the floor or banging the desk with your fist. Before you take the monitor to a repair shop or junk it, however, you may want to investigate a bit further.

1 Check the power cord on the back of the display, as well as the data cord connecting the monitor to your computer. Both should be tightly secured; loose connectors could easily cause on-screen abnormalities.

2 If your PC has a dedicated graphics card, it may need to be reseated in the slot. You can usually tell what type of graphics adapter a computer uses by examining the rear panel: If the connector the data cord goes into is mounted vertically amid several aluminum expansion slot covers, the PC is equipped with a graphics card. If it is mounted horizontally, that usually means you have a built-in graphics processor, so there is no card to reseat.

3 If your computer does have a graphics card, disconnect the PC's power cord and remove the case's side panel. Locate the graphics card by following the connection from the port. Remove the card by working it up while tilting it from side to side. Then reinsert it using the same motion in reverse. Push down on the card to make sure it is fully inserted in the slot. Close the case, replace the power cord, and restart your system. The problem should be solved.

4 If that doesn't solve the problem, there's still one more thing you may want to try before you invest in a new display: Connect a different monitor to your system. If the color shift persists with the new monitor, the problem is caused by a faulty graphics card, which will need to be replaced.

 ProTip

CLEAN THE PAPER PATH

A good way to clean the full paper path of your printer or plain-paper fax machine is to use a cleaning sheet, which comes premoistened with a mild cleaning solution and uses a patterned surface to scrub away dirt and residues caused by ink and toner from the rollers and other parts. Use a cleaning sheet about once every three to four months. You can get them at office-supply stores for about $9 per dozen.

You can also make your own cleaning sheet to clean the paper path of a top-feeding inkjet printer. Simply moisten a sheet of copy paper with some Windex or other ammonia-based glass cleaner. Don't saturate the paper, however; it will only fall apart. Push the paper-feed button to cycle the paper through the printer; you can repeat this step with a new sheet of paper if needed. Then run a sheet of dry paper through the printer a few times to absorb any leftover cleaner. Let the printer dry for at least an hour before using.

Keep printer ink flowing

The best way to avoid problems with your inkjet printer is to use it on a regular basis. This keeps ink flowing through the print heads and prevents heads from drying out or getting clogged. On average, experts recommend using your printer at least once a week to print both black text and color patterns.

Avoid back-to-back printer cleaning cycles

If your printer has a print-head cleaning routine, it's a good idea to use it when you see streaky colors or broken text on your printouts. But don't overdo it; uninterrupted cleanings can actually make matters worse by gorging the print heads with ink—which will eventually wind up on the paper rollers or other mechanisms inside your printer. After running a cleaning cycle, print out a nozzle-check pattern to gauge its effectiveness. (You can run the nozzle-check pattern from the dialogue box that comes up when you print or from the software you installed when you first got your printer.) Wait a few minutes; then make two or three prints of a color image. This will force out any air bubbles in the ink left behind after a cleaning cycle.

Don't remove Lexmark or HP printer cartridges

If your inkjet uses a cartridge with a built-in print head, such as models made by Lexmark or Hewlett Packard, never remove the cartridge from your printer except when it's clogged and requires cleaning or you are replacing it. The cartridge's nozzles and internal sponge can dry out in a surprisingly short time. If you need to take the cartridge out of the printer, place it with a slightly moist paper towel inside a sealed plastic bag.

Fix a clogged print head

Occasionally, the print head on a cartridge may get clogged. If the printer's cleaning cycle does not correct the problem, you can usually fix it by removing the cartridge and gently wiping the print head with a soft cloth dipped in water. Don't use facial tissue or alcohol. Other printers, those made by Epson, for example, employ fixed print heads. If the print head gets clogged, don't try to clean it yourself, because you could permanently damage the printer. Instead, pick up a special cleaning cartridge or kit specifically designed for your printer model. They cost less than $15 and can be purchased in office-supply stores or online vendors.

Extend the life of an ink cartridge

If you are like many people and refill your printer's ink cartridge to save the high price of buying a new one, you can get more life out of the cartridge by never letting it run completely dry. Cartridges use resistors to control the current to each outlet jet. When a cartridge runs out of ink, the resistors can overheat and you'll need to buy a new cartridge. Most printers will warn you before a cartridge runs out of ink. As soon as you see the ink is running low, refill or top off your cartridge to prevent it from burning out.

Telephones

Phones need little maintenance beyond keeping them clean. Often when they stop working, there is a simple reason. Here's how to keep connected.

Clean and disinfect a phone

You use it every day—and so do all your family members and, often, visitors to your home. It's therefore essential that you occasionally clean and disinfect the phones around your home. Pour a little isopropyl alcohol onto a soft cloth (never apply the alcohol directly to the phone), and wipe both the receiver and the base. (Try testing the alcohol on an inconspicuous area of the phone first, just to make sure it won't react with the plastic.) Then wipe all parts of the phone with a dry cloth.

If you don't mind trading a little more cost for a little more convenience, you can clean and disinfect your phone with pre-moistened towelettes that are especially made for cleaning phones. You can buy them at many office-supply stores.

Replace a worn cord

Static on the line of your wall or desk phone might not be due to a bad connection, or even the phone. You might have a worn-out or faulty handset cord. Over time, phone cords—especially coiled cords—may get tangled, and the wires inside loosen or become frayed. Replacement cords are inexpensive and are readily available at electronics and department stores, and even many pharmacies.

Hang on to your old phone

Did you just replace your trusty old push-button or perhaps even an ancient rotary-dial phone with a new cordless or digital model? Don't toss that reliable old phone. It could come in quite handy the next time you have a power outage. Those newfangled cordless phones become useless the moment power is cut to their stations. But corded phones draw their power from the phone line and will continue to work during a power outage.

Restore the tone to a phone

For some inexplicable reason, all the phones in your home work except the one in your master bedroom. First check that the phone cord is solidly connected, both in the wall phone jack and in the phone itself. If that doesn't solve the problem, switch the phone with one of the working ones in your home. If you hear a dial tone, you need a new phone. If not, the problem is either in the phone jack or in the line coming into the room. Remove the cover from the jack and make sure that all the wires are properly connected. (If you have only one line, only the red and green wires need to be attached; the yellow and black combination is for a second line.) If all appears to be in order, you may want to try replacing the jack anyway before you call for repair. Also, trace the line coming into the room to make sure that it is not damaged or somehow disconnected.

Put the charge back in a cordless phone

The battery packs inside many cordless phones are notorious for rapidly losing their charge as they get older. Before you head out to the store to buy a new cordless, first check with the manufacturer to see how much a replacement battery will cost—or stop by RadioShack or another local electronics store to see if they carry a compatible pack. Sometimes it's cheaper to replace the battery; sometimes it's cheaper to replace the entire phone.

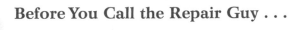

Before You Call the Repair Guy . . .

It's been known to happen: All the phone lines in your house suddenly go dead. Before you pull out the cell phone and call the telephone company, check to see on whose end the problem lies. If the trouble originated at the phone company, it's the company's responsibility to repair at no charge to you. If the problem is on your end of the line, however, you can expect to pay at least $40 per half hour's work for a call by a telephone service person. Here's what to do:

1 Start by locating a small gray box known as the network interface; it's probably on the outside of your house where the phone wire comes in, or it might be in the basement.

2 The network interface box typically has two separate sides. One side is sealed and is strictly for use by the phone company; the other side can be accessed by the consumer. On the consumer side, you should see at least one standard phone jack—the same size and shape as a modular phone jack—with a short cord attached. This is your phone line.

3 Disconnect the cord from the jack and plug in an old push-button phone; if you don't have one on hand, you'll either have to buy one or try to borrow one from a neighbor.

If you don't hear a dial tone when you lift the receiver of the push-button phone, that's good news. It means the problem has occurred outside your home.

If you hear a dial tone, however, the problem is your responsibility. Before you pull out your checkbook, disconnect all of your phones one at a time to see if a faulty unit is the cause of the problem. Also check the phone lines in your house for breaks or something that might be causing a line to short. If you do need to call for help, you may be able to save some money by shopping around for telephone repair other than your service provider. Look for telephone-equipment service and repair in the yellow pages.

Laptops, Cell Phones, and Other Portable Gear

When you start porting around delicate electronic equipment, you greatly increase the chances that it will get damaged—or stolen. Fortunately, you can prevent both from happening with the right precautions.

Don't put off buying extra batteries

The only way to make sure your notebook PC or cell phone will always have adequate power is to purchase a few extra batteries for it. If you hope to stock up on extra batteries, however, the best time to buy them is when you purchase your portable gear or shortly thereafter. Given the rapid turnover rate in most manufacturers' product lines, it may be difficult to find a replacement battery for some models as little as two years after you make your purchase. Also, always make sure you fully charge all of your batteries just before you travel...and don't forget to pack your charger.

Reinforce a carrying case

You can convert a regular shoulder bag or knapsack into a padded carrier for your laptop, PDA, cell phone, or other peripheral gear by cutting pieces of upholstery foam to line the inside of the bag. The foam, available at fabric stores, is easy to cut with scissors. Before you start, though, place the notebook, for example, inside the bag and take note of how much room is left. You want the computer to compress the foam for a snug fit, but you also want to be able to slip the computer in easily.

Protect your laptop from theft

Notebook PCs are easy pickings for most thieves. This is especially true in airports and other public places, where you should always be on your guard. While there are never any guarantees that someone won't try to make off with your laptop, here are several simple steps you can take to protect your notebook and your data.

• *Use a system password.* This will prevent Windows from loading until the proper password is entered. To find out how to create a password for accessing your system, check your User's Manual. (You usually need to hit the DELETE, ESCAPE, or F1 key immediately after powering up, which accesses the start-up menu.) Although password-protecting your system won't deter theft, it will make it harder for a thief to access your system. (And you, too, if you forget the password, so be sure it's a password you can remember.)

• *Have it engraved.* It may sound a bit extravagant, but engraving your name on the front of your laptop may just be enough to deter a thief from swiping it. At the very least, it will certainly make your notebook more difficult to fence.

• *Use removable media.* When it's time to hit the road with your notebook, be sure to copy your essential files to CD-Rs, keychain-type flash drives, or some other form of removable media, and keep them in your pocket or packed in a separate case. That way, you'll still have the information you need if your laptop goes missing. (You may even opt to leave the files off your laptop's hard drive altogether.)

• *Carry it in an inconspicuous bag.* Avoid computer bags emblazoned with a manufacturer's logo on it—they simply call attention to the fact you're carrying a laptop. Instead, carry your notebook in a modest-looking, adequately padded shoulder bag. There are plenty of different types of computer bags to choose from—and many nondescript ones that could easily pass for ordinary briefcases or knapsacks.

• *Encrypt sensitive data.* Using encryption software won't guard your system against theft, but it can protect your sensitive business and personal files—which can often be more valuable than the notebook on which they're stored. Good encryption programs includes PGP (Pretty Good Privacy, available at www.pgp.com and many shareware sites) and the utility included with Windows XP.

• *Register it.* Registering your system's serial number with the manufacturer will not only ensure that your laptop is covered by the manufacturer's warranty, but in the event that it's stolen, the manufacturer will be able to trace the notebook back to you if it comes in for repairs. Also, don't forget to write your notebook's serial number in your user manual and on an index card to be kept with your important records.

Calling all cell phones

Was it really only a few years ago that we got along fine without these little gadgets? Many of today's cell phones do much more than place and receive telephone calls. They include digital still and video cameras, personal digital assistants, and even Internet browsers and e-mail programs. Yet as much as we rely on them, cell phones are among the most fragile electronic items out there, with improper handling and storage

✦ BEST ADVICE ✦ **Cell Phones**

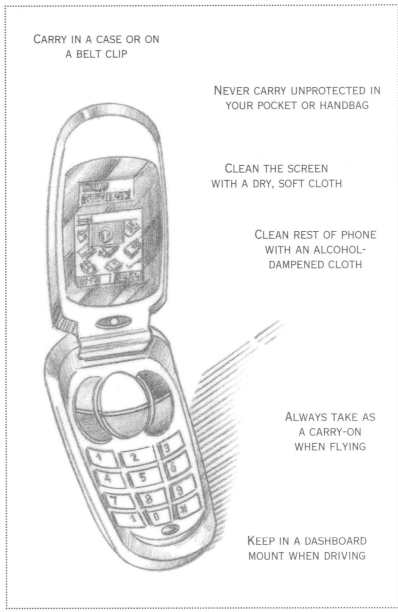

CARRY IN A CASE OR ON A BELT CLIP

NEVER CARRY UNPROTECTED IN YOUR POCKET OR HANDBAG

CLEAN THE SCREEN WITH A DRY, SOFT CLOTH

CLEAN REST OF PHONE WITH AN ALCOHOL-DAMPENED CLOTH

ALWAYS TAKE AS A CARRY-ON WHEN FLYING

KEEP IN A DASHBOARD MOUNT WHEN DRIVING

accounting for most of the damage. With that in mind, here are some ways you can prevent your cell phone from winding up in the repair shop:

• Never leave your home or office without placing your cell phone on a belt clip or inside a protective case. Don't place it unprotected in your pocket or inside a purse. In addition to the risk of impact damage, an unsecured phone is easier for pickpockets to steal.

• When traveling by plane, always include your cell phone

in your carry-on luggage. Packing it with your checked luggage is the best way to find a broken phone when you arrive at your destination.

• If you use your cell phone while driving, be sure to securely mount it where it is easily accessible from the driver's seat. Don't leave it lying on the passenger seat or armrest, because it is likely to fall on the floor or against the door every time you make a sharp turn or sudden stop. Also, don't forget that for safety, many states require you to use a headset if you talk on the phone while driving.

Cleaning your cell phone

Like every other phone, your cell phone will require the occasional cleaning and disinfecting. Never use abrasives or strong chemicals to clean your phone. Instead, wipe it down with a soft cloth dampened with a bit of isopropyl alcohol. Take care not to touch the display screen (LCD or liquid crystal display) with the damp cloth; it can leave streaks or damage any protective coating on the screen. If you need to clean the screen, wipe it with a soft, dry cloth or use any cleaning cloth supplied by the phone's manufacturer.

Patching a cracked cell screen

If you get a small crack on your cell phone's display screen, but it still works fine, try covering the crack with transparent tape or the stronger clear packaging tape. This should prevent the crack from spreading and keep the panel from popping out.

Get a solid case

They say an ounce of prevention is worth a pound of cure, and that is certainly true when it comes to protecting all the valuable data on most PDAs. Given the universally fragile nature of these devices, one of the best ways you can safeguard your investment and your important information is to keep yours housed in a protective carrying case. There are a number of different styles and materials to choose from; most are priced between $15 and $40.

Sync your PDA frequently

If you carry a lot of valuable addresses, phone numbers, appointments, and other important information on your PDA, be sure to sync it with your computer frequently—every day if you input new information all the time.

Shout out to a Samaritan

Although there's no guarantee that someone will return your PDA if you lose it, there is one way that you might help facilitate its safe homecoming. Set a repeating alarm to go off once a week that displays your name, address, and phone number.

Protect a PDA screen

By far, the most important—and most delicate—feature of any PDA is the LCD screen. To maintain its "fresh out of the box" clarity and to ward off scratches and dirt, cover it with a transparent screen protector, which can be purchased in boxes of 12 for as little as $10. If price is no issue, Boxwave's ClearTouch screen protector provides superior visibility and fit. But at $12.95 for one, it's an expensive piece of plastic.

You can also make your own screen protectors by cutting up a sheet of clear vinyl (available from most fabric stores for less than $2 a yard). First clean the PDA screen with a bit of glass cleaner applied to a soft lint-free cloth. Then cut the material to fit your screen, place a few drops of water on the vinyl, and attach it to the PDA. Don't lay the vinyl down all at once, because that tends to trap large pockets of air between the surfaces. Smooth out any air bubbles with a credit card.

Home Electronics

Televisions

Gone are the days of replaceable tubes and rotating on-board channel selector knobs that frequently broke off. Today's TVs need little maintenance, but there are a few important things to do to make sure you keep getting the picture.

Beware of static electricity

Always turn off your tube or plasma TV and make sure the screen has "cooled down" (that is, it doesn't crackle with static electricity) before you clean it—especially if you plan to use a dry cloth. If you don't, the back-and-forth motion you make with the cloth while cleaning the screen can build up static electricity inside the picture tube. This static electricity can cause serious damage to your TV. Also, when you finish cleaning, be sure to discharge any static on your hands by touching a doorknob, a screw, or other grounded, metallic object before you touch the set's controls, to avoid damage.

Dust off a TV screen

No, it's not your imagination. Your television screen and computer monitor are actually dust magnets thanks to their electrical charges. If you have a TV with a conventional CRT (cathode ray tube) or a plasma screen, you can make dusting the screen easier and actually cut down on your regular dustings by recycling some used softener sheets from your clothes dryer. These sheets are designed to reduce static cling. They not only remove the dust, but they keep it from resettling for several days or longer. You can also clean a CRT or plasma-screen model with a clean, lint-free cloth dampened with glass cleaner, denatured alcohol, or rubbing alcohol. Liquid crystal display (LCD) screens, which include not only LCD TVs but projection TVs with digital light processing (DLP) screens, should only be wiped clean with a soft, dry cotton cloth. Check your owner's manual to see what the manufacturer suggests. If your TV came with a cleaning kit, use its cleaner and cloths.

Clean your TV's case

A television's screen may attract the lion's share of household dust, but its enclosure is never far behind. An accumulation of dust is not only unsightly and unhealthy; it can hinder your TV's performance by insulating the electrical connections inside the box. Whether you keep your TV on a freestanding cart or housed in an entertainment unit or other enclosure, don't forget to sweep out those dust bunnies hiding on the back of the set at least once a month. To clean the case of a CRT or plasma screen TV, dampen a soft cloth slightly (pick a fabric that won't unravel to avoid having ragged ends catch in the ventilation slits) with glass cleaner or a general household cleaner—both have relatively quick evaporation. Follow up with a rubdown using a clean, dry cloth.

☞ NEVER
clean a TV case with alcohol

Although water- and ammonia-based cleaners are fine for cleaning a TV case, alcohol-based solutions should never be used. They can react with the plastic and may leave stains and discoloration—especially on dark-colored cases—that will be impossible to remove.

Say "no" to power surges

Plugging your television's power cord into a surge protector is a good way to protect it from potential damage resulting from power surges during electrical storms or from faulty wiring. Using a surge protector with all sensitive electronic devices is essential if you live in an area that's prone to thunderstorms.

Let a wet TV dry

If liquid finds its way to the inside of your TV set—either from an accidental spill or from

✦ BEST ADVICE ✦ **Television Set**

TURN OFF TV AND LET
IT COOL BEFORE CLEANING IT

WIPE THE SCREEN OF A TUBE TV WITH
USED FABRIC SOFTENER SHEET

WIPE THE TV'S PLASTIC CASE
WITH CLOTH DAMPENED WITH
GLASS CLEANER

PLUG INTO A
SURGE PROTECTOR

NEVER WIPE THE
TV CASE WITH SOLUTIONS
CONTAINING ALCOHOL

mischief with a water gun—unplug the set and let it thoroughly dry out for at least a week. If the TV still doesn't work properly when you plug it back in, it may need to be serviced.

Keep speakers away

The CRT picture tube inside your conventional TV—or computer monitor, for that matter—is extremely vulnerable to exterior magnetic forces, especially children's magnet sets and stereo loudspeakers. Placing a magnet too close to a TV screen can produce uneven colors and distorted images that may be difficult to correct. If you need to place loudspeakers near your TV, make sure they are magnetically shielded. Keep all other magnetic items—including headphones, loose magnets and electromagnets (that is, any electrical devices containing motors) as far away as possible from the TVs in your household.

Let it vent

Those vents found on the top, sides, or back of TVs, VCRs, and game-console cases provide needed air circulation that cools the circuits inside and prevents them from overheating. Never place cloth, paper, or other materials over these vents or block them if you put the units into cabinets or other enclosures; it could cause the devices to malfunction and may even ignite a fire.

Never spray your TV

Never spray liquid cleaner directly onto a television screen or onto the case of a TV, VCR, or game console—any moisture that makes its way into the interior of an electronic device can cause the circuit board to short out, which may result in permanent damage. Instead, spray cleaner onto a clean, dry cloth to moisten it slightly, and use the cloth to wipe down the surface of the unit.

Video Cassette Recorders

Take care of that old VCR—you might not be able to buy a new one once DVDs take over. Give the machine a little attention, however, and you'll be watching tapes of your grandkids for years to come.

Run a head-cleaning tape regularly

Use a head-cleaning tape to clean your VCR's video heads after every 100 hours of operation (about every four or five months of average use). More frequent cleaning is recommended if you rent a lot of tapes. Rental tapes usually shed more oxide flakes from being played so many times and they bring in dust they've picked up from the other decks that they've been played on. Cleaning is also required when the picture quality drops off or when you get a blue screen indicating that the heads are dirty.

For regular cleanings, a good-quality *dry* head-cleaning tape will usually be sufficient. Never use a *wet* head-cleaning tape, because the liquid cleaner may not evaporate before another tape is played. That could make things much worse by spreading grime from the tape to the playback heads, resulting in a set of clogged heads. If this happens, you'll need to clean the heads manually or make a trip to the repair shop—or maybe to the mall for a new VCR.

In a pinch, you can even use a new, blank tape to clean your VCR's heads. Simply let the tape play for a couple of hours. The prolonged contact with the tape will usually remove any soft deposits from the heads. This is reported to be effective approximately 70 percent of the time. Discard the tape afterward.

Manually clean neglected heads

If your VCR refuses to play—or if a couple of passes with a commercial video cleaner does not help—you may need to manually clean the video head and tape path inside your VCR. Here's how:

1. Unplug the unit and remove the screws holding the case in place—be sure to keep different-sized screws together to make sure they go back in the right places. Some units may additionally require you to remove the front panel to access the interior.

2. Moisten a few chamois swabs with some denatured or isopropyl alcohol—don't use cotton swabs—you don't want loose fibers floating around inside your VCR. Clean the capstan, rollers, and other components along the tape path. Chamois swabs are sold at audio and electronics stores.

3. Locate the head drum: It's a round, shiny disc with several small notches on the bottom (those notches house the video heads, so be careful when working around them). Dampen a fresh swab with alcohol and then slowly rotate the top of the head drum with your fingertips—don't touch the sides of the drum—and clean the entire circumference once or twice. Never move the swab in a vertical (up-and-down) direction, because you're likely to damage a head if your swab accidentally comes in contact with one. If the swab is dirty when you're done, repeat the process as many times as it takes, using clean swabs, until no dirt is visible.

Don't leave a tape inside

It's not advisable to leave a videocassette in your VCR between viewings. Even if you turn off the VCR's power, the tape is left wound around the heads (it's automatically un-spooled when you insert the videocassette into the VCR). In addition to putting unwanted wear on the VCR's video heads, this can result in stretching or wrinkling the tape, which reduces its longevity and increases the likelihood of it getting jammed in the player later on.

Don't freeze the frame

To get the longest life from your VCR's video heads and videotapes, try to limit pausing the playback—using the so-called "freeze frame" feature—and previewing tapes with the fast-forward or rewind controls. Both of these actions place considerable stress on the videotape, and usually cause oxides to wear off much faster, which, in turn, increases the risk of clogging up your machine's video heads.

Remove trapped objects

Whether it gets there by acci-dent, such as an old label peeling off a videotape, or is a toy, crayon, or food inserted by a curious child, you need to remove foreign objects, because they invariably cause mecha-nism jams and other problems.

Unplug the unit, remove the cover and inspect the inside of the VCR. When removing the object, be careful not to detach any wires or break any leads on the circuit board (use a tweezers if possible). After the object has been removed, clean up debris particles or residue with a soft brush or with denatured alcohol applied to a soft cloth.

Use a tape rewinder

Take some of the wear and tear off your VCR by using a video-tape rewinder. Purchase a two-direction model if you own a lot of tapes, because it's best to store tapes forwarded to the end of the reel. Get a good-quality rewinder. Some cheaper models may wind tapes too fast and damage them.

Before You Call the Repair Guy . . .

Few nonliving things can be as aggravating as a videotape that refuses to be ejected from your VCR—especially when it's a rental tape that should be on its way back to the video store. Before you pack the VCR off to the repair shop, try this:

1. Disconnect the VCR's power cord for about 30 seconds; then plug it back in again. This sends a reset pulse to the unit's onboard-computer chip. If the VCR is locked up, this will usually fix it; such lockups are caused by minor power surges or a buildup of static electricity. (This is actually the first step taken by many repairmen, who may charge you about $100 for the operation if they're successful—and you wouldn't be the wiser.)

2. Other possible causes of a tape not ejecting include a warped cassette case, the metal basket that the cassette fits into being bent, or a foreign object blocking the tape path or jamming a gear. Unplug the VCR and disconnect the cables and take off the top cover (it's usually held on by a few screws along the bottom edge and at the back). Then try to wiggle the cassette free. Using both hands, apply gentle pressure on the cassette, being careful not to bend the metal basket. As you do so, look for places where the cassette might be binding. If the videotape is caught in the transport mechanism, free it first. If you must touch the tape, first put on cotton gloves.

Game Consoles

Here are a few pointers to make sure your game console keeps zapping the bad guys.

Take the heat off your game console

Overheating probably causes more problems—including lock-ups, drive errors, and lack of sound or video—than anything else when it comes to game consoles like Microsoft Xbox and Sony PlayStation. Good ventilation is necessary for these devices to function properly, because they generate considerable warmth. Keep game consoles freestanding, if possible. If you need to place them in a cabinet, make sure there's adequate room behind and above the console and that there's nothing blocking the vents. Bear in mind that lockups can also be caused by dirty or damaged discs and by problems with the DVD drives.

Dealing with "disc error" messages

They're the bane of gamers, and appear all too often when the game console is kept in a dusty environment or in cramped quarters. If you've already established that the problem isn't caused by overheating or a damaged disc, the next most likely cause is dust inside the DVD drive. Although it may be tempting, *do not* try to clean out the dust using a can of compressed air; that will only worsen the problem by driving the dust to the inside of the drive, making it more difficult to clean. Instead, try using a laser-lens cleaner. It looks like an ordinary CD, but has several small brushes on the surface. This will only clean the lens, not the mirror, but often that's all that's needed.

Problems with power

If your game is called off due to a power outage in your game console, it could be a faulty power cord. First, make sure the unit is plugged into the wall and that the cord is connected properly to the rear terminal on the console, then try to turn the power on again.

If the console still won't power up, you may need to replace the cord. (This is a particularly serious issue with older Xbox systems. In 2005, Microsoft announced a recall of power cords for all Xbox consoles made before October 23, 2003 because of potential fire hazards. If your console meets those criteria, you can contact Microsoft about getting a free replacement console at www.microsoft.com and search for "recall." Still no power? The unit may need to be professionally serviced.

ProTip

SPLICE A DAMAGED GAME CONTROLLER CORD

Did Rover just chew through the cord of your Xbox or PlaysStation controller? Before you rush out to buy a new one, try cutting the cable and evenly stripping about 1/4-inch (6 mm) of insulation off each wire. Solder each like-colored wire together, and then cover each repair with a small piece of electrical tape. Use a larger piece of electrical tape to wrap the entire splice tightly. You, uh...your kids should be back in the game in no time.

CD and DVD Players

These amazing players, which use lasers to read those shiny discs, are the first link in the chain that brings you great sound and images. Here's how to keep them working their best.

Clean the player's lens

If your CD or DVD player frequently skips during playback or has difficulty reading discs, it's probably the result of a dirty lens. Most of the time, you'll be able to solve the problem by using a laser-lens cleaning CD, sold by most electronics retailers. Carefully follow the directions on the disc's packaging to get the best results. Cleaning the lens of an optical-disc player about once a year should keep it in good working condition, although more frequent cleanings may be needed, depending on usage and the amount of dust in the environment.

Manually clean a lens

The buildup of dust on a player's lens may be so thick that it prevents the player from "seeing" the cleaning disc when it's inserted. In such cases, you'll need to remove the unit's cover and manually clean the lens. *Note:* Do this only with players that are no longer covered by a warranty. Probing around the interior of any piece of home electronic equipment will usually void the warranty.

If you're cleaning a single-disc player, leave the unit plugged in and press the *Open/Close* button to open the tray. Then unplug the device, remove the housing screws, and slide the cover away from the front panel; you may also have to remove the front panel and tray assembly to access the lens on some units. Once you've located the lens, use a soft brush—the type used for cleaning optics is best—to clear away heavy accumulations of dust. Then, very gently, clean the lens with a piece of camera-lens tissue or a foam swab moistened with lens-cleaning fluid. Don't use eyeglass tissue (it's too coarse) or a cotton swab, which could leave fibers behind.

Replace a worn belt

If your CD or DVD player powers on, but nothing happens when you push the *Open/Close* button, the most probable cause is a broken tray motor belt. Fortunately, replacing the belt isn't all that difficult, and it's much cheaper than buying a new player. (Finding the right-size belt is usually the most challenging part, however, so

it's always best to start your search by contacting the player's manufacturer.) With the unit unplugged, remove the housing screws and take off the cover. Locate the spindle of the tray motor, and use tweezers to remove the broken belt. Don't handle the new belt with your fingers; wear cotton gloves or use a tweezers. Attach the new belt by first placing it on the tray gear and then extending it to the motor spindle.

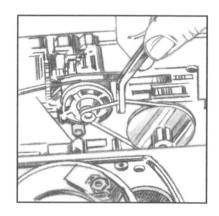

As a player ages, the tray may work, but move erratically. This is an indication that the belt is slipping. You're probably better off replacing the belt in this instance as well. However, cleaning the belt with some rubber revitalizer may buy some time before you order a new one. The revitalizer removes deteriorated rubber from the surface of the belt, leaving a clean, new surface. You can purchase rubber revitalizer at most electronics supply stores.

DVD Players

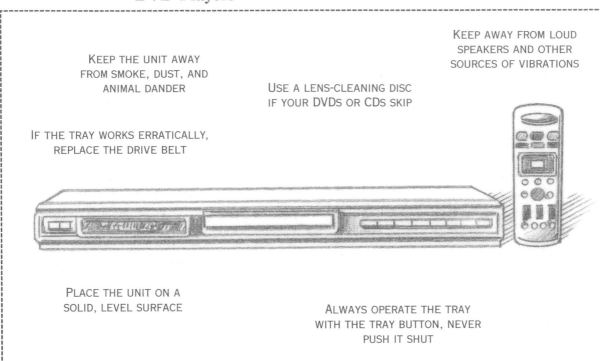

KEEP THE UNIT AWAY
FROM SMOKE, DUST, AND
ANIMAL DANDER

KEEP AWAY FROM LOUD
SPEAKERS AND OTHER
SOURCES OF VIBRATIONS

USE A LENS-CLEANING DISC
IF YOUR DVDS OR CDS SKIP

IF THE TRAY WORKS ERRATICALLY,
REPLACE THE DRIVE BELT

PLACE THE UNIT ON A
SOLID, LEVEL SURFACE

ALWAYS OPERATE THE TRAY
WITH THE TRAY BUTTON, NEVER
PUSH IT SHUT

Steady that CD player

To avoid skips during playback, place your CD or DVD player on a stable surface. Putting a player on a flimsy shelf—or even close to a booming loudspeaker —leaves it vulnerable to jolts and vibrations, which can result in faulty playback and even cause scratched discs. If you occasionally hear subtle vibrations from your player, and moving it is not an option, try placing some inexpensive anti-vibration feet or an isolation mat under it. You can order these products from audio specialty retailers. Check the Yellow Pages. Or do an online search for a retailer in your area.

Use the CD tray button

Always use the tray button to open and close the drawer on your CD or DVD player. Pushing the motorized drawer closed with your hand can strip the plastic gears that move the tray, or it can wear out the drive belt, which can cause disc jams and other malfunctions down the road.

Don't smoke near a CD or DVD player

Smoking isn't only bad for you and others around you; it's harmful to most home electronic devices. The tar and other chemicals contained in cigarette and cigar smoke

adheres to circuit boards and other components and forms a sticky surface. Add some dust, pet dander and other foreign particles, and you have a grimy mess capable of causing over-heating and other problems. To be sure, smoky conditions of any kind—including those of kitchen areas—can damage sensitive electronics. Smoke can be especially hazardous to CD and DVD players. Any dust or dirt that gets on the player's lens will prevent it from properly reading discs, resulting in skips and "unreadable disc" errors. What's worst, smoke residue on the lens is difficult, if not impossible, to remove.

Stereo Components and Other Sound Gear

Whether you treasure your faithful receiver, turntable, tape deck, and speakers or are more likely to take your sound on the road with a portable cassette or MP3 player, you want to keep the music playing as long as possible.

Don't stack stereo components

It may have been all the rage back in college, but stacking your stereo components on top of one another is never a good idea. In addition to the risk of damage caused by the accumulated weight and built-up heat, stacking your equipment leaves it prone to vibrations of all sorts and, of course, accidental toppling. Always house your stereo components on separate shelves in a sturdy rack or cabinet—and be extra careful not to cover the air vents or to crowd the cables against the back of the units.

Drop the dime on dust

Dust is the enemy of all your household possessions and stereo receivers are no exception. Use a soft cloth misted with glass cleaner to regularly clean off the case and front panel (never spray anything directly onto either surface) and always wipe *away* from the air vents to prevent pushing dust into the inner workings. Dust can impede your receiver's performance by coating the circuits and controls. So it's also a good idea to clean out the chassis every few years:

1. Unplug the receiver and disconnect the cables one at a time (use masking tape to label where each one goes).

2. Place the receiver on some spread-out newspaper and remove its cover. Be careful not to touch any of the small, barrel-shaped capacitors when exploring the inside of a receiver; although the unit may be unplugged, these components can still hold a powerful charge.

3. Use a soft, clean paintbrush or artist's brush to agitate the dust, then blow it out with a can of compressed air (avoid using AC-powered vacuums because they can generate a lot of harmful static electricity). If you've been experiencing any erratic behavior from the controls, this would also be a good time to clean off the contacts and potentiometers (see the next tip).

Silence noisy switches and controls

Do you hear static when you turn the volume control or other knobs on your receiver? Or are the receiver's switches behaving erratically or need to be jiggled or tapped to make them cooperate? The likely cause of all of these symptoms is dirt inside the potentiometer. Remove the external knobs and switches to access the potentiometers or levers behind the controls (some have tiny screws in the sides of the knobs), and spray the problematic part with contact cleaner. The cleaner is available in spray cans at most electronic supply stores. To deliver the cleaner more precisely, attach the strawlike extension tube, which comes with the can, to the nozzle and snake it into or near any visible access holes. Turn the control or flip the switch to help the cleaner soak in. Don't overdo it, though; if you can get the cleaner into the potentiometer, you'll only need a little. *Note:* Do not use WD40 or a similar product. In addition to being flammable, such lubricants damage some components.

Improve your FM reception

Is your receiver's inconsistent FM reception driving you up the wall? Relax; chances are that the problem lies not in your receiver, but in the antenna. First, make sure that the antenna is connected properly. If so, try placing it in different locations around the room while the radio is on to see if the reception is better in another area (metal beams can sometimes cause interference or reflections). If that doesn't work, try purchasing a replacement antenna of the same type, or an FM booster antenna. As a last resort, you may want to consider mounting a rooftop radio antenna.

REVIVE A DEAD RECEIVER

Before you junk your lifeless receiver, remove the cover and locate the internal fuse (it may be soldered to the circuit board, so you may need to de-solder it by heating the connection with a soldering iron and pulling the wires apart). Examine the fuse to see if it's blown—this is usually obvious by a burned or blackened appearance. Even if it appears to be intact, you may want to test it with a digital multimeter: On the RX1 scale, it should register 300 ohms or less. If the fuse is blown or fatigued, take it to a Radio Shack franchise or other electronics supply store and get a replacement. Your receiver is likely to spring back to life—as good as new.

Use heavy-gauge cables

Okay, so you have top-shelf stereo equipment and a terrific set of speakers, and yet the sound quality still isn't quite up to snuff. What's the problem? It just might be your speaker wire. If you're using thin, poorly made cable, the sound will suffer. You don't have to go overboard and buy the most expensive speaker wire out there (it can be surprisingly expensive), but you should choose a nice, heavy-gauge cable, preferably from a recognized manufacturer. Also, be sure to keep your speaker leads as short as possible; the added length will only make the signal work that much harder to get to the speaker, and it may pick up extraneous signals. And don't forget to always turn off the power to your stereo receiver or amplifier when adjusting the speaker wires to avoid damaging your system, your speakers, or both.

A cure for speaker cutouts

Does your hi-fi system suffer from wobbly sound? You know, this is when one or both speakers cut in and out for no apparent reason while playing. First check the wire at the speaker terminals. A poorly connected or extremely frayed wire at the terminal will cause it to respond intermittently. You can solve this problem by re-stripping the wire and attaching crimp-on terminals to prevent the wire from slipping off in the future. Or you can place a bit of solder on the

exposed wire tips; melt just enough solder to coat the strands evenly. If the speaker connection isn't the problem, however, the source may be in your amplifier or receiver (some contact cleaner on the volume control may solve the problem). It could also be caused by a defective driver or crossover in the speaker, which may require professional servicing or replacing.

Revive or replace a blown speaker

Nothing can put a damper on your listening experience like a blown speaker, which usually announces itself with loud crackling and greatly diminished output and sound quality. Most speakers are blown by overloads resulting from excessive volume, but they can also be damaged by improper handling and even old age. If you have a high-end speaker system, it's usually best to have it repaired by a professional or the manufacturer. This will ensure that the speaker is properly balanced and tuned (although it may cost almost as much as a new speaker). If you have an inexpensive speaker system, there's no harm in trying to repair the damage yourself, although it may ultimately need to be replaced.

❶ Make sure that the speaker is damaged. You can easily determine this by first swapping the speakers and then the wires to eliminate the possibility that the wires or the receiver is causing the problem. To determine this, first switch the speaker wire connections in the back of the receiver. If the problem changes from one to the other speaker, you know it is the wire or the receiver. Now try disconnecting the wires and swapping them. If the problem changes from one to another speaker again, you are in luck—it's just a faulty wire. Otherwise there's a problem with one of your receiver's channels.

❷ Once you have determined the problem is in the speaker, pry off the cloth grille and examine how the drivers are mounted. Lay the speaker on its back to loosen the fasteners, and lift out the damaged driver and the crossover network that's attached to the speakers. Disconnect the wires by grasping the driver terminal with a pair of needle-nose

pliers, and then use a second pair of small pliers to pull off the wire connectors. If there's a small hole in a paper-type cone, you may be able to fix it by using some rubber cement and a kraft-paper patch (you may need to experiment with a few layers to achieve the right balance). If it's a large hole, try to get a replacement speaker from your local stereo shop or from a Radio Shack franchise or other electronics store for lower-end speakers. The store may even be able to custom-order a match for your system.

Match speakers correctly

When replacing the speakers for your stereo system, make sure they match the wattage and ohm rating (a unit of electrical resistance) of your receiver or amplifier (it may be noted on the back of the unit). If you don't, you're running the risk of damaging your system or your new speakers. Most speakers are rated at 8 ohms, but if you have any doubts about compatibility with your hardware, contact the receiver or amplifier manufacturer.

Replace a broken turntable belt

If you go to play a record on a turntable and the platter doesn't spin, it's probably due to a broken or stretched belt. The only way to tell for sure is to unplug the turntable and remove the dustcover and platter mat. Then, rotate the platter to access the pulley through the access hole and use your finger (wear gloves, if possible, to prevent

True-Life ✦ *Long* Life

Matthew Klein of San Francisco, CA, counts his old Rotel RP-1100Q belt-driven turntable among his most prized possessions. Although it's not a high-end piece of equipment, it has plenty of sentimental value; Klein received it as a gift from his grandmother, who won it in a raffle in1970. Klein didn't use the Rotel until his old, integrated receiver/turntable stopped working in the late 1970s, but he has been using it ever since. "I've changed the turntable belt twice, and replaced the stylus several times, but that's about it," he said. While he doesn't listen to LPs as often as he used to (he has about 1,200 of them), Klein says the turntable still performs flawlessly. "I give it the periodic dusting and treat it gently, but I don't go overboard on the maintenance. I'm hoping it lasts forever, though. I always think of my grandmother whenever I put on an album."

unnecessary handling of sensitive parts) or a screwdriver to lift the belt off the motor pulley. This should allow you to remove the platter.

Some turntable platters are also held in place by a tiny fastener, called a C-clip, on the spindle. If this is the case, insert a small flat-bladed screwdriver between the clip and the spindle, and slowly twist the screwdriver until the clip slides up. Hold one hand over the clip in case it pops off. Lift up the platter and remove the belt. Clean the platter rim and pulley with a chamois swab dipped in denatured alcohol. If the belt is just slightly loose, you may be able to restore it with some rubber revitalizer. If the belt is stretched out or broken, replace it with one that is exactly the same size (required to maintain the proper speed). If the belt appears to be OK, the problem may be caused by a frozen or faulty motor, a dirty idler tire, or a defect in the speed controls. You would probably be better off having these professionally serviced rather than attempting to repair them yourself.

Stop turntable rumble and hum

Rumble is a very low frequency noise introduced to the audio signal by vibrations within the turntable. It's an intermittent, low-pitched booming sound. Don't confuse it with hum,

which is constant, and a higher pitched sound that can be caused by a variety of reasons. All but the most expensive turntables suffer from some amount of rumble. You can minimize it by placing an isolation mat or rubber feet under your turntable and making sure that the turntable isn't too close to your speakers. Keeping the dustcover in the up position while playing a record can also reduce the amount of rumble picked up by the needle.

Pinpointing the cause of hum can be difficult, however; it may be caused by a defective transformer anywhere in your hi-fi system. Often, you can minimize hum, or eliminate it altogether, by using well-made, shielded cables to connect components to the receiver.

Adjust tone arm tracking

To get the best sound quality from your records, you need to have the proper weight, or tracking, on the tone arm. This is essential for keeping the stylus in the grooves of the record, and too little weight is as bad as too much. If you don't have guidelines from the stylus or cartridge manufacturer, you can fine-tune the tracking yourself by slowly adjusting the weighted knob on the back of the tone arm. You'll need to use a record to test the tracking, preferably one that's not a collectible. Start with a light setting that just

allows the tone arm to make contact with the record surface and increase the weight on the arm until you eliminate any skipping or excessive distortion.

Sometimes the tone arm's tracking may be fine, but it will still miscue. The cause is likely to be the needle itself. Either the tip is worn out, broken off, or it might be dislodged from its holder. Lift up the arm and carefully examine the needle. The diamond tip is on the end of a short shaft, which rests in a fork-shaped rubber holder. This shaft can often be easily dislodged from the holder. If that's the case, simply ease it back into place.

☞ DON'T
touch the needle

Never touch the diamond tip of the stylus with your bare fingers. The oils left behind by your hands can decrease its sensitivity and result in accumulations of dust and grime that will reduce its sensitivity. You can also inadvertently dislodge the needle from its holder or even knock off the tip. If you need to clean the stylus, try blowing on it or using a soft, clean brush.

Clean up scratchy, erratic turntable sound

Is your turntable suddenly putting out distorted "fuzzy" sound, or are the left and right

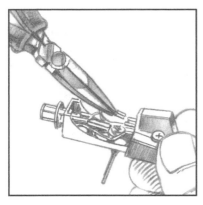

channels fading in and out? Check the wire connectors on the cartridge. Many cartridges use small clip-on connectors that sometimes become loose. Remove the stylus and set it safely aside on a soft cloth, then loosen the locking band around the cartridge head shell, and remove it from the tone arm. Make a wiring diagram of how the wires connect to the cartridge. Gently remove each one, using a pair of tweezers or a pair of needle-nose pliers. Spray a little contact cleaner on a swab and use it to clean off the metal contacts on the cartridge before reattaching the connectors. Once they're attached, make sure they are on tight. Reinsert the needle and reassemble the tone arm.

Don't rush tape playback

Want to avoid mangling or ripping your audiocassettes? It's easy. Just remember to *always* press the *stop* button before pressing the *fast forward* or *rewind* buttons, and before pressing the *play* button when the unit is rewinding or fast-forwarding. Pretty simple, huh? Tape tangles often occur from sudden changes in speed or direction while the tape is moving. The change in motion causes a small tape loop to form, which subsequently gets caught in the pinch roller or some other part of the tape transport mechanism.

Swab the tape deck

If your tape deck, boom box, portable cassette player, or open-reel deck is sounding muddy or losing its highs and lows, the problem is probably caused by particles obstructing the playback heads or tape path. A tape deck records sounds by magnetizing tiny particles of metal oxide that are glued to the tape; those particles are subsequently read by the deck's playback head to recreate the sounds. Over time, the oxide particles come loose from the tape and collect on the tape heads, guides, rollers, and other parts along the tape path. The particles are microscopic with weak magnetic fields, but they can degrade sound quality if allowed to accumulate. It's a good idea to clean the heads and tape transport mechanism in your tape deck after every 10 to 20 hours of use. If you can't access the heads, such as those in a car stereo, a cleaning cassette should get the job done. Typically, you apply the cleaning solution to the chamois brushes on the cassette and "play" the tape for 10 to 20 seconds. On most cassette decks, however, the heads are readily accessible and can be cleaned following this procedure:

1 Open the door and wipe down the heads and all metal parts with a chamois swab dipped in some denatured or isopropyl alcohol.

2 Turn on the deck and hold the swab against each capstan and pinch roller as it turns (commercial rubber cleaner is preferable for cleaning the rubber roller, if you have it on hand).

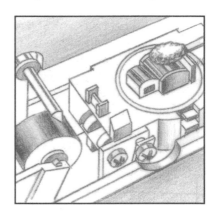

3 Go over the cleaned parts with a clean, dry swab to absorb any leftover liquid.

Demagnetize tape heads

Cleaning the tape path is only half of the equation for getting the best performance from your cassette or open-reel tape deck. The other half is demagnetizing the record and playback heads. With frequent use, the heads and other metal parts may pick up some residual magnetism, which can add noise during recording and even progressively erode the signal on recorded tapes. You don't need to demagnetize the heads as often as you clean them, but you should break out the demagnetizer before cleaning the heads whenever you hear any sound degradation. Many demagnetizers are capable of creating a strong magnetic field, so handle these devices carefully and be sure to keep them away from your other audio equipment and tapes at all times. Here's how to use one:

1. Turn off the tape deck. Switch on the demagnetizer when it's positioned about 2 feet (60 cm) away from the deck. Slowly move it closer—but take care not to let the tip of the demagnetizer touch the heads.

2. Gently move the demagnetizer back and forth over all the metal surfaces along the tape path; avoid any fast or jerky motions (they can actually strengthen the magnetic fields inside the deck). When finished, slowly move the demagnetizer a couple of feet away from the tape deck before turning it off.

Note: Demagnetizing heads is a delicate process. If it's not done right, it can actually do more harm than good. If you need to demagnetize the heads of a cassette deck rather than an open reel deck, you're probably better off using a special battery-operated cassette shell designed strictly for that purpose. You can usually purchase one for under $15 in most electronic-supply stores. Warning: Never use a demagnetizer with the video heads inside a VCR; it will destroy them.

Adjust the azimuth

If your prerecorded tapes start sounding muddy or muffled, it may be time to adjust your tape deck's azimuth alignment. The azimuth is the angle created by the gap of the playback head and the tracks recorded on the tape. It should be precisely 90 degrees. If not, tapes made on other recorders will sound muffled when played back on the misaligned deck—and vice versa. To determine if an adjustment is needed, record some music on your tape deck and then play it back. If the recording sounds good on your deck, but sounds muffled when played on another deck, the azimuth needs to be adjusted. But keep in mind that, after you've adjusted the azimuth, any tapes that you've recorded on the deck prior to making the adjustment may sound muddy. So weigh your options before adjusting.

If you decide to realign the azimuth on your tape player, here's how to do it:

1. Play a prerecorded tape with lots of high notes (classical music or jazz are usually good choices).

2. Locate the azimuth screw—it's typically a spring-loaded or fixed screw below the record/playback head. You may be able to access the screw through a hole on or under the loading door. If there isn't an access hole, you'll need to remove the door (or even the case and front panel).

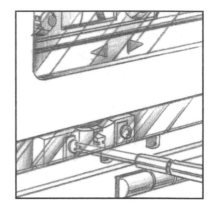

3. While the tape is playing, turn the screw to set the azimuth for the strongest and most-natural sounding treble response. Turn slowly; move the screw in small increments. Leave it set in the best-sounding position. If possible, place a small drop of clear nail polish over the screw to discourage it from moving.

Connect your personal player to your home stereo

Headphones or ear buds are fine for plane rides and the morning train commute, but did you ever consider listening to your MP3 player, personal stereo system, portable CD player, or even your laptop computer through your home stereo? It's really easy to do. All you need is an unoccupied input on your stereo receiver or amplifier and something called a mini-plug-to-RCA adapter cord. This 3- or 6-foot (1- or 2-meter) cord has a small mini-plug on one end, which should fit the headphone jack of your portable device, and a pair of red-and-white RCA plugs on the other. The RCA plugs go into the input on the receiver (do not plug into the phono input, however, unless you want to blow out your speakers).

Before you attach the player, set its volume to about three-quarters and leave it there. Once the player is hooked up, make all volume adjustments on the receiver. This prevents sudden volume spikes that might damage the receiver. Make sure everything is powered off when you connect the player to your stereo, and when you unplug the player from the adapter cord. It's fine to leave the RCA adapter cord attached to the stereo when your portable player is on the road.

Make a personal stereo deck

You can turn your portable music device into a hi-fi system for a bedroom, workspace, or kitchen area. Although special, pricey decks are sold for Apple iPod and Sony MP3 players, all you need to turn your portable player into a small-area stereo is to connect it to an inexpensive two- or three-piece speaker system—the powered type sold for computers at Best Buy and other electronic retailers. These speakers connect to your portable player with the same jack used for a computer, so that you don't need any special cables.

Portable players require care

Just because a music system is portable, it doesn't mean that it's maintenance-free. In fact, just the opposite is true. Most personal and portable music devices (except for MP3 players) receive more steady use than their on-the-shelf counterparts and need more frequent cleaning (for portable cassette decks, follow the directions for cleaning tape decks on page 231). Portable CD players can be dusted off with a can of compressed air, and then cleaned with a chamois swab moistened with denatured alcohol; use a dry swab to wipe off any excess fluid. Be sure to clean units with the power switched off or with batteries removed.

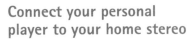

INFO STATION

FINDING REPLACEMENT PARTS

Are you having a hard time finding that replacement part you need to repair your tape deck—or any other piece of electronic gear? You'll find plenty of parts suppliers online. Five of the best are:

> **All Electronics Corporation**
www.allelectronics.com
888-826-5432

> **Electronics Parts Center**
www.electronicsic.com
800-501-9888

> **MCM, an InOne company**
www.mcmelectronics.com
800-543-4330

> **Pacific Coast Parts Distributors**
www.pacparts.com
800-421-5080

Use rechargeable batteries in personal players

When it comes to battery usage, all portable music systems are not created equally. The lack of moving parts in MP3 players, for example, helps many models achieve impressive battery lives—although there is some debate about the lifespan of the permanent, rechargeable batteries in some early model Apple iPods. Other devices, such as portable audiocassette players, can go through their weight in AA or AAA batteries every other month or so. If your music player will accept rechargeable batteries—and most will—pick up some nickel metal hydride (NiMH) rechargeable batteries. These rechargeable batteries, which come in all standard battery sizes, are a vast improvement over the old nickel cadmium (NiCd) types. They're easier to charge, hold their charges for longer periods of time, and provide more power than alkaline batteries. In short, they can save you plenty of money over the long haul. Remember that you will need to buy a small charger unit in which to recharge your batteries—and that's a good idea even if you have a player that is designed to recharge batteries.

Clean battery leads

Keeps the juice flowing in your portable music players by occasionally cleaning oxidation or residue, and especially any corrosion that accumulates on the internal battery contacts, with a few gentle strokes from a pencil's rubber eraser. Don't clean spring contacts, however, they can easily get bent out of shape or break off, and don't let any eraser rubbings fall onto the player's circuitry.

Rescue a soggy portable player

There's nothing like enjoying some tunes at the pool or the beach—that is, until your boom box or personal stereo decides to take a dip in the water, or winds up buried in the sand. In many cases, this will not only bring an abrupt end to the music, but the player as well; salt water can be especially corrosive to small metal parts. There is some emergency first aid you can perform, although the chances of survival vary greatly from player to player and depend on the extent of the water damage.

1. Immediately remove the batteries or disconnect the plug (toss all wet batteries; they will leak if reused).

2. Remove any housing screws and disassemble the player as best as you can. If the unit fell into fresh water, just dry the sections with a hair dryer or gently towel them off and let them air-dry for at least 48 hours before restoring power. If the unit landed in salt water, soak the disassembled pieces in fresh (preferably distilled) water for at least 20 minutes before drying them with the hair blower.

3. Did sand get in there? The procedures above will remove some of it, but you should also thoroughly sweep out any remaining sand with a soft brush.

4. Clean off any belts and other moving parts with some denatured alcohol and add a bit of lubrication.

Cameras and Camcorders

Whether it's a simple point-and-shoot film camera, a full-featured SLR, or the latest digital camera or camcorder, a little care goes a long way toward keeping your camera in good working order.

Clean the lens

Never use anything to wipe off a camera lens other than a special lens-cleaning cloth or tissue; both are available at most photography stores. That means no paper towels, facial tissues, shirts (yes, even your softest cotton t-shirt), or jackets. Also, don't use chemically treated eyeglass cleaning cloths. They may also scratch the lens or harm its protective coating.

Before you wipe the lens with either a lens cloth or tissue, however, it's always best to turn your camera upside down and use a blower bulb or blower brush (found in most photo shops and electronics stores) to remove any dirt, dust or sand from the lens. A combination of blowing and brushing usually

works best, although you should always start by using just the blower, because it can remove loose material without coming into contact with the glass. When using a blower brush, take care to protect the brush from dust and oils (including those on your fingers). If you suspect a brush may be dirty, clean it with rubbing alcohol and let it dry before using it.

👉 DON'T
touch the lens

It's the first law of photography, and it's worth repeating: *Keep your fingers off the lens.* A greasy fingerprint on your camera or camcorder lens can distort photos and videos, and most attempts to clean it off will probably result in scratching the glass.

Wipe off that fingerprint

Okay, so you've *never* touched your camera's lens, but somehow a fingerprint managed to find its way onto it nonetheless. Don't panic, you can remove the fingerprint. Apply a few

drops of photo-lens cleaning fluid or ethanol alcohol onto a lens-cleaning cloth (choose a micro-fiber cloth, if available), and gently wipe the lens with the cloth in a circular motion. Never apply the fluid directly to the lens; it will make it more difficult to clean by spreading any dirt into the edges. High concentrations of cleaner may also damage the len's coating. Be sure to wipe off any remaining cleaner with a dry part of the cloth. Letting cleaner evaporate can leave streaks on the glass.

ProTip

USE A FLASHLIGHT TO INSPECT DETACHABLE LENSES

Want to see exactly how much dirt and dust is on the lens, or perhaps nail down the exact location of that annoying fingerprint? Try shining a high-powered flashlight through the back of your detached lens. If the lens were perfectly clean, the light would travel straight through the lens. Of course, unless you live in a sterile environment, you're likely to see something, and anything that's illuminated by the flashlight doesn't belong there. A few miniscule dust particles won't necessarily interfere with your pictures (if you can count the number of dust specks on your lens, no action is usually necessary). If there are too many to count, however, or if you see smudges or blockages over a discernable area of the lens, you probably should clean it.

KEEP YOUR CAMERA WARM OUTDOORS ON COLD DAYS

PUT SILICA GEL PACKETS IN YOUR CAMERA BAG ON HUMID DAYS

WIPE THE CASE USING ONLY A SOFT, DRY CLOTH

USE A LENS-CLEANING CLOTH AND LIQUID TO REMOVE FINGERPRINTS ON LENS

PUT A LENS CAP ON A NONRETRACTABLE LENS

USE A PADDED CARRYING BAG

ALWAYS PUT YOUR CAMERA IN YOUR CARRY-ON LUGGAGE WHEN FLYING

NEVER LEAVE YOUR CAMERA LOCKED IN THE CAR ON HOT DAYS

USE A BULB BLOWER TO REMOVE LENS DIRT, NEVER TOUCH THE GLASS

Always use a lens cap

As soon as you're finished shooting, put on your camera's lens cap or close the built-in lens cover. On an SLR also do so when changing lenses. This will minimize the lens's exposure to dust and dirt, and could protect it from scratches and impact damage. If you own high-end equipment, you should also consider using lens hoods on all your lenses, as well as an eyecup for your camera's viewfinder (make sure the accessories are made for or compatible with your camera before buying them). Such options can add years of use to your gear by protecting it from skin oils, dust, and airborne pollutants. They can also reduce the amount of extraneous light reaching your eye and your photos. With a lens hood especially, you'll get fewer washed-out looking outdoor shots.

Load film and tapes indoors

Whenever possible, load your film camera or cassette camcorder in an enclosed environment—such as in your home or car—before you head into the great outdoors. This will minimize the chances of getting wind-bourne moisture, dust, dirt, or other foreign particles inside the film or cassette compartment.

Clean cameras with care

A soft, dry cloth is usually all you need to wipe a camera or camcorder body. To remove stains and sticky residues, however, you may need to use a cloth that has been slightly dampened with water (be sure to squeeze out any remaining liquid before wiping your camera). Don't use soap, alcohol, or any harsh chemicals. They can ruin the surface and possibly even damage the viewfinder. Water should never be applied directly to your camera. It may cause some camera parts to rust and can seep into the inside mechanisms where it can cause serious harm.

If you need to clean the film compartment of a camera, fight off the temptation to try to blow out the dust with your mouth; the introduction of any saliva or water vapor will only make the problem worse. Use a blower bulb or blower brush instead. If that doesn't work, bring the camera to a trained specialist for a thorough cleaning. With a camcorder, use a wet-type head-cleaning cassette to clean the tape path (be sure to give the unit adequate time to thoroughly dry before you insert a tape—at least an hour; see the directions that come with the tape). You can also use a few chamois swabs with some denatured or isopropyl alcohol to clean the tape path, but because of a camcorder's many miniaturized components, manual cleaning is only recommended for experienced users. In most cases, you would probably be better off getting the unit professionally serviced.

Keep cameras warm in cold weather

Moisture can do more damage to photographic equipment than almost anything. That's why it's essential to always store a camera or a camcorder in a safe, dry place. Be especially careful when bringing a camera indoors after using it outdoors on a cold day, because condensation can form inside the camera body when the cold camera encounters the warm air. To prevent this, keep your camera warm while you are outdoors by tucking it under your coat or keeping it in an insulated bag when you are not using it.

Coping with condensation

If you notice condensation develop on the outside of your camera or camcorder, odds are good that it's also forming inside the camera. As soon as possible, bring your camera indoors and remove the batteries and film or tape. Then, open the film or cassette compartment and let it air-dry for several hours. If you're in a hurry, you can use a hair dryer on its lowest, coolest setting, using short blasts of air. In the case of ice, however, it's advisable to let the camera air out for at least 24 hours before using it. For a digital camera, follow the same procedure by removing the memory card and letting it air-dry; don't use a hair dryer.

Help cameras beat the heat

Excessive heat is bad news for cameras and film, and it can result in cloudy-looking images or malfunctioning or damaged equipment. If you need to lock your camera inside your car on a hot summer day (or even in an non-air-conditioned environment for a prolonged period of time), wrap the camera and film canisters in a couple of tightly sealed plastic bags and place them in a insulated picnic cooler with a single cooler pack (one of those small, self-contained cold packs used for camping or picnicking). Don't use more than one pack, and don't place the pack directly on top of the bag. You don't want the camera and film to get so cool that condensation forms on them when the hot air hits them.

Pro Tip
DEALING WITH STICKY SITUATIONS

Photographers in humid locales are at an increased risk of seeing condensation develop inside their cameras. When pros head to tropical climes, they keep a few silica gel packets in their camera bag at all times. The silica will usually absorb any moisture in the air before it reaches the camera. Once they're done shooting, many of these professionals also store their gear in airtight containers with several small silica packets inside.

You can follow the pro's example without spending a dime. Simply recycle the silica gel packets that come packed into shoeboxes and with small electrical appliances. Replace the packets every three months or so in areas where the humidity is high year-round, or once a year in temperate climates. Keep your recycled silica packets fresh and ready to use by storing them in a dark, dry location inside your home.

Bag photo gear at the beach

Sand is the enemy of all photographic equipment. Unless you're using a cheap disposable camera, you'll need to take some added precautions to protect your photo gear when taking it surfside. Many manufacturers offer optional sand- and water-proof casing for their cameras and camcorders, with prices running as high as several hundred dollars. But many photo stores and websites (and photo magazine listings) do sell a less expensive covering that is little more than a zip-shut plastic bag with a glass window for the lens.

If you don't have time to get a protective covering, try placing your camera or camcorder inside a transparent plastic bag; sturdy zip-close sandwich and freezer bags tend to work best for this application. Make sure there are no creases or holes in the plastic and try to position the bag so that it fits snugly over the lens (take care that it doesn't rub *against* the lens, however). The chief trade-off of this approach is that shooting behind the plastic is likely to result in some loss of detail and sharpness in your pictures. Experiment with this technique to see if the photographic quality is acceptable to you. Moreover, while the plastic provides considerable protection against water and sand, it's not 100 percent effective—and even a little sand is enough to harm the optical zoom mechanisms on most of today's digital cameras.

Keep photo gear in reinforced cases

You paid plenty for your photo equipment. So it's worth investing a bit more to protect it from the rigors of the road. Select a padded bag or case that can comfortably accommodate your camera, lenses, flash units, memory cards, film, tapes, and other accessories, but avoid bags that are so roomy that your camera or lenses will be jostled. Also, be sure to choose a bag with a strong, cushioned shoulder strap (or purchase the strap separately) for easy and blister-free use on the move.

Carry on cameras when flying

Always include all your photographic gear in your carry-on luggage when traveling by plane. Never put it through as checked baggage. Besides the possibility of it getting lost, few cameras, zoom lenses, or flash units can withstand the rough treatment doled out by baggage handlers or of being crammed into an extremely cold luggage compartment.

Use a high-quality UV filter

If your camera lens is threaded to accept filters, safeguard the lens by keeping an ultraviolet (UV) filter in place. Not only will the filter protect the lens glass from dust, unexpected splashes and skin oils, but it may even spare the lens from damage if it suffers an impact. Since UV filters are designed to be left on lenses indefinitely, it pays to buy a well-made, optical-glass filter (inexpensive ones may result in unwanted reflections or distortions in your photos). Even the best-made UV filters can cause sun-flare on outdoor photos, however. If it's a concern, you can simply remove the filter, take your pictures, and then replace it.

Clean viewfinders regularly

Photographic viewfinders fall into one of three categories: The traditional viewing window found on most 35mm cameras and many digital ones; an eyepiece viewfinder like those on many older camcorders; and a small LCD screen found on digital cameras and on newer camcorders. Both viewing windows and LCD viewfinders are easy to clean. Simply use a soft cloth or chamois to periodically wipe fingerprints and grime from the plastic or glass surface (many camcorders and digital cameras come with a cloth that's especially made for cleaning the LCD screen).

The eyepiece viewfinder can be trickier to clean. It typically consists of two surfaces: A small CRT-type viewfinder and a diopter lens, which is positioned above it to magnify the images on the viewfinder. Often the lens is housed in a tube that slides up and down to let you focus. Once you've detached the tube, you can easily clean any dust or dirt from the viewfinder with a blower brush or even a short blast of canned air. The lens, however, comes into continuous contact with the area around your eyes, which leaves deposits of eyelashes, skin oils, dust, and other contaminants. It should be regularly cleaned with a lens cloth or lens tissue (apply a few drops of lens-cleaning solution, if necessary).

Clean SLR mirrors with caution

The internal mirror is the most delicate component of an SLR camera. In addition to being very fragile, it must be in the proper position to accurately show you through the viewfinder what it is going to record on film. It is therefore essential to never wipe it with a cleaning cloth or tissue. If you absolutely need to remove dust from the mirror, use a handheld blower or a clean, soft camel's-hair brush. Never use canned air as it produces too much force. If your mirror is still dirty after using the brush or blower, take it to a camera specialist to be professionally cleaned.

Camera batteries need care, too

While many 35mm cameras still use photocell batteries, digital cameras typically rely on rechargeable ones. As any digital camera owner quickly discovers, however, caring for and maintaining rechargeable batteries constitutes an entire subset of camera usage. Here then are some essential tips for getting the best performance out of all types of camera batteries:

• Always shut off your camera when you are done taking pictures. Leaving the power switch in the *on* position can quickly drain the batteries and leave you scrambling for the charger or replacements the next time you need to use your camera.

• Don't plan to use your camera or camcorder for a while? Regardless of whether your camera takes photocell or rechargeable batteries, remove them from the camera before you pack it away. Batteries left in cameras over extended periods of time slowly lose their charge, and may even leak after they are depleted—which can result in permanent damage to your camera.

• Most digital cameras can accept rechargeable nickel metal hydride (NiMH) batteries, which are relatively inexpensive and provide a significant increase in the number of pictures per charge over

competing battery types, including alkaline. Moreover, nickel metal hydride batteries don't suffer from the "memory" problems that plagued earlier types of rechargeable batteries and prevented them from fully charging. For maximum performance, recharge NiMH batteries both before and after long-term storage.

• Store batteries in a dry, cool place, preferably in a refrigerator, if you don't intend to use them right away. Never expose batteries to temperatures above 110°F (43°C); that includes leaving them inside a car on a hot summer day. Doing so can result in permanent damage to them.

• Make sure the batteries in your digital camera are adequately charged before you start to download photos to your computer. If your batteries run out during the download process, the camera will automatically shut off and may corrupt the image files. Even better, use a card reader to download the images so that you don't have to use your camera-battery power at all (see the next tip).

Don't download from the camera

Downloading images directly from your camera into your PC eats up a lot of battery power and is a fairly slow and tedious

process. There is a faster, simpler way to download your images: Buy an inexpensive memory card reader that plugs into your PC and use it to download photos rather than downloading them from the camera. Just take your memory card out of the camera and insert it into the reader; usually the software that you use to download the camera will recognize the card and start up. Many computers made in the last few years come with built-in memory card readers.

Buy an adapter kit when traveling overseas

If you're planning a trip overseas, take note: You will need an electrical adapter with a universal plug (or a set of plugs) and voltage adapter to use battery chargers and most other small appliances. The voltage standard in North America is based on 120 volts and a 60Hz frequency. Electrical systems in most other parts of the world, however, are based on 220 volts and 50Hz frequency. Plugs also vary from place to place. Consult your camera manual or contact the manufacturer for specific instructions and equipment recommendations.

Never try to open a digital camera

Unlike most 35mm cameras, which provide easy access to the interior through the film compartment, digital cameras are closed systems. Except for changing lenses on a digital SLR, never try to take the camera apart. You'll run the risk of severely damaging the camera.

Don't leave tapes in camcorders

Take the tape out of your camcorder—that is, assuming it's not a digital camcorder—whenever you've wrapped up shooting. Soon after a cassette is placed in the camcorder, the videotape is automatically wound around the tape drum. A tape left wrapped around the drum can develop creases that may result in problems when you record or play back, and the tape can even become stuck inside the camcorder.

Practice proper label placement on tapes

Labeling your camcorder tapes can make them *much* easier to identify later on, but be careful where you place the labels. Try to use pre-labeled cassettes whenever possible. If you use a stick-on label, position it on the edge opposite the tape cover (which hides the actual tape). Make sure the label is firmly affixed, and that none of the adhesive backing hangs over the edge of the cassette. If the label does hang over, it's a safe bet that the cassette will become jammed inside the camcorder.

Home Interior

table of contents

Walls and Wall Coverings

Here are some tips on protecting, patching, and painting your walls to keep them looking great.

Dust walls regularly

Dusting will make your paint and wall coverings last longer by keeping dirt from building up and grinding in when you wash them. A lamb's-wool duster works well. Or wrap a microfiber dust cloth or clean white cloth around a broom and dust with that—a technique that's especially handy for high spots and the ceiling. Vacuuming with a soft-brush attachment is another effective means to dust your walls, especially when removing cobwebs in corners.

Wash with the right solution

When it's time to wash your walls, you want to clean them thoroughly without harming the paint or wallpaper. Here are two solutions you can mix up yourself that are cheaper and at least as good as anything you can buy:

• Mix 1 cup of borax and 2 tablespoons of dishwashing liquid in 1 gallon (4 liters) of warm water. Borax is sold in the detergent section of the super-market.

• Mix 1 cup of ammonia, 1 teaspoon of dishwashing liquid, and 1 gallon (4 liters) of water.

Wash the walls with a natural sponge, available at hardware or home improvement stores, or use a white cloth.

Wash wall coverings carefully

Most modern wall coverings are treated with vinyl to make them washable. But many other wall coverings are often not washable, including delicate papers, fabrics, and natural organic coverings made from grass, reeds, hemp, cork, or leather. To determine whether a wall covering is washable, wet an inconspicuous area with a solution of a little dishwashing liquid and water. If the paper absorbs water or darkens or if the colors run, it's not wash-able, because the cleaning solution will damage it.

If the wallpaper proves wash-able, clean it just like a painted wall with these precautions:

• Don't flood the surface with water, overwet the seams or edges, or leave water on for more than a minute.

• Don't scrub unless the manu-facturer says that the covering can be scrubbed.

• Don't use harsh, abrasive cleaners on any covering.

Cleaning nonwashable wall coverings

Regular dusting and vacuuming is, of course, the first step in keeping nonwashable wall cov-erings clean. For dirt that can't be dusted or sucked away, use wallpaper dough, which you can find at hardware, home improvement, and paint-and-wallpaper stores. Roll the dough into a ball, and then roll it onto the dirty area. When the dough ball gets dirty, knead the dirty part back into the middle, make a new ball, and continue. You can use fresh, crustless white bread in the same way.

Erase spots with the right stuff

For run-of-the-mill spots on the wall—a kid's dirty hand print, for example—mix baking soda with water to form a paste. Apply it to the spot with a soft cloth, then wipe clean with a damp sponge. To remove small wall smudges, just rub gently with an art-gum eraser. Did the kids go crayon crazy on the walls? Spritz with WD-40, and the crayon will wipe right off. Ink or marker? Use rubbing alcohol. For grease, mineral spirits is the solution.

Wash before repainting

"Hey, why wash a wall before painting?" you ask. "The paint will cover the dirt anyway, right?" That's true. The problem, though, is that the paint may not stay on the wall as long as it should. For a long-lasting job, the paint needs a clean surface to cling to. Trisodium phosphate (TSP) is a strong cleaner that will remove all foreign matter from your walls. It will also make glossy paint dull, which is good before repainting because new paint will adhere better to a dull surface. But it's also the reason you shouldn't use TSP for general wall cleaning. Make sure to wear vinyl gloves when using TSP.

Re-adhere wallpaper

As the years roll by, wallpaper paste can begin to lose its grip, causing the seams to lift. If the paper still looks good, you can fix the problem and prolong the wallpaper's life. All you need is some lap-and-seam adhesive, which you can buy at any wall-paper store. First moisten the seam with warm water, and very carefully lift the softened wallpaper away from the wall. Apply a thin coat of the adhesive, and gently press the paper back into place. Roll the seam with a seam roller, and wipe up any adhesive that squeezes out with a damp sponge.

Spray-starch high-traffic areas

A light coating of spray starch on hallway and stairwell walls will make it easier to clean grime off and prolong the life of your paint job.

Install doorstops

What a drag! The doorknob has punched a hole in the wall. When you finish fixing the hole, prevent it from happening again by installing a doorstop. The most common type is just a brass rod or flexible spring with a wood screw on one end and a rubber tip on the other. You can find variations in oak or maple instead of brass to match your decor. These stops are just screwed into the baseboard where the corner of the door would hit it.

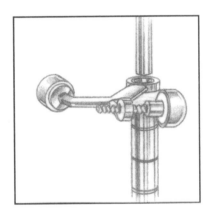

There are also doorstops that screw to the floor instead of the wall. Or you can use a hinge-pin doorstop that attaches to a hinge; it has a small adjustable arm.

Protect outside corners

You've seen them in many older homes—particularly Victorian homes with ornate moldings. They are wooden corner beads, often embellished with turnings, and they were designed to protect the delicate corners of

plaster walls. Modern drywall is installed with metal corner bead that offers some protection, but corner bead can still be bent from impact and paint can chip off it. Wooden corner bead is still available at home centers and lumberyards. It can be applied over plaster or drywall. For a slicker, more modern look, you can protect corners with transparent plastic corner bead.

Use screws to hang pictures on plaster

Banging nails into plaster can crack it or cause it to come loose from the lath. Use short drywall screws instead to hang your pictures. Or if you do use a small nail, protect the wall with an X of masking tape.

Repair bulging plaster

Sometimes, most often on ceilings, plaster comes loose from the lath. If plaster is bulging or sagging but is not crumbling, you can usually reattach it to the wood lath with a gadget called a plaster washer. Attach

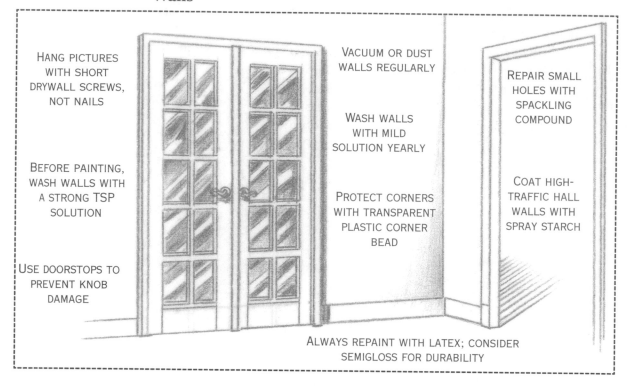

HANG PICTURES WITH SHORT DRYWALL SCREWS, NOT NAILS

BEFORE PAINTING, WASH WALLS WITH A STRONG TSP SOLUTION

USE DOORSTOPS TO PREVENT KNOB DAMAGE

VACUUM OR DUST WALLS REGULARLY

WASH WALLS WITH MILD SOLUTION YEARLY

PROTECT CORNERS WITH TRANSPARENT PLASTIC CORNER BEAD

REPAIR SMALL HOLES WITH SPACKLING COMPOUND

COAT HIGH-TRAFFIC HALL WALLS WITH SPRAY STARCH

ALWAYS REPAINT WITH LATEX; CONSIDER SEMIGLOSS FOR DURABILITY

a washer with a drywall screw about every 4 inches (10 cm) in all directions starting at the outer edge of the loose area and working toward the center. Once the plaster is firmly reattached, hide the plaster washers with several coats of drywall compound. Then sand and paint.

Choose the right patching materials

There are lots of joint compounds and other wall-repair materials out there. For a lasting repair, it's important to use the right stuff. Here's a rundown of what to use when:

• Fill small holes in drywall or plaster with spackling compound. Drywall joint compound, designed for finishing new drywall joints, also works fine, but it dries more slowly and shrinks more, so you may need more coats than with spackling compound. Also, joint compound comes only in 1-gallon (3.8-liter) and 5-gallon (18.9-liter) buckets, so it is not a good option unless you have some around already.

• Get a drywall repair kit if the hole is bigger than about 1 inch (25 mm) across. A typical kit contains a piece of drywall you

can cut to fit the hole, powdered patching compound, a combination tool for cutting the drywall and spreading the compound, drywall screws, a mixing tray and stick, and a sanding pad. The compound is quick-setting and easy to sand.

• Repair hairline cracks in plaster by embedding fiberglass mesh joint tape in a layer of drywall compound and then going over it with a second layer. Be aware, though, that plaster cracks are caused by movement such as the house settling. Unless you correct the cause of the movement, the crack will return.

• For large holes in plaster walls, spritz the lath with water so it doesn't suck all the moisture out of your patching compound. Then fill the hole with a premixed gypsum-base coat plaster with perlite—it comes in bags that you mix with water. Structolite and Gypsolite are two common brands that you'll find at lumberyards and home centers. Apply a couple of coats, filling the hole partway with the first and letting it dry before adding the second. Then give it a third finish coat; this can be joint compound, but if you really want to match the texture of plaster, mix up some plaster of paris.

Buying long-lasting paint

Color is only one of the choices you have to make when choosing paint. When considering durability, you have a few other choices that are more important.

• When it comes to paint, more money usually does buy you more durability. A top-quality can of paint will contain a higher percentage of titanium oxide—the solid pigment. As a result, a can of top-quality paint will actually weigh more than cheaper paint. Besides, cheap paint may not really be so cheap, since it takes more paint and more work to get good coverage.

• Once upon a time there was only oil-base paint. Then latex paint came on the scene. Latex can be cleaned up with water, but many pros stuck with oil-base because it was more durable and flowed on better. Today oil-base paints use a synthetic oil called alkyd and still require paint thinner to clean up. Natural latex also has been replaced with synthetic materials, usually acrylic, though most paint cans still say latex on them. Today these latex paints are so durable that there is no reason to use alkyd paints indoors. (For information about outdoor application, see page 264.)

• The level of gloss you choose can be very important to durability. Most paint cans are labeled high-gloss, semigloss, eggshell, satin, low sheen, or flat. Recognize that these are general labels—the semigloss from one manufacturer might be similar to the gloss of another. Glossier paints resist marks better, are easier to clean, and usually last longer, but they make any dents or other unevenness in the wall more apparent. Touch-ups also blend in better with less gloss.

• If you are painting an area that will be submitted to high humidity, such as a bathroom, have the paint store add mildewcide to the paint.

Yes, you can patch wallpaper

That is, as long as you have a small leftover piece of the same paper. If you don't, your wallpaper dealer might still have the pattern. Just follow these two steps:

❶ Put the scrap piece over the hole and line up the pattern. Then lightly tape the scrap in place. Use a utility knife and straightedge to cut out a rectangular patch while cutting through the wallpaper below at the same time. Now you have a rectangular hole and a patch that fits it exactly.

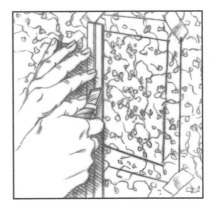

❷ Apply wallpaper paste to the patch, and place the patch over the hole to transfer paste to the wall. When the paste gets tacky, smooth the patch in place with a wet sponge.

Floors

Want your floors to last? The key is to keep them clean. This is particularly true for wood floors, but it applies to other types as well.

Keep out grit

The Asian tradition of taking off your shoes when entering the house is a great way to preserve wooden and vinyl floors. Like sandpaper, the grit on your shoes abrades the floor finish, shortening its life. If you are not up to going shoeless, clean the floor frequently to prevent grit from getting ground in.

Choose a good doormat

Any dirt you can keep outside is dirt you won't have to clean up, so doormats are the first line of defense in extending the life of your floors. The traditional welcome mat is helpful if people remember to rub their feet on it. Better is a "walk-off" mat—an extended mat that is at least long enough so that both feet rub across it. Mats for outside your door are usually made of rubber- or vinyl-backed synthetic turf. The indoor variety is available in several dark, dirt-defying colors to coordinate with your décor.

Vacuum and mop—a lot!

No matter what your floor is made of, frequent vacuuming or sweeping will prevent dirt from grinding in. Wipe up any spills immediately, and clean the floor with a damp mop at least once a week. Use plain water, and change the water when it gets cloudy.

Make your own floor cleaner

When floors get too dirty for damp-mopping with plain water, you can use a commercial cleaner designed for floors, such as Murphy Oil Soap. Or literally brew your own cleaner by seeping 2 teabags in 1 quart (1 liter) of hot water. Another option is to mix 1/2 cup of cider vinegar in 1 gallon (4 liters) of warm water. Whatever cleaner you choose, don't slop water all over the floor. Instead, dip a soft cloth or sponge in the solution, wring it out, and wipe the floor. Buff with a soft, dry cloth.

☞ DON'T
use caustic cleaners on marble

Acids (such as vinegar) will etch marble, and strong alkaline solutions (such as washing soda or trisodium phosphate) will break down the surface and leave it rough.

Bring brightness back to marble

To clean marble, just add a couple of squirts of mild dishwashing liquid soap to a bucket, and fill with warm water. Frequent washing over time will actually brighten a marble floor as the floor absorbs oils from the soap. Don't use wax on marble.

Clean stone floors with sawdust

It's low-tech and effective: Sprinkle damp sawdust over your stone floor, scrub with a stiff brush, and then sweep up the sawdust with a broom and dustpan. Follow up with a good vacuumming.

Keeping ceramic-tile floor clean

Ceramic tile usually needs nothing more than a quick pass with a damp mop to clean it. Indeed, cleaning ceramic tile would be a breeze if tile were all you had to clean. It's that pesky grout between the tiles that's the problem. One way to prolong the life of grout is to seal it (see "Seal the grout" on page 254). When damp-mopping isn't enough, mix one of these cleaning solutions:

• 1 capful of rubbing alcohol in 1 gallon (4 liters) of water

• 1 teaspoon of borax and 2 tablespoons of ammonia in 1 gallon (4 liters) of water.

Keep vinyl flooring vital

When it comes to vinyl flooring, the key to longevity is to use the mildest cleaning method possible. Sweep or vacuum frequently so that dirt doesn't get a chance to grind in. Clean up spills right away. Use a warm, damp mop for dirt that you can't sweep or vacuum away. If dirt still remains, try mixing 1 cup of vinegar into 1 gallon (4 liters) of water. Dirt too stubborn for vinegar? Then try 2 tablespoons of borax in 1 gallon (4 liters) of water. In either case, apply a small amount with your mop; then rinse thoroughly by mopping with plain water.

Know your finish before rejuvenating wood floors

Floors installed or last refinished before the mid-1960s are most likely coated with varnish or shellac. These finishes were often waxed and require different care than a modern polyurethane finish, which should never be waxed. You can tell one finish from the other by scratching the surface with a coin in an inconspicuous place. If the finish flakes, it is probably shellac or varnish. If the finish doesn't flake, it is probably polyurethane. To check for wax, put a couple of drops of water on the floor. Wait 10 minutes. If white spots appear under the water, the floor has been waxed.

◆ BEST ADVICE ◆ **Hardwood Floors**

INSTALL A WALK-OFF MAT TO CLEAN SHOES ENTERING ROOM

VACUUM FREQUENTLY, DAMP-MOP WEEKLY

USE WRUNG-OUT SPONGE MOP WHEN MOPPING DIRT AWAY

SHINE POLYURETHANED FLOORS ONLY WITH NON-WAX FURNITURE OIL

FIX SMALL NICKS AND SCRATCHES WITH CLEAR NAIL POLISH

USE WAX ONLY ON OLDER VARNISHED OR SHELLACKED FLOORS

REPAIR DEEPER GOUGES WITH FURNITURE MARKER AND POLYURETHANE

If the floor is varnished or shellacked, give it new luster with a solvent-based liquid wax. The solvent will dissolve and remove most of the old wax, along with the dirt embedded with it. You'll be left with a thin protective coat of new wax. Polyurethane is tough stuff and doesn't need additional protection. But you can restore the shine by rubbing with a cloth containing a little furniture oil. Read the label to make sure that the furniture oil doesn't contain any wax. Be sure to use just a little—too much will attract dirt and can turn your floor into a skating rink.

Nail polish can fix floor nicks

No matter how careful you are, small nicks and scratches on your wood floor are an inevitable fact of life. As long as the damage has not penetrated through the finish, you can make these small blemishes disappear by filling them with clear nail polish.

Make deeper gouges disappear

If the scratch is lighter in color than the floor, it means it went through the finish and any stain to expose bare wood. In this case, dab the gouge with a furniture touch-up marker (from a home center) in a color that matches your floor. Stain from a can will work too, although it is less convenient. Cover the repair with polyurethane, using two or more layers to build it up flush with the existing finish.

Minimize flooring gaps

It's inevitable. Wood will expand across its width when it's humid and shrink when it's arid. When it comes to real solid-wood flooring, this can

---

Buy to Keep: Wood Floors

If you like the look of wood floors, there are three ways to get it. Here are pros and cons for each:

Solid wood	This traditional flooring—usually 3 /4 inches (19 mm) thick—is the most durable and beautiful choice, but it is also the most expensive to buy and to install. Installation is best left to pros. Solid-wood flooring often is sanded and finished in place, but it is also available in prefinished planks. (Prefinished planks meet with a V-groove that can collect dirt.) When the finish wears off, you can strip it off and refinish the floor. Wide flooring boards evoke old-fashioned charm but will shrink in dry weather, causing dirt-grabbing cracks. Solid-wood parquet won't shrink, because it is made of small strips—usually in 12-inch (30-cm) squares. But parquet is extremely difficult to sand for refinishing because the strips change direction every few inches.
Engineered wood	This is essentially plywood. It consists of three or five thin plies of wood glued together in a crisscross pattern that makes the product strong and more stable than solid wood—you won't have to worry about gaps forming. The top layer is hardwood, so the look is nearly indistinguishable from solid-wood flooring. The drawback—you usually can't refinish the floor, because you'd quickly sand through the top layer.
Laminate	This manufactured flooring consists of a thin layer of plastic laminate—the same stuff countertops are made of—bonded to a composite material. The surface feels like a countertop. The wood look comes from an image printed onto the top layer, which is then treated with a plastic-wear layer. Laminate flooring is very tough—it will still look good when it would have been time to refinish a solid-wood floor. That's fortunate, since laminate can't be refinished. Laminate is easy to install—the planks interlock, some without glue, and they are not attached to the subfloor. Laminate flooring is actually flatter than solid wood, which can make it look more artificial, especially in large areas.

---

cause gaps between boards in dry weather when the wood shrinks. There is no way to completely prevent gaps in solid-wood flooring, but there are a few things you can do to keep gaps tiny and unnoticeable when you install new solid flooring:

• Use narrow flooring boards. Each board will shrink proportionally less, so the narrower the boards, the narrower the gaps.

• Bring the flooring into the room a few days before it will be installed. If it is wrapped, unwrap it. This will let the flooring acclimate to the humidity level in the room.

• Don't install flooring on humid days.

Paint old linoleum

Pulling up old linoleum that's glued down is a real drag. Maybe you don't have to. If the linoleum is old and dingy but not worn through, you can give it a new life with paint. Keep in mind, we are talking about real old-fashioned linoleum here—paint won't stick to vinyl-sheet flooring.

First put on a dust mask, and lightly abrade the surface using 80-grit sandpaper in a rotary sander. Then paint the floor with enamel floor paint. (Don't do this if there is any possibility that the linoleum contains asbestos. Abraded asbestos will

become an airborne health hazard.) You can use a brush or a roller depending on the texture you want. Get creative: Mask off squares or a border. Use stencils or create textures or patterns with a sponge or rag. Finish up with a couple of coats of polyurethane, and your "new" floor will last for years.

Reuse those vinyl scraps

Cover plywood utility shelves with leftover scraps of vinyl flooring to create a durable, easy-to-clean surface. Attach the flooring to the plywood with leftover flooring adhesive.

Seal hard floors

Tile and stone floors are porous. To prevent dirt from grinding into the pores and permanently discoloring the floor, be sure to seal it when first installed. Recoat with sealant occasionally, up to every year for high-traffic area like mudrooms.

Patch a vinyl floor

Got a rip or an indelible stain in your vinyl-sheet flooring? No problem, you can easily patch it. No extra flooring put aside? Steal a piece from inside a closet or under the fridge. Here's how to make the repair.

❶ Place the patch piece over the damage, line up the pattern, and tape it in place, as shown for wallpaper on page 245. Use a straight-

edge and utility knife to cut a rectangle through the patch and the damaged area simultaneously. Pull up the damaged piece, using a hair dryer to soften the adhesive, if necessary. Scrape up the old adhesive.

❷ Test-fit the patch. Put new adhesive on the subfloor with a floor-adhesive spreader, wait the length of time recommended on the can, and then put the patch in place. Press it down with a rolling pin, and use a rag, water, and detergent to clean up any adhesive that squeezes out. Weight down the patch for a day while the adhesive cures.

Tighten loose treads

Want to renew those creaky old stairs? It's usually easy to tighten them up, but the method you use depends on the stair construction:

• If the underside of treads and risers are accessible, take a look underneath. You may notice that the treads are fit into grooves in the stringers. Often in this design, forward-thinking carpenters, knowing that threads would shrink in time, make the grooves—called dadoes—a little large and then secure the treads with shims. If you see shims under each tread, just give them a tap with a hammer to tighten up the treads.

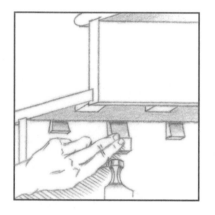

• If there are no shims in place, have someone walk on the stairs while you are underneath listening for squeaks. When you identify a loose tread, drive a shim into the stringer dado along the bottom of the tread. It can also help to drive a wedge between the tread and riser if that joint is loose. Put a little glue on these wedges. (Don't glue wedges into the stringer dadoes in case you need to tighten the joint again.)

• If your stairs are an open stringer design in which the treads sit on big notches cut into the stringer, drive trim-head screws through the tread into the stringer. Conceal the screw heads with wood putty. You can also use trim-head screws through the top if the dadoed stringers are inaccessible from the bottom. In this case, start the screws right at the joint between the tread and the stringer. Angle the screws, so they'll bite into the stringer.

Fix a wobbly newel post

There's no single solution for wobbly old newel posts, because posts were installed in a variety of ways. Here are the three most common installations and how to resecure them.

• In newer homes, most posts are bolted to the framework or to the short shirt wall that follows the angle of the stairs. In either case, the original screws were concealed behind wood plugs and are almost impossible to get to for tightening. You'll have to install additional lag screws from each side to firm up the post.

• If the post goes into the floor and is attached to a joist, you can add blocking, shims, or additional screws from below. This procedure may require you to remove a section of a finished basement's ceiling.

• If the post was secured to the floor with a metal plate, the only way to steady it is to install larger screws in the stripped-out holes. First cut back the carpet or remove the tile and remove the newel post. Next install bigger screws, and then reattach the post to the floor.

Fix a wobbly baluster

If a baluster is coming loose from the handrail, you can fix it in two quick steps:

1 Cut a wedge to the width of the baluster. Put some glue on it, and wedge it in the space between the baluster and handrail.

2 Predrill a countersunk hole for a wood screw angled up through the baluster into the handrail. Finally, cut off the excess wedge flush with the baluster using a trim saw.

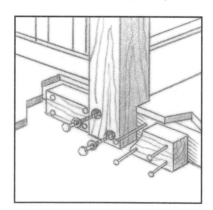

Carpet

Ahh, the luxurious feel of carpet underfoot. Follow the advice you'll find here, and your carpet will last for many years.

Keep your socks on

Sure, it feels great to pad around barefoot on carpet. Trouble is, oil from your bare feet rubs off onto the fibers. Dirt sticks to the oil, shortening the life of your carpet. So while it is kind to your floors to take your shoes off when you enter the house, leave your socks on to protect the carpet.

Don't vacuum antique Oriental rugs

The strong suction and rotary brush on your vacuum will shorten the life of valuable Oriental rugs. Instead of vacuuming, send these rugs out to be professionally cleaned. Look under the listing for carpet and rug cleaners in the yellow pages. Make sure they know how to handle Oriental rugs.

Vacuum—whether it needs it or not!

A good vacuum will remove 85 percent of the dirt in a carpet, so frequent vacuuming—perhaps weekly depending on traffic—is the best way to make your carpet last. It's important to have the right vacuum—the best is an upright designed for carpeting, but a motorized attachment for a canister-type vacuum is almost as good and has the advantage of being able to reach farther under furniture. Both types have a rotary brush, designed to loosen the dirt in carpet. Keep in mind that as the bag fills up, the suction power reduces, so change your bags when they are about half full.

Steam-clean for new life

Even with regular vacuuming, dirt eventually works its way deep into the pile where the vacuum can't reach. To really renew your carpet, steam-clean it every 6 to 18 months. You can rent a steam cleaner and do the job yourself, but for the best results, hire a professional carpet-cleaning company. The pros will swoop in with a big truck, get the job done, and get out of your way. The big truck contains a heating unit, which keeps the water very hot throughout the cleaning process, and a very powerful vacuum, which will suck up all the water that the cleaner puts down.

Change traffic patterns

Changing the traffic pattern on the carpet will distribute the wear, making the carpet last longer. If it is a movable rug, rotate its position in the room.

For wall-to-wall carpeting, move your furniture to change the traffic pattern.

Avoid direct sunlight

To keep carpet from fading, protect it from direct sunlight by closing drapes or blinds during peak sunlight hours.

Don't skimp on the padding

Besides making carpet feel more luxurious, top-quality padding will make your carpet last longer.

Steam out furniture footprints

Are you left with furniture footprints in your carpet after rearranging the room? Use a steam iron to bring the crushed fibers back to their original shape. Just set the iron on steam, and hold it about 1/4 inch (6 mm) above the carpet. Use a screwdriver to help flush out the fibers.

DON'T
drag furniture over carpet

Be sure to pick up the furniture the next time you rearrange a carpeted room. Dragging furniture over carpet causes unnecessary wear. Moreover, if the carpet is nylon, the friction caused by dragging can actually melt the fibers.

Repair loose or missing yarn

Level-loop carpet consists of long lengths of yarn installed in loops. If something—say, a furniture leg—snags and pulls a loop, you can wind up with a couple of inches of loose yarn. Fortunately, this is easy to fix. If the yarn is still attached to the carpet, all you need are a nail set (a tool you can get at a hardware store) and some carpet-seam adhesive. First protect the area around the run with masking tape; then put a heavy bead of adhesive into the run. Use the nail set to press each "scab" (where the original adhesive clings to the yarn) down into the carpet backing until each new loop is at the right height.

If the loose yarn is missing, count the number of carpet loops it will take to fill the run. Then pull a piece of yarn from the edge of a scrap piece of carpet, count the curls in the loose yarn, and cut it to provide the right amount of yarn to fill the run.

Snip off burns

Singed carpet is no tragedy. Just snip off the charred tips of the tufts with a pair of sharp scissors. If the carpet is plush, it helps to feather out the area by lightly tapering the nap in a circle a little wider than the damaged area.

The cookie-cutter patch

If a small section of carpet is so badly stained that you can't clean it or is burned too deeply to snip off the damage, you can still fix it easily enough, thanks to spot-patch repair kits. The kits come with a circular tool with a center pivot and a blade attached to the outside. You just rotate the tool to cut out the damaged area; then do the same to cut a patch from spare carpet. Put down double-stick tape that comes with the kit, plug in the patch, and that's it! If you don't have spare carpet, you can steal a patch from a hidden area. The inside of a closet is usually a good choice.

Sew up seam tears

Most carpet tears happen along seams where two pieces were originally glued or sewn together. To fix a tear along a seam, thread some heavy fishing line through a curved upholstery needle. Stitch the tear together, pushing the needle through about 1/2 inch (13 mm) from the edges of the tear and spacing the stitches

about 3/4 inch (19 mm) apart. The top of the stitches should be square to the tear—the underside diagonal—for the least visibility. If you are rejoining a seam that was once glued together, you'll find the old glue tape tough to work the needle through. Use needle-nose pliers to help push the needle.

Buying a long-lasting carpet

There are two types of carpet pile—cut and loop. Cut pile is plusher, but you'll get more years of service from loop carpet, especially in high-traffic areas. Another key to long carpet life is to choose the right material for the situation. Here, according to the Carpet and Rug Institute, are your choices and their characteristics:

• More than two-thirds of the carpet used in North America is made of nylon. It's no wonder, since nylon is wear-resistant, resilient, and withstands the weight and movement of furniture while

REMOVING STAINS ON CARPETS

Modern carpeting is designed to resist stains, so you can usually remove them if you use the right method. Refer to this chart, and remember—the sooner you get to a stain, the easier it will be to remove.

Cause	Solution
Animal urine	Immediately blot up excess with paper towels; soak with club soda; blot again; scrub with diluted carpet shampoo.
Blood	If fresh, blot up with cold water (not hot). If dried, cover with equal parts cold water and meat tenderizer. Let set for 30 minutes. Sponge off with cold water.
Chewing gum	Freeze with ice cubes in a plastic bag; then scrape off with a butter knife and blot with trichloroethylene (dry-cleaning fluid, available at drug and hardware stores).
Coffee, beer, milk	Blot up excess with paper towels, scrub with diluted carpet shampoo; cover with paper towels and weight down for 2 to 3 hours.
Fruit juices, soft drinks	Blot up excess; sponge with a solution of 1 teaspoon of powdered laundry detergent and 1 teaspoon of white vinegar dissolved in 1 quart (1 liter) of warm water.
Grease, oil, lipstick, butter	Blot up excess with paper towels; sponge with dry-cleaning fluid; work from edges to center.
Shoe polish, ink, dry paint	Dab with paint remover; if that fails, use dry-cleaning fluid.
Wax	Scrape off as much as possible; then place a brown paper bag over the area and run a warm iron over it. The bag will act as a blotter and absorb the wax.

providing brilliant color. Nylon resists soils and stains and can stand up to heavy-traffic areas. Solution-dyed nylon is colorfast because color is added in the fiber production.

• Olefin (polypropylene) is the stuff indoor/outdoor carpeting is made of because it resists wear and permanent stains and it is easy to clean. It is colorfast because the color is added when the fibers are made.

• Polyester carpet has a luxurious soft feel when used in thick cut-pile textures. It has excellent color clarity and retention. It's easily cleaned and is resistant to water-soluble stains.

• Acrylic offers the appearance and feel of wool at a lower cost. It has a low static level and is resistant to moisture and mildew. It's commonly used in velvet and level-loop carpets and in bath and scatter rugs.

• Wool is very durable and luxuriously soft and thick. It's available in many colors, but it's much more expensive than synthetic carpets.

• A wool-nylon blend combines the excellent look and comfort of wool with the durability of nylon. Other common carpet blends that combine good characteristics include acrylic-olefin and nylon-olefin.

Tile

Maintain the grout joints of properly installed tile, and you've got a surface that's a snap to clean, impervious to stains, and bound to be around for another generation to enjoy.

Seal the grout

Tile doesn't wear out—the grout is the weak link. Whether the tile is on a floor, counter, or wall, you can prolong the life of the grout and make it easier to clean by sealing it with a penetrating sealer. For new tile, wait a week or two for the grout to dry before applying the sealer. Reapply sealer annually. Unless you have done the test described just below, apply sealer only on the grout, as it may dull the tile.

Seal some types of tile

In general, there's no reason to seal glazed tile, but most types of unglazed tile will benefit from a coat of sealer. To check if your tile should be sealed, put a little water on it. If the tile darkens, it's absorbing the water and should be sealed.

Softer tile, such as Mexican Saltillo, should be sealed and then coated with an acrylic floor finish to protect the sealer. There are also sealers that incorporate finish. Harder tiles are fine with just sealer. Check with your tile dealer or manufacturer to determine the best coating to ensure a long life for your particular tile.

Replace the grout

When grout gets stained and cracked, you can replace it, giving the tile a new lease on life. Here are three simple steps to laying down new grout:

❶ The easiest way to remove old grout is with one of those little rotary tools. Hold the tip of the tool against the grout line and pull down. You can also scrape the grout out with a grout saw or an old-style pointy can opener. Vacuum the dust and debris out of the joints between tiles. Then use a tile cleaner to wash off any mineral buildup, soap scum, or grout residue.

❷ Mix a batch of new grout to the consistency of toothpaste. Apply the grout with a rubber float, covering about 2 square yards (2 square meters) at a time.

❸ Smooth and pack the grout lines with the handle of a toothbrush. Allow the grout to set for 30 minutes; then wipe off any remaining film with a clean, dry cloth. Wait for two or three weeks before applying grout sealer.

Borrow a tile

You've got a cracked tile conspicuously located in the middle of the bathroom. You don't have an extra tile, and you can't find a matching one to purchase. You have two options short of replacing the whole floor. First see if you can remove a tile from an inconspicuous spot like behind the toilet. Be aware, this is often very difficult or impossible to do. The second option is to replace a few tiles with a different color to create a new pattern of tiles.

Paint, don't replace

You don't need to replace tile for a new look. With the proper prep, prime, and paint you can change the color. First make sure the tile is very clean. Then scuff it slightly with fine sandpaper to help the primer adhere. Now the important part: Use a bonding primer/sealer designed to adhere to slick, hard-to-paint surfaces—the can should list tile among the surfaces it will adhere to. Then you can paint with regular interior wall paint.

Caulk is key

It's important to understand the difference between grout and caulk. Grout is a hard, inflexible cement. In effect, it turns a wall of tiles into one solid surface. Caulk is soft and flexible—it can expand and contract without cracking or losing its bond. That's why caulk is the ticket for sealing the joint between two surfaces that may expand and contract at a different rate, such as where a wall of tile meets the bathtub. Silicone caulk is the most durable, waterproof type of caulk to use for joints around water. It comes clear or in a few colors and in a mildew-resistant formula.

 ProTip

ICE SKATES OVER CAULK

An ice cube is the perfect tool for smoothing a caulk joint. Melt a corner of the cube in your hand to form the radius you want for the joint. Then run it over the joint—it will never stick to the caulk.

Choose the right base for your tile

When installing new tile, you have two decisions to make that will affect the longevity of the job. First, what substrate will you use—in other words, to what will you attach the tile? And second, what adhesive will you use?

If the tile will be attached to a wall that never gets wet or damp, the substrate can be regular drywall. If occasional moisture is an issue and you are building a new wall, use moisture-resistant drywall— sometimes called greenboard because of its color. For walls and floors that will regularly get wet, such as shower stalls

and bathroom floors, use cement backer board.

For floors that will not get wet regularly, tile can be attached directly to a plywood subfloor. Of course, it is fine to attach tile directly to a concrete floor.

When it comes to adhesives, you have two choices: organic mastic or thinset mortar. Organic mastic is easier to work with, but it weakens with time if it is allowed to remain damp. You can use it in wet situations as long as you maintain the caulk and grout. Thinset is trickier to use, especially on walls, because you have to mix it to just the right consistency and use it quickly, but it is impervious to water.

Plumbing and Plumbing Fixtures

Faucets, sinks, tubs, and toilets, all make our lives easier and healthier. Until the day they stop working, that is. Here are the easy ways to keep your plumbing system in tiptop working order.

Dissolve mineral deposits with vinegar

Is your showerhead clogged with mineral deposits? To make the water flow again, fill a plastic bag with vinegar, put the bag around the shower-head, tape it in place, and let it soak overnight.

Tape tools to preserve chrome

To prevent scratching your beautiful chrome or brass fixtures, wrap the jaws of your pliers with adhesive tape. Do the same with the tips of screwdrivers that you'll use for prying.

Here are a are a few simple things to check that might save you from calling the plumber:

• Low water pressure at the kitchen faucet? Unscrew the aerator from the end of the faucet. If the pressure improves, you just need to unclog the aerator.

• Water dripping from your toilet tank? If the whole outside of the tank is wet up to the tank's water level, it's just condensation—nothing to worry about. Otherwise, make sure the water-supply connection under the tank is tight and not leaking.

Fixing a leaky compression faucet

These faucets turn off the water by compressing a rubber washer when you twist the handle. (If your faucet has only one handle to control the hot and cold, it's not a compression faucet.) If you fix a compression faucet leak immediately after it starts, you'll just need a new washer—which costs about a nickel. If the sink has been leaking for a while, the seat may need to be replaced—a more involved job that requires a specialized seat wrench. Here's how to change the washer:

❶ Turn off the water under the sink; then unscrew the faucet handle. Sometimes a screw is exposed at the top of the handle; other times

you need to pry off a cap. If you see plastic parts when you take a handle off a two-handled faucet, you have a cartridge faucet. See "Fix a leaky cartridge faucet."

❷ Use channel-lock pliers to loosen the retaining nut and remove the brass stem assembly. If you see a plastic retaining ring instead of a brass nut, you have a cartridge faucet.

❸ Remove the stem screw from the bottom of the stem assembly. Remove and replace the washer. Reassemble the faucet and you are back in business.

Fixing a leaky cartridge faucet

Cartridges are found on many single-handled faucets and some two-handled models. When the faucet starts to leak, the cartridge is a snap to replace:

❶ Start by turning off the water under the sink and removing the handle as described in step 1 of "Fix a leaky compression faucet."

❷ On single-handled faucets you'll find a large plastic retaining ring. Two-handled faucets often have a metal nut. Use channel-lock pliers to remove the plastic ring or an adjustable wrench to remove the nut. Remove any clip holding the cartridge. Then use pliers to grab the top of the cartridge and pull it out.

❸ Take the old cartridge to the hardware store to make sure you get the right replacement. Use plumber's grease to lubricate the O-rings on the new cartridge, put the cartridge in place, and reassemble the handle.

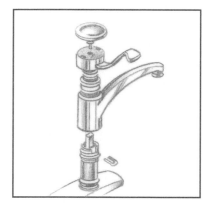

Try tightening the cap

If your leaky single-levered faucet has a rounded cap with knurled edges just under the cap, it's a ball-type faucet. Replacing these is a bit trickier because there's a bunch of little parts inside—you may want to call a plumber unless you are handy. But before you do, try this: Put some adhesive tape on the jaws of your channel-lock pliers, put the pliers around the knurls, and tighten clockwise. There's a good chance the leak will stop.

Cure a running toilet

Despite the strange gurgling and swooshing noises emanating from your toilet tank, there's

nothing very mysterious going on in there. In fact, if your toilet is running, it's an almost sure bet you can fix it yourself in a matter of minutes.

When you flush your toilet, the lever pulls up the flapper that stops the water from flowing down the flush valve. Sometimes there is a plastic or rubber ball instead of a flapper. If your toilet is running, it's likely because the flapper or ball isn't seating fully into the valve. Usually you can just bend the lift arm or adjust the length of the lift chain to make the flapper seat more accurately.

Another possibility is that sediment on the flush valve is preventing the flapper or ball from sealing. Turn off the water going into the toilet; there's a valve with a knob just below the tank. Flush the toilet, and wipe out the remaining water with a sponge. Clean the valve with a cloth. For stubborn deposits, use fine steel wool for a brass rim or a pad made for cleaning vinyl-coated cookware if the rim is plastic.

The toilet might be running because the float ball needs to be adjusted. This ball is attached to an arm that is attached to the ball cock. The ball cock is the device that turns the water supply on and off. If the ball cock is adjusted too high, water will leak into the top of the overflow pipe.

Bending the float-ball arm down a little will usually solve this problem. Occasionally the overflow tube develops a leak along its side. If that's the case, just replace the overflow tube.

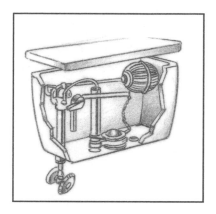

Keep drain systems clear

Here's an easy way to keep your drains free of clogs: Mix 1 cup of baking soda with 1 cup of salt and 1/4 cup of cream of tartar. About once a week pour 1/2 cup of this mixture into each drain, followed by 1 quart (1 liter) of boiling water. Be careful pouring the hot water.

Keep grease out of your septic system

The anaerobic bacteria that break down septic waste can't digest grease, so the stuff just floats to the top, clogging the leach field of your septic system. To prolong the life of your septic system, scrape all grease from your dishes and pans into cans and toss it into the trash. Or have a grease trap installed in your waste line and clean it regularly.

Don't use a garbage disposal with a septic system

If your sink has a garbage disposal, you'll naturally dump more solid stuff down the drain. Even though it's ground up, this stuff will put an excess load on your septic tank's filtration system, allowing some solids into the leach field. Once your leach field clogs up, the septic tank follows, and it's time to call those expensive guys with backhoes to dig it all up.

☛ **DON'T**
drive over your septic field

> Septic leach fields need oxygen to work. If you drive over the field, you'll compress the soil, squeezing out the air and shortening the effective life of the field.

Prevent rust buildup in galvanized pipes

Galvanized pipes have a zinc coating designed to resist rust. Trouble is, after a couple of decades, the flow of water wears away at the pipes and rust starts to build up. You can prolong the life of the pipes by having a plumbing service ream out and flush the pipes annually. You can also slow down the rust by turning the water heater down to about 85°F (30°C), which you shouldn't do if you have a dishwasher, which needs a higher temperature to clean

properly. Of course, the most permanent solution is to install copper pipes that don't rust.

Repair a cracked tub

If your porcelain bathtub develops a hairline crack, fill it with caulk to prevent the crack from enlarging. Rub regular bathtub caulk into the crack, and then wipe off any excess with a damp cloth. Allow the caulk to cure overnight; then skim off any excess with a single-edged razor blade.

Sprinkle a little baking soda

Keep baking soda in a recycled plastic spice jar on the sink. Sprinkle on the sink basin and fixtures, and wipe with a sponge once a day to keep them sparkling.

Treat porcelain with care

Porcelain is easy to clean because it presents a smooth, impervious surface. Your porcelain can look like new for decades if you are careful to keep it smooth and impervious. Once the porcelain gets scratched, dirt can grab hold of it, and the porcelain requires more scrubbing to clean; the scrubbing causes more scratches, and a cycle of decline begins. So rule number one is to never use abrasive cleaners on porcelain. Here's how to preserve your porcelain surfaces:

• For routine cleaning, get out the liquid dishwashing soap,

liquid laundry detergent, or all-purpose cleaners (such as Formula 409 and Dow Bathroom Cleaner). If you use detergent, mix 1 tablespoon with 1 gallon (4 liters) of hot water. Clean with a soft sponge and rinse thoroughly.

• If the porcelain is lightly stained, clean it with baking soda or trisodium phosphate (available at home improvement and hardware stores). Sprinkle either powder on the surface, and then rub with a damp sponge. Rinse with vinegar or lemon juice to neutralize the alkaline cleaner; then rinse thoroughly with water.

• To remove heavy stains, even rust, rub the fixture with a paste consisting of 1 cup of powdered borax (available in the supermarket laundry section) and 1/4 cup of lemon juice. Dab a cloth, sponge, or, if necessary, a scrubber sponge in the paste, rub the paste on the stain, then rinse with running water.

Remove copper stains from tubs

Water with high copper content can leave blue-green stains on your tub. To remove these stains, make up a paste: Combine equal amounts of cream of tartar and baking soda (usually 1 tablespoon of each is enough), and add some lemon juice drop by drop until you have a paste. Rub it into the

Kitchen Sinks

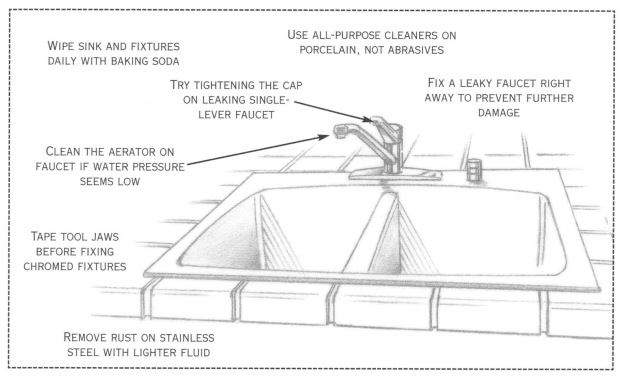

WIPE SINK AND FIXTURES
DAILY WITH BAKING SODA

USE ALL-PURPOSE CLEANERS ON
PORCELAIN, NOT ABRASIVES

TRY TIGHTENING THE CAP
ON LEAKING SINGLE-
LEVER FAUCET

FIX A LEAKY FAUCET RIGHT
AWAY TO PREVENT FURTHER
DAMAGE

CLEAN THE AERATOR ON
FAUCET IF WATER PRESSURE
SEEMS LOW

TAPE TOOL JAWS
BEFORE FIXING
CHROMED FIXTURES

REMOVE RUST ON STAINLESS
STEEL WITH LIGHTER FLUID

stain with your fingers or a soft cloth. Leave it for 30 minutes, and rinse well with water.

Clean fiberglass tubs without scratching

Fiberglass can be difficult to clean because mild cleaners have little impact on a seriously soiled unit, and abrasive cleaners applied with too much scrubbing pressure will quickly dull the finish. For everyday cleaning, spray on a household cleaner or a tub-and-tile cleaner, and wipe with a nonabrasive sponge. If you need to bring out the big guns, use a powdered cleaner, such as Comet, and a light-duty scrubbing sponge, but don't overdo the scrubbing pressure.

Be sure to rinse well with water so that the chemicals won't stay on the surface.

Use lighter fluid on a rusty steel sink

Got some rust on a stainless steel sink? Rubbing with lighter fluid will dissolve the rust and renew the steel.

Heating and Cooling

Doing simple, regular maintenance on your heating system will keep it reliable and extend its life. And if that's not enough incentive to do these easy tasks, all the fuel money you'll save should be!

Have your heating system checked annually

Oil-fired furnaces require more maintenance than gas-fired furnaces do. But whichever type you have, it will last longest and cost you the least to run if you have it checked annually by a professional—you can usually contract with your fuel supplier to automatically do the work each year.

Check your heat distribution system, too

Just like the furnace, the heat distribution system should be professionally serviced each year. There are three common heat delivery systems:

• In a forced hot-air system, heated air is forced through ducts and comes out of registers, usually in the floor. In addition to annual professional servicing, you should change the air filter each month during the heating system. Usually you'll find it just inside the furnace housing or in a slot between the furnace and the main duct. Your service technician can tell you where it is. It's also a good idea to vacuum your registers before the start of each heating season.

• In a hot-water system, hot water gives off heat through radiators—either the large cast-iron kind usually found in older homes or the newer baseboard-convector type. In an even more recent variation, the water circulates through hoses looping through the floor so that the heat radiates up from the floors. If you have cast-iron radiators—"bleed" any air out of them before each heating season. This involves using a special key or a screwdriver to open a little valve at the top of the radiator. At first, hot air will come out of the valve. Close it when a steady stream of water comes out.

• Steam systems are found almost exclusively in older homes and use cast-iron radiators just like the ones in a hot-water system. They need to be bled the same way.

Have the ducts cleaned

Hot-air ducts should be cleaned about every five years or whenever a dust-producing renovation is done.

Ease your furnace's workload

A layer of dust acts as a layer of insulation. If your radiators or the convection fins of your hot-water baseboard are dusty, your furnace will need to run longer and more often to force heat through them. Of course, this not only wears the furnace out sooner but also costs you more fuel as well. So save money by regularly vacuuming your radiators' baseboards. Be sure to take the covers off to get to the fins.

Keep fins straight

Those thin metal convection fins under the covers of your hot-water baseboard are easily bent or crushed together. This greatly decreases their efficiency. Fortunately, they are just as easy to straighten when you take the covers off to vacuum.

Seal your chimney

Brick is pretty tough stuff, but water can bring on its eventual demise. Over the years rain can roughen the surface of your chimney brick—or any outdoor brick, for that matter—and then the bricks begin to absorb water. In cold weather the moisture in the brick expands, and the brick starts to crumble. To arrest this problem, coat your chimney with a clear masonry sealer. Be sure the sealer is labeled for use with brick—some clear sealers are not.

Take down that old antenna

It's probably been years since you took your television reception from that antenna strapped to your chimney. It's kind of ugly, and you've been meaning to take it down. Well, here's another reason to do so: The strapping on the mortar can stress the mortar joints. Also, in a strong wind the straps and antenna are pushing the chimney sideways. Both factors can loosen the brick.

Burn seasoned hardwood only

If you use a woodstove, burn only hardwood that has been seasoned for at least a year. Green unseasoned wood contains up to 50 percent water. It takes a lot of energy to drive off this water before the wood can burn. So green wood is hard to light, doesn't produce much heat, and creates a lot of smoke. The smoke solidifies in your stovepipe and chimney in the form of creosote that can ignite and cause a chimney fire. More creosote means you'll need to have the chimney cleaned more often. And if your stove has a catalytic combuster, as newer stoves do, low temperatures and creosote buildup can render it useless.

The problem with burning softwood like pine is a little different: Seasoned softwood—like construction scraps—is perfect for lighting your stove.

It starts easily and burns hot and fast. But once the fire gets going and you want to close up the stove for a slow, steady fire, don't feed it with softwood—the stuff doesn't produce that much heat, and you'll create the very same creosote problems as you do with green hardwood.

Warm up your woodstove

Cast-iron stoves can crack if you build a raging fire in a cold one. Warm it up with a small fire first.

Clean your chimney frequently

How often you need to clean your chimney depends on whether you use a woodstove or a fireplace and, of course, how often you make fires. One thing is certain, creosote buildup causes extremely dangerous chimney fires.

Woodstoves and fireplace inserts are much more efficient heaters than fireplaces because you can severely limit the air intake. As a result, wood burns slowly without sucking a lot of air out of the room. Unfortunately, a slow draft means the smoke has plenty of time to cool and solidify on the walls of your chimney. A roaring open fireplace, on the other hand, sucks air out of the room and shoots smoke up the chimney before much of it gets a chance to solidify.

So if you burn your woodstove throughout the heating season, have it cleaned at least once a year. (Don't be surprised if your chimney sweep advises an additional midseason cleaning.) On the other hand, if you burn your open fireplace for occasional entertainment, your chimney might be fine for three or four years. Find a reliable chimney sweep and follow his advice.

Install a chimney cap

It's a good idea to install a cap to keep water out of your chimney. Water dripping into the chimney combines with creosote to create acids that can corrode brick and mortar, as well as galvanized chimney pipe.

Check the firebox liner

Your woodstove has an interior liner that does two things: It increases the stove's mass so it radiates heat more evenly, and it protects the stove's outer walls from getting damaged by high heat and logs banging against them. The liner might be cast iron, firebrick, or refractory cement. To make your stove last for generations, check the liner for cracks before each heating season. Replace any cracked brick or iron, or patch cracks in the cement.

Keep your air conditioner's fins fit

The key to making an air conditioner last is to keep air

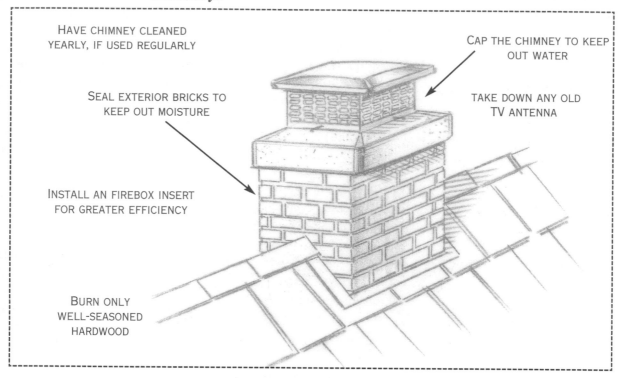

HAVE CHIMNEY CLEANED
YEARLY, IF USED REGULARLY

CAP THE CHIMNEY TO KEEP
OUT WATER

SEAL EXTERIOR BRICKS TO
KEEP OUT MOISTURE

TAKE DOWN ANY OLD
TV ANTENNA

INSTALL AN FIREBOX INSERT
FOR GREATER EFFICIENCY

BURN ONLY
WELL-SEASONED
HARDWOOD

flowing through it as easily as possible. In the case of a window air conditioner, the air is pulled in through tiny fins at the back and pushed out through tiny fins in the front. Remove the unit from its case, and vacuum these fins with a soft brush attachment. If the rear fins are really dirty, you can rinse them out with a garden hose. You can access the fins of a central-air system's outdoor unit by removing the cover. Vacuum the fins from the outside, and rinse them with a garden hose, spraying from the inside.

Clean your air-conditioner filter often

The filter at the front of a window air conditioner is really easy to remove—usually you just pull it out. So do just that every month or so, and rinse the filter in warm water with a squirt of dishwashing liquid. It's just as important as keeping the fins clean.

Don't cover your air conditioner

The outdoor unit on your central AC unit is designed to withstand the weather. Covering it could trap moisture and actually rust the unit's case.

House Exterior

House Siding and Trim

Your home is your biggest investment. Taking care of the exterior of your home is essential to protecting that investment. Plus, you're doing your part to ensure your beautiful home survives for many generations to come.

Preserve paint with an annual washing

Washing your house once a year will keep the paint job looking bright longer. Use 1 cup of extra-strength detergent and 1 quart (1 liter) of chlorine bleach to 3 gallons (11 liters) of water. Scrub with a long-handled sponge mop, and rinse well with your garden hose.

Latex or alkyd?

When you are considering what paint to use on your house, it comes down to this: Latex paint is more flexible than alkyd paint, but alkyd, also commonly called oil paint, penetrates better into bare wood. For this reason, you'll get the longest-lasting job if you prime bare wood with alkyd primer and then use top-coats of latex, according to the experts at Benjamin Moore paint company. Alkyd topcoats used outdoors tend to become brittle, and they chalk (that is, shed powder) and don't hold their color as well as latex. Plus, latex paints clean up with water instead of messy mineral spirits. Latex paints are also kinder to the environment.

Don't paint alkyd over latex

Never use alkyd primer or paint to recoat latex. The flexible latex layer will cause the brittle alkyd topcoat to crack.

Keep water away from fresh latex paint

Latex paint is water-based—which means that, until it dries, latex paint is soluble in water. So to ensure the paint will stick for many years to come, make sure that the surface you are painting is perfectly dry when you apply the paint and will remain that way until the paint dries. This means you don't want to start painting in the morning until the dew burns off, and don't paint at all if rain is predicted for that day.

Paint when the temperature is right

Hot, dry weather is perfect for painting—the paint will suck right into the dry wood, creating a strong, long-lasting bond. If your climate has cool nights and hot days, however, be careful. If you paint a cool surface that will become hot in a few hours, the paint may blister within a couple of days.

Don't paint over weathered wood

Gray weathered wood is not a sound surface for paint. You must sand weathered wood down to a new bright surface. Otherwise the paint will peel.

 ProTip

LITTLE THINGS ADD UP TO A DURABLE PAINT JOB

Every professional house painter knows that the right tools and techniques are just as important as the right paint. Here are three simple pointers for a long-lasting job:

• Buy the best paintbrush—expect to pay about $20. Use natural-bristle brushes for alkyd paint, and a synthetic bristle one for latex. A good brush will pick up lots of paint and lay it down thick and smooth.

• Thoroughly stir the paint before you use it, drawing the solids up from the bottom until you achieve a smooth consistency.

• To minimize unsightly lap marks, always maintain a wet edge—that is, always work out from the wet edge of a recently painted area.

Is stain the right choice?

If you are applying a finish to bare exterior wood siding and trim, you have the option of using stain instead of paint. You can use semitransparent stain, which colors the wood but leaves the grain visible. Or you can use solid-colored stain—essentially thinned paint that obscures the grain without completely obscuring the texture of the wood.

The advantage of stain is that it has an oil or resin base that penetrates into the wood instead of simply adhering to the surface like paint. This means stain won't peel off as paint may do if there is a moisture problem. (Solid-colored stain penetrates less than semitransparent because pigment stays on the surface, so it can peel, but not as readily as paint.) Unlike paint, you can use stain on weathered wood. And because stain is thinner than paint, you can recoat many more times before you have enough buildup to require stripping. The disadvantage is that stain is much less durable than paint and must be recoated more often. Depending on conditions—perhaps every three years for semitransparent or five years for solid-colored stain. A good paint job, by comparison, can last up to a decade.

☞ DON'T
paint vinyl a darker color

Never paint vinyl siding a color that is darker than the original color. The darker color will absorb more heat, and this may cause the siding to buckle.

Yes, you can paint aluminum and vinyl siding

Sorry, but when it comes to exterior siding, there really is no such thing as maintenance-free. Just like any other outdoor surface, the sun will eventually fade vinyl and aluminum siding. The good news is that prepainting prep work for vinyl or aluminum is usually easier than it is for wood.

The main thing is to make sure the surface is completely clean before you paint it. Use a scrub brush with laundry detergent mixed with water. Or if the surface is very dirty and you want to save some elbow grease, rent a power washer. If you do power-wash, be careful to moderate the settings so that you don't damage the siding or blast good paint off aluminum siding.

New vinyl siding has color throughout, so there is no paint to blast off. This means you don't need to prime vinyl siding unless it is pitted or porous. In that case, use a latex primer. Once it is clean, you can give it two coats of latex house paint. Don't use alkyd primer or paint—vinyl expands and contracts with temperature changes. Alkyd is much less flexible than latex and might crack and peel.

Aluminum siding is painted at the factory. If the original paint is in good shape, you can clean it and then use two coats of latex paint. Otherwise scrape off any loose paint, and spot-prime the bare metal with latex primer before painting.

Caulk siding joints

Watertight caulk joints are key to keeping your wood siding and exterior trim in good shape for generations. Each spring, check the caulk joints on the outside of your house. If the caulk is brittle or cracked, dig it out and replace it. You'll cut down on drafts and save on your energy bills, too.

When to keep your caulk gun in its holster

Exterior caulk helps stop drafts and seals the end-grain of clapboards where they meet windows, doors, and corner boards. But it's not necessary to seal the bottoms of boards where they lap the board beneath. In fact, this actually could create a problem by trapping interior moisture in the boards, causing paint to peel.

Shapely caulk joints last longest

Your caulk joints will last longest if you give them an hourglass shape. In other words, you want the caulk to be thick where it adheres to both sides of the joint but thinner in the middle. The thicker sides adhere well, while the thinner middle lets the caulk stretch

Making a good caulk joint is half the equation. The other key to a long-lasting caulking job is selecting the right caulk for the job. Here's a rundown of your choices:

Type	Advantages	Disadvantages
Silicone caulk	The most flexible caulk, and it stays flexible for decades. Adheres well to nonporous surfaces, such as glazed tile, glass, and plastic, and water won't undermine it. Holds up well outdoors and is great for tough, wet spots indoors and out.	Expensive. Paint will not adhere to it. Comes only in clear and a few colors.
Acrylic latex caulk	Often labeled as "painter's caulk," it is great for filling gaps before an indoor paint job. It is inexpensive, takes paint well, is easy to work with, and will last 20 years or more in a dry indoor location.	Not good outdoors or for other locations that are subject to moisture or wide temperature swings. Doesn't adhere to tile, glass, and other smooth surfaces as well as silicone caulk.
Acrylic latex caulk with mildewcide	Often sold as bath caulk, it's useful for moisture-exposed indoor locations that need to be painted, such as where tub enclosures or tiles meet the wall.	Not good for locations subject to moisture or wide temperature swings. Doesn't adhere to smooth surfaces as well as silicone caulk. Not suitable for kitchen counters, where it may come in contact with food.
Siliconized acrylic latex caulk	The addition of silicone can add 10 years to the life of the caulk, and you can still paint it. For outdoor joints that will be painted—where siding boards meet casing, for example.	High priced and doesn't adhere to smooth surfaces as well as silicone caulk.
Butyl rubber caulk	Specially formulated to withstand wet and subfreezing conditions—use on gutter seams and lap joints, and for joints where metal meets masonry and foundations.	Messy to apply and has tarlike appearance. Not suitable for siding.

more easily, reducing the chance that the caulk will separate from the sides of the joint.

Flexible joints are most important when caulking outdoor wood, such as where siding meets window and door casing. That's because outdoor wood expands and contracts a lot, and good caulk seals are important to long-lasting house exteriors. So rather than just filling up these joints with caulk, fill most of the space with foam backer rod. Run your bead of caulk; then smooth the joint with a wet finger to create the outer concave shape.

Make sure siding can dry after rain

No matter how well you take care of it, siding can rot if it stays constantly wet. Make sure your siding can dry out quickly when the sun comes out after a rain. Don't let bushes and vines grow up against the side of your house. Shady spots will stay damp, ultimately promoting rot.

Remove moss or algae from shingles

Moss and algae can grab onto the textured surface of wood shingles or shakes. The growth retains moisture, promoting rot. This is true whether the shingles or shakes are used as siding or roofing. To remove moss, algae, and dirt, wait until the siding or roof has been dry for several days; then brush with a stiff push broom. This is often enough to clean the siding.

If brushing doesn't do the job, rent a power washer. Be careful with this tool—shingles are soft, and if you use too much pressure, you can damage them. Keep the spray nozzle about 18 inches (50 cm) from the siding or roof as you work, and be careful not to aim at doors, window, vents, or plants. Always wear safety goggles.

Cure the cause of moss and algae

The fact that these plants are thriving on your siding is probably evidence of a moisture problem that you need to solve. If bushes or trees are growing against the house, keeping the siding wet, cut them back. If a gutter is leaking on the siding, fix it.

Patch vinyl siding

If vinyl siding is cracked or badly stained, get a replacement piece from a siding distributor.

Replace a piece that's at least 4 feet (1.2 meters) long. While you are at the siding store, pick up a "zip tool"—you'll need this specialized tool to unlock the old siding. If your siding has weathered, a new section of siding won't match well. So take a section from an inconspicuous spot, and use that for the replacement. Then use the new piece to fill the inconspicuous spot. Here's how to proceed:

❶ Use a combination square to mark cutting lines on the damaged panel. Let an edge fall along an existing joint if one is close.

❷ Work the zip tool under the edge of the panel above the damaged one. Pull down on the zip tool, and draw it along the panel to unlock the panel above.

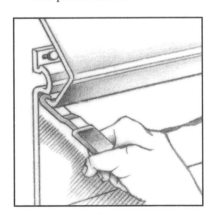

❸ Prop the unlocked panel open with blocks of wood. Remove the nails in the damaged panel's top edge. Cut out the damaged area with tin snips.

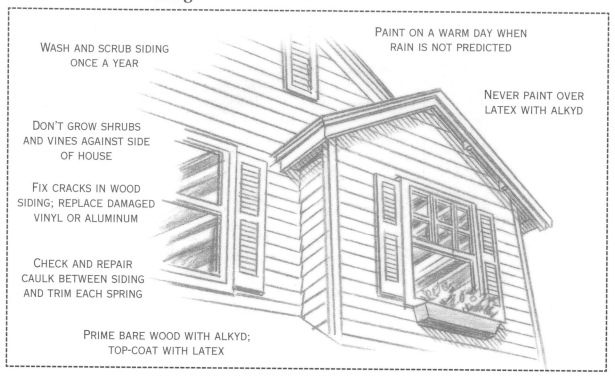

WASH AND SCRUB SIDING
ONCE A YEAR

PAINT ON A WARM DAY WHEN
RAIN IS NOT PREDICTED

NEVER PAINT OVER
LATEX WITH ALKYD

DON'T GROW SHRUBS
AND VINES AGAINST SIDE
OF HOUSE

FIX CRACKS IN WOOD
SIDING; REPLACE DAMAGED
VINYL OR ALUMINUM

CHECK AND REPAIR
CAULK BETWEEN SIDING
AND TRIM EACH SPRING

PRIME BARE WOOD WITH ALKYD;
TOP-COAT WITH LATEX

④ Cut the replacement panel about 1 1/2 inches (4 cm) longer than the opening to allow for 3/4-inch (2-cm) overlap at each end. Slip the panel under one adjacent panel's edge, and overlap the other following the existing pattern of overlaps. Make sure the panel's bottom edge locks in place.

⑤ Secure the panel's upper edge with aluminum nails at 16-inch (40-cm) intervals. Center each nail in an oval slot. Stop nailing just when the head touches the siding. If you nail it tight, the panel won't be able to expand in warm weather, and it will

buckle. Relock the panel above with the zip tool.

Patch damaged aluminum siding

It won't crack like vinyl or split or rot like wood, but aluminum siding will dent, as you will discover the first time a kid whacks it with a baseball. Here's how to replace a dented section:

① Use a zip tool, available at siding suppliers, to unlock the damaged piece of siding from the piece below and above. Pull down as you slide the tool along. Pull the nails that secure the damaged section from the house.

② Prop the upper piece of siding up and out of the way with wood blocks for easier access. Use aviation snips to cut out the damaged section of siding. Be sure to wear heavy gloves—the metal edges are sharp.

❸ Cut the replacement piece so that it overlaps the existing siding 3/4 inch (2 cm) on each side. Notch the nailing strip at the top to accommodate the overlap.

Fix cracked wood siding

Small cracks in wood siding can trap water, causing paint to peel and inviting rot. Fortunately, they take minutes to fix. Just squirt in a little acrylic latex "painter's caulk," smooth with your finger, and paint. If the split runs most of the width of a clapboard, wedge it apart with two or three screwdrivers. Fill it with a waterproof glue such as resorcinol. Press the split shut, and nail the board's lower edge with galvanized or aluminum nails. Sink the nail heads with a nail set, and fill the holes with wood putty before painting.

Replace damaged clapboard

If a section of clapboard is rotted or damaged beyond repair, you can cut out the section to replace it. Here's how:

❶ Use a combination square to mark cuts at both sides of the damage. Drive wooden wedges under the damaged area to separate the clapboard from the one below.

❷ Make your cuts with a backsaw; then use a chisel to break away the exposed part of the piece.

❸ Drive your wedges between the clapboard above and the remaining section of the overlapped board. Slip a hacksaw blade under it, and cut the nails holding the remaining piece.

❹ Replace damaged building paper, or fix it with roofing cement. Cut a replacement piece of matching clapboard to fit snuggly side to side, and then, protecting the bottom of the replacement piece with a wood block, tap the new piece into place. Nail it along the bottom and through the board above.

Replace a shingle or shake

Wood shingles and shakes are the easiest types of siding to repair because you don't have to cut out sections.

❶ Use a flat pry bar to carefully pry up the shingles just above the damaged shingle that overlap the damaged shingle. Insert wedges to keep the shingles pulled out.

❷ Use a hammer and chisel to split the damaged shingle into several sections that you can pull out from around the nails. Use a flexible hacksaw blade to cut out the nails—wear heavy gloves, wrap one end of the blade with tape, or use a hacksaw-blade handle designed for this job.

❸ Insert the new shingle, and gently tap it into place. Nail the new shingle just below the butt of the shingles above. Sink the nail heads with a nail set, and fill the recess with caulk.

Roofs

The roof is your home's first line of defense against the elements. It really asks for little attention when you consider the important job it does.

Give wood roofs a clean sweep

Wood-eating fungus needs moisture to thrive. Of course, you can't keep a roof from getting wet. The trick is to keep your wood roof clean so the shakes or shingles can dry before fungus can set up housekeeping. This means getting up there with a broom and sweeping off leaves, pine needles, and other debris that can capture moisture.

Prevent moss, lichens, and algae

While moss, lichens, and algae don't directly damage your wood roof, they trap moisture—never a good thing on any roof and especially bad on a wood roof, where persistent dampness may attract wood-eating fungus.

Flashing your roof ridge with copper or galvanized steel will help discourage growth of these organisms. Rain leaches down small amounts of the metal that will discourage growth for 10 to 15 feet (3 to 4.5 meters) down the roof. For larger roofs, you can string copper wire across the roof.

Kill accumulated moss

If moss has accumulated on your roof, treat it with zinc sulfate, which is relatively safe around plants and comes in granules for dry application. Follow package directions. You'll find it at hardware stores and home centers. Note that zinc corrodes copper, so don't use it if you have copper gutters and roof flashing.

Go for the growth-resistant shingles

Many manufacturers of asphalt shingles now add zinc- or copper-oxide-coated granules to the surface of their shingles to discourage growth of moss, lichens, and algae. If you have growth on your old roof, use these shingles when you reroof.

Laminated lasts longest

Also called architectural or dimensional shingles, laminated shingles have become more popular than the once ubiquitous three-tab shingles. There are good reasons: Laminated shingles last longer because

---

❓ How Long Do Asphalt Shingles Last?

ANSWER: 14 years to 45 or more

Asphalt shingles always cite a life span right on their packages—20, 25, 30, or 40 years. If you read the fine print, these life spans are not guaranteed. So what do they really mean?

Well, they mean that if the shingles are properly installed in *average* climate conditions, they should last approximately the number of years stated. The problem, of course, is that there is no such thing as an average climate. In general, a hot climate is bad for shingles, and even worse is a climate with dramatic shifts between hot and cold temperatures, which causes the shingles to expand and contract in a short period of time, causing cracks and buckles. Another important variable is roof pitch. Everything else being equal, shingles will last longer on a steep roof than on a roof with shallow pitch.

All told, your "25-year" shingles might last 17 years, or they might last 35 years. Still, the stated life span is a very important tool to use when comparing shingle prices. On any given roof, you can expect a 25-year shingle to last longer than a 20-year shingle.

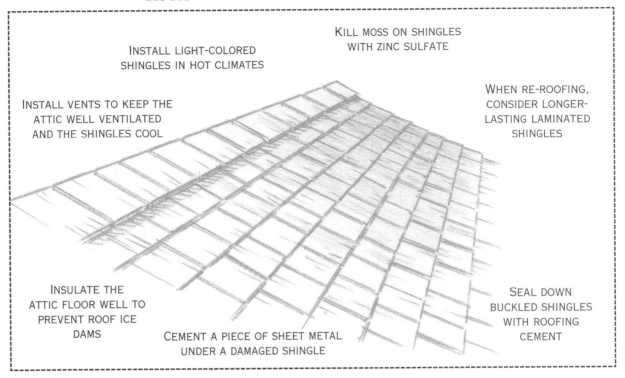

INSTALL LIGHT-COLORED
SHINGLES IN HOT CLIMATES

KILL MOSS ON SHINGLES
WITH ZINC SULFATE

WHEN RE-ROOFING,
CONSIDER LONGER-
LASTING LAMINATED
SHINGLES

INSTALL VENTS TO KEEP THE
ATTIC WELL VENTILATED
AND THE SHINGLES COOL

INSULATE THE
ATTIC FLOOR WELL TO
PREVENT ROOF ICE
DAMS

CEMENT A PIECE OF SHEET METAL
UNDER A DAMAGED SHINGLE

SEAL DOWN
BUCKLED SHINGLES
WITH ROOFING
CEMENT

they consist of two layers of shingle glued together. They cost more than single-layer three-tab shingles, but they may be cheaper in the long run when you factor in labor-cost savings from less frequent replacement. Most people find laminated shingles more attractive, and installers like them because there is no pattern to line up.

Buy time with roofing cement

If roof shingles are beginning to buckle, start saving up for a new roof. If only a few are buckled, you can stave off the need to replace the roof by seal-ing them down with roofing cement. The cement comes in caulking tubes. Just squirt some cement under the buckled area, and press the shingle down. You might need to keep the shingle pressed down with a brick or similar weight until the cement cures. Work on a warm day so the shingles will be flexi-ble and the cement will flow easily. Otherwise the shingles might crack when you press them down.

Repair a shingle with sheet metal

If part of an asphalt shingle has fallen off or is badly damaged, you can fix it quickly with a piece of sheet-metal flashing. Use tin snips to cut the metal to size so that it will slide under the damaged shingle and also be overlapped by the adjoining shingles. Put roofing cement on top of the flashing, and slip it under the damaged shingle.

Go light in hot climates

If you live in a hot climate, use light-colored asphalt shingles to reflect sunlight. This will slow deterioration of the shingles and save your air-conditioning bill as well.

Provide proper roof ventilation

Prolong the life of your shingles and lower your cooling bills by installing ridge vents in your roof. If the attic is a finished space, you'll need to install soffit vents in order for the ridge vents to work. (The soffit vents suck in cool air to replace hot air flowing through the ridge vents.)

Check flashing seams on flat roofs

Because water can collect on them, flat roofs are more prone to leaks than sloped roofs. The good news is that the leaks are usually caused by water seeping under the edge flashing. If the cracks are thin, a generous coating of roof cement will usually solve the problem.

Prevent ice buildup

If your attic floor is not sufficiently insulated, warm air rising through your home will warm the bottom of your roof in the winter. This will cause snow on the roof to melt, flow down the roof, and then refreeze on the cold eave overhang, creating an ice dam. The

dam traps water flowing down the warm roof and forces the water under the shingles, causing a leak that can stain walls, soak insulation, and rot rafters. The best way to prevent ice dams is to improve attic-floor insulation and ventilation in the attic itself so that the bottom of the roof stays cold and the snow doesn't melt. You'll reduce your heating bill, too.

Flat roof bubbles can be patched

Very often, leaky flat roofs can be patched, adding several years to the life of the roof. Patching a flat roof is a messy job that you might not want to take on yourself. Before you let a contractor sell you a new roof, make sure he has explained to your satisfaction why patching is not an option.

Gutters and Downspouts

Water is public enemy number one as far as your house siding and foundation are concerned. Well-maintained gutters and downspouts will whisk water from the roof and deposit it where it can do no harm.

Clean gutters are happy gutters

Debris in your gutters shortens their life in two ways: First it slows the flow of water, keeping them wet inside. If you have metal or wooden gutters, this moisture will promote rust or rot. Second, the debris adds weight. This can cause the gutters to sag and eventually come apart. If you live in a climate that has autumn, it is especially important to clear your gutters after the leaves fall and before the winter.

To clean your gutters, you'll need a pair of heavy work gloves, a ladder, a garden trowel, a whisk broom, and a bucket with a metal hanging hook. Starting near one downspout, sweep debris into a pile away from the downspout outlet. Scoop up the debris with the trowel, and dump it into the bucket. Clean as far as you can comfortably reach; then move the ladder along.

Clear a clogged downspout

After a gutter is cleaned, run water from your garden hose into it to check for leaks or sags and to make sure the down-spouts are clear. If you find a clogged downspout, first try to clear it with a strong direct blast with your garden-hose nozzle. If that doesn't work, downspouts are pretty easy to disassemble and clean. Just remove the sheet-metal screws that hold the parts together and pull them apart.

Consider gutter caps

If you have many large trees that lose their leaves in the fall, consider investing in gutter caps, especially for gutters that are hard to reach for cleaning. The best caps completely cover the gutters with solid metal pieces that have slots just under the downslope edge. Debris washes over the caps and off the roof while surface tension draws the water into the gutters. Top-quality gutter caps can cost more than the gutters, but they make the gutters stronger and less likely to sag, prolonging their life and saving you endless hours of gutter cleaning over the years.

Get the sag out

While cleaning your gutters, you might notice water collecting at one point. When the sag gets worse, you might notice it from the ground. Either way, a sag signals the beginning of the end for a gutter unless you fix it.

Your gutters are most likely held up either by spikes—you'll see the spike heads on the outer lip of the gutter—or by brackets that you don't see from the ground, because they clip into the inside of the gutter.

With the spike system, a long spike is driven through the top edge of the gutter, then slipped through a tube called a ferrule before being driven through the back of the gutter, through the fascia board and, let's hope, into the end of a rafter. The first thing to do is simply to hit the spike head with your hammer to see if you can tighten it and remove the sag.

If the spike won't pull tight, it might be because the installer missed the rafter end—the fascia board alone is not thick enough to provide a strong attachment. Look closely at the fascia; you'll see the heads of the nails used to attach it to the rafter end. If

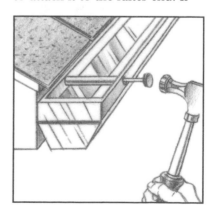

Buy to Keep: Gutters

Most gutters are made of vinyl, aluminum, galvanized steel, or copper. Each type of material has its advantages, but each also has its vulnerabilities:

Top of the line	At the high end of the price scale are soldered copper and galvanized steel. These systems are custom-fitted on site and are usually the strongest and most attractive. Left unpainted, copper weathers to a dull brown. Soldered galvanized steel gutters must be painted.
Seamless sheet metal	Moderately priced "seamless" aluminum or steel gutters are formed on-site on a machine that molds factory-coated sheet metal. Single sections can run almost any length, so the system has fewer joints. (It's not really seamless.) Fewer joints means fewer opportunities for leaks. Aluminum is more popular than steel because it won't rust. Steel is a bit sturdier, but aluminum is usually sturdy enough.
Assemble-it-yourself	Multipiece aluminum, vinyl, and steel gutters are the least expensive, and you can install them yourself. They are assembled from 10-foot (3-meter) lengths of gutter and joined with fittings and caulk. Most metal types have a baked-on finish that resists corrosion. However, some cheaper lines suffer from leaky joints and look flimsy. If you opt for this type, look for heavier-gauge systems.

the spike is not in line with those nails, pull it out, drill a new hole through the top edge of the gutter, insert the spike and ferrule, and drive the new spike in. (It will easily pierce the back of the gutter—no need to drill there.) If the spike is properly aligned but won't grab, water damage may have rotted the end of the rafter. Call a carpenter unless you are handy enough to remove the gutter and fascia and repair the rafter.

If brackets were used, they clip inside the front of the gutter and are nailed to the roof sheathing under the shingles or in some cases, to the fascia. First check to see if the bracket is bent or came loose at the front. If so, just bend it back into shape or reattach. The nails under the shingles rarely come loose—a good thing, since they are tough to hammer without breaking shingles or removing the gutters. If a bracket is loose, your best bet is to resupport the gutter section with a spike. If the brackets are nailed to the fascia, you can either unclip them and remove the gutters or resupport them with a spike.

Repair a metal gutter

No need to replace a whole section if there's a hole in one of your steel or aluminum gutters. You can do an excellent job of patching the hole. Start by using a wire brush to clean and scuff the inside of the gutter around the hole. Cut a patch of the same metal, put it in position, and predrill four pilot holes for pop rivets. Caulk the perimeter of the patch area and the bottom of the patch itself with silicone. Secure the patch with pop rivets.

House Foundation

As long as water isn't undermining your foundation, there's usually nothing you need to do to ensure its long life. Here's how to make sure your foundation is healthy.

Monitor your foundation

Normally your home's foundation needs no attention to last for generations. But if you notice cracks in the basement walls, keep an eye on them. Most cracks are nothing to worry about unless they are very large or they are expanding. To monitor cracks, mark their length on the wall and note the crack's width at its widest point. If cracks are expanding, consult a structural engineer. Even if a crack is not expanding, it should be repaired. Patch a dry crack with mortar. If a crack is leaking water, use hydraulic cement (as described in "Patch water leaks," page 276).

Diagnose moisture source

Before you can dry wet basement walls, you need to know where the water is coming from. Most often it is caused by condensation—moist vapor hits the cool wall and turns into water. Sometimes the water is the result of hydrostatic pressure. This occurs when poor drainage traps water around your foundation. Pressure builds until the water is literally forced through the walls and sometimes the floor.

If water is obviously seeping through a crack, you know it is caused by hydrostatic pressure. If the wall is just wet, do this simple test to determine the cause: Secure all four sides of a rectangular piece of aluminum foil or plastic wrap to the basement wall with duct tape. Remove the patch after two days. If the wall behind the patch is dry, you've got condensation. If the wall behind the patch is wet, hydrostatic pressure is the problem.

Curing condensation

Condensation in the basement won't seriously harm your foundation, so you could do nothing. If you want to prevent it, first make sure that all of the bathroom, kitchen and dryer vents in your home are venting to the outside. If any of these air-exhaust vents runs through the basement, make sure all the pipe joints are airtight. It may also help to insulate cold-water pipes in the basement. Otherwise a dehumidifier will solve the problem.

Curing hydrostatic pressure

Water pressing against your foundation is not a good thing—in extreme cases, it can collapse a wall—though water will usually start pouring through a crack first. Hydrostatic pressure is so tremendous that coating and patches applied from the inside usually fail eventually. So it's best to prevent hydrostatic pressure in the first place. Here's what to check in order from simplest to most difficult to correct:

• Check to make sure that leaky gutters or downspouts are not dumping water directly onto the foundation.

• Use splash blocks under your downspouts or roll-up hoses attached to them, if necessary, to direct water farther away from the foundation.

• Don't pile shoveled snow against the foundation.

• If your basement has window wells, keep them free of snow in winter. If you get a lot of snow, consider installing window-well covers—clear plastic bubbles that let light in but keep snow, rain, and debris out. Make sure that the wells have at least a few inches of gravel in the bottom for drainage, and keep their bottoms free of leaves and other debris.

• Keep water flowing away from the house. You may have to redo the landscape so the ground slopes away from the house; a minimum slope of 6 inches over 10 feet (15 cm over 3 meters) is advised.

• In extreme cases, you may need to have a trench dug around the foundation to install gravel and drainpipes. If this is done, the outside of the foundation wall should be coated with a waterproofing compound.

To waterproof from inside

Digging trenches to improve drainage is a very expensive proposition, and often you have no choice—if hydrostatic pressure is great enough over a large area, no interior basement wall coating will stop it. But before you resort to the backhoe, have a professional assess whether coating the inside of your concrete or block foundation with crystalline waterproofing material might do the job. This stuff actually penetrates several inches into concrete and makes it waterproof.

Patch water leaks

If water is leaking through a crack in the foundation, not seeping through the whole wall, you can usually solve the problem with hydraulic cement. This material, available at any hardware store or home center, hardens fast (even under water), expands as it cures, and will plug even a gushing leak in minutes. Of course you are better off using it to plug cracks and holes before water starts pouring in. Here's how:

1. Chip off any loose material around the hole with a cold chisel and a ball peen hammer. Make the opening larger inside than at the surface to lock the cement in place. Wear safety goggles. Brush away debris.

2. Mix a heaping handful of hydraulic cement with water. When it becomes stiff enough to form into a ball— after a minute or two—it's ready to use.

3. Wearing rubber gloves, push the cement into the hole, and hold it there for a few minutes until it hardens.

Windows

Old windows aren't just charming. They can be surprisingly efficient, too. Here's how to keep yours around for another generation.

Super–glue that cracked glass

You might not even notice it at first—a tiny seemingly harmless crack in a window pane. Then suddenly the little crack morphs into a dangerous monster, snaking its way across the glass and forcing you to replace the pane. The culprit is seasonal temperature changes that cause the glass to expand and contract. But with the help of a little super glue (cyanoacrylate, better known by the brand names Krazy Glue and Superglue), you can keep the crack small and prolong the window's life indefinitely. Just squirt the glue directly from the container into the crack—capillary action will suck the glue right in. If a little glue remains on the glass, don't wipe the sticky stuff away; it dries clear and hard anyway. Works for car windshield dings, too!

Erase glass scratches with toothpaste

A little toothpaste is all you need to make scratched windows look new again, provided the scratches are not too deep. "Extra-whitening" brands work best because they contain the most abrasive. Gel toothpastes contain little or no abrasive and won't work. Just dab the toothpaste on a soft cloth, and rub the scratch vigorously for a minute or two. Wipe clean with a damp rag.

Don't wash natural–finish window frames

You wouldn't use harsh detergent and water on your fine furniture, would you? If your home is graced with wooden windows that have a natural varnished finish, not a painted one, treat them with the same care. To make sure the windows are around for the next generation to enjoy, vacuum the wood rather than washing it with detergents that will eventually dull the finish and dry out the wood. If a really grimy wooden sash (the frame around the glass) needs washing, use a mild oil-based wood cleaner labeled for use on natural wood finishes, such as Murphy Oil Soap.

Lubricate window channels

If you're shoving and jerking a window to get it to slide up or down, you're shortening its life with undue wear. First clean out the channels on either side of the window with fine steel wool, and then vacuum away all debris and dust. Then make life easier for your windows, not to mention yourself, by rubbing the channels with a white wax candle. Or better yet, spritz the channels with silicone spray, available at hardware stores. The spray will last longer and will lubricate better than the wax.

Replace old window putty faster

If your window putty is brittle and cracked, replace it to prevent water from seeping in and rotting the window sashes. You can chip out the putty with an old chisel, but a multipurpose "five-in-one" tool works better. This inexpensive painter's tool is also useful for spreading putty, opening paint cans, scraping peeling paint, driving screws, and squeezing paint out of rollers. You can get one at a paint or hardware store or a home center.

Make putty last long

If you have to replace a windowpane, brush a generous coat of boiled linseed oil onto the raw wood the putty will go on. Let the oil soak in for about half an hour. This will prevent the wood from sucking the linseed oil out of the putty, prolonging the life of the putty and the window sash.

Save a rotted sill with epoxy

Windowsills get hit with a lot of water and this makes them vulnerable to rot. Replacing a windowsill takes considerable carpentry skill. The good news is that as long as the sill is mostly intact—even if it is soft—you can repair it yourself. Ask your local home center for a kit that contains two forms of epoxy—liquid wood consolidant and structural adhesive putty. You drill holes in the sill and squirt the liquid consolidant into them to harden the wood. Then you use the putty to seal over the holes and to fill any missing areas. Detailed instructions come with the products.

Don't put off replacing broken sash cords

Traditional double-hung windows use a counterweight system to make them easy to raise and to hold them up: A cord or chain attached to the top of the sash runs up to a pulley and down to a weight in a cavity at each side of the window. When the cord or chain breaks, some folks just shrug and prop open the window with a stick. Not only is this unsafe and inconvenient, it's a sentence for slow death for the window as you rock it back and forth, struggling to raise it. This is a shame, since replacing the cord or chain usually is an easy job.

Replace window cords with chain

When one sash-weight cord breaks, the others are surely on their way out, so replace them all. When you do, use flat-link brass or steel sash chain; it will last years longer than cord. Here how to change a cord:

❶ Carefully pry off the wood stop, or parting strip, just in front of the sash that holds the sash in place. Disconnect the cord from the each side of the sash, and lower the weight inside the weight chamber.

❷ Open the small panel near the bottom of the channel, and take out the weight. Cut off and discard the old cord.

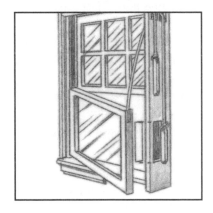

❸ Feed the new chain over the pulley into the weight chamber and pull it out of the weight-access hole. Loop the chain through the top of the weight, and secure the end to the chain with wire.

❹ Pull on chain, raising weight close to the pulley. Put a nail

through the chain to hold it in place.

❺ Snip off excess chain, and attach the end of the chain to the side of the sash.

Consider friction channels

During the 1970s energy crunch, misguided remodelers sometimes removed the counterweights and filled the weight chambers with insulation. If you discover insulation instead of weights in the jamb pockets, your best bet is to install vinyl or aluminum friction sash channels sold in kits.

Don't rush to replace old windows

While it is true that modern windows are more energy efficient than their predecessors, it usually takes about 20 years to

recoup the cost of the windows through savings in heating and cooling, according to *Consumer Reports* magazine. So instead of investing a lot of money to replace windows that work perfectly well, invest a little time and money to make sure your existing windows are in good working order and as airtight as possible. Add new weather-stripping and replace any that is old and worn.

Weather-strip old double-hung windows

You can quickly make those charming but rattling old windows airtight again. You'll need two types of weather-stripping—self-adhesive foam strip and vinyl V-strip. Both are very easy to apply.

❶ Apply a self-adhesive foam strip to the bottom of the lower sash. First make sure the bottom of the sash is clean, so the adhesive will stick. Then cut the foam to the length you need with scissors, remove the protective paper from over the adhesive, and stick the foam strip to the bottom of the sash. If the upper sash is operable, apply foam to its top edge as well.

❷ Apply a strip of vinyl V-strip to the channels on either side of the sash. Again, make sure the channels are clean, and cut two pieces of the weatherstripping to the

◆ BEST ADVICE ◆   **Double-hung Windows**

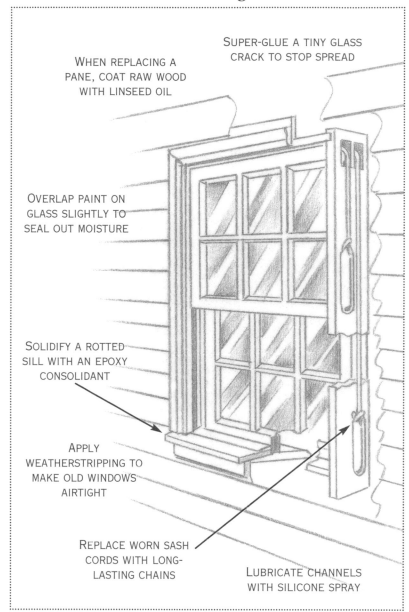

WHEN REPLACING A PANE, COAT RAW WOOD WITH LINSEED OIL

SUPER-GLUE A TINY GLASS CRACK TO STOP SPREAD

OVERLAP PAINT ON GLASS SLIGHTLY TO SEAL OUT MOISTURE

SOLIDIFY A ROTTED SILL WITH AN EPOXY CONSOLIDANT

APPLY WEATHERSTRIPPING TO MAKE OLD WINDOWS AIRTIGHT

REPLACE WORN SASH CORDS WITH LONG-LASTING CHAINS

LUBRICATE CHANNELS WITH SILICONE SPRAY

length of the channel. Most V-strip is self-adhering. Even if it is, when using V-strip on window channels, it's a good idea to anchor it with a few brads. Use a nail set to make sure the brads are flush, so the sash won't catch on it. If the upper sash is operable, you can weather-strip its channels, too.

3 If you notice a draft coming from the parting rails—the rails on the upper and lower sashes that overlap—you can put a piece of V-strip along the inside top edge of the lower sash. If the upper sash doesn't

move, use self-adhering V-strip—you'll never get a hammer in to drive nails. Make sure the crease in the V-strip is facing down.

Calm cranky casements

The secret to long life for modern casement windows is to lubricate their mechanisms as soon as you notice the cranks are becoming difficult to operate. The same goes for jalousie windows, which have several louvered panes. First loosen the setscrew, and remove the handle so you can pop off the cover. Then squirt the gears with a little silicone spray, and

spritz all the pivot points on the crank arm and the top and bottom guide arms. Don't see any gears? That means the gears have been permanently encased and lubricated. Just spray the pivot points.

Buy to Keep: Windows

When buying replacement windows, you have a number of choices that will last you a lifetime or more. Here are some factors to consider:

Wooden windows	The traditional choice, wood windows are still the sturdiest and most handsome you can buy, and when maintained, they can last for centuries—as the ones in historic houses attest. However, their exteriors must be painted regularly.
Vinyl windows	These windows need no paint and require little maintenance. Good-quality, well-installed vinyl windows are sturdy and energy efficient. But if they are cheaply made and poorly installed, they can leak air like a sieve. Look for good strong welds at the corners. You won't have much color choice—some come only in white.
Clad windows	Wood windows covered on the outside with vinyl or, less often, aluminum are a popular compromise. A vinyl-clad or aluminum-clad window gives you a relatively maintenance-free exterior with the elegance of wood on the interior.
Aluminum windows	These are a sturdy, economical alternative, but aluminum readily conducts heat and cold, so these have become less common. If you do buy aluminum windows, look for ones with thermal breaks—a core of insulation that stops much of the heat loss and keeps your energy bills lower.

Doors

No other moving part of our homes sees as much use—and sometimes abuse—as the doors. We shove them, slam them, even kick them shut. No wonder doors need a little adjustment now and again.

Cure a door that's tough to close

Do you really have to shove that door the last little bit of the way to get it to close? First rule out a warped door: With the door closed, check to make sure the door hits the stops all the way around. If the door is fine, the hinges probably are bound—that is, the hinge closes completely before the door does. Cut pieces of matchbook cover that are as long as the hinges and half as wide. One at a time, detach each hinge from the jamb and place a piece of matchbook into the hinge mortise, against the hinge barrel side. You may have to experiment a bit—perhaps you need two thicknesses of matchbook or just one thickness of heavy paper.

Toothpicks cure loose hinges

When door hinges are loose in their mortises, it's because the screws are stripped in their holes. To give the screws new grip, detach the hinges from the doorjamb. Fill the holes snuggly with toothpicks or a wooden matchstick dipped in white household glue. (One or two toothpicks usually do the trick.) Cut the toothpicks or matchstick flush with a utility knife or chisel. Replace the door—no need to redrill the holes where you've filled them; just drive the screws right in.

Adjust the strike plate

If the latch bolt doesn't catch when you close a door, most likely the bolt and the strike plate are misaligned, so the spring-loaded bolt isn't fitting into the hole in the plate. Close the door slowly to see if the bolt is positioned above, below, or to one side of the plate hole. If the misalignment is slight, the easiest solution is to file one edge of the strike-plate hole until the bolt drops in. If the misalignment is too great to file, take the strike plate off and chisel the strike-plate mortise bigger so you can move the plate and reinstall the screws in new holes.

Sometimes the door has shrunk so that the latch bolt no longer reaches the strike plate. In this case, take the strike plate off and use it as a template to cut one or two pieces of cardboard to the strike-plate shape, including the hole. Put the cardboard into the mortise to "pack out" the strike plate.

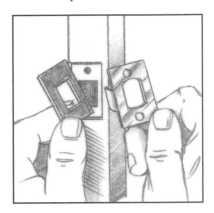

Prevent doors from swelling

Do your wooden doors swell on humid days to the point where you have to bang them with your shoulder to get them open? Check to make sure the top and bottom of the doors have been painted or varnished. If not, exposed end-grain may be sucking in moisture. A coat of primer and a couple of coats of paint or a few coats of varnish probably will solve the problem. If the problem persists, see the next tip.

Cure a sticky door

If a door sticks even in dry weather—or if painting the top and bottom doesn't cure humid weather sticking—the problem may not be the door at all. Your house may have settled or the framing may have shrunk, changing the door opening slightly. You can't easily adjust the door opening, but you can plane the door a little to fit the opening. First do a little detective work: With the door closed, check to see that there is a slight gap between the top and sides of the door and the frame, and between the bottom of the door and the floor or door sill. If you find a place with no gap, mark it with chalk. Then open the door, and look for places where the paint or varnish has rubbed off the edge of the door and mark these places. Use a hand plane or a belt sander to reduce these spots.

Doors that won't stay open

If a door swings shut on its own, it means the door frame isn't plumb—either because your house has settled or the installer didn't plumb it in the first place. Fortunately, there's an easy solution: Remove the hinge pins, and bend them slightly so that they fit more tightly in their holes. The extra resistance should solve the door's problem.

Fix a door rattle in no time

To stop a rattling door, remove the strike plate and use pliers to slightly bend the flange toward the hole. Another solution is to move the doorstop tighter against the door at the bottom. Use a utility knife to cut through the paint or varnish on both sides of the stop so it can break free. Then use a block and hammer to move the stop over

about 1/8 inch (3 mm). When you test it, the door should hit the stop and latch at the same time. Finally, drive a couple of 1 1/2-inch (38-mm) finish nails through the stop to anchor its new position.

Lubricate with graphite

The working parts of a door—hinges, latches, and locks—will work smoothly for generations if you lubricate them occasionally. It's especially important to do this if you notice a squeak. Light machine oil will work fine for hinges or latches, but don't squirt it into a lock, where it will collect dirt that may gum up and prevent the lock from working. Use powdered graphite instead—it doesn't collect dirt. You can use the graphite on hinges and latches, too. It comes in a plastic bottle with a small nozzle for squirting into tight places.

Peg loose door joints

On a traditional paneled door, the raised panel is in a frame consisting of horizontal rails and vertical stiles. Usually the rails have tongues called tenons that are glued into pockets called mortises in the stiles. After many years of use, these mortise-and-tenon joints can become loose and separated. The fix is easy if you are getting ready to repaint the door. Clamp the joints tightly closed. Drill a 1/2-inch (13-mm) hole

through the stiles at each corner so the holes will go through the mortises and tenons.

Put some yellow carpenter's glue in the holes; then tap in 1/2-inch-diameter hardwood dowels. Cut the dowels flush on both sides, and sand smooth. Paint will hide the repair.

Renew a door with a brass plate

Another way to reinforce loose bottom joints is to screw on a brass plate that spans the bottom rail and the bottoms of the adjoining stiles. Put one on both sides for extra strength. It's also a great way to protect the paint or finish on that door you tend to kick open when your arms are full of groceries.

Make your old door airtight

After many decades of use, that old wood front door is leaking air and causing major drafts. You could replace it with one of those tight-as-a-drum new steel or fiberglass entry doors. But that old door is part of the original architecture of your home—you hate to see it go. Don't fret. There's usually no reason to replace a historic entry door. You can eliminate most, if not all, of the draft leaks with new weatherstripping at a tiny fraction of the cost of a new door. Here's how:

• Most of the air infiltration probably comes under the door.

To solve this, you can install either a door sweep or threshold weatherstripping. A door sweep (A), which attaches to the bottom of the door, consists of a strip of rubber attached to a metal flange. The rubber presses against the threshold, creating an excellent seal. It is easy to install—you cut it to length and attach it to the bottom of the door. The drawback is that sweeps must be placed on the interior of an inward-swinging door. They are also very visible and may not be the decorative touch you have in mind for your foyer.

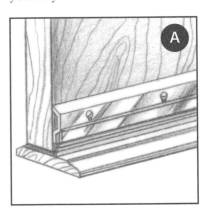

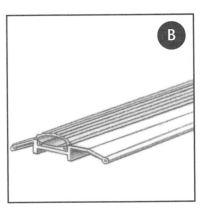

Threshold weatherstripping (B) is less obtrusive but harder to install. There are several types, but the most common uses a rubber gasket, usually set in a metal or an oak threshold. You'll need to pull up the old threshold and cut the new threshold to fit. For the threshold to work best, the bottom of the door should also be beveled slightly in the direction of the swing. If your door is not already beveled, doing this involves removing the door so that you can make the bevel with a plane or belt sander.

Also weather-seal between the door and side and top jambs. There are several products you can use. Metal tension strips are the most durable. Cut the metal strips to length with a tin snips. Then nail the strips in place through the holes in its flange. Finally, bend the strip out a bit so it will press against the door when it closes.

Add a storm door

Another option to replacing a nice old exterior door is to add a storm-screen-combination door. Models with full-glass panels can show off a historic old door while protecting it from the weather. A top-quality storm-screen door, however, can cost nearly as much as a new main door, but it's easier to install and will be just as airtight as a new door.

Tighten up a screen door

Wooden screen doors take a lot of abuse, especially when they are attached to a spring that slams them shut. It's not surprising that they warp or suffer from loose joints. To straighten a warped screen door, install a tension rod with a turnbuckle diagonally across the door. Tighten the turnbuckle to pull the door flat. To reinforce loose joints, you can use the strategies described earlier in "Peg loose door joints" and "Renew a door with a brass plate." Another easy, cheap, but less attractive solution is to use L-shaped steel mending plates. Just put one mending plate across each joint on one side of the door, and fasten them down with the screws provided.

Get rid of the spring

To keep the joinery in your wooden screen door from loosening up in the first place, replace the spring closer with a piston closer, like those found on most aluminum screen and storm doors. Piston closers will make the door close gently, but they allow the door to open only 90 degrees.

Shutters and Awnings

Shutters were invented to protect the fragile windows in early homes from storms. Today most exterior shutters are purely decorative, but they still need some attention to keep them looking great.

Clean outdoor shutters

To clean shutters, remove the shutters from the windows and lay them flat. Wet them down with a solution containing an all-purpose cleaner, such as Fantastik or Formula 409, or use a spray bottle of water with a squirt of dishwashing liquid added. Make sure that you get cleaner into every crevice. Leave the cleaner on for 5 minutes or so. Then use a screwdriver wrapped in a towel to attack hard-to-reach spots. Rinse with a garden hose, using as much water pressure as your hose can muster. Dry the slats with a towel. Let the shutters finish drying in the sun.

Reinforce sagging shutters

If the joints have come loose on your old shutters, you can easily give them new life with L-shape mending plates. In most cases these days, shutters are kept permanently open, so place the mending plates on the side that won't be seen. Just remove the shutters, and push the joints tightly together—it's a good idea to use pipe or bar clamps if you have them. Or you can make a tourniquet clamp with rope. Then screw the plates into position. If a shutter is sagging, fasten a wire diagonally across it to make it square, as you would with a sagging screen door. Attach the wire on the hidden side, with the top of the wire on the hinged side.

Clean acrylic awnings

These awnings are usually a breeze to clean because most have a soil- and stain-resistant finish. When dirt accumulates, just wash it off using a sponge and a solution of warm water with a few squirts of dishwashing liquid. Rinse thoroughly with fresh water and air-dry. For stubborn stains, use a fabric stain remover, following the directions on the label.

Remove mildew from acrylic awnings

Mildew usually is a snap to remove from acrylic awning because mildew doesn't grow on the acrylic itself; it grows on the dirt, leaves, and other materials that have accumulated on the fabric. To remove both the mildew and the dirt, mix 1 cup of bleach with a squirt of mild dishwashing liquid in 1 gallon (4 liters) of warm water. Apply it to the entire area, and let it soak in (but not dry). Then scrub with a sponge. Rinse thoroughly and air-dry. Don't use bleach on awnings with logos or prints; just use soapy water.

Clean vinyl or fabric awning

Use a garden sprayer to apply vinyl and fabric cleaner (such as SkyClean 2 in 1 Vinyl Cleaner & Protectant) evenly in a saturating mist. Don't wet the awning with water first. Start from the bottom of the awning and work up. Before the cleaner dries, scrub the awning with a soft sponge or soft- to medium-bristle brush. (Brushes work best on fabric awnings.) Rinse by spraying with a garden hose until the runoff water is clear. You'll want to remove all the cleaner because leftover cleaner will leave a chalky film once it dries.

Remove mildew on a vinyl or fabric awning

Mix 1 cup of bleach into 1 gallon (4 liters) of warm water. This solution will do a great job of removing mildew. The problem is that there is a slight possibility it will cause the colors to fade or run. So test it by running a solution-soaked cotton swab on a hidden section of awning. If colors are fast, scrub the awning with a sponge and then rinse it off completely with water before the bleach solution has a chance to dry.

Porches and Decks

Keep your deck or porch clean, dry, and sealed. You'll be rewarded with many years of rocking on the porch or sunning on your deck.

Sweep for long life

Sweep your porch or deck clean on a regular basis—weekly or more often if leaves, pine needles, or other debris tends to collect. It's the simplest, most important thing you can do to prolong its life. Debris collects moisture, and moisture promotes rot and encourages termites. So pay particular attention to nooks and crannies where debris can collect, like the bottoms of posts. Get the broom bristles between the deck boards to remove debris that can collect on top of the joists below the decking.

Select the right cleaning solution

Deck cleaners are designed to clean away grime and to remove loose wood fibers on the surface of the deck boards and railings. There are a variety of formulas to choose from at your home center or hardware store. Some cleaners contain only detergents; others may contain oxalic acid or bleach or a combination of these ingredients. Unless you have mildew, moss, or berry stains, you won't need a cleaner that contains bleach (sodium hypochlorite). Avoid the bleach if you can; heavy concentrations of it can damage the wood. Read the labels and choose a cleaner that best suits the discoloration or staining problems on your deck.

Your deck: to finish or not to finish?

You can be taken aback by the variety of deck-finishing products that you'll find at the hardware store or home center. But just like the 30 varieties of yogurt you find in the supermarket diary case, there really aren't many variations in suitable wood finishes. In fact, you really only have three choices:

• One choice is to apply no finish. This is a perfectly valid choice if you live in a relatively dry climate and you don't mind the deck turning gray.

• The most popular finishes for decks are clear penetrating wood finishes, sometimes called sealers. These usually darken the wood's natural color in a way most people find pleasing. Clear finishes contain a water repellent—usually paraffin wax, as well as a mildewcide and ultraviolet stabilizers to slow deterioration from the sun.

Clear finishes need to be reapplied each year. It's easy—just use a paint roller attached to a pole for the deck boards and a natural-bristle brush for the railings and anyplace else the roller can't reach. Use a roller designed for textured paint finishes—it holds the most finish.

• If you want to change the color of your deck, you can use a semitransparent stain. The major difference is that the pigment in the stain provides more protection from the sun than a clear finish can provide. You'll need to recoat only about every two or three years. To apply, use the same technique as for a clear finish.

Don't paint your deck

Paint and solid-colored stain (essentially thinned paint) form a film on the surface of wood rather than a penetrating layer. This is fine for vertical surfaces like the side of your house, and it provides the most protection from the sun. It's also okay to use these finishes to add some color to the railings of your deck. But they are not a great idea for deck boards. Foot traffic wears away paint and solid-colored stain, and these finishes become unattractive in a hurry. Water eventually finds its way under the finish, causing it to crack and peel. Worse, the trapped moisture promotes rot. There are paints, usually labeled

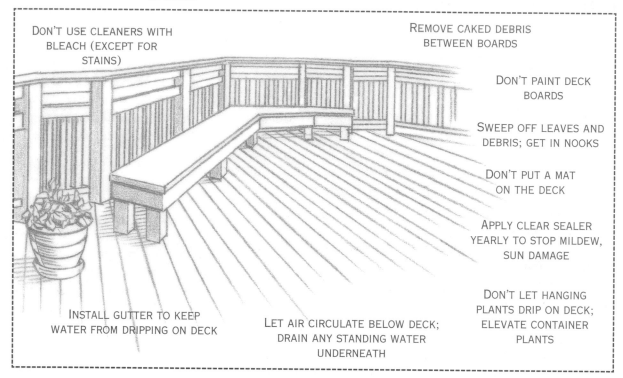

DON'T USE CLEANERS WITH BLEACH (EXCEPT FOR STAINS)

REMOVE CAKED DEBRIS BETWEEN BOARDS

DON'T PAINT DECK BOARDS

SWEEP OFF LEAVES AND DEBRIS; GET IN NOOKS

DON'T PUT A MAT ON THE DECK

APPLY CLEAR SEALER YEARLY TO STOP MILDEW, SUN DAMAGE

DON'T LET HANGING PLANTS DRIP ON DECK; ELEVATE CONTAINER PLANTS

INSTALL GUTTER TO KEEP WATER FROM DRIPPING ON DECK

LET AIR CIRCULATE BELOW DECK; DRAIN ANY STANDING WATER UNDERNEATH

"porch paints," that are designed to stand up to foot traffic, but these should be used only on surfaces that will be protected by a roof.

Vent your deck

Water dripping from the roof can cause deck boards to rot with surprising speed. The best solution is a gutter to carry the water away. But if that is not possible, consider installing a grill vent along the drip line to let the water drip through.

Scrape debris from between boards

When wet pine needles and other debris get caked between deck boards, you probably won't be able to clear the spaces with a broom. Use the teeth of any old coarse saw blade to pull out the debris. A drywall jab saw is perfect for the job.

Pros and cons of pressure-treated wood

It's a common misconception that pressure-treated wood is the most durable you can buy for outdoor use. But depending on the application, that's not always the case. In the pressure-treatment process, chemicals that are toxic to termites and fungi are forced into the wood under pressure. This means the critters won't eat the wood.

Keep in mind, though, that termites and fungi also need a moist environment—they won't eat wood that doesn't stay damp. So if you are building something that will remain damp or will be in contact with the ground, such as the frame of a deck or porch—nothing will last longer than pressure-treated wood.

For your deck or porch floor, however, pressure-treated wood may not be the ideal choice. Water can't collect on a well-designed and well-maintained deck, so fungi and termites won't come to dine anyway. Plus, pressure-treated wood is usually made with southern yellow pine, which is denser than lighter woods like redwood and cedar. This means southern yellow pine is more likely to warp and splinter from humidity changes and the effects of wetting and drying—an especially important consideration for decks that get rained on. Porch floors are usually covered by a roof, so rain shouldn't be a problem. Choose tongue-and-groove mahogany porch flooring, which looks much better than pressure-treated boards. The mahogany is more durable, too, and you will be pleased to discover that it costs no more than pressure-treated wood.

Keep it tight

When your deck was built, the wood probably wasn't completely dry—especially if pressure-treated wood was used. As the wood does dry over several years, connections that have been bolted together (beams or joists to posts) or nailed (deck boards to joists) can become loose. Besides being disconcerting, a deck that wobbles and creaks can cause parts to break eventually. Plus, loose connections collect debris that stays wet and causes rot. If you have this problem, get underneath the deck and tighten every nut and bolt you see. Tighten nails with a couple of hammer whacks, using a nail set to avoid denting visible areas of deck boards and railings.

Flip deck boards

Deck boards getting worn, weathered, and splintery? Just take them up, flip them over, and reinstall. You might still have to replace a few, but it's a cheap way to double the life of most of them.

☞ DON'T
block air circulation below

Air circulation below your porch or deck prevents moisture buildup that causes rot and encourages termites. If you want to screen the area below a deck or porch, use lattice so that air can move through freely. Keep the lattice about 1 inch (25 mm) off the ground so it doesn't rot on the ends.

Don't let hanging plants drip onto your porch

If you hang plants from your porch overhang, make sure they are far enough out so that water drips on the ground, not the porch.

Elevate your flower pots

Although this won't increase the life of your containers or your plants, you'll extend the life of your deck boards if you keep all your pots on rolling plant stands instead of setting them directly on your deck. Even if you put saucers underneath your containers to catch water, the saucers themselves

will leave marks, but water will drain away from rolling stands almost completely.

Skip the welcome mat

Don't put mats on your porch or deck. They collect rot-inducing debris and moisture. If you must have a doormat on the porch, be sure to clean under it regularly and pick it up and dry it out after a rainy period.

Replace step treads with multiple boards

Are the treads rotting on your porch or deck steps? If the stringers that support the treads are in good shape, it is usually very simple to pull off and replace the old treads. But this time, replace each tread with two or three narrower boards—two 2 x 6s (38 x 140 mm) or three 2 x 4s (38 x 89 mm) usually will do the job—leaving about 1/4 inch (6 mm) of space between each board. The space will allow water to drain through, rather than collect and cause rot that shortens the life of the treads. Less water also means less dangerous ice buildup.

Consider skipping the risers

Vertical riser boards placed between each step do provide a finished look. But on outdoor steps, the joint where risers butt the tread below always collects rot-inducing moisture and debris. There is no structural need for riser boards, so consider eliminating them if you are building or restoring an outdoor stair. If you do include risers, leave at least 1/2 inch (13 mm) of space between the bottom of the riser and the tread.

Open stringers last longer

There are two ways you can configure the stringer boards that support the treads of your outdoor stair.

• In an open design (A), the stringers are cut out to receive the treads (and the risers, if you are using them). Although it is more difficult to build, the joint is protected from water buildup and will last longer.

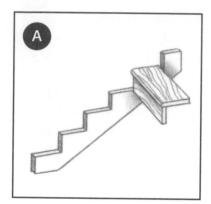

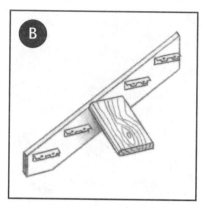

• In a closed design (B), the treads fit between the stringers, sitting on a cleat or metal support attached to the inside of the stringers. Closed stringers provide a more finished look, but water will seep into the joints between the treads and the stringers, making the treads vulnerable to rot. If you do opt for closed stringers, use metal support hardware instead of wooden cleats. The cleats, hidden from the drying effects of the sun, will be even more vulnerable to rot than the treads. Also, it's best not to support the treads in dadoes (grooves) cut into the stringers. That's excellent indoor construction but a sure recipe for rot outdoors.

Yard & Garden

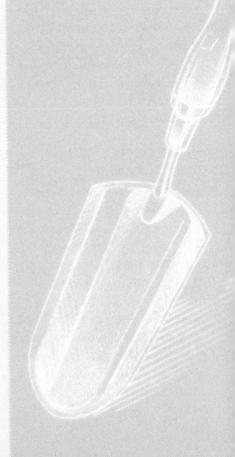

Your Yard

There's no getting around it: It takes work to maintain a yard that provides pleasure year after year. But with a little smart planning you can turn the toil into tasks that are easy and, yes, even fun.

Make a maintenance schedule and stick to it

Plants, like all living things, appreciate tender loving care and will reward you for providing it. Conversely, neglecting lawn and garden maintenance can do lasting damage to the landscape. Protect your landscaping investment just as you would your good clothes, your car, or your house. Familiarize yourself with the needs of your plants, including watering, weeding, pruning, and fertilizing. Then literally mark dates on the calendar to remind yourself when each type of job needs to be done.

Group plants with similar maintenance needs

Birds of a feather flock together, the old saying goes—and it's true for plants, too. Plants that need good drainage, for example, should be planted together (in a location with excellent drainage, of course) and not mixed in with plants that need very moist soil. Otherwise, at best, you'll be making a lot of work for yourself trying to give each plant just what it wants, and at worst, the garden will

sustain some casualties. If you chose plants to match the conditions on your site, you'll find that these groupings happen naturally, but if you bought some plants impulsively and now you're wondering where to put them, this is where to start: Group them by their growth and care needs.

Plant only what you can manage

Because maintenance is so critical to keeping plants healthy over time, make sure not to overextend yourself by planting too much. Fewer plants and smaller gardens make for less work, and if you don't feel overwhelmed, you're more likely to do the work there is to do.

Visit your garden frequently

There's an old adage that goes "The best thing for a garden is the shadow of the gardener," meaning that gardeners who spend a lot of time in their gardens notice problems while their gardens are still small and manageable. Regular monitoring is how to detect pests and diseases before they get out of control, and what could be

nicer than a daily stroll through your own little paradise?

Prepare soil before planting

The biggest mistake home gardeners make is to plant in unprepared soil. Pros know that nothing, absolutely nothing, will do more to promote plant health and longevity than lovely, friable (crumbly) soil that provides plenty of nutrients, lets roots grow freely, and holds water, yet drains adequately. The only problem is that most soils aren't like that naturally! If your soil is like most, you'll be adding generous quantities of compost, rototilling compacted soil, or doing other preparatory work. Plan to do this *before* planting because the job is nearly impossible to do after plants are in the ground.

Keep the water flowing

Most garden plants prefer a constant amount of soil moisture instead of infrequent drenching alternating with droughts, and regular soil moisture is critical to establishing new plantings—the first step in ensuring a long life. To make the job easy, install a simple irrigation system (it could be nothing more than a soaker hose winding through the beds just underneath the mulch) and put it on a timer. The watering will take care of itself, and your plants won't have to survive on the whims of the weather.

Learn your NPKs

Those numbers on bags of fertilizer hold a wealth of information. "N" stands for nitrogen, which stimulates leafy growth. "P" is for phosphorus, which promotes flowering. Finally, "K" represents the potassium content; plants need potassium for a host of functions, including root formation. Nitrogen, phosphorus, and potassium are called the plant "macronutrients" because plants need these three in large quantities. They also need so-called "micronutrients," such as iron, but in smaller amounts. A bag of 10-10-10 fertilizer contains 10 percent each of nitrogen, phosphorus, and potassium by weight. The higher the numbers, the more "potent" the fertilizer, but buy only what you need because overfertilizing is as bad as underfertilizing. Your local garden center or Cooperative Extension can advise you on what and how much to fertilize.

Plan your landscape as a whole

If you landscape right the first time, you'll get to enjoy it longer because you shouldn't ever have to rip it out and redo it. Don't leave "getting it right" up to chance; get a satisfactory design for your entire property on paper before you turn a shovelful of soil—even if you'll be installing it over the course of many years for budgetary

reasons. This approach works because it makes you think about your landscape pragmatically, which will lead you to plant purposefully; it discourages impulsive plant choices and purchases; and it defines your costs more clearly.

Consider hardscaping

Plants can't solve every landscaping problem. If a fence is really what's needed, trying to make do with a hedge instead may be a waste of money and time. It's a mistake to choose plants over hardscaping simply because they sometimes cost less and seem more "natural." Instead, use restraint and practicality to allocate landscaping dollars where they're really needed. The sooner you make effective choices, the longer you'll get to enjoy them.

Don't put new mulch over old

When you replace an organic mulch (such as anything made from wood products), be sure to remove all the old mulch first unless it's so decomposed it's hardly distinguishable from the soil. If you put new mulch over old, it just becomes harder for the bottom layer to decompose. Over time, a mat of mulch can build up that literally suffocates plants and prevents water penetration, shortening the life of your garden. In most climates, 2 inches (5 cm) of mulch is plenty and applying more may be detrimental.

Steer clear of trends

The gardening world is subject to trendy fads just as high fashion is. It's fun to try new plants, but unless you have the patience and the bank account to withstand high losses, don't build a whole garden around them. Use reliable materials and techniques for the majority of your landscape, so if some small experiment doesn't work out, you'll still have laid the groundwork for a sustainable garden.

Learn to like the weathered look

It's not necessary to replace an organic mulch every year unless it has fully decomposed. Wood chips, for example, should give you several years of service, but in a moist climate they'll weather and turn gray their first season on the ground. Although they may not look fresh and new, if they're still doing their job, leave them in place until you've gotten your money's worth.

Let autumn leaves lie

If there isn't a good reason to remove fallen leaves, don't. Leaves compost by themselves, providing beneficial humus for trees over time. Think of it as the trees feeding and mulching themselves. So unless the leaves are smothering something

planted underneath the trees, this is definitely one legitimate way to minimize maintenance—you can't ask for less work than *no* work!—while actually promoting plant health.

Never compost diseased plant cuttings

One way to keep your garden healthy and long-lived is to remove diseased plant parts as soon as you detect a problem. While it's a wonderful idea to compost any *healthy* vegetative

material you remove from the garden—you'll save money making your own compost instead of buying it, and your garden will thank you—home compost piles are unlikely to produce the high heat necessary to kill disease-causing organisms. So take those mildew-covered phlox leaves and throw them in the trash, not the compost.

Choose amendments with care

Don't spend money on expensive soil amendments if you don't have to. If your objective is just to lighten the soil, your plants are best served by simple compost or aged manure. Reserve amendments with special properties (such as peat moss, which lowers soil pH for acid-loving rhododendrons and azaleas) for situations that require it.

Use the right mulch

Pick a mulch based on its application, not its cost, color, or longevity. Vegetable and perennial gardens, in which you dig and turn the soil regularly, should be mulched with light-textured composts that decompose quickly, such as leaf mold. Shrubs and trees, whose root zones should not be disturbed after they are planted, should be mulched with long-lived shredded bark or bark nuggets.

Your Lawn

Lawns provide not only an open green space but also a pleasing backdrop for showier perennial gardens and container displays.

Buy the right grass

For a healthy lawn that will survive the seasons, use a turf grass seed or sod suitable to your geographic area and your growing conditions. For instance, fescues do best in shade, while Kentucky bluegrass needs lots of sun to grow well. Very hot climates require so-called "warm-season" grasses (such as *Zoysia)* that thrive in heat. At northern latitudes, you're better off with "cool-season" grasses that grow in spring and fall, slowing down in summer, because they will survive harsh winters. And if at all possible, use a blend of grasses instead of just one type. That way, if an insect or disease attacks one grass, you're unlikely to lose the entire lawn.

Buy only as much nitrogen as you need

If you fertilize your lawn—and lawns don't automatically need fertilizing—don't be taken in by products billed as lawn fertilizers that have a very high "N" (nitrogen) number, especially if they come at a premium price. Nitrogen is a nutrient that moves quickly through soil; heavy rains or an excessive amount of irrigation can wash it away. Using only as much fertilizer as your plants need and applying it only when the plants can use it will keep your lawn healthier by promoting moderate, sustainable growth.

To dethatch or not to dethatch

Some grasses—Kentucky bluegrass, in particular—tend to build up a layer of stems and woody roots called thatch. Water and nutrients have a tough time penetrating this layer, starving and dehydrating the lawn. Some lawns may never need dethatching, while others will need it every few seasons. To see if you need to dethatch, take up a 3 x 3-inch (7 x 7-cm) square of lawn. If you see more than 2 inches (5 cm) of thatch—it will look

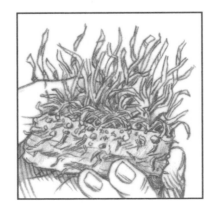

almost like thick woven fabric— it's time to dethatch. Rent a dethatching machine, and make plenty of room in your compost pile for all the material it will pull out of your lawn. Your grass may look raggedy for a week or two after dethatching, but it will benefit from the grooming.

🖝 DON'T
mow too low

Cutting grass too low can harm it, causing brown patches and dieback. Set your lawn-mower height to 2 1/2 to 3 inches (6.5 to 7.5 cm). That will leave the blades long enough to photosynthesize and regrow healthily.

Grass loves lime

In general, lawn grasses prefer moderately alkaline soil, and that's what lime provides. That's why twice-a-year liming is recommended in areas where acid soils predominate. Get a soil pH test to see if you need to lime your lawn at all. If you do need to lime, make it part of your regular maintenance schedule, applying the lime as recommended for your local area. At just a few dollars per bag, agricultural lime is a cheap way to help your lawn thrive. Just don't apply too much; if you raise the pH above 7.5 or so, you'll actually start to harm your lawn.

Outdoor Plants

Here's the lowdown on picking plants that will enhance your home for many years, as well as how to keep them happy and healthy.

Am I really going to prune that thorny shrub?

Before you invest in a shrub, consider the amount and kind of maintenance it will require, especially if you're buying it because it's billed as a "low-maintenance" plant. Barberry is a good example. The only maintenance it really needs, beyond watering, is a good pruning once or twice a season. But it's covered with nasty spines that make the job daunting. A sturdy pair of gloves will keep your hands free of punctures, but if some jobs are so unpleasant you opt not to do them, you'll end up with an overgrown garden that won't last long. So get the whole story before you buy.

Fit plants to your yard

If you choose acid-loving shrubs, such as rhododendrons and azaleas, for your landscape but your soil isn't acidic, understand that you're creating a lifelong maintenance chore for yourself. Sure, soil pH can be adjusted, but only temporarily. Products that lower soil pH do so only for a season, if that long, so you'll have to apply them year after year, forever. A garden that requires extra care can still have a long life, but the chances decrease as the maintenance load goes up. Keep this in mind before planting a sun-loving shrub in a shady yard or a moisture-loving plant in semi-arid terrain.

Say "no" to invasive plants

No matter how much you like a pretty but invasive plant, you and your garden are probably better off without it in the long run. Plants that can rapidly overrun their neighbors probably will, and once that happens, the whole garden may have to be torn out. So for the long-term health of your garden, pass on the invasives and stick with well-behaved plants that make good neighbors. A reputable nursery can help you sort out the two.

Examine roots when buying

Whether you're buying a tree or a perennial, look for a plant that is well rooted but not root bound. It will transplant the best and have the greatest chance of survival. Ask a nursery staff member to tip the plant out of its pot for you so you can examine it. The roots should be visible at the surface of the soil all around the root-ball, but there should not be a solid mat of roots (see picture) anywhere. Avoid trees and shrubs with major roots that seem to wrap around the root-ball. These roots can "girdle" a plant, killing it.

Divide and thrive

Most herbaceous perennials, such as aster, daylily, and phlox, need regular division. That means digging them up every three to five years, literally dividing the roots into smaller clumps by cutting or by shaking them apart, and replanting them. Division promotes profuse flowering and new, vigorous growth. Astilbes are a case in point. If left undivided, they tend to flower less and less over the years, as their roots get crowded and woody. The same clump, once divided, can explode with blossoms. But don't automatically divide everything. Some perennials simply don't need division, and a few downright detest it. Check a good reference book before dividing any perennial whose preferences you don't know.

ProTip

PICK THE RIGHT PLANTS

Landscape and professional gardeners know that plants that are not suited for your yard's conditions won't last a long time no matter how much care they receive. This is true for any plant capable of living more than one season and even, to some extent, for the annuals that will grace your yard for only a few months. Make a list of the conditions at your home: the pH and workability of your soil, sun and shade, rainfall, winter cold hardiness, summer heat and humidity, and anything else you think might be important. Good reference books list the needs of common garden plants, but common sense will get you far. For example, if you live near the Great Lakes, use plants native to that area or to other parts of the world with similar conditions and you can't go far wrong. Also be mindful of what is likely to get eaten by wildlife in your area, such as deer. If you don't know, inquire at your local nursery.

Give plants the space they require

If you plant trees or perennials so close together that they shade one another as they grow, eventually one of them will have to make way for the other. Although it's hard to imagine a tiny seedling as a full-fledged plant, determine plant spacing according to the plant's mature size, not its size when you get it. This is even more critical for trees than for perennials, since they are tougher to move once established. Any good plant reference book will tell you a plant's size at maturity.

Bring tender plants in from the cold

Hardy plants are happy to go dormant and spend the winter outside, but some garden favorites, such as dahlias, cannas, and gladioli, aren't tough enough to survive very cold winters. If you grow them outside their range, remember to dig them up in fall just when frost cuts down their leaves. If you forget to, plants that could have given you pleasure year after year will turn to mush when they freeze. These tender bulbs and tubers all have different needs for winter storage, so do an online search, consult a book, or check with your local garden center for more specific instructions.

Wait on those bulbs

Spring bulbs are a joy—it's undeniable. That burst of color when most other plants are still dormant is just the remedy for the winter blahs. But if your perennial garden is new, wait a season or two before planting bulbs. You want to make sure you're happy with the overall layout and won't be making big changes, because if you decide to move things around midseason, you may find yourself spearing bunches of brand-new bulbs with your spading fork. Rather than have to replace them, be patient and put bulbs in when you know everything else will stay put.

Find that special plant online

In the days before the Internet, gardeners had to search high and low for unusual plants. Now even the smallest growers are likely to have websites, and performing a quick search of the Internet can turn up dozens of sources for plants you'd given up on finding. To have the greatest chance of success, try doing separate searches using the botanical name and then the common name of the plant you want. If it's a specific variety you want, include that in your search terms, too.

Tree trunks and string trimmers don't mix

Tree trunks sustain more injuries from the lashing of string trimmers than from anything else. The damage may seem minor, but it can cause major problems if it happens repeatedly. An easy way to avoid the problem is to prevent grass, which needs to be trimmed, from growing up to the trunk of a tree—or a shrub—in the first place. Install shallow edging a few feet from the trunk to keep grass at a

BE ON THE LOOKOUT
FOR DISEASE AND
TREAT IT EARLY

PRUNE BROKEN BRANCHES
NEATLY WITH A SHARP TOOL

MULCH UNDER THE
TREE TO KEEP AWAY
GRASS—AND
TRUNK-DAMAGING
TRIMMERS

DON'T DRIVE OR PARK—
OR PUT A PATH—OVER THE
TREE'S ROOTS

DON'T HEAP DIRT
AROUND TRUNK OR
OVER THE ROOTS

NEVER GARDEN AGGRESSIVELY
OVER A TREE'S ROOT ZONE

healthy distance, and apply a layer of maintenance-free mulch inside the edging or plant the area with a low-growing shade-loving groundcover. It will look neater and keep your woody plants healthier.

Take care with tree roots

Where trees are concerned, prevention is the best medicine, and that means protecting their roots from damage.

• Make sure that cars don't drive over or park in the root zones of trees. Also make sure that people don't habitually walk over the same area.

• Never heap soil over the roots of trees or around their trunks. It may take years for mounded soil to suffocate a tree, but it most assuredly will.

• Don't garden aggressively directly beneath trees. The constant digging and disturbance are damaging to roots. Keep trees and gardens at a respectful distance from one another, and both will benefit.

• If you are planning major work on your house, fence off the root zone of any trees in the vicinity so that heavy equipment operators won't drive over the roots. This will also help ensure that the trunk isn't damaged by equipment or materials getting too close.

Put a tree tour on your schedule

Homeowners often walk through their gardens looking at the herbaceous flowers, but it's all too easy to ignore trees and shrubs—the woody backdrop. Every so often, make a point of "touring" your home landscape looking for woody plant problems that are starting to develop.

• If you find branches broken or torn by heavy winds, prune them neatly with a sharp blade to minimize the opportunity for infection.

• Look for signs of disease—discoloration or disfiguration of leaves, defoliation, or masses of insects—and take steps to treat them. But don't go overboard. A few tent caterpillars aren't an infestation. Consult your local Cooperative Extension if you have doubts about how or whether to treat insect problems.

• For major tree work, consult a licensed arborist, not just any garden service.

? How Long Will A Tree Last?

ANSWER: From 30 years to hundreds of years

Just like animals, trees have life expectancies, and some trees are genetically predisposed to live longer than others. Birches and shadblows may give you 30 to 50 years, while oaks will outlive not only you but also a few generations of your descendants. There's also a trade-off between growth *speed* and longevity. Trees that grow quickly typically do not enjoy long lives, in part because fast-growing trees form relatively weak wood that can't stand up to the ravages of time. Remember this when you're choosing trees to create a privacy buffer or for any long-term purpose.

Clearly define groundcover plantings

What makes a groundcover beautiful is the visual mass of a large planting and its clear separation from the surrounding area. If you maintain a sharp boundary, you'll also increase the life of the planting by preventing grass or other plants from invading your groundcover. Create a line of demarcation with hardscaping products, such as brick or metal-strip edging, or by using a spade to cut a clean edge twice a season.

 ProTip

LET GROUND-COVERS GO SOLO

People who design landscapes for a living say that planting two different groundcovers together or in adjacent areas is like trying to wear two outfits simultaneously. It just doesn't work. Groundcovers are supposed to spread, so eventually two different ones in the same area will grow together, look like a mess, and have to be torn out. Let each groundcover shine in its own dedicated space.

Patio and House Plants

For an apartment dweller, a few containers may be the whole landscape, while at a country house, they are more likely to be the finishing touch in a larger design. Either way, the small size and transitory nature of container arrangements make them the perfect place to experiment with design ideas and splurge on must-have plants.

The perpetual pot

Terra-cotta pots can last essentially forever…with proper care. If you live in a climate that produces freezing temperatures in winter, remove all plants from outdoor pots in late autumn. Move the pots to a frost-free place (such as a warm cellar), using a dolly or cart if you need to, leaving the soil inside. If the pots are too heavy to move with the soil inside, empty them first. Soil can be shoveled into heavy contractor garbage bags and stored anywhere. If you can't store your pots at above-freezing temperatures, they *must* be emptied; otherwise moisture in the soil will expand when it freezes and crack them. To store terra-cotta pots outdoors, turn them upside down so snow and ice don't accumulate inside, and raise them off the ground by putting blocks of scrap wood under the rims. If possible, store them under an eave or a carport for added protection. Your terra-cotta pots may one day become treasured family heirlooms.

Selecting containers

Containers can be a considerable investment, so think before you buy. Real terra-cotta pots are lovely and can last a long time, but they require winter protection in cold climates; their weight makes them hard to move and store; and if you drop them, they will break. If you can't give them the care they need, foam or resin pots may be a better, more long-lasting choice. Although these materials also need some care, they can withstand more abuse. When buying pots, whatever they're made of, look them over for cracks and reject any that have significant flaws.

Keep plastic perfect

Plastic pots—whether described as foam, resin, or vinyl—offer a good compromise between quality and convenience. They won't last for generations, but they are lightweight, inexpensive, and often just as attractive as terra-cotta. Plastics degrade more from exposure to light than anything else, so store plastic pots out of direct sun-

shine. While it's best to empty them before the thermometer drops below freezing, it's not absolutely critical to do so. To overwinter a pot filled with soil, pull a trash bag over it, securing the bag's edge to the ground with rocks, or cover it with a piece of scrap plywood cut large enough to overhang the pot's edge, also secured with a rock. Finally, remember that at cold temperatures, some plastics become very fragile. If dropped, a cold plastic pot can shatter.

Stay clean, be green

A little hygiene goes a long way toward ensuring a full season of life for your container plants. At the start of each season, sterilize pots by immersing them in a mixture of 1 part bleach to 10 parts water for 20 minutes or so. Rinse them off, and let them dry before filling with soil and planting. The bleach will kill disease-causing pathogens from last year still lurking on your pots, waiting for an opportunity to infect a new crop.

Keep potting mix, but use caution

Whether to reuse potting mix is a question you have to answer each and every year. A good rule of thumb is this: If it's not broken, don't fix it. In other words, if there's no problem with snails, slugs, fungal diseases, or anything else that can be harbored in potting

Container Plants

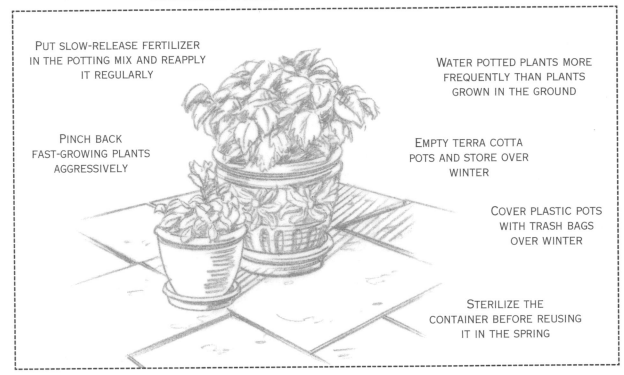

PUT SLOW-RELEASE FERTILIZER IN THE POTTING MIX AND REAPPLY IT REGULARLY

PINCH BACK FAST-GROWING PLANTS AGGRESSIVELY

WATER POTTED PLANTS MORE FREQUENTLY THAN PLANTS GROWN IN THE GROUND

EMPTY TERRA COTTA POTS AND STORE OVER WINTER

COVER PLASTIC POTS WITH TRASH BAGS OVER WINTER

STERILIZE THE CONTAINER BEFORE REUSING IT IN THE SPRING

mix, don't replace it. Instead, amend it each spring with some compost, and incorporate some slow-release fertilizer before filling your pots and planting. Reassess its condition each year until it's clearly time to buy new.

Water generously

Potted plants need to be watered more frequently than those in the ground because their limited rooting area can't hold as much water as a patch of garden soil. Pots drain quickly because they are elevated, and terra-cotta pots actually wick moisture away. A simple irrigation system might consist of a thin hose that drapes from pot to pot with small emitters in each pot that release water. Add a timer to such a system, and you've got a totally automatic way to quench the thirst of container plants.

Don't be afraid of pinching

That's right, container plants should be liberally pinched, pushed, pulled, prodded, and pruned to keep them the size and shape you want. Don't let the fast-growers overshadow the laggards, and avoid having heavy stems snap by using stakes and twine, as necessary. Containers, much more so than in-ground gardens, are little compositions where proportion is of paramount importance.

Don't spare the pruners

Similarly, cut back houseplants occasionally to rejuvenate them and improve their appearance. Regular pruning encourages denser growth and is a good way to eliminate old, woody stems that have become leafless and unsightly. Not all houseplants can be pruned the same way, however. Consult a good reference book to find out how to prune the plants you have, and any time you find yourself thinking that a plant could use some sprucing up, rather than automatically reaching for the fertilizer, ask yourself if a good pruning would do the trick.

Keep the food coming

Plants in containers need more food than plants in the ground. That's because they have a limited rooting area, most potting mixes don't contain any of the nutrients found in real soil, and any fertilizers you apply get washed away quickly by irrigation and rain. Feed container plants liberally to keep them looking good all season long. Perhaps the easiest way to make sure your container plants get their three squares a day is to mix a good slow-release fertilizer right into the potting mix at planting time. Reapply using label directions as your guide.

Keep your houseplants comfortable

Houseplants respond beautifully to the right light level, humidity, and temperature, and all plants have their preferences. Here are some pointers to keep your plants perky:

• Light level ranges from the dimness of a north-facing window to a bright conservatory awash in sunlight. If no location in your house is bright enough for a favorite plant, invest in a lighted plant stand.

• Raising the humidity can be as easy as filling a tray with pebbles, pouring water in, and placing your potted houseplants on top. As the moisture evaporates, it will humidify the air around the plants.

• Be aware of temperature differences around your home, and place plants accordingly. Close the door of a spare room in winter to create a cooler environment, or set up a mini-greenhouse for plants that like very moist, warm conditions. Two things to avoid with all plants: heating registers in winter and drafty locations any time of year.

• Finally, remember that some plants can't set flowers without long nights or cooler temperatures at night, meaning you may have to move them daily or otherwise accommodate their special needs.

Some plants need rest to do their best

Many houseplants do just fine if they get the same care year in and year out, but others need a regular period of rest or dormancy. Poinsettias, for example, leaf out and flower, but then want cutting back and some "time off." Cyclamen and gloxinia are other common houseplants that appreciate an annual vacation. Most houseplants aren't that particular, but if you want them to last a long

---

new uses for Old Clay Pots

When those long-lasting terra-cotta pots do finally crack, they can still serve a useful purpose.

• Try using them indoors filled with dried flowers. They make perfect theme decorations on screened porches or in sunrooms.

• Invert one and use it to support a lightweight sculpture or a small potted plant, especially one that trails. You can even top an upside-down pot with a round trivet and a doily to make a small table. If the pot is especially beautiful, display it all by itself on a shelf or stand, perhaps draped with some faux ivy and lit like a piece of fine art.

• If the pot is a total loss, break it up with a hammer and give the shards a second life by placing a few curved pieces over the drain hole at the bottom of a new pot before filling it with soil. They'll keep the soil from clogging the drain hole.

---

time, learn your plants' unique growth cycles.

Don't be overprotective

It's possible to give your houseplants too much care. More houseplants die from overwatering than underwatering. Likewise, overfeeding can burn delicate plant roots, and applying food to a dormant plant forces growth at the wrong time of year. Of course, a lack of water and food is also bad. Excesses of both kinds stress plants, leaving them prone to pest and disease infestation and increasing mortality. To keep houseplants thriving year after year, try to strike the right balance between smothering and neglect.

Give them the once-over once a month

In the protected environment of a house, insect populations can

explode seemingly overnight. Aphids, mealybugs, and scale are just a few of the insect pests that regularly plague houseplants. Once a month, check your plants for unwanted guests by looking under leaves, along stems, and on the soil surface for the bugs themselves, as well as egg masses, insect droppings, or anything else unusual.

Turn, turn, turn

If you sunbathe, you know you've got to turn regularly to get an even tan. And although

houseplants don't tan, they will grow lopsided if they keep the same face to the sun all the time. To keep them attractive and balanced through the years, pick a direction (clockwise or counterclockwise) and spin your houseplants a quarter turn the same way every week or two.

Give them some rooting room

While a few plants, such as the magnificent *Clivia*, actually like to be pot bound, most plants don't. If you can see roots growing out the bottom of a pot or if a mat of roots is forming on the soil surface, it's time to repot. Make a "root review" part of your regular inspection of your houseplants for pests and other problems. After increasing pot size a few times, plants that are small today can become spectacular specimens.

Garden Hand Tools

Hand tools that you use in the yard and garden don't demand a lot of attention and should perform well for years. But with a little extra care, they can last a lifetime–and be much more enjoyable to use.

Keep spades and hoes rust-free

After use, digging tools will often be encrusted with soil. This will not usually promote corrosion, but will take some of the pleasure out of using the tool next time. The quickest way to thoroughly clean your tool is to make a pit stop at your hose and spray it clean. If the soil has hardened, use a stiff brush or paint scraper to remove it. Once or twice a season, spray or wipe the metal parts of your tools with penetrating oil to help keep them from rusting.

Renew wooden handles

The best way to preserve the wooden handles on shovels, rakes, wheelbarrows, and other yard tools is to store them in a shed or the garage where they are protected from the elements. But if you have left a tool outdoors and the handle has begun to check and splinter, restore the wood by sanding to remove splinters and roughness. Then brush on several coats of boiled linseed oil, letting each coat soak in before applying the next. Wipe off the excess oil before using the tool.

Replace broken garden-tool handles

Don't toss a garden tool, such as an ax, hoe, or spade, just because you've broken its wooden handle. Replacement handles are readily available at hardware stores and home centers. To remove the old handle, take out any wedge, pin, or bolt that holds the metal tool head to the handle. Then pull the handle out, working it from side to side. If it doesn't slip free easily, drill several 1/4- or 3/8-inch (6- or 10-mm) holes into the top of the old handle to loosen it. Fit the new handle into the tool. If the handle does not fit completely into the tool, use a file or rasp to shave wood from the new handle until it fits. Resecure the handle by driving the wedge back into the slit at the top or by drilling a hole and replacing the pin or bolt.

Sharpen gardening tools regularly

It's a sad and all-too-typical story. A pair of shears, loppers, or pruners gets dull and no longer cuts well. Then the frustrated owner relegates the tool to jobs it wasn't designed to do, like lopping off a thick dead branch. The excessive torque causes the tool's joint to loosen. Then the user tosses it or hangs it in a dark corner of the shed and forgets about it. Keeping your tools sharp will avoid this untimely demise—and it's easy, as long as you do it regularly.

 ProTip

SHARPENING YOUR TOOLS

Sharpen all of your garden cutting tools with a file or grinder using the manufacturer's factory-set blade bevel as a guide. If there is no bevel on the tool, a 30-degree edge is the rule of thumb, although the bevel on pruners tends to be narrower, closer to 15 degrees. Be careful: If you put too sharp an edge on your tool, it will dull, dent, and chip easily. If you put too blunt an edge, it will not perform efficiently. Don't be afraid to go to a professional to get a good precision cutting tool sharpened.

Bright spray paint colors prevent small tool loss

It's extremely easy to leave hand garden tools, such as hatchets, bow saws, and crowbars, lying in the grass, where they stay forgotten and rusting until the next time you mow the lawn. Jog your memory— and make them easy to spot when mowing—by spraying a streak of bright orange Day-Glo paint on them.

◆ BEST ADVICE ◆ **Garden Hand Tools**

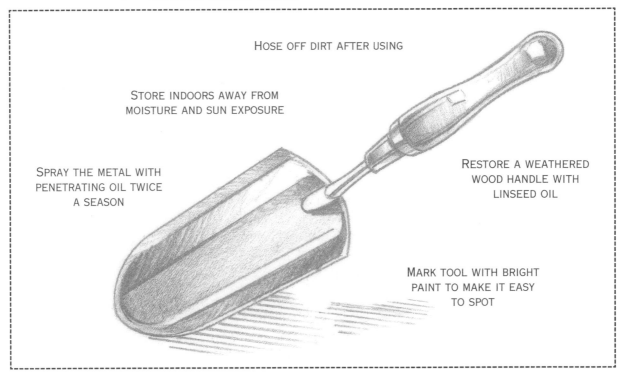

HOSE OFF DIRT AFTER USING

STORE INDOORS AWAY FROM
MOISTURE AND SUN EXPOSURE

SPRAY THE METAL WITH
PENETRATING OIL TWICE
A SEASON

RESTORE A WEATHERED
WOOD HANDLE WITH
LINSEED OIL

MARK TOOL WITH BRIGHT
PAINT TO MAKE IT EASY
TO SPOT

Lube tools with moving parts

Every time you sharpen your pruners, shears, and lopping tools, put a few drops of oil on each operating joint and spring. Use a multipurpose oil, such as 3-IN-ONE.

Wash your gardening gloves

Cotton garden work gloves will last longer—and be a lot more pleasant to use—if you wash them regularly. Washing removes abrasive dirt particles that tear at the fabric of the gloves like sandpaper.

Make a yard tool caddy

You are less like to misplace or lose your tools if you keep them with you as you move from job to job in the yard. If you have an old unused golf bag with a pull-cart attachment, give it new life as a roll-around carrier for your yard and garden tools. Store long-handled tools where you formerly kept your woods and irons, and stash your work gloves and small tools in the zipper pockets. An old plastic trash can with rollers can also serve as a yard tool caddy.

Garden Power Tools

Match the dollar investment you've made in your garden equipment with a few hours of maintenance every year, and you won't be frustrated by equipment that won't go when you need it to.

Find your grease fittings

Even in this age of sealed self-lubricating joints, many riding mowers, garden tractors, snow-blowers, tillers, and other outdoor power equipment require a regular squirt of grease to keep running smoothly. Check your owner's manual, and seek out the grease fittings (small metal nipples). Purchase a grease gun with a flexible hose to make the job easier.

Avoid overheating small engines

Whether a two-stroke or four-stroke engine runs your equipment, it is likely to be damaged if the engine runs too hot. To avoid this, subscribe to these rules:

• If the engine is a four-stroke, keep the oil reservoir filled to the correct level and change the oil at the intervals specified by your owner's manual.

• Clean the engine of sawdust, clippings, and other debris to facilitate cooling.

• Cool the engine slowly. Engines run hot. You can increase their life expectancy by letting the engine idle for several moments after you've given it a tough workout.

• Mix fuel and oil thoroughly for two-stroke engines, or the oil may pool at the fuel tank bottom, where it can't help keep the engine running cool.

Replace and gap spark plugs

To ensure quick starts and to keep your small garden equipment engines in peak running condition, change the spark plug after every season or two. First clean around the old spark plug so that debris doesn't fall into the hole when you remove it. Then remove the plug with a socket wrench and a spark-plug socket correctly sized for the plug. Gap the new plug according to the specs in your owner's

manual. The gap is the space between the plug's center and the L-shaped side electrode. You'll need an inexpensive feeler gauge, sold in auto supply stores, and pliers to set the gap. Screw in the new plug so that it's snug but not tight.

Don't leave the mower in the sun

Don't store gasoline-powered garden equipment in sun-light—even from a window. Repeated warming and cooling of the metal parts can cause water condensation inside the machine, which can lead to mechanical problems. The best storage place is cool and shaded. Barring that, toss a tarp over your machine.

Add a fuel preservative

If you use gasoline-powered equipment infrequently or will be storing it for the season soon, add a fuel preservative, such as PRI-D or STA-BIL, to your gas, using the amount recommended on the can label. Preservatives lengthen the shelf life of gasoline and help prevent engine corrosion from fuel deterioration caused by the buildup of gum and other deposits in the fuel system. Preservatives also improve engine performance and ensure faster starts.

Get fuel-to-oil ratios right

The easiest way to ensure the proper ratio of fuel to oil for two-stroke engines is to buy small containers of two-stroke oil that are sized to automatically give you the correct ratio when mixed with a gallon of gasoline. Choose a two-stroke oil that comes with a fuel stabilizer. It will protect your engines from rust, wear, and corrosion in addition to maintaining fuel quality.

☞ DON'T
use the wrong oil

> Never use automotive engine oil when mixing fuel and oil for a machine with a two-stroke engine. Use two-stroke engine oil or whatever other oil is specified in your owner's manual.

Note the warranty when buying

It's surprising how much warranties vary for similar products. In a recent survey of electric power-tool manufacturer's, for example, warranty periods ranged from one to three years. Of course, the warranty is not a perfect indicator of quality—it often has as much to do with marketing as product durability. However, you should still consider the warranty length when purchasing equipment. Save receipts and warranty information. It's also a good idea to mail in warranty registration postcards (or register online) when making a

purchase of any significance. While it is not usually mandatory to do so, it won't hurt to have your name on file with the manufacturer. Plus the manufacturer will be able to notify you should there be a recall.

Put a file box in the garage or shed

The end of the road for many tools comes when they stop working or a part is lost. Many of these tools can be easily fixed, but the owner's manual that would spell out how, or provide a parts list, is missing. Don't let this happen to you. Get a file box for all of your garden equipment manuals, and keep it where you store your tools. Most owner's manuals have troubleshooting sections that will solve most of the problems you run into. They will also spell out the best maintenance schedule for your tool.

Grandpa Says...

"Add life to your mower blade by sharpening it regularly. Be sure to retain the same cutting-edge angle as the manufacturer (usually 30 degrees) and to remove equal amounts of metal from both sides of the blade. Check for blade balance by resting the blade's center on a dowel or marble."

○○○

Getting a replacement manual

Lost the owner's manual to your mower or other piece of power equipment? Type the manufacturer's name into an Internet search engine such as Google, Yahoo, or MSN to find the company's website. You can usually order a new manual or look up a part online. In some cases, you can even view and print out the manual.

Put your name and address on expensive tools

Your outdoor machines will stick around a lot longer if you make a point of writing your name, address, and phone number on them with a permanent marker. This will help to remind neighbors to return them. If theft is a problem where you live, buy an engraving tool and mark each machine in two places, one hidden and one apparent.

Consider a high-tech theft deterrent

Tool theft causes millions in losses in the construction and yard-maintenance industries. Several manufacturers have developed systems to help contractors prevent theft. You may want to check these out to prevent the theft of a valuable piece of outdoor power equipment, such as a garden tractor that you store in a shed. The systems include transceivers

Power Mowers

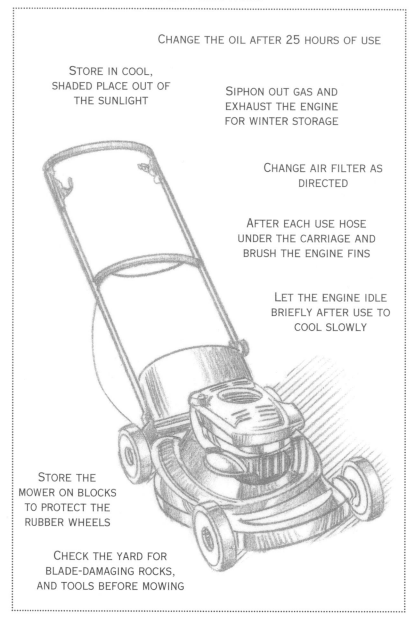

CHANGE THE OIL AFTER 25 HOURS OF USE

STORE IN COOL, SHADED PLACE OUT OF THE SUNLIGHT

SIPHON OUT GAS AND EXHAUST THE ENGINE FOR WINTER STORAGE

CHANGE AIR FILTER AS DIRECTED

AFTER EACH USE HOSE UNDER THE CARRIAGE AND BRUSH THE ENGINE FINS

LET THE ENGINE IDLE BRIEFLY AFTER USE TO COOL SLOWLY

STORE THE MOWER ON BLOCKS TO PROTECT THE RUBBER WHEELS

CHECK THE YARD FOR BLADE-DAMAGING ROCKS, AND TOOLS BEFORE MOWING

Stretch tire life

Moisture, heat, and sunlight can damage rubber. Store power equipment with rubber tires in a dry, cool place, away from sunlight. Place blocks under the equipment to raise it off the floor to promote air circulation around the tires and to prevent damage from moisture. If storing equipment outdoors, protect tires with a tarp and raise them off the ground. Do not store equipment where the tires will rest on heat-absorbent or reflective surfaces, such as asphalt, packed snow, or sand.

Keep cables lubricated

Many controls on outdoor power equipment are operated with cables that are not unlike bicycle cables. Take precautions against snapped cables by occasionally putting a drop or two of oil at the points at which the cable enters or exits the cable sheathing.

Keep old chain-saw blades

It's a shame to dull a nice sharp chain-saw chain by using it to cut tree roots or for demolition work. Keep your old chains handy for such occasions.

Prevent trigger burnout

Triggers and on-off switches in general are a frequent cause of an electric tool's demise. To avoid switch problems, avoid turning off a tool while the

planted on the machine. Should a theft occur, the transceivers can be activated and will begin to emit an inaudible signal. Police can then track and recover your equipment. Whether or not you want to invest in such a high-tech solution, you will find it helpful to have the receipt, identification or serial numbers, and a photo when making your report to the police and claim to the insurance company.

motor is working hard. This may cause arcing that can damage the switch's contacts. Instead, allow the tool to run a few seconds with no load and then switch off the tool.

Maintain brushes on electric tools

For homeowners who enjoy doing their own gardening chores, buying professional-quality tools is often a wise choice. They will last much longer, perform better, and make chores go quicker. In addition to costing more than homeowner-grade equipment, these tools will eventually require maintenance and service to keep them in top shape. Pro-quality electric tools, such as hedge trimmers, chain saws, and mowers, for example, have replaceable motor brushes. These carbon-block contacts press against the motor's armature and deliver current to the motor's electromagnets. If they wear too thin, the motor will run poorly or stop altogether. Replace them according to the instructions and schedule in your owner's manual.

Rags are valuable

Never toss an old cotton garment, such as a T-shirt or old towel. Cut it up into rags. Use the rags to wipe away debris, such as grass clippings or sawdust, from electrical- or gas-powered equipment. Pay particular attention to switches, vents, and the cooling fins found on gasoline engines. Also, be sure to wipe around the openings for oil and fuel so that as you remove the caps, debris won't find its way into the tanks.

Keep your mower in top shape

Lawn mowers are not disposable! Double the life of your mower by following this simple routine:

• Before you begin to mow, check the lawn for stones, tools, branches, or other objects. Running over a toy can turn it into a missile. Running over a root or stone can severely damage your mowing machine.

• Clean your mower after each use. For a push mower, keep a brush handy for the task. For cleaning gas or electric power mowers, a blast from your garden hose under the carriage will do the trick. Disconnect the spark plug before your begin, wait until the engine is cool, and avoid getting the engine or spark plug wet. If you forget to clean it once or twice, you may need a scraper to loosen the dried accumulations.

• To prevent the engine from overheating and becoming damaged, use a long-bristle brush or stick to clear debris that has been caught between the engine's cooling fins after each use.

• Keep the engine housing and all mechanical connections clean. A rag and an old toothbrush simplify this task. Lubricate cables where they enter and exit cable sheathing to keep them from getting stuck and breaking.

• Change oil according to your manual or after every 25 hours of use. To get to the oil drain plug, usually located under the mower carriage, prop your mower on concrete blocks. Catch the dirty oil in an oil pan so that you can take it to your recycling center. If your engine has an oil filter, change that as well.

• Change or clean the air filter according to the instructions in your manual. Simply replace a paper filter with a new one; clean the filter housing and insert the filter, pleat-side up. If your filter is foam, soak the new filter in oil and squeeze out excess with a rag before inserting it.

• When you put away your mower or lawn tractor for the winter (or your snowblower for the summer), siphon out most of the fuel and then run the equipment until the tank is dry. You can use the leftover gasoline that you siphon out in your auto as long as it has not been mixed with oil.

Selecting a snowblower

A two-stage snowblower will generally last longer—and have greater snow-moving capacity—than a single-stage snow thrower. Two-stage blowers remove snow in a two-step process: A screwlike auger feeds the snow into a high-speed impeller that blows it away. Single-stage machines gather and throw snow in one action. They operate at higher speeds and are more susceptible to damage. Opt for at least an 8-horsepower engine and a worm-driven auger.

Reverse snowblower scrapers

The scraper bar, located at the bottom of the auger housing, gives your snowblower its cutting edge. But all that contact with asphalt, concrete, and gravel will cause the bar to wear. For this reason, most blowers are designed so that you can reverse their scraper bars. If you do this whenever your blower comes into contact with an abrasive surface, you can double the life of the scraper bar.

Use the correct shear pin

Snow throwers are equipped with shear pins. These little bolt-shaped parts are designed to break if the load becomes too much for your machine, saving you an expensive repair. Keep spares handy—and don't substitute just any bolt or screw, or you could be asking for trouble.

Outdoor Structures

Fences, Trellises, and Other Wood Structures

Whether it's a fence, shed, or arbor, the eye is drawn to the structures we place in our yards. And a little regular maintenance will keep these focal points looking their best.

Go with latex paint, oil primer

The most durable finish for your outdoor wood is a couple of coats of acrylic latex paint. Oil-based paints tend to become more brittle, which can cause them to loose their grip when wood shrinks and expands. Oil-based paint is also more likely to trap moisture, which leads to blistering and rot. However, if your structure has never been painted, experts recommend that you prime it first with alkyd oil-based paint. Alkyd primers penetrate wood fibers best and provide a strong, smooth surface for your finish coats.

Solid-color latex stains, which can be used over an existing painted finish, will also give satisfactory results, but the finish won't last as long as paint. An opaque stain finish, however, will be easier to prepare than a painted fence when restaining it the next time because it won't peel or blister.

Don't wait too long to paint

Be sure to paint or stain your new fence, shed, or playhouse soon after it's built. If you let the wood weather, it will decrease the life expectancy of your paint job. Instead, allow the fence to go through a couple of drying cycles (where it gets wet and then dries). You don't have to wait for rain—just wet the structure with a hose. Then lightly sand, and apply paint right away.

Tighten outdoor nails

Wood on outdoor structures, such as fences, gates, trellises, and decks, expands and contracts with the seasons, and this causes nails to work loose. Loose nails mean loose joints. Loose joints collect debris and allow water to infiltrate—a combination that promotes rot. Make it an annual springtime habit to inspect your outdoor structures with hammer in hand to reset any loose nails. If the nail has become too loose to reset, remove it and replace with a bigger rust-resistant nail or screw.

With vinyl, don't overdo it

More and more vinyl products are finding their way into the backyard. They include fencing, arbors, and garden sheds as well as playhouses and toys. Since vinyl is a virtually maintenance-free product, there's not much you need to do to keep it looking good. In fact, it's easy to do too much to it.

• When cleaning vinyl, don't use stiff brushes or abrasive cleaners, because they may scratch the surface, creating a blotchy, uneven look.

• Remove crayon, asphalt, and grease with mineral spirits or a naptha tar remover. Use a soft cloth to apply the cleaning agent and only enough pressure to do the job. Rinse the cleaned area with water.

• When feasible, cover the vinyl item to keep the sun from causing its color to fade. Stake the item to the ground to prevent it from being blown about by sudden wind gusts.

Paint before assembly

If you are putting up a new fence using unfinished lumber, paint or stain the posts, trim, and pickets before you put them together. The same is true of unfinished preassembled sections. For one thing, brushing on the paint or stain will be much easier. But more importantly, you'll get better paint or stain coverage where it's really needed—inside joints, where moisture collects. This translates into a longer life for the fence and paint job. For really

◆ BEST ADVICE ◆ **Picket Fences**

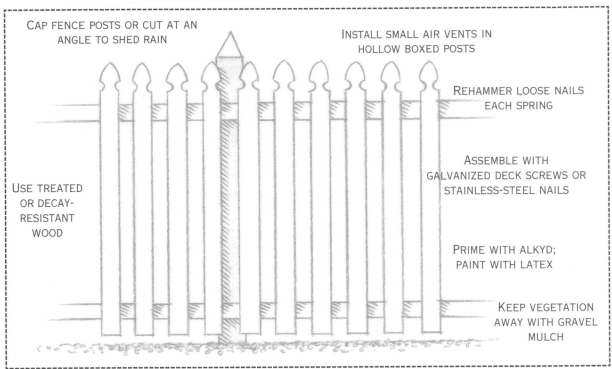

CAP FENCE POSTS OR CUT AT AN ANGLE TO SHED RAIN

INSTALL SMALL AIR VENTS IN HOLLOW BOXED POSTS

REHAMMER LOOSE NAILS EACH SPRING

ASSEMBLE WITH GALVANIZED DECK SCREWS OR STAINLESS-STEEL NAILS

USE TREATED OR DECAY-RESISTANT WOOD

PRIME WITH ALKYD; PAINT WITH LATEX

KEEP VEGETATION AWAY WITH GRAVEL MULCH

long-lasting results, brush on a coat of paintable water-repellent preservative at joints and on exposed end-grain before you paint or stain the pieces.

Defend your fences

Fences are expensive to construct and time-consuming to maintain. To protect your investment and keep your fence looking good for many years, follow these guidelines:

• Use pressure-treated or naturally decay-resistant woods. Avoid ground contact for non-pressure-treated components.

• For boxed posts, install small, screened vents to prevent moisture buildup inside the hollow post. This will help prevent rot.

• Use galvanized deck screws to assemble a fence. Using screws instead of nails will make future repairs and maintenance a lot easier. If a few pieces become damaged by rot

or insects, it is relatively simple to unscrew the ailing parts and replace them, lengthening the useful life of the rest of the fence. Similarly, if the fence is damaged by a fallen branch, the broken section will be easier to unscrew and replace without damaging other parts.

• For fences built with newer pressure-treated woods, such as ACQ (alkaline copper quaternary) and CBA (copper boron azole), use stainless steel fasteners. They're expensive, but the new rot-resisting chemicals are reported to be corrosive to other types of fasteners and may cause them to fail prematurely.

HOW TO RECOGNIZE TERMITES

These destructive insects need water to survive. If they're chewing away inside your shed sill plate, chances are a telltale earth-colored tunnel outside your foundation wall will give them away. Scrape away the tunnel and treat the affected area with a termite soil treatment (termiticide) and/or a termite bait—jobs best left to professional exterminators. The website below provides detailed information and photos that will help you identify termites and the damage they do.

> The Pennsylvania State College of Agricultural Sciences Cooperative Extension
www.ento.psu.edu/extension/factsheets/termite.htm.

• To make fence posts last longer, saw off their tops at an angle so that they will shed rain rather than absorb it. Another option is to cover the post tops with a pyramid-shaped metal cap. You can buy caps at lumberyards and home centers, or fashion your own from copper or aluminum roof flashing.

Create weed- and plant-free zones

Keep weeds and plants, especially vines, from growing too near your fence. Good air circulation will keep your fence in its prime longer. A good way to do this is to lay a heavy-duty weed barrier—roofing felt or landscape fabric—a few inches below grade to either side of your fence. Cover with gravel. If your fence is adjacent to your lawn, this will make your weed-whacking sessions easy—and shorter, as well.

Use pressure-treated wood for sills and sleepers

When laying the foundation for lightweight outdoor structures, such as greenhouses, sheds, and sunporches, use pressure-treated lumber laid on a 6- to 8-inch-deep (15- to 20-cm) bed of gravel for drainage. To prevent warping and twisting of boards, double up members and join them together with lag screws, overlapping at joints. Screw or bolt the structure to the foundation to keep it from shifting in heavy winds.

Keep vines pruned on trellises and arbors

Trellises and arbors can become overloaded and stressed by vines after two or three growing seasons. And depending upon how sturdy the structure is, the extra weight can damage it. Avoid this problem by pruning back the vegetation regularly—or prune as recommended for the vine you are growing.

Make trellises detachable

Vines that grow on deck balustrades and house siding lend grace and charm to outdoor structures, but they can cause damage in the long run because they hold moisture that promotes rot and they block periodic maintenance of the host structure. You can solve these problems by growing vines on detachable trellises. When it's time to paint, unscrew the fasteners and lay the vegetation-entwined trellis on the ground, or if you are worried about breaking the vines, just lean the trellis against a ladder. Also use standoffs of 3 to 4 inches (8 to 10 cm) to let air circulate between the structure and the trellis.

Play Sets and Swimming Pools

Keeping your outdoor recreational equipment in top condition means it's ready for you and your kids when you want to play—which is why you spent all that money on it in the first place!

Coat play sets with preservative

For nonpainted wooden play sets, brush on a protective coat of water-repellent, UV-blocking preservative every couple of years. Use one that's nontoxic so you don't have to worry about your kids touching it and eating with contaminated fingers afterward. A good choice is Thompson's Water Seal Advanced Natural Wood Protector, which is water based and nontoxic once it has dried.

Get the best play set

The best wooden play sets are made from kiln-dried wood. This helps prevent shrinkage, the loosening of joints, warping, and checking. The new pressure-treated lumber types are made without toxic chemicals. (Older pressure-treated wood, treated with copper, chromate, and arsenic, or CCA, has been linked to an increased risk of lung and bladder cancers). The new treatments, while considered safe, have their own problems. They are reported to corrode fasteners, even coated fasteners. Opt for corrosion-resistant stainless steel or heavy-duty fasteners when possible.

While most residential play sets on the market today are made of wood, consider a heavy-duty metal play set for the last word in durability. These are super strong and will not warp, twist, or splinter. Be certain, however, that the unit and all hardware are made with heavy-gauge galvanized steel. Some galvanized steel units are coated with polyester for additional protection.

Cover your pool

Taking the time to cover your pool pays dividends in longer pool life and less pool maintenance. Covers reduce UV damage to vinyl liners and plaster walls—and will keep dirt and debris out, so you will spend less time cleaning and you'll use fewer chemicals. A good choice is a mesh-type cover. It won't collect puddles of water as do solid covers.

Patching puts your pool back in the pink

A patch in time, just like the proverbial stitch, will keep your pool looking good for years— and save big repair bills. If you can find your leak, see below for what to do. One way to find leaks is with food dye. Place dye at suspected trouble spots, such as cracks or blistered areas. If it moves through the wall, you've found a leak.

• In pools with vinyl liners, attend to tears or punctures as soon as possible. Repair tears with a manufacturer-supplied patching kit, many of which can be used above or below water so you won't have to drain the pool. Some repair kits come with a small can of adhesive and a vinyl liner patch. Simply brush on the adhesive, and apply over the tear. Others have the adhesive preapplied to the patch. Just remove the paper backing and press in place. Liner tears longer than 2 to 3 inches (5 to 8 cm) may not be repairable, in which case you'll have to replace the liner.

• In pools finished with plaster, repair hairline cracks in the plaster at least once a season. The plaster is the layer—usually applied over Gunite or Shotcrete pool floors and walls—that forms the waterproof membrane around your pool. To repair it, lower the water level below the damage. Clean loose pieces from cracks and fill them with plaster, marine-grade caulking compound (don't use ordinary house caulk), or a two-part epoxy putty. Smooth with a trowel or your fingers, and allow the patch to cure before refilling the pool. Call in a pro to handle large cracks. Some wear scuba gear to make the repair underwater, avoiding the expense and time involved in draining the pool.

• Fiberglass pools can also be patched if the damaged area is small. Drain the pool to below the damage, and let it dry. Abrade the damaged area with 100-grit sandpaper. Mix and brush on a two-part liquid epoxy, and lay on your patch of fiberglass cloth. Smooth with a bristle brush, making sure you haven't left any air bubbles under the cloth. When the adhesive dries, brush on another coat of epoxy liquid. Sand to feather the edges of the patch. Reapply the liquid epoxy one or two more times. Then sand lightly, and paint to match the rest of the pool. If the damage is extensive, the entire pool may have to be recoated. A coat of epoxy paint will improve the appearance of an older fiberglass shell.

Replaster or repaint
Plastered or painted pools chip and flake due to pool chemicals and the large swings in water temperature. Replaster concrete pools about every 10 to 15 years, or repaint every three to five years.

Don't drain a pool too low
Some pool owners drain their pools to below skimmer level for the winter. While this is a good strategy for preventing cracked skimmers due to freezes, it stresses the pool's cover, which causes tears. It also exposes the pool liner to air, causing it to degrade. Instead of draining the pool, use Gizzmo skimmer guards to prevent skimmer damage. Gizzmos are made of plastic and look a little like a hollow dumbbell. They are designed to absorb the pressure from the expansion of freezing water in the skimmer. These low-cost, popular products come in large and small sizes and are easy to screw into the skimmer ports.

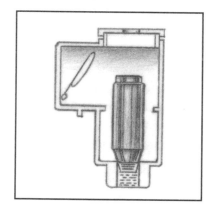

Protect your pool from ice expansion
Fill three or four plastic jugs about one-quarter full with water, and float them in your pool when you close it for the winter. If ice forms in the pool, it will crush the jugs instead of the walls of your pool.

Use the same principle at skimmers. Insert smaller, empty plastic soda bottles, with caps screwed on tightly, into skimmers to prevent them from cracking due to freezing water.

Winterize your pool
To ensure many happy summers by the pool, protect it from freeze damage, unnecessary wear, and water contamination during the off-season. You may try doing some or all of the following yourself—or call in a professional and work up a maintenance schedule.

• Lower the water to the proper level for your pool, typically 3 to 6 inches (8 to 15 cm) below tile level for solid covers and 12 to 18 inches (30 to 45 cm) for mesh covers. For pools with a tile deck in freezing climates, it's especially important to keep the water from infiltrating the tile bed, where it can freeze, popping or cracking the tiles.

• Backwash to clean or replace the filter according to the maker's directions. Drain DE (diatomaceous earth) filter tanks, and leave the backwashvalve open. Unplug the drain on sand filters.

• Disconnect the pump, and turn it upside down to make sure it is drained of all water.

• Remove and store baskets, fittings, plugs, automatic cleaners, gauges, hoses, and filters. Store small parts in the pump basket so you can find them easily come spring.

• Use an air compressor or powerful shop vacuum to blow water from belowground plumbing. Plug lines with rubber expansion plugs or Gizzmo plugs to create a vacuum, thereby preventing the reentry of water. Don't use antifreeze, which can be a mess to clean up in the spring.

• Use your air compressor or shop vacuum to blow water from the plumbing of aboveground equipment, such as heaters, filters, auto vacs, and slides, as well.

• Thoroughly clean your pool with a vacuum, skimmer, and brush. The pool should be clear and free of algae.

• Mix winterizing chemicals and water in a large container, such as a drywall bucket, prior to adding them to the pool. Otherwise some granules are likely to fall to the pool floor and cause staining.

• Use a test kit to determine any necessary adjustments you should make to the water's pH level. The pH should be between 7.2 and 7.6. Adjust alkalinity and chlorine levels as well: 100 to 150 parts per million for alkalinity and 3.0 for chlorine. (These levels are for winter only.)

• Secure your cover carefully to prevent animals or debris from getting in. Remove accessories, such as ladders and handrails, if they're in the way of the cover.

• Prevent stains by adding chlorine or algaecide every month during the off-season or as needed to keep water fresh and free of algae.

• During the winter season, increase the life of your pool cover by regularly clearing it of debris. Pump puddles off solid covers. Check water level regularly, and add or remove water as necessary.

Fountains, Lawn Ornaments, and Watering Systems

Lawn ornaments and water features add a sense of serenity to a nicely landscaped backyard—but not when those features look worn or aren't working properly.

Renew concrete fountains

Slow the aging of concrete fountains by brushing on a coat of concrete sealer, available at most home centers and hardware stores. If your fountain is badly stained and discolored, you may want to paint it with an acrylic paint formulated for masonry. Two coats will generally have it looking like new. Or if you like the fresh concrete look, blast your fountain with a pressure washer. The water pressure alone is often enough to lift dirt and grime.

Winterize fountains and lawn ornaments

If you live in a harsh climate and can store your fountain or birdbath indoors for the winter, do so. Use burlap layered between masonry components to prevent accidental scratches and chipping. If you must leave lawn ornaments outdoors, drain them thoroughly and cover with a waterproof tarp.

Rid fountains of unsightly mineral buildup

Fountain bowls are susceptible to mineral buildup because of the constant splashing and evaporation. Specially formulated fountain cleaners and lime removers, such as Crystal Clear Fountain LimeSolve, will remove the scale if used on a regular basis and restore your fountain to its original splendor. You can purchase these products at a pond supply dealer or online.

Use epoxy to fix damaged fountains

A fallen branch or unexpected freeze may cause your fountain (or lawn ornament) to break or chip. Most breaks can be repaired with epoxy glue or, if there is missing material, an epoxy patching compound. The surfaces to be rejoined must be clean and dry. Let the repair cure for at least 24 hours before putting your fountain back into service.

Care for garden pumps

Pumps are at the heart of garden fountains, ornamental ponds, and fishponds. To keep a pump running efficiently, follow these tips:

• Maintain adequate water heights; a pump that runs dry (without water) will be quickly damaged.

• Dirt and debris can accumulate inside a pump and cause it to stop working. Keep this from happening by cutting off a tube-like section of sheer panty hose. Slip the pump inside it, and tie the ends.

• Clean pumps regularly, especially if there is high mineral content in your water. Soak the pump for about 10 minutes in a solution of 2 cups of white vinegar mixed into 2 gallons (7.5 liters) of water. Then run the pump for about 30 minutes while submerged in the solution. If your pump has stopped working due to severe buildup on the impeller, use a product specifically formulated for removing mineral buildup from kitchen appliances and dehumidifiers.

Avoid damage to outdoor spigots

Water can freeze inside the pipe that leads to an outdoor spigot, damaging the line and spigot. Most homes have a valve that lets you shut off the water to each spigot for the winter. Typically, you'll find the valve in the basement, near the spot where the spigot is located on the exterior wall. After turning off the valve, open the outdoor spigot and leave it open for the winter. If your home doesn't have a shut-off valve and pipes freezing are a concern, consider replacing your faucet with a freeze-proof faucet (also known as a freeze-less or frost-proof hose bib, sill cock, or faucet).

Yard watering systems

When it comes to keeping your yard green and healthy year after year, there's no one perfect system. You'll probably find a combination is best to meet the particular needs of your yard. Here are your main choices:

• A simple, old-fashioned sprinkler is usually best for large grassy patches of lawn. You can adjust its arc, move it to any location, and position it to reach out-of-the-way corners.

• A soaker hose may be best where a more thorough drenching is demanded, or where you want to set the hose down and leave it all season—in your garden or a flowerbed or around new plantings.

• A drip irrigation system permits a slower flow of water and can be altered as your gardening needs change.

• Underground sprinklers are convenient and efficient but are the most costly of the bunch.

Stretch hose life

If you live in a cold climate, you can extend the life of your garden hoses for many more

◆ BEST ADVICE ◆ **Garden Fountains**

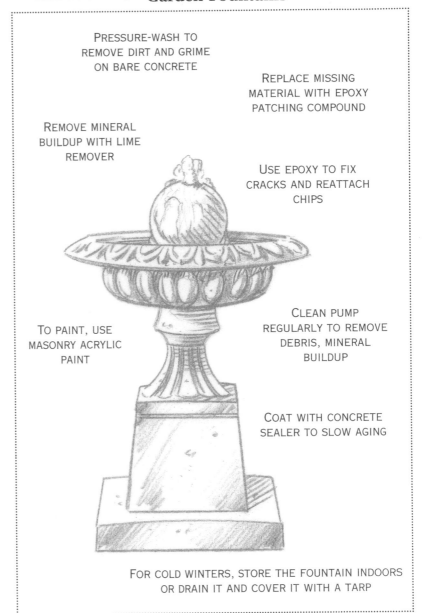

PRESSURE-WASH TO REMOVE DIRT AND GRIME ON BARE CONCRETE

REPLACE MISSING MATERIAL WITH EPOXY PATCHING COMPOUND

REMOVE MINERAL BUILDUP WITH LIME REMOVER

USE EPOXY TO FIX CRACKS AND REATTACH CHIPS

TO PAINT, USE MASONRY ACRYLIC PAINT

CLEAN PUMP REGULARLY TO REMOVE DEBRIS, MINERAL BUILDUP

COAT WITH CONCRETE SEALER TO SLOW AGING

FOR COLD WINTERS, STORE THE FOUNTAIN INDOORS OR DRAIN IT AND COVER IT WITH A TARP

seasons by not leaving them outside during the winter. On the day you shut off the water to your outdoor spigot, make it a habit to drain your hoses, coil and hang them in a shed, garage, or basement—preferably on a hose hanger, not on a damp concrete floor.

Walls and Paved Surfaces

Outdoor walls, walks, patios, and driveways are typically built to last for many decades. But that doesn't mean you can ignore them. Here's how to keep them in tip-top condition.

Build timber retaining walls to last

Timber retaining walls are an attractive way to terrace a hill to create level gardens. Whether you are building one yourself or having it built for you, here are some guidelines to make sure your wall will hold up for the long haul:

• Install deadmen or tiebacks to make sure that the wall will stay in place. These anchors, typically 6-foot-long (2-meter) 4 x 4s (89 x 89 mm) with a short perpendicular section fastened to one end, help to prevent water and freeze-thaw pressures in soil from pushing the timbers out of position. Use large spikes to fasten the base of the T-shaped anchors to the wall in the third or fourth course at 8-foot intervals.

• For walls taller than 4 feet (1.2 meters), install a second row of deadmen, six or seven courses from the base. Also be sure to slant the wall back into the hillside, about 1/4 inch (6 mm) for each course.

• Backfill against the wall with gravel to facilitate drainage. There's enough space for water to seep between timbers so you don't need to provide weep holes as you would for a masonry wall.

Build masonry retaining walls to last

Poor drainage behind stone and masonry retaining walls can allow water to build up immense amounts of pressure. If the saturated soil then freezes, the pressure will be enough to move or crack almost any wall. Avoid this by installing drains in walls (perforated PVC drainpipes work well) and keeping them clear of debris and silt. Here are some other essentials to look for in a well-built masonry retaining wall:

• Provide a footing (a stable bed of tamped gravel, stone, or concrete) for your wall. In areas where the ground freezes, the footing should be to the frost line—the lowest point to which the earth freezes in your locale.

• Lean walls 1 inch (25 mm) for every foot toward the soil you wish to retain.

• Use gravel as fill behind the wall so water can drain away and won't collect there.

• Keep the gravel and drainpipes from becoming clogged with soil and silt by using water-permeable landscape fabric between the gravel and soil (three sides, but not between the wall and gravel).

Remove unwanted vegetation

Stone walls can last for centuries, surviving wind and storm. But it's often something as simple as a sapling that will bring them down. Don't allow plants, especially trees and vigorous vines, to get a foothold between the stones. It's easiest to pull them out when young; otherwise use your lopper.

Tapered freestanding stone walls

When building a traditional stone wall, either dry-stacked or mortared, don't forget to begin with a solid footing (tamped gravel to frost-line depth). Then start building with a large base, and taper the sides slowly inward as the height increases. Cap the walls with flat stones to

help prevent damage from water infiltration and freezing.

Replace popped stones immediately

Stone walls, even those with mortar, are subject to the domino effect: Lose one or two stones because a car hits the wall or there is a freeze, and more stones will soon loosen. Replace a fallen stone as soon as possible to prevent a much bigger job later.

Avoid chipped and cracked patio slates

Slate and brick often chip and crack because of inadequate drainage. If this is happening to your patio, lift the still good slates and lean them against a wall to dry. Dig up the patio area to about 3 inches (8 cm) deep. Fill the area with crushed stone or sand, and make sure it is level and tamped in place. Then reset the slate or brick. Also consider installing a weed barrier under the stones as described in the next hint.

Use weed barriers under slate and flagstone

Weed barriers can help keep a patio or walkway looking like the day you installed it. The idea is to use a water-permeable polypropylene landscape fabric under a layer of gravel or bark to keep weeds from sprouting between the slate, brick, or flagstone pieces. Many such schemes fail because the gravel layer is too thin or too thick. If it's too thin, the unsightly fabric is exposed when the gravel is kicked or washed aside. If it's too thick, the gravel layer itself becomes a medium for growing weeds as it accumulates dirt. Landscape-fabric manufacturers recommend a depth of 3 to 4 inches (8 to 10 cm).

Banish weeds without herbicides

Keep the spaces between pavers, slate, and brick weed-free without herbicides by pouring just-boiled water on them. If you don't want to handle hot water, mix 1 cup of salt and 1 teaspoon of dish-washing liquid into 1 gallon (4 liters) of vinegar. Pour a thin stream of this solution directly on the weeds.

Get the right pavers

Whether you choose brick pavers, concrete pavers, or tile for your new patio or walk, it's crucial to use paving units that are designed to withstand your climate. Here are some guidelines:

• No matter where you live, don't try to pave with building bricks, also often called common bricks. Even building bricks designated for severe weather applications aren't designed to hold up as pavers.

• If you live in a freezing climate, make sure you get pavers designated as SX. If it doesn't freeze where you live, you can use MX pavers. NX pavers are for use only indoors, where freezing conditions are not present.

• Concrete pavers are the most durable type of paving unit—and usually the cheapest, too. They are made of a dense, pressure-formed concrete that will hold up in any climate.

• Tile usually needs to be set in a bed of mortar atop a solid concrete slab. For cold-weather climates, quarry tile is usually the best choice. It has a rough surface that makes it skid-resistant—just make sure the tile you buy is designed to withstand freezing. Glazed tiles are also available for freezing climates, but the glossy glaze is slippery when wet. Saltillo and terra-cotta tiles have a beautiful red color but should be used only in warm climates. Cold weather can cause them to crack.

Preserve concrete walkways and driveways

Yes, it looks like it's impervious and will last for ages, but concrete needs care to keep it looking good and to help prevent cracks and flaking. Here's how to add years of life to your concrete walk, patio, or driveway.

• Clean concrete once a year to avoid dirt and grime buildup. Use low-pressure water—from a hose or a pressure washer at 3,000 psi (210 kg/square cm)—with a stiff brush or broom (not a wire one). For stubborn spots, use a light-duty cleaner designed for masonry. Avoid harsh detergents.

• Patch any existing cracks. There are many patching compounds available. Typically, you clean the crack's edges thoroughly and brush on a bonding adhesive prior to applying the patching compound.

• Seal joints with joint sealant to help prevent too much water from working its way under the concrete, where it can freeze and crack the concrete. Joint sealant is available in cartridges. Apply it with a caulk gun just like caulk.

• Seal concrete surfaces when water no longer beads up on them. Sealer does many good things: it provides resistance to water infiltration, repels dirt, resists staining, and minimizes the damaging effects of deicing salts, oil, and antifreeze. Clean concrete surfaces thoroughly before applying sealer with a brush or sprayer.

Seal and patch your asphalt driveway

Sealing an asphalt driveway is not difficult, but it takes time. For the sealer to adhere well, wash the driveway thoroughly first. Also dig out any weeds or grass sprouting from cracks, and chop off surface roots from nearby trees that may cause the driveway to crack. Then patch all cracks with patching compound. Apply at least two coats of sealer for long-lasting results. No time to do the job right away? Dig out the weeds or grass from cracks and patch the breaks. This will prevent further damage until you can reseal it and may save you the cost of a new driveway.

Outdoor Lighting and Sound Systems

A little dramatic lighting. A bit of music. It doesn't take much to create the right atmosphere for an outdoor party. And it doesn't take much to maintain your equipment.

Protect electrical lines

It's very easy to forget where you've buried an outdoor electrical line, only to rediscover it with a spade or tiller. When installing outdoor lines, use UF (underground feeder) cable and bury it to a depth of 24 inches (30 cm). According to the National Electrical Code, it can be less deep if run through rigid plastic conduit—18 inches (46 cm)—or coated rigid metal conduit—6 inches (15 cm). For directly buried cable, leave expansion loops where it exits and enters the conduit. Should the earth move, the cable will have some slack to move with it. Paint any plastic conduit that's exposed to the sunlight to keep it from degrading due to exposure.

Renew outdoor lamppost

An outdoor lamppost or porch light is often the first thing guests see as they arrive at your front door, so don't neglect it. If yours is rusted, you can extend its life in an hour or two. Turn off the power to the light at the service panel by flipping off the circuit breaker or removing the fuse. Remove the rust with steel wool or a wire brush. Then apply a rust inhibitor to any bare metal surfaces. Finally, brush on two coats of a rust-resisting enamel paint. Replace any broken glass panels to prevent further damage.

Buying low-voltage lighting

Low-voltage (12-volt) outdoor lighting is a great improvement to almost any yard. It can set the mood when entertaining, improve safety and security, and showcase your home, garden, and pool at night. The low-cost outdoor lighting kits found at most home centers, however, have a limited life span. And they don't allow for much flexibility in designing your landscape lighting.

Powder-coated aluminum fixtures are more durable and look a lot better. For a system that will really last, however, choose fixtures made of solid copper, brass, bronze, or stainless steel, and opt for stainless steel fasteners. Buy lenses that are made with tempered glass and have gaskets that are rated to withstand high temperatures. Look for fixtures that are rated water-resistant and UL approved for outdoor use. When choosing a transformer, buy one big enough to handle any lights you might add in the future.

Protect outdoor receptacles

Check to be sure the hinge and gaskets that protect outdoor receptacles are functioning properly. If not, cover with a sturdy plastic food bag and secure with twine or a hefty rubber band until you can repair or replace the cover. You can also use a plastic bag to protect the plug and receptacle when leaving ornamental lights plugged in for a while, especially in snowy climes. Run the cord through the bag opening, and secure the bag over the plug and receptacle with twine.

Flag the plowman

Outdoor lighting is vulnerable to errant snowplows. Protect it with reflector-topped metal stakes, so that you and your plow operator know where they are when the next snowstorm hits.

Check speakers for water

Outdoor sounds systems have improved dramatically since the days when you pointed your speakers out your college dorm-room window. Today speakers are designed to withstand the elements. The housings are molded from durable plastics.

Outdoor Lampposts

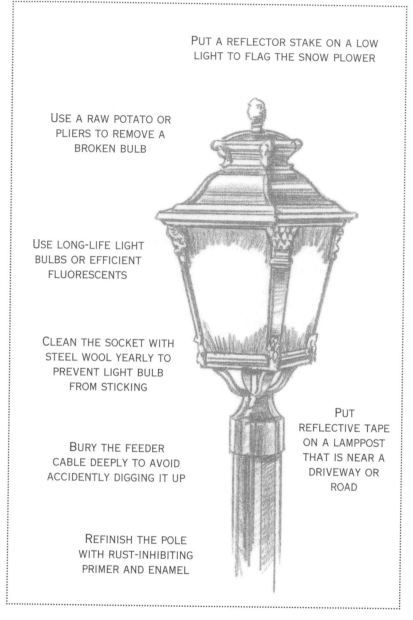

PUT A REFLECTOR STAKE ON A LOW
LIGHT TO FLAG THE SNOW PLOWER

USE A RAW POTATO OR
PLIERS TO REMOVE A
BROKEN BULB

USE LONG-LIFE LIGHT
BULBS OR EFFICIENT
FLUORESCENTS

CLEAN THE SOCKET WITH
STEEL WOOL YEARLY TO
PREVENT LIGHT BULB
FROM STICKING

BURY THE FEEDER
CABLE DEEPLY TO AVOID
ACCIDENTLY DIGGING IT UP

PUT
REFLECTIVE TAPE
ON A LAMPPOST
THAT IS NEAR A
DRIVEWAY OR
ROAD

REFINISH THE POLE
WITH RUST-INHIBITING
PRIMER AND ENAMEL

bring along long-life bulbs. They last ten times as long as conventional floodlights—up to 20,000 hours, so you shouldn't have to change the bulb again for many years. Long-lasting—and energy-saving—fluorescent floodlights are also now available. They're approved for outdoor use, provided you have a weather-protected fixture.

Preserve outdoor lights

Unplug or switch off the breaker to outdoor lights at least once a year, and clean any corrosion from the inside of the bulb socket with a ball of very fine (0000) steel wool. This will help prevent bulbs from jamming in sockets and make removal easy. Avoid touching the bulb with your hands. The oils from your skin can create stress points on the bulb glass and cause premature bulb failure. This is especially true for halogen bulbs, but the oils can shorten the life of incandescent bulbs as well.

Removing a broken lightbulb

Outdoors lightbulbs sometime burst because of moisture or sudden large swings in temperature. If this happens, turn off power, cut off the end of a potato, and press it into the bulb base. Twist to unscrew the old base. Once the base is removed, clean the socket thoroughly with steel wool and a cotton rag.

The grills provide stiff resistance to moisture infiltration. Bass drivers are also made from moisture and humidity-resistant materials. To keep your system humming, however, it's wise to check regularly for water accumulations due to condensation.

Open the cabinet, swab out any water you find, and check to be sure the weep holes are clear.

Choose long–life bulbs

Tired of climbing up a ladder to change outdoor floodlights? The next time you make the climb,

Gas Grills

There are a few simple things you can do to make outdoor dining and entertaining pleasant and problem-free. All it takes is a little elbow grease and some simple household products, such as silicon spray, soap, and car wax.

Keep grills dry

A gas grill can last for 10 or 15 years, and still look like new. Or it can look like it's ready to be shipped to the dump after just a few seasons. Of course, it's important to buy a good-quality grill in the first place. But just as important is to keep your grill covered when it's not in use and to store it in a dry place during the off-season. Covers are available from the grill manufacturer, or make your own from a waterproof tarp. In addition to keeping your grill dry, a cover will help prevent bugs, such as spiders and earwigs, from nesting in the metal tubes under your grill's burner.

🖝 DON'T
brush hot porcelain

> Although drippings are easier to remove while the grill is hot, don't wire-brush or scrape a porcelain coating when it is hot. It's more likely to chip, and once chipped, it will start to rust.

Get a grill that will last

A gas grill has a hard job to do, dealing with high temperatures and splattering grease. Here's what to look for in a grill that will stand up to tough use:

• Cheap burners will rust or burn through. Look for burners made of stainless steel, cast brass, or cast stainless steel for long life. They should be protected from direct drippings.

• The most durable cooking grates are made of porcelain-coated cast iron or stainless steel.

• Enameled and stainless steel hoods will look great for years. With stainless steel, look for an insulated hood—or else the finish will discolor from high temperatures.

• Wood sideboards look great in the showroom but are almost impossible to keep from being stained by drippings. A stainless steel one is a better choice.

• Look for a grill that is welded to the cart. It will last longer than one that's bolted on.

• A mechanical igniter will last longer than a battery-powered electric one.

• Make sure the warranty covers the burner if it fails due to burn-through or rust.

Keep the flame burning

It's easy to keep your grill ready to go season after season by following these suggestions:

• Scrub the grill rack after each use with a nylon scouring pad. It's easiest to do while the grate is still warm (but not hot enough to burn you).

• Wash the metal grill bars frequently. Grease and salts from foods are corrosive.

• Once a season, clean the grill box as well. Turn the unit on for a few minutes to soften the grease. When it's cool enough to touch, scrub with a stiff brush using a bio-safe detergent and hot water. Do the same to the burner. Dry thoroughly.

• If your burner won't light, which often happens after it hasn't been used for longer periods of time, brush the burner clean with a stiff brush and use a wire or pipe cleaner to clear the holes. Carefully replace the burner in its original position.

• Wash and wax the cover of your grill to keep it sparkling.

Easy way to clean briquettes

Even the permanent briquettes in a gas grill need to be cleaned after having grease dripped on them a few dozen times—but there's an easy way to do it. Simply turn over the briquettes so that their greasy sides are face down. Then light the grill, set the temperature on high, and close the cover. Let the fire burn for 15 to 20 minutes; your briquettes will be as good as new.

Leave cleaning for the morning

While you should really scrub off the cooking rack on your gas grill soon after every use, often you really don't have time. Instead of facing a tough cleanup next time you're ready to grill, try this trick: Take the cooled rack from your grill and drop it in the grass, cooking side down. Let it sit there overnight, and in the morning, wipe away the dew—and the grease—with a few damp paper towels.

Soak hardened grease

For really tough baked-on grease, put your dirty rack inside a heavy-duty plastic garbage bag. Mix a solution of 1/2 cup liquid dishwashing detergent and 1 gallon (4 liters) of water. Pour the mixture over the rack and seal the bag with a twist tie. Let it sit overnight. The next day, use a stiff brush to remove the residue. Rinse the rack thoroughly.

WASH AND WAX COVER OF GRILL

NEVER WIRE-BRUSH A PORCELAIN SURFACE WHEN IT IS HOT

SCRUB THE FOOD GRATE WITH A NYLON PAD AFTER EACH USE

BURN THE GREASE OFF BRIQUETTES AFTER EACH USE

KEEP GRILL DRY; COVER IT FULLY WHEN IT IS NOT IN USE

STORE GRILL INDOORS DURING THE OFF-SEASON

CLEAN AND WASH THE INTERIOR BOX AT SEASON'S END

Your Car

Operating Your Car

A car may be a machine, but it's sensitive to the way you drive it. Learn how to be a gentle driver and you'll be lucky in love—at least when it comes to automobiles!

Be patient during the break-in period

You've bought your dream car and now you want to make it last at long as possible in top condition. Here are some things to remember as you pull it out of the dealer's lot:

• During the break-in period, typically the first 1,000 miles (1,600 km), keep your speed under 55 mph (88 kpm) or to the speed recommended by your car's manufacturer.

• Avoid heavy loads on the drive train, such as towing trailers, and loading the roof rack or trunk with heavy construction materials.

• Do not allow your new car to idle for long periods—this is good advice for the life of your car, but especially during break-in. The oil pressure generated by doing so may not be sending oil to every part of your engine.

• Use only light to medium acceleration, keeping the engine rpms below 3,000 for the first few hours of driving.

Drive with care everyday

Being car considerate shouldn't stop after the break-in. Drive with care every day and your car will reward you with longer intervals without repair.

• Do not race your car's engine during start-up. This is a quick way to add years of wear to your engine, especially if it's cold outside.

• Accelerate slowly when you begin your drive. The most wear to the engine and drive train occurs in the first ten to twenty minutes of operation.

• Warming the engine by letting it idle in the driveway is not a smart idea. The engine doesn't operate at its peak temperature, resulting in incomplete fuel combustion, soot deposits on cylinder walls, oil contamination, and ultimately damaged components.

• Put less strain on your engine and automatic transmission by shifting to neutral at red lights. Otherwise, the engine is still working to push the car even while it's stopped.

• Avoid driving at high speeds and accelerating quickly, especially when it's very hot or very cold outside. Such driving behavior will result in more frequent repairs.

• Extend the life of your tires with careful driving. Observe posted speed limits. Avoid fast starts, stops, and turns. Avoid potholes and objects on the road. Don't run over curbs or hit the tire against the curb when parking. And, of course, don't burn rubber.

• When turning your steering wheel, don't hold it in an extreme right or left position for more than a few seconds. Doing so can damage the power-steering pump.

• Consolidate your short driving trips. Most of the wear and tear—as well as the pollution your car generates—takes place in the first few minutes of driving. Doing several errands at once, during low traffic hours if possible, will keep your engine happier longer.

Buy gas at reputable service stations

Ask whether the gas you buy is filtered at the pump and if the station has a policy about changing the pump filters regularly. If you get a song and dance, find another gas station. Some stations don't have pump filters, making you more vulnerable to dirty gasoline. Other stations may not mix alcohol and fuel properly—or worse, water down their product. Find a station you trust and stick to it.

Buy to Keep: Cars

Choosing a car, and the options that come with it, is as much an emotional decision as it is a practical one. Many people want their car to reflect their personality. There are some options, however, that you may want to avoid if you don't like bringing your car to the dealer every month or two for repair work. Make your buying decisions on value-oriented facts unless, of course, you don't care how long your car lasts. Keep this list in mind the next time you buy a car.

Windows	Less can go wrong with manual window openers and mirror adjusters. Opt for tinted windows to cut down on UV light and excess heat that can damage interior surfaces.
Brakes	The parking brake in some models will automatically release when the car is placed in drive or reverse. This feature can slow the wear on brake shoes and pads.
Exhaust	Opt for a stainless steel exhaust system. It will put an end to visits to muffler repair shops and pay for itself in spades over the course of the life of your vehicle.
Transmission	Standard transmissions will generally last longer than automatic transmissions, and they are usually less costly to repair.
Interior	Leather upholstery will look better and last longer than synthetic fabrics and vinyl. It's also easier to clean.
Engine	Demand long-life spark plugs for your new car. You won't have to worry about changing them for many years.
Bumpers	Choose a car with bumpers rated for 5 mph (8 kph) impact or better. The mandated impact standard is only 2.5 mph (4 kph), but some makers give you more. Avoid low-riding bumpers. They're bound to snag on a curb or road debris sooner or later.

Don't fill up if you see the tanker

If you happen to see a gasoline tanker filling the tanks at your local gas station, come back another day or go to a different station. As the station's underground tanks are being filled, the turbulence can stir up sediment. Sediment in your gas can clog fuel filters and fuel injectors, causing poor performance and possibly necessitating repairs.

Go easy when you're stuck

When stuck in mud or snow, don't make the problem worse by damaging an expensive component. Gently rocking in an attempt to free the car is fine. But if it looks as though you're really stuck, don't keep at it. Throwing your car from forward to reverse repeatedly, as well as spinning tires at high speeds, can generate lots of heat and spell trouble for transmissions, clutches, and differentials. It may be cheaper in the long run to call the tow truck rather than risk big repair bills down the road. It's a good idea to carry a traction aid in the trunk, such as sand, gravel, or cat litter.

Lighten up your key chain

Does your car key share a chain with a dozen or more other keys? That's a pretty heavy load hanging off the car key when it's in the ignition. The weight, combined with bouncing while you drive, can wear out the tumblers inside the ignition and eventually lead to ignition switch failure. To add years of service to your ignition switch, purchase a lightweight key chain that allows you to separate your ignition key from the others. Drive with only the ignition key in your ignition. If your ignition key "sticks" when you try to turn on the car, it's a warning that your ignition switch is about to fail. Replace it before you get stranded.

Choose a good car insurer

Sometimes, no matter how careful you are, disaster inevitably strikes—typically in the form of an accident. Make sure that your car will be repaired to the best possible standard by finding an insurer that will pay for parts from the original manufacturer and guarantee the repairs it authorizes.

Keep an auto log

Keep a pad and pencil in the glove compartment and use them to record your gas fill-ups and mileage. If you notice that your gas mileage worsens, mention it to your service man. It may be an early warning sign that something is wrong with your car.

Preserve your car during long-term storage

If you are not going to use your car for more than a month, store it properly to prevent unnecessary damage and repairs upon your return.

• Fill the gas tank to help prevent condensation from accumulating in the gas tank. Add a fuel stabilizer and drive the car around a bit to distribute the additive to engine parts.

• Wash and wax the car thoroughly to protect the finish.

• Place a vapor barrier on your garage floor. A 4-mil polyethylene drop cloth will do.

• Disengage the parking brake to help avoid brake corrosion.

• Put the car on jack stands to take the weight of the vehicle off the wheels and tires.

• Disconnect and remove the battery to keep it from draining. Place the battery on a trickle-type charger. Or periodically drain the battery, using a small light bulb, and then recharge it with a low-volt charger.

• Plug the tailpipe with a rag to prevent moist air from infiltrating into it.

☞ DON'T
drive with your foot on the brake

Don't rest your foot on the brake pedal as you drive. Even slight pressure can cause a drag that will wear out your brakes and waste gasoline.

Car Interior

Some of us spend so much time in our cars that the interior becomes our second living room. And, indeed, the inside of your car needs and deserves the same attention you give the furniture in your home.

Park in the shade

Of course, a garage is always the ideal place to park your car. But if one isn't available, minimize interior damage from UV sunlight and heat by always trying to park your car in the shade. If no shade is available or if you find parking under a tree results in bird droppings, use a car shade to minimize the sun's impact. As a bonus, you'll have a cooler car to step into on hot sunny days. Car shades come in two basic types: those that you unfold and place on the front windshield and rear window, or pleated types that attach to the windshield posts (with adhesive), window frames (with Velcro), or the windows themselves (with suction cups).

Clean the inside, too

Vacuum and sponge your interior every time you wash your car. Dirt particles are abrasive, and spilled liquids, such as soda, can be corrosive. Vacuum your interior thoroughly with a powerful vacuum (small cordless models are generally too weak). Use the appropriate wand heads when vacuuming. The bare metal wand can mar and scratch surfaces. Sponge vinyl surfaces clean with a solution of mild detergent and water.

Clean dash gauges carefully

Use a soft damp cloth to lightly wipe dust from the clear plastic lenses on your dashboard. Too much pressure will scratch them. Too many scratches can make it difficult to read your gauges under certain lighting conditions.

Let floor mats take winter's beating

Use floor mats to protect carpeting. The best type for controlling salt, slush, and mud in winter are rubber waffle-style mats. They stay in place, don't allow the water to seep through, and are easy to wash clean. Carpet-style mats are helpful, too. Shake, vacuum, or wash as needed; replace them as they wear through.

Blast mats with the hose

When washing your car, drag out the rubber or carpet floor mats and blast them with the hose. This will dislodge dirt particles that, if allowed to

INFO STATION

RESTORE DAMAGED LEATHER

Don't give up on leather car upholstery even if it is stiff and cracking. There are products available to restore damaged leather, including a cleaner that preps the leather for reapplying dye; fillers that cover scratches, tears, and small holes; and dyes for re-coloring the leather. To learn more about these products, visit the websites below:

> **Leather Magic**
www.leathermagic.com

> **Leather World Technologies**
www.leatherworldtech.com

Car Seats

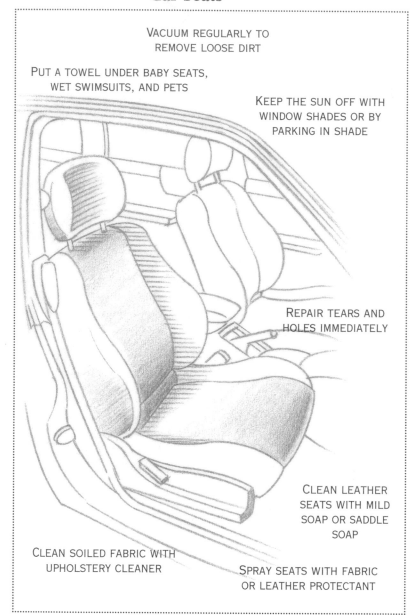

VACUUM REGULARLY TO
REMOVE LOOSE DIRT

PUT A TOWEL UNDER BABY SEATS,
WET SWIMSUITS, AND PETS

KEEP THE SUN OFF WITH
WINDOW SHADES OR BY
PARKING IN SHADE

REPAIR TEARS AND
HOLES IMMEDIATELY

CLEAN LEATHER
SEATS WITH MILD
SOAP OR SADDLE
SOAP

CLEAN SOILED FABRIC WITH
UPHOLSTERY CLEANER

SPRAY SEATS WITH FABRIC
OR LEATHER PROTECTANT

build up, will grind holes in your mats. Let the mats dry thoroughly in the sun before reinstalling them.

For stubborn carpet or mat stains

After vacuuming floor mats or interior carpeting, apply foam rug cleaner to resistant stains as directed by the maker. Work the foam into a few square feet at a time, using a wet sponge or brush. Vacuum when dry.

Preserve door and window seals

Wipe a rubber protectant (such as Armor-All) or silicone on door and window weatherstripping to keep it in good condition. Don't use an oil-based product, such as WD-40, because the oil will damage the rubber. Regular cleaning and treatment of your car's weatherstripping will also lessen the likelihood of your door sticking to its rubber seal in cold weather, a common cause of damage to the rubber.

Fix bad weatherstripping immediately

If your weatherstripping is letting rainwater leak into the interior of your car, take a look at it and decide if you can repair it or if it needs to be replacd. Small leaks can be handled with brush-on seam sealers. Re-secure loose sections, not otherwise damaged, with trim adhesive. Torn sections may be repaired with special caulking available at auto parts stores. You may also be able to extend the life of worn-but-intact sections by inserting foam rods, available at automotive stores, into the hollow section of the weatherstripping. If you decide to replace entire sections of gasket, don't simply buy generic stuff such as you'd use around the house. Buy a product that matches your car's original weatherstripping—it's available in a wide variety of profiles from dealerships and automotive mail-order catalogues.

☞ DON'T
play locksmith

If you've locked your keys in the car or trunk, call a professional locksmith or a local dealer for help. Fishing around with a coat hanger can damage weatherstripping and lead to nagging leaks and water damage.

Keep leather from drying out and cracking

Leather cars seats are durable and don't require a lot of maintenance. After a few years, however, the seats can become soiled. Use a leather cleaner to remove dirt and stains. Then apply a leather protectant formulated for pigmented or top-coated grain leather (the leather used for most leather car upholstery). Protectants will resist stains and make the upholstery easier to clean in the future. Choose a protectant that includes conditioners to keep your leather supple.

Use upholstery cleaners on soiled seats

The same upholstery cleaners you use at home can be used on your car's upholstery. Use them sparingly, however, to avoid saturating the fabric. Use a clean cloth to wipe away the foam. On velour seats, brush the fibers gently to avoid matting them

and to preserve the original texture of the fabric.

Renew fabric upholstery

Spraying fabric car seats and carpets with a fabric protectant, such as Scotchgard, will make them resist dirt and stains, and make them easier to clean. Thoroughly clean the fabrics before using one of these products and then test the product on an inconspicuous place to be sure the treatment will not discolor the fabric.

Place a towel under baby seats

All manner of food bits and liquids can accumulate under a baby seat, where they can permanently stain the upholstery. Place a sheet of heavy plastic and an absorbent towel under the seat to prevent damage, and re-secure the seat according to the manufacturer's directions.

Car Exterior

Need an incentive to wash and wax your car? Just price a new one. Here's how to keep your faithful "classic" as shiny as a new penny.

Protect car paint from the sun

Paint does more than make your vehicle look great. It's also the first line of defense against rusted body panels. Of course, the best way to protect the paint is to park the car in a garage. If that is not possible, park in the shade or purchase a car cover. The sun's ultraviolet rays break down paint and cause it to fade. Some car covers protect your car from more than sun, moisture, bird droppings, and dust—they also have a thin layer of cushioning that will guard against light impact, such as from a tipped bicycle or small falling tree branch.

Touch up nicks sooner rather than later

Touch-up paint won't adhere well to rust. So be sure to keep some matching touch-up paint on hand so you can touch up any minor nicks, often found around door edges, before rust has a chance to form.

Tape saves light covers

A cracked taillight or turn-signal cover, if left alone, may allow your light compartment to fill with water and cause some real damage. A good short-term fix is to tape over the crack. Use the red or orange tape that's made for this purpose. You can purchase it at many automotive parts stores.

Avoid light fixture problems

When changing a bad bulb, clean dirty or corroded sockets with fine steel wool or a small wire brush. Wipe the socket clean of debris before installing the new light bulb.

Fix small windshield chips

Got a rock chip, crack, or ding in your windshield? Bring your car to a windshield repair shop. For far less cost than replacing the windshield, they can fix chips and cracks, even quite long ones. The repairs not only keep the chips and cracks from spreading and restore structural integrity, they also improve clarity.

Fill with washer fluid only

Don't add water to the windshield washer reservoir. It won't clean as well as washer fluid, and it may freeze in cold weather and damage the system. Don't try to run your windshield washer system once you suspect there's no more fluid in the tank, or you may damage the washer fluid pump.

Fix the washer fluid tank

Cracked washer-deicer fluid tanks are fairly common once a car is of a certain age. A good remedy—until you can buy a new tank or find one at the junkyard—is to insert a plastic freezer bag into the tank and fill it with the washer fluid.

Don't try to carry too much

Never exceed your car's roof load specifications or weight limits. You can find them in your vehicle owner's manual. Check the weight limitation of your roof rack as well. Typically the range is from 150 to 200 pounds (68 to 90 kg). That's the equivalent of eighteen 8-foot 2 x 4s (2.4-meter 38 x 89s) or three sheets of 3/4-inch (17-mm) plywood. If you have to deliver a heavy load from the home or garden center, consider having it delivered. It will save wear and tear on you as well as your car.

Keep an old blanket handy

Protect your car's roof from scratches with an old blanket before tying lumber, bicycles, or luggage to your roof rack.

Secure loads to avoid dents and scratches

The beginning of the end for the finish on many cars and trucks—

♦ BEST ADVICE ♦ **Car Exteriors**

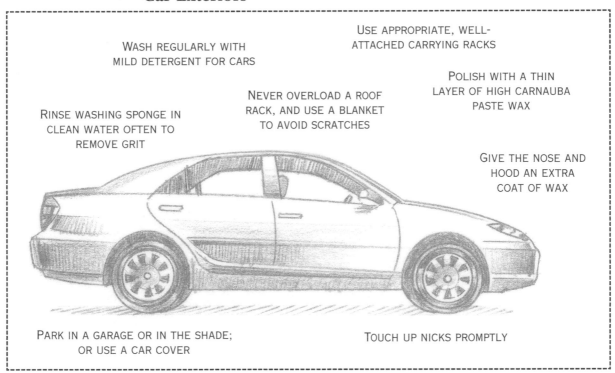

WASH REGULARLY WITH MILD DETERGENT FOR CARS

USE APPROPRIATE, WELL-ATTACHED CARRYING RACKS

POLISH WITH A THIN LAYER OF HIGH CARNAUBA PASTE WAX

NEVER OVERLOAD A ROOF RACK, AND USE A BLANKET TO AVOID SCRATCHES

RINSE WASHING SPONGE IN CLEAN WATER OFTEN TO REMOVE GRIT

GIVE THE NOSE AND HOOD AN EXTRA COAT OF WAX

PARK IN A GARAGE OR IN THE SHADE; OR USE A CAR COVER

TOUCH UP NICKS PROMPTLY

and for wagon and hatchback interiors for that matter—is an improperly stowed load. Invest in the appropriate racks for bicycles, cargo, and luggage. A good trick to keep tall objects from sliding around in a pick-up truck bed is to use a shower curtain rod (or two) as a brace. Just push the cargo against the front wall of the truck bed and install the rod behind it. Twist to secure. Cargo nets will also help keep objects from banging around and damaging a truck bed.

Inspect wheel–well splashguards

These guards, however flimsy on many of today's cars, help keep water and winter's salty slush from splashing up into the engine compartment, where it can damage sensitive electrical components. Unfortunately, these guards tear off easily— sometimes without the driver knowing it. Check for damage to these guards when you wash your car. Re-secure with the appropriate fasteners or replace as needed. As added protection from splashed-up muck, slush, and debris, install mud flaps (also called splash guards) on your vehicle.

Wash in winter, too

If you rarely wash your car during messy winter weather, you are not alone. The cars you see on the road make it obvious that lots of folks figure, "Why bother? The car is going to look awful the next time I drive it." The problem with this thinking is that washing is more important in the winter than other times of the year. All that sand, slush, and ice mixed with road salt is exactly what makes your car rust. The fastest corrosion occurs when the temperature repeatedly rises above and then falls below freezing. Especially during the messy months, be sure to rinse the undercarriage and hard-to-reach areas that are susceptible to rust, such as the bumpers and inside the wheel wells. If the temperature outside is going to stay above freezing long enough for your car and driveway to dry, fill a bucket with warm water and tackle the job at home. If not, pay a visit to your local car wash and be sure they dry the car thoroughly.

Wax to protect your car's paint job

No way around it! Waxing your car is work. But it's satisfying work that will help keep your car looking new. Car wax preserves paint by slowing oxidation and forming a barrier against bird droppings, sap, and pollution. Plus driving a nice shiny car is just plain fun. Here's what to do to ensure the maximum in protection:

• Liquid and spray waxes are tempting to use—they make the car shiny with less work than rubbing in paste wax. But there's still no beating paste wax for the hardest, longest-lasting finish. Look for paste with a high carnauba wax content.

• Apply a thin, even coat of wax to the car's surfaces with a damp sponge. Avoid applying too much, or it will be difficult to remove and some residue will inevitably mar your finish.

• To avoid fine scratches, use a clean, soft cotton or microfiber cloth to remove wax once it has dried.

• Apply an extra coat of wax to the nose and hood. The wax film in these areas wears away quickly.

Give your car a new skin

New self-adhering urethane films have been developed to protect the most vulnerable painted areas on your car from stone chips and other minor abrasions. You can wash and wax these surfaces, just as you would the rest of the paint job. While it's best to have these films professionally installed, you can peel them off yourself. One product is made by 3M, and you can learn more by going to 3m.com and searching for Scotchgard Paint Protection Film Solutions.

Don't let tools mar your car's finish

If you plan to service and make repairs to your car, invest in a fender cover. It drapes over your fender, providing a safe place to rest your tools without causing scratches. It will also prevent your belt buckle from marring your paint as you lean into the engine compartment to work.

ProTip

WASH YOUR CAR LIKE AN EXPERT

Washing your car regularly will go a long way toward keeping the body in tiptop shape. But besides doing it regularly, you need to do it right. Here's how to do the best job:

• Wash your car with a mild detergent that's formulated for car finishes. Don't use dishwashing liquid. It's harsher and will remove the protective wax coating on your car. Some detergents even contain salt that will corrode metal.

• Wash your car in sections, beginning with the roof, and rinse as you go. Otherwise, a soap film will dry on the finish before you rinse. The film will make the finish look dull.

• Keep a second bucket of clean water handy and use it often to rinse your sponge. This will ensure that you are not using a gritty sponge that can put tiny scratches on your car's finish.

• Avoid using the same sponge for painted surfaces as you use for wheels. The dirt particles embedded in the wheel sponge will add hundreds of fine scratches to painted surfaces with every swipe.

Tires, Wheels, and Brakes

This is where the rubber meets the road. Even the hottest sports car won't handle well and safely if you ignore these essential components.

Keep the caps on

You step out into driveway ready to start your morning commute only to discover a flat tire. How in the heck did that happen overnight? If the tire valve is missing its cap, the culprit might be a leaky valve. Those little caps keep out dirt and moisture that can cause leaks, so be sure to keep caps on all your tire valves. Another tip: When you replace tires, remind the tire shop that you expect new valves with the tires.

Maintain proper inflation

Under-inflated tires are a tire salesman's best friend. They create excessive heat and stress that can lead to tire failure. If you want to get every last mile out of your tires, get yourself a tire pressure gauge and use it at least once a month (more in hot weather) to keep your tires inflated to the recommendation in the vehicle's owner's manual. Check tires when they are cold (driven for less than one mile) for an accurate reading.

Beware the wet thumb

If you top off your tires at a service station, check to see if there's moisture coming from the air pump. Simply depress the pin inside the inflator valve with your thumbnail. If your thumb gets wet, advise the station manager that his tanks need to be drained and go to a different station. Moisture, trapped inside a tire, can cause pressure variations and corrode rims.

Check for uneven wear

Check tires for uneven wear. If you've maintained tire inflation properly, uneven wear may indicate the need for a wheel realignment. It can also mean improperly operating brakes or shocks, a bent wheel, internal tire damage, or worn bushings.

Check tread for safety

Most states require tires to be replaced when they have worn down to 1/16-inch (1.5 mm) of remaining tire depth. Tires sold in North America are required to have "wear bars" molded into them to make it easy to see when tire replacement is legally required. However, if you'll be driving in the rain, you should change your tires when there is 1/8-inch (3 mm) of tread left. Otherwise, water may not escape from under your tires fast enough and you risk hydroplaning—a dangerous situation in which your car loses traction and literally floats on the water. Stick an American quarter between the treads in several places. If part of Washington's head is always covered, you have enough tread to drive in the rain. If you drive in snow, you'll need at least 3/16-inch (5 mm) of tread to get adequate traction. Stick an American penny between the treads. If the top of the Lincoln Memorial is always covered, you're ready for winter driving.

Rotate your tires

Rotating your tires helps to distribute tire wear evenly and ensures that you'll get the maximum road life out of them. The first rotation is especially important. Your owner's manual should specify both rotation period and pattern. If not, rotate your tires every 6,000 to 7,500 miles (9,700 to 12,000 km)—your tire dealer should know the correct pattern of tire rotation.

When temperatures affect tire inflation

When outside temperatures drop or soar, tires tend to lose pressure. A drop of 10 degrees F (6 degrees C), in fact, will decrease a tire's air pressure by 1 or 2 pounds. Tires can lose even more air in hot weather. Under-inflated tires can result in accelerated wear and poor driving performance. If you live in a place where temperatures vary a lot, check your tire pressure often and add air as needed.

Buy used tires

If you own a car that you plan to drive only for another year, the last thing you want to do is to buy a new set of tires. If it's time to replace those tires though, it's really time. Rather than hesitate, buy a set of used tires. Call local tire dealers to see what's available. You'll be surprised by how much wear is left in tires that are turned in by image-conscious car owners. Have your tire size handy.

Fix a flat with a rubber plug

It's perfectly OK to have your flat tire fixed by plugging the puncture with a rubber plug, assuming your tire has good tread left. Beware, however, of add-on charges for this service when it's done at a tire dealer, where the primary goal is usually to get you to buy new. Prices literally range from $5 to $40.

Use wheel cleaner

Your car's wheels are down there on the road, taking the brunt of road dirt. Add in the dust that wears off your brake pads and you've got a formula for stains that are tough to remove when you wash your vehicle. Car-washing liquid won't do the job. You need a wheel cleaner specifically formulated to remove such stains. Be sure to buy the correct formulation. Some cleaners are designed for metal wheels, and others for painted or clear-coated wheels. The metal wheel cleaners come in various formulations as well, depending upon whether your metal wheel has a satin, aluminum, or chrome finish. Protect metal wheels with wheel polish, painted wheels with a coat of wax.

Lube your lug nuts

Lug nuts, if not lubricated occasionally, can seize or "freeze" to the studs due to corrosion. Repairing them can be expensive. Having to call a tow truck for a flat you can't remove is even more expensive. The next time you change or rotate your tires, pick up some anti-seize lubricant at your local auto supply store. Clean the stud threads with a wire brush and wipe them with the lubricant. It's formulated to prevent the lug nuts (spark plugs, too) from seizing and won't allow them to loosen as you drive, the way other

lubricants might. If a lug nut does freeze to a stud, try spraying the nut and stud with WD-40 or Liquid Wrench. Allow it to penetrate for 10 or 20 minutes. Use a heat gun to apply heat. Then use a ratchet wrench to remove the lug.

Hang on to your hubcaps

Clang, clang, clang! There goes your hubcap, rolling off to destination unknown. Hubcaps, wheel covers, and center caps can pop off your car's wheels as you're driving if they were not reinstalled correctly, have loosened over time, or if they were damaged by being jammed against a curb while parking. Here are some things you can do to keep these expensive parts on the car:

• If your older metal hubcap has loosened, remove it and pry the metal clips outward slightly. This should fix the problem.

• Newer plastic-type hubcaps and some wheel covers are usually held in place by a retaining wire ring that snaps into tabs on the wheel. When installing such a cap or cover, take care that you do not bend or break the tabs.

• One way to make sure your expensive hubcaps aren't damaged by a repair shop is to remove them yourself before taking your car in for a repair that requires wheel removal, such as a brake job or new

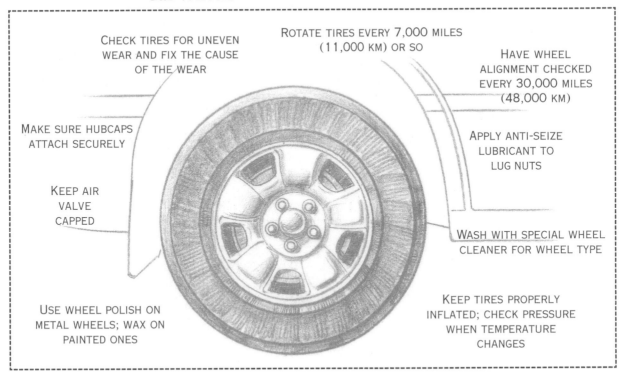

CHECK TIRES FOR UNEVEN WEAR AND FIX THE CAUSE OF THE WEAR

ROTATE TIRES EVERY 7,000 MILES (11,000 KM) OR SO

HAVE WHEEL ALIGNMENT CHECKED EVERY 30,000 MILES (48,000 KM)

MAKE SURE HUBCAPS ATTACH SECURELY

APPLY ANTI-SEIZE LUBRICANT TO LUG NUTS

KEEP AIR VALVE CAPPED

WASH WITH SPECIAL WHEEL CLEANER FOR WHEEL TYPE

USE WHEEL POLISH ON METAL WHEELS; WAX ON PAINTED ONES

KEEP TIRES PROPERLY INFLATED; CHECK PRESSURE WHEN TEMPERATURE CHANGES

tires. When reinstalling hubcaps, rest the hubcap in place and then tap it gently with a rubber mallet. Don't hit the hubcap hard, or you might break the clips underneath. If you prefer to have your repairperson remove the covers, check to make sure they were reinstalled properly. They should look even and flush.

Have wheel alignment checked

Have your car's wheel alignment checked every 30,000 miles (48,000 km), or as recommended in your owner's

manual. Also have it checked after buying new tires and when you replace a rack-and-pinion steering unit or other steering parts. Improper tire alignment will shorten the life of your tires as well as cause poor handling. If your steering is stiffer than normal or the vehicle pulls to one side, you probably have an alignment problem.

Top off your brake fluid

Check brake fluid monthly. Wipe dirt from the master cylinder lid before you open it. If you need fluid, add the type recommended by your car's maker. Never

substitute other fluids, such as transmission or power-steering fluid. And don't use brake fluid from a previously opened container. Once exposed to air, brake fluid absorbs moisture and contaminates easily.

Care for anti–lock brakes

An anti-lock brake system is sensitive to moisture, which can ruin the expensive ABS pump and rot the brake lines from the inside. Since brake fluid attracts moisture, it should be "bled" or purged at least every three years, or as specified in your owner's manual.

Car Engine and Other Systems

Gone are the days when your car needed a tune-up every 10,000 miles. Today's cars are durable and relatively trouble-free, so it's easy to forget that they still need regular maintenance. Paying regular attention to the parts under the hood will ensure that your car hums along the highway for hundreds of thousands of miles.

Check engine oil at every other fill-up

For an accurate reading, follow this procedure:

• Run or drive your car for about 15 minutes to warm the oil; then park the car in a level place. Turn off the engine and wait 15 minutes to allow the oil in the engine to drain back to the oil pan.

• Remove the dipstick and wipe it clean with a paper towel or rag. Reinsert the dipstick, being sure to push it in all the way, then pull it out again to check the oil level. It should be somewhere between the hash marks on the dipstick.

• Add the type and amount of oil as specified in your owner's manual, if necessary.

Change oil frequently

Your dad knew that frequent oil changes were key to keeping his Buick on the road another year. And while owner's manuals for today's cars recommend increasing long intervals between oil changes, the fact remains—frequent changes flush abrasive dirt and metal particles out of the engine, prolonging its life. Most owner's manuals recommend a more frequent interval for "severe conditions." To maximize the life of your engine, follow the severe intervals recommendations, especially if drive regularly in stop-and-go traffic.

Avoid overfilling your crankcase with oil

Don't overfill your engine crankcase with oil. If you do, the oil can rise into the crankshaft, where air bubbles will get churned into the oil. Your oil pump can't do a good job of circulating oil with air bubbles. The result can be overheating and stress on engine components. Overfilling can also foul your sparkplugs. In fact, overfilling is a bad idea with all automotive fluids.

Wipe oil pan plug clean

If you do your own oil changes, clean the drain plug and washer with rags before reinstalling your oil pan. Some plugs are magnetized to trap metal particles.

Don't forget the filters

There are several filters (the main ones are oil, fuel, transmission, and air) important to preserving your car engine, and they should be changed according to the schedule in your owner's manual or as follows:

• Change the oil filter at least at every other oil change—every change is even better because the old filter contains nearly a quart of dirty oil that will remain with the new, clean oil. If you change your oil yourself, wipe the filter threads with an anti-seize lubricant, available at auto supply stores.

• Check the air filter every two months and replace it when dirty or as part of a tune-up. Air filters are generally easier to get to than oil filters. You find them under the big metal lid in a carbureted engine or in a rectangular box in a fuel-injected engine—check your owner's manual for the exact location. Extend the life of air filters by blowing them clean with compressed air.

• Despite claims by makers and dealers that some newer fuel filters never need changing, it's smart to have it done once a year. A clogged fuel filter will cause poor engine performance (hesitation and starting difficulties) and is an early warning that there may be corrosion in your gas tank.

• Change your transmission fluid filter after the first 5,000 miles (8,000 km) of driving and every 25,000 miles (40,000 km) or two year thereafter. (See "Maintain your transmission," at right.)

Don't forget the PCV valve

The PCV (positive crankcase ventilation) valve is an emissions control device on older cars—check your service manual to see if your car has one. The valve recirculates partially burned gases from the engine's crankcase to the combustion chamber. Important to a properly functioning engine, the valve should be changed every 30,000 miles (48,000 km) or as specified in your owner's manual. In addition to helping you get the most from a tank of gasoline, it helps to prevent the buildup of harmful sludge and corrosion. When replacing your PCV valve, be sure you use the correct one or you may damage your engine.

Heavier is not always better

Use the oil viscosity grade that's recommended in your owner's manual for the temperature range you expect for the coming season. Lighter grades (lower viscosity, such as SAE 5W-30), often specified for

today's smaller car engines, will deliver easier starts and better engine protection in winter and improved gas mileage throughout the year, thanks to less internal engine friction. Do not use a heavy grade of oil in cold winter climes or you will risk damage to your engine.

Maintain your transmission

Change automatic transmission fluid and filter after the first 5,000 miles (8,000 km) and after every 25,000 miles (40,000 km) or two years thereafter, or as recommended in your owner's manual. If you use your vehicle for towing, change the fluid and filter every year. For manual transmissions, change the lubricant (motor oil or gear oil, depending on the car) after the first 5,000 miles and after every 50,000 (80,000 km) thereafter. Use synthetic motor oil or gear lube for longer transmission life unless the manufacturer recommends otherwise.

Consider adding oil coolers

If you plan to do a lot of towing and your vehicle is not already equipped with coolers, consider having them added. Aftermarket engine oil and transmission fluid coolers are simple, low-cost add-ons that operate on the same principle as your car's radiator. The fluid flows through them, and many small fins absorb and dissipate heat. Cooler operating

temperatures of engine oil and transmission fluid can add significantly to the life of your engine and transmission.

ProTip

SYNTHETIC OIL IS BETTER

Use synthetic lubricant when you change your engine oil. It's more expensive, but your engine will thank you. Synthetic oils last longer, stand up to high heat and extreme conditions, and have better flow rates when cold than regular oils. Take care, however, not to void your warranty. Follow the schedule for oil changes specified in your manual—at least through the warranty period.

Spark plugs do need changing

The advent of electronic ignition and on-board computers has eliminated the need for regular tune-ups, but you still need to change your spark plugs. Many manufacturers recommend changing plugs every 30,000 or 40,000 miles (48,000 or 64,000 km) to ensure good fuel mileage and engine performance. Some new cars come with long-life plugs (sometimes called double platinum plugs) that can last for 100,000 miles (160,000 km). If your car isn't so equipped, make the switch after 30,000 miles. The extra cost is only a few dollars per spark plug. While you're at it, change your

spark plug wires as well. Their typical life is 50,000 miles (80,000 km). Deteriorated wires can cause those high-tech new spark plugs to foul.

Avoid hose hassles

Check the hoses under your hood every month or two to avoid the hassle of a broken hose while you're on the road. With the car cool and off, squeeze the hoses. If they are hard or make a crunching sound, replace them. Ditto if they are extremely soft or sticky. With the car warm but off, examine hoses for bulges and collapsed sections. If you find any, the hose walls are weak, and it's time to replace the hose. Never drive with a ruptured coolant hose, or you are liable to overheat the engine and damage it. Other hoses are crucial to operation of your power brakes and cruise-control systems.

Test drive–belt tension

Check the tension and condition of your drive belt (or, with many cars, multiple belts) every month. Belts that are too tight can wear out the bearings in accessory components, such as AC compressor, water pump, and power-steering pump. Belts that are too loose will wear out faster and may fail prematurely. Perform your examination before you start the car to avoid injury due to a hot belt

or moving engine part. Check for tension by pressing in the center of the belt's longest exposed run while holding a ruler next to it. If you can depress the belt 1/ 2 to 1 inch (13 to 25 mm), but not more or less, the tension is good. If not, adjust the belt tension yourself according to your car's service manual, or have your dealer or auto repair service do it. Also check for belt damage, such as glazing (often due to oil leakage), fraying, and cracks. If you spot damage, have the belt checked by a pro and replaced if necessary.

Don't forget the timing belt

On many cars, it's the belt you can't see that is the most critical. If your manual says, as many do, that you should replace the timing belt at 50,000 miiles, do it! A failed timing belt can, depending on engine type, cause thousands of dollars worth of damage to your engine.

Clean your engine

There are several reasons to wash your engine at least every year or two. A clean engine will run cooler than a dirty one. You'll be more apt to tackle routine belt and hose checks and the like if you know you won't get covered with grime every time you do so. A clean engine will also make it much easier to spot leaks and to service components. Remember to protect sensitive engine components—including the air intake, distributor, and electrical parts—with plastic bags before getting started. Use dishwashing liquid or other grease-cutting detergents and a bristle brush to scrub engine and components surfaces. Rinse thoroughly. Heavy-duty engine cleaning products are available at automotive parts stores. Follow the directions carefully. You may also have your engine professionally steam cleaned.

Run your AC in winter

To keep your car's air-conditioning system fit for the next warm season, run it a few times throughout the winter. This will prevent moving parts in the compressor from seizing. Also, circulating the refrigerant will help keep the seals soft and pliant.

Maintain your car's battery

Maybe the manufacturer says your battery is maintenance-free, but don't you believe it! Check your battery regularly to extend its life and avoid the hassle of being stranded with a dead battery.

• Begin with the simple: keeping your battery clean. A dirty case can actually cause current to drain. Wipe with a damp rag. Use a mild detergent if necessary.

• Next, clean the battery posts or terminals. Loosen and remove the negative cable (black or minus sign) first, then the red positive cable. Use a brass wire battery brush dipped in a paste made from a few tablespoons of baking soda and a little water.

• Inspect the battery case for damage, such as cracks or bulges—signs that a battery needs to be replaced.

• Reinstall the cables, positive first, and coat the terminals and clamps with a thin coating of grease to prevent new corrosion.

Some batteries need water

If your battery has vent caps, remove them to check the level of the electrolyte. It should rise 1/2 inch (13 mm) above the battery's top plates. If it doesn't, use distilled water to raise the level to 1/4 or 3/8 inch (6 or 10 mm) below the bottom of the vent cap. Don't use tap water, as it may contain minerals that can damage your battery. Mechanics should check your battery as a part of your regularly scheduled maintenance, but they often skip the procedure. Be sure to ask to have it done.

☞ BE CAREFUL
when working with a battery

Handle batteries with care, wearing safety glasses and gloves. Batteries are filled with acid and explosive gases. Never smoke while working near a battery.

Be kind to your battery

If you inadvertently leave your lights on and drain your battery, take the following precautions to prevent damage to the battery and the starter when jump-starting your car:

• Don't risk causing the battery to explode. With both cars off, connect a positive cable end to the positive battery terminal of the dead battery.

• Connect the other positive cable end to the positive terminal of the source battery.

• Connect a negative cable end to the negative terminal of the source battery.

• Attach the remaining negative cable to unpainted metal on the car engine (as far from the dead battery as possible).

• Wait a few minutes and try to start the disabled car. If it doesn't start, start the source car and then try starting the dead one again.

• When the car starts, be careful to disconnect the cables in the reverse order.

• If the car still doesn't start, don't keep trying to charge it or you are liable to damage the starter. Bring the battery to an automotive shop to see if it can be recharged.

• Even if you're successful, ensure a full recharge by hooking up the battery to a charger overnight or by driving the car for 5 or 10 miles (8 to 16 km).

Seal a leaky radiator

Save the high expense of a new radiator by trying to seal a leak with a radiator sealer, such as Alumaseal from Gold Eagle Co. Available in powder or liquid form, the product circulates in the radiator until it gets to the hole, where it sets up and fills the hole upon contact with the air. Alumaseal may be used to stop heater core leaks as well.

Dilute your coolant

Your cooling system needs both coolant-antifreeze and water, so don't pour undiluted coolant into your cooling system. Dilute it with water to the commonly recommended 50-50 ratio. Similarly, don't use straight water in your system either. The coolant protects against corrosion and freezing. The water ensures good heat transfer from the coolant to the radiator.

Keep your cool

Check the coolant-antifreeze level weekly that shows on the translucent coolant-antifreeze overflow tank. If low, fill to the maximum fill mark on the tank with a 50-50 solution of coolant-antifreeze and water. Some coolant manufacturers now sell premixed coolant and water for the motorist who wants a quick and easy way to top off.

Don't forget to flush

Coolant-antifreeze eventually degrades and becomes contaminated. Flush it from your cooling system as recommended in your manual (typically every two years; every five years for newer coolants). Failing to do so can damage your radiator, clog your heater core, and cause the thermostat and water pump to fail.

Don't mix coolants

Avoid mixing coolants that are different in color. If your coolant is pink, don't add a green formulation to it. Otherwise, you'll end up with a thick solution that won't do its job. Use only the coolant specified in your owner's manual.

Check power-steering fluid

Check the power-steering fluid once a month with the car warmed up. If the level is low, have the hoses and pump inspected for leaks. In addition to making your car difficult to steer, low power-steering fluid will damage the power-steering pump. Be sure to use the power-steering fluid recommended for you car.

Tools &
Workshop

Workbench and Tool Storage

Many homeowners assemble a workshop in their homes. It's a great place to pursue hobbies, such as woodworking or model making, as well as an ideal space to repair and maintain your possessions. Here are some tips that will help you keep your workshop ready in the battle to make everything you own last longer.

Preserve your workbench

Cut sheets of tempered hardboard to the size of your workbench top, and tack it in place. Once it's gouged or loaded up with glue drips, flip it over for a clean start. This will keep your workbench surface looking new.

Fabricate a tougher top

If you need a bench for messy jobs, such as cleaning greasy parts, sharpening tools, and mixing paint, have your local heating and air-conditioning shop fabricate a top from sheet metal. Give them a piece of medium-density fiberboard (MDF) the size of your bench top, and ask them to make a snug-fitting cover for it. Make sure the metal gets bent over and under the MDF edges to avoid getting snagged or cut on sharp edges.

HD is the way to go

Heavy-duty benches need to be heavy in order to be stable enough for pounding, jointing, and planing tasks. This makes them a bear to move. If you use knock-down assembly hardware, however, you can easily disassemble your prized bench and take it with you should you have to move.

Build drawers with heavy-duty glides

Woodworking and mechanics' tools are heavy. If you're building a workbench with drawers, use heavy-duty drawer hardware for years of smooth, trouble-free operation.

Prevent rust in the shop

If moisture is a problem in your workshop, store your small metal hand tools, small electric tools, and your steel hardware in airtight containers. Toss in a packet or two of desiccant (clay or silicon) for good measure.

Cushion your hand tools

Cut pieces of carpet to fit inside drawers where you store your hand tools—especially sharp-edged tools, such as planes and chisels. This will prevent the tools from getting scratched or nicked. Spray the carpet with WD-40 to help prevent rusting. Keep a piece of carpet or carpet liner on your workbench for resting your cutting tools as well.

Dehumidify a basement workshop

A dehumidifier is a smart way to protect your tool investment if your shop is in a damp basement. It will prevent rust from forming on the surfaces of your hand tools and inside power-tool motors. Choose one that's large enough for the job. You can find the manufacturer's sizing recommendation in the owner's manual or on the company's website. For most basements, you'll need a 30-pint (15-liter) unit. For extremely large or damp basements, you may need a 40- or 50-pint (20- or 25-liter) unit.

When dehumidifying, keep windows closed

You can't expect a dehumidifier to last long if it's straining to dehumidify the great outdoors. So keep your windows closed. Also make sure your clothes dryer is not venting into the basement. Keep doors to unused areas closed as well. To eliminate the nuisance of having to empty your dehumidifier by hand, install a hose so that it empties automatically into a floor drain. Keep your humidifier working longer by washing the air filter frequently and cleaning dirt and lint from the coils.

Maintain your ladders

Ladders are among the simplest of tools, but unless kept in top shape, they can be among the most dangerous. Protect wooden ladders with a clear varnish, shellac, linseed oil or other wood preservative. Don't paint a wooden ladder, because the paint could hide defects. Sand splinters until smooth, and reseat, replace, or resecure any loose fasteners. Inspect metal ladders for burrs and sharp edges, and file them smooth. Check the protective lacquer coating on fiberglass ladders. If it's scratched or abraded, sand lightly and apply a coat of lacquer. Regardless of what your ladder is made of, lubricate the hardware, such as pulleys and spring-loaded rung locks. Replace rope if you notice it's fraying.

Add life to sawhorses

A pair of sawhorses is an invaluable addition to any workshop. Use them as the base of a worktable or to support lumber while sawing with a circular saw. Attach a 3/4-inch (19-mm) thick sacrificial wood strip to horizontal members to protect them from being sliced up by saw blades. Fasten the strip from below so that the blade won't hit the fastener when you set your saw to cut slightly deeper than the workpiece. When the strip gets chewed up, toss it and install a new piece. This tip works for most resin and steel sawhorses as well.

Hang your shop broom

The lowly shop broom requires some care if it's to perform well. When it's not in use, hang it on the wall with a spring-loaded broom clip (available at most hardware stores). It will keep the bristles from curling. Brooms with nylon bristles last the longest and are not affected by moisture or chemicals.

Choose a rechargeable fire extinguisher

A fire extinguisher is a must for any workshop. For years of service, buy a commercial-quality rechargeable model. It should be rated ABC for fighting all common types of fire, including ordinary materials (type A fire), flammable liquids (type B), and electrical (type C).

Preserve your extension cords

Wind your workshop extension cords onto a reel to protect them from damage due to spills, burns, and abrasion. Another way to keep extension cords out of harm's way is to hang them overhead. Install several bicycle hooks in your workshop ceiling. Loop the extension cord over the hooks while you work.

Mount outlet strips on a vertical surface

Outlet strips are real timesavers in the workshop. You can have several tools plugged in at once so you don't waste time plugging and unplugging them. To prevent the sockets from becoming fouled with sawdust, dirt, and spills, don't mount the strips horizontally. Instead, mount them on the side of your workbench, on a wall, or under a shelf above your bench.

Extend the life of fluorescent tubes

If the fluorescent bulbs in your work area are darkening, try reversing them end to end. Although this is a temporary solution, you're likely to get several months of additional service from your bulbs.

Hand Tools

Hand tools are our simplest but most valuable machines. Buy good ones, and they'll last a lifetime—maybe even two—if given a little care.

Don't misuse tools

The top causes for the demise of most hand tools are misuse and abuse. Here are some common examples:

• Use the right tool to hit chisels. If the chisel is made of hardened steel, such as a cold chisel, strike it with a ballpein hammer, not a nail hammer or brick hammer. Plastic-handled carpenter's chisels that have a metal cap on the end are designed to be struck with a nail hammer, but plastic- or wooden-handled chisels without metal caps should be struck only with wooden mallets.

• Don't use specialty hammers, such as a bricklayer's hammer, to strike steel tools or nails. You may damage the hammer.

• Don't use a screwdriver as a chisel, pry bar, punch, scraper, or paint stirrer. You will ruin the screwdriver.

• Don't use an extender, such as a pipe, to increase torque on any wrench. You are liable to damage the wrench if you do. Never strike a wrench with a hammer, either.

• Always adjust a wrench so that it tightly grips the object you are using it on. If it's loose, the jaws may become misaligned when you pull on it.

• Don't expose pliers to excessive heat, or you may draw the temper from the steel and ruin the tool.

• Don't use pliers to cut or bend wire if you have to use excessive force.

Buy replacement blades with the tool

These days, manufacturers are making many variations of basic cutting tools, such as hacksaws, utility knives, and paint scrapers. It is wise to buy the replacement blades when you buy the tool to ensure you'll have them when you need them. If the store doesn't sell the replacement part, don't buy the tool.

Remove rust and paint

Depending on storage conditions, your hand tools may develop rust despite your best efforts. Removing it is relatively easy if the rust hasn't gotten out of hand. Just rub lightly rusted surfaces with some steel wool dampened with a squirt of WD-40. Use Naval Jelly or a similar product to remove heavier layers of rust.

Paint and glue spatter removal may be a little more difficult. One method is to submerge the sullied tools in a pot of boiling water. After a few minutes, the paint will have loosened and will be easy to scrape or wipe away. Afterward, dry the tools thoroughly, and wipe or spray them with a penetrating oil. However, don't do this with any tool that has a wooden handle or any kind of foam or plastic cushioning or insulation.

※

Grandpa says...

"You can buy cheap handsaws that are intended to be tossed when they become dull. But you probably won't have a sharp saw on hand when you need it for a fine cut. Buy good-quality handsaws, which are more comfortable and accurate from the start, and learn how to sharpen them. All it takes is a round file and some patience. With the saw secured teeth up in a vice, use the file to dress the edge of each tooth. You'll know it's sharp when you see it shine."

ooo

High-tech rust preventer

If you live in a warm humid climate, especially if you're

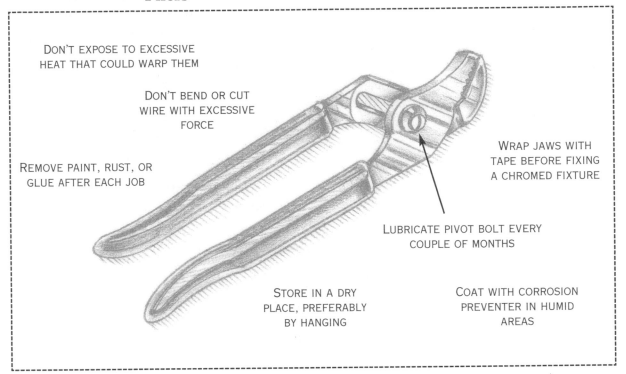

DON'T EXPOSE TO EXCESSIVE
HEAT THAT COULD WARP THEM

DON'T BEND OR CUT
WIRE WITH EXCESSIVE
FORCE

REMOVE PAINT, RUST, OR
GLUE AFTER EACH JOB

WRAP JAWS WITH
TAPE BEFORE FIXING
A CHROMED FIXTURE

LUBRICATE PIVOT BOLT EVERY
COUPLE OF MONTHS

STORE IN A DRY
PLACE, PREFERABLY
BY HANGING

COAT WITH CORROSION
PREVENTER IN HUMID
AREAS

near salt water, you may have to take special measures to keep rust from forming on ferrous metal surfaces, such as drill and router bits, chisels, and pliers. One highly effective product, used by NASA and the U.S. Navy among many others, is called CorrosionX. You spray or wipe it on and wipe it off the excess. The thin film left behind actually disrupts the corrosion process rather than just inhibiting it. Learn more about this product from Corrosion Technologies Corporation at 1-800-638-7361 or www.corrosionx.com. It's also great for locks and other exposed hardware.

Protect saw blades

Handsaws, whether of the rip, crosscut, back, or hack variety, are usually too large to store in a drawer. Fashion a tooth guard for them with pieces of old hose. Simply cut the hose to a suitable length, split one edge with a utility knife, and slip the guard over the saw's teeth. For smaller blades, such as for a hacksaw, use plastic report-cover spines. Cut the spine to length, and fit it over the blade's teeth.

Keep tools sharp

Tools that you keep well honed so that they cut smoothly last longer than ones that you let get dull. When sharpening cutting tools, such as chisels and axes, use the bevel set by the factory as a guide. Grind lightly (using a grinder or a belt sander with a 100-grit belt) so the metal doesn't become too hot, or it will lose its hardness. Dip the tool into water frequently to cool the metal at regular intervals. You can, of course, opt to have your blades professionally sharpened as well.

Level your level

Periodically, check to see that your level is on the level. You can do this by using it to draw a horizontal line on a piece of paper taped to the wall. Make sure the bubble is aligned between the two hairlines at the center of the vial. Then reverse the level, end to end, so you're reading the other side of the same vial. Hold the level against the line. If the bubble is no longer in the center, you have a problem. If you purchased a level with an adjustable or replaceable vial, you can fix it. If not, the level is junk.

Handle levels with care

Keep levels accurate by handling them carefully. Never leave one where it can fall or where something can fall on it. Avoid getting glue or paint on a level, because even a small accumulation on the edge can affect a reading. Keep levels away from heat and rain, especially levels made of wood. Use the hang hole for storage. Regularly rub linseed oil into wood levels.

Care for your C-clamps

Store your C-clamp collection by clamping them to a rack. Don't store clamps on pegboard hooks, where they are likely to fall and break. Don't store them in a drawer either, where the clamp screw can be damaged from getting banged about.

Use the right clamp

Use a heavy-duty clamp, such as a bar clamp, when you need a lot of pressure. Use a light-duty clamp, such as a C-clamp, only for light-duty jobs. Never use an undersized clamp for a big job, or you are liable to break it.

ProTip

CARING FOR SQUARES

No carpenter, no matter how skilled, can produce good work without accurate squares. Carpenter squares, combination squares, and try squares are all precision tools that must not be abused if they are to perform well. Protect them from moisture, glue, and paint splatters with a coat of car wax. On the job site, protect them from being scratched, or the markings will become difficult to read. Store them in a drawer rather than hanging them on the wall to lessen the chance that they'll fall on the floor. Spritz the moving parts of your combination square with silicone so that the steel rule will slide easily without jamming.

Get an angle square for rough work

Angle squares, often known by the brand name Speed Square, are triangular chunks of aluminum designed to withstand the rigors of rough framing work. They'll remain accurate enough for framing even if you drop yours from the second floor. So if you do any framing, put an angle square in your pouch and save the combination and try squares for finer work.

Replace hammer handles

Wooden handles on mallets, sledges, and framing hammers take a lot of abuse. If the handle loosens in the eye of the tool head, resecure it with a small steel wedge. If that doesn't do the trick, or if you've damaged the handle, replace the handle.

Lubricate anything that moves

Hand tools with moving parts, such as wrenches, pliers, wire cutters, and tin snips, will wear out faster if you don't lubricate them. Spritz them with WD-40 every month or two. This will help prevent rust as well.

Keep your tape measure sliding along

A coat of paste wax on your tape-measure blade will keep the retractor working smoothly and will prevent grease and dirt from sticking to the blade.

Power Tools

Today's electric drills, circular saws, sanders, and other power tools have more features and power than the ones your dad carried around in his toolbox—but if you want them to last as long as his, you'll have to pay attention to proper use and maintenance.

Use the right extension cord

Use the appropriate gauge of extension cord when you need to use one with an electric power tool. An undersized cord can cause loss of power, overheating, and premature motor failure. Owner's manuals specify the cord gauge to use with the tool in question according to its length. Table saws rated for between 12 and 16 amperes, for example, require a 14-gauge extension cord at 25 feet and a 12-gauge extension at 50 feet. When in doubt, use the next heavier gauge. But don't get confused: The smaller the gauge number, the heavier the cord.

Attach the chuck key to the power cord

Many of today's drills are keyless, but heavy-duty corded drills still require keys for opening and tightening the drill chuck. Such tools are rendered useless if you can't find the key. Upon purchasing such a drill, use the rubber key tie to attach the key to the cord. If your model doesn't come with a tie, use cloth-type electrical tape to attach the key to the tool's cord. Tape it close to the plug for ease of use and so it doesn't get in the way when you're operating the drill. This is also a good safety measure because it ensures that the cord is unplugged when you are changing bits.

ProTip

POWER-TOOL UPKEEP

Dalton Ghetti, a carpenter in Westport, Connecticut, says that he never has to replace any of his power tools. After each use he dusts off them off with a paintbrush, and occasionally he runs a shop vacuum over the tools' vents. Most important, Ghetti says, is to keep the owner's manual. "When something breaks, I order the part and fix it," he says. "It's simple to install new brushes or a new trigger."

Avoid using an extension cord with a charger

Plug a charger directly into a wall outlet instead of into an extension cord. Not only will this help preserve the charger, it will reduce the risk of fire and personal injury. If you must use an extension cord, it should be 16 gauge or large enough for the AC ampere rating of the charger. Make sure the extension cord has the same number of pins as the plug on the charger and that the pins are the same size and shape.

Be careful where you place batteries

Do not place a rechargeable tool or its battery near heat or fire. The battery could explode. Do not place a rechargeable battery near metal objects, such as coins or nails, which could cause the terminals to connect. A shorted battery will be ruined at the very least; it can cause a fire at worst.

Know your cordless tools' limits

Do not use a rechargeable drill or saw to perform tasks that require high torque (turning power)—you'll shorten the life of the tool. Corded tools are better suited to such tasks.

Sharp edges mean long life

Keep cutting edges on drill bits and saw blades sharp. This will keep them from binding, avoid motor strain, and lengthen the life of your tools. It will also make the tools safer to use, and they'll produce better results.

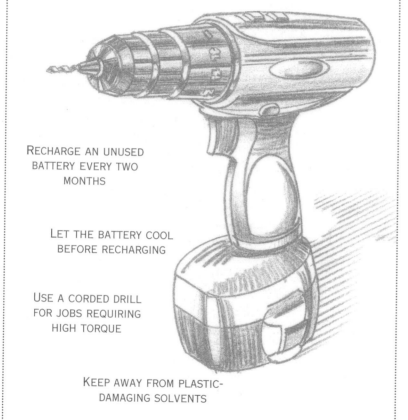

KEEP RECHARGEABLE BATTERY AWAY FROM HEAT, FIRE, AND NAILS

USE THE CORRECT GAUGE OF EXTENSION CORD

ATTACH CHUCK KEY TO THE POWER CORD

AVOID EXTREMELY COLD OR HOT STORAGE CONDITIONS

USE SHARP BITS TO AVOID MOTOR STRAIN

RECHARGE AN UNUSED BATTERY EVERY TWO MONTHS

LET THE BATTERY COOL BEFORE RECHARGING

USE A CORDED DRILL FOR JOBS REQUIRING HIGH TORQUE

KEEP AWAY FROM PLASTIC-DAMAGING SOLVENTS

☛ DON'T
use cordless tools near fire

Never use a cordless tool near an open flame or pilot light or even sparks. Batteries produce highly explosive hydrogen gas.

Give your batteries a cool-down

Batteries in cordless tools will become hot when the tool has been used continuously. In such situations, prevent damage to your battery pack by letting it cool for at least 30 minutes before recharging it.

Pamper your cordless tool batteries

Prolong the life of your rechargeable batteries by storing and charging them at room temperature. High or low temperatures will shorten battery life. Don't store batteries in a discharged state. Always recharge them immediately. If tools are stored unused for long periods, recharge the batteries every month or two to prolong battery life.

Pull the plug properly

Unplug tools and chargers by pulling on the plug, not by yanking on the cord. Doing this will lengthen the life of any electric tool or appliance.

Avoid solvents when cleaning tools

Keep your power tools clean, but don't use solvents to do the job. Solvents can damage the plastic housings used on most tools today. Similarly, keep tools from contact with brake fluid, gasoline, and penetrating oils. They can damage and weaken plastic parts, too. Use a mild detergent to remove grease; otherwise, wipe them clean with a dampened rag.

Watch for sparking in motors

Many good-quality electric power tools have replaceable carbon motor brushes. Excessive sparking may mean the brushes are worn out and need replacement. Check brush thickness periodically, and replace brushes when they get down to 1/4 inch (6 mm) or the thickness recommended in your manual. The brushes are spring-loaded, so take care when removing them.

Compressors demand maintenance

Compressors, long a favorite of professional builders and cabinetmakers, are finding their way into home workshops and garages. They can be used with sprayers to refinish kitchen cabinets, with power nailers and impact wrenches, or for sanding and grinding. Along with their versatility and convenience, however, comes the need for regular maintenance.

• If your unit is oil-lubricated, change the oil at the intervals recommended in your manual. Although the oil will not look dirty, as it does in your car, it still should be changed. Change oil filters and air filters as recommended.

• Drain condensation from the air storage tank after each use. There is usually a petcock located at the lowest part of the tank that releases the air in the tank, along with moisture contained in the air. If you don't drain the tank, it will rust from the inside and eventually begin to leak air.

Protect circular saw blades

The best way to keep those expensive circular saw blades sharp is to store them carefully. Sandwich them with cardboard, and put them in a drawer.

Rid blades of gum

Resins from wood will build up on your saw blades, causing them to perform poorly and overheat. Extend the life of circular saw blades and table saw blades by removing gum and resins with pitch-and-gum remover. Soaking blades in turpentine and then rubbing them with steel wool once the gum has softened will work, too.

Painting Tools and Supplies

Painting is one of the most popular do-it-yourself home improvement projects. To do it right, you need to invest in good-quality tools and supplies. With a little care, you can make sure your brushes, paints, and other supplies will be ready for duty the next time you need them.

Make drip holes in paint cans

If you have ever hammered the lid back onto a can of paint only to have paint squirt out in every direction, you'll love this tip: When you first open the can, use a nail or a nail set along with a hammer to punch six or seven holes into the groove in the top of the can into which the lid seats. The holes allow any paint that collects in the groove to drain back into the can. Besides preventing the messy squirt of paint, the can will seal better and you won't get a buildup of dried paint that can drop into the can.

Keep latex paints from freezing

Repeated freeze-and-thaw cycles will ruin latex paint. Store paint in a dry place where temperatures stay above freezing, such as a basement. Don't store paints in sunlight or near a heat source, either.

Wrap and freeze rollers

You can clean a paint roller, but it's usually more trouble than

it's worth. But if you plan to continue painting with the same color within a day or two, you can reuse a roller several times without the cleaning hassle. Just squeeze excess paint back into the can and then wrap the roller in plastic wrap or aluminum foil and put it in the freezer. The roller will be okay for continued use for up to several days. In fact, if you wrap it thoroughly with plastic, the roller will be fine overnight without freezing. This tip works for rollers used with oil or latex paints and for brushes, too.

Clear spray nozzles

When using a can of spray paint, hold it upside down upon completion of your paint session and press the button or trigger until no more paint sprays from the nozzle. This cleans out the nozzle so that it won't be clogged the next time you go to use the spray can.

Simple habits save paint

You thought you were all set. You went to the trouble to label and store the leftover paint so that you would have it on hand for touch-ups. Now you open the can only to find a congealed lump. Here are some tips on how clean up and store paint that so it will be fresh when you need it.

• First of all, mark the lid of the can with the name and number of the color, along with the date of purchase. It may be helpful to brush a small swatch of the paint on the lid as well. Lots of paint gets tossed because people forget what color is inside and so can no longer buy more matching paint when repainting.

❓ How Long Will Paint Last?

ANSWER: Up to 10 years for latex; 15 for alkyd

Oil-base alkyd paints can last for up to 15 years, while water-base latex paints can keep for up to 10 years. With either type, test old paint before using it by stirring it for several minutes. If the paint mixes well and any lumps disappear, it's probably okay to use. Try brushing it onto newspaper and check for lumps. If there are none, feel free to use the paint.

• When you pour from a paint can, hold the can so that any drips will fall away from the instructions portion of the label. This will allow you to read important information about coverage, application temperatures, thinning, and such the next time you need this color. Wipe drippings from the outside of the can before they dry.

• Upon completing your job, use a roller squeegee, available at most paint stores, to squeeze excess paint from roller-cover fibers. You'll be surprised at how much paint can be recovered from a roller cover. Use an old kitchen spatula to scrape paint from the roller tray back into the can.

• Use a brush or rag to wipe paint that collects inside the groove of the paint can. Otherwise dry paint will build up and prevent you from being able to reseal the can properly. Wipe paint from the rim of the lid as well.

• Add to the shelf life of any paint by resealing the can properly. First position the lid on top of the can. Cover the lid with an old rag to catch any splatters. Then tap lightly with a hammer around the rim until the lid is securely seated. Another trick is to cover the open can with a piece of plastic wrap prior to reseating the lid. This controls splatters and gives a tight seal.

• If a can of paint is fouled by dirt or paint crud, don't toss it. Use a paint filter to strain it into a clean container.

Get the last drops

It's frustrating. There is no paint coming out of the spray can, but you can still feel paint sloshing around inside. The paint pickup tube may be on the side opposite the direction you are spraying (A). Twist the nozzle half a turn and try again (B).

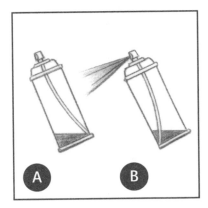

Use tray liners

There's no need to keep buying new paint trays for rollers. Just be sure you have a good supply of plastic tray liners on hand.

Make roller frames last

Brushes and roller covers aren't the only things you should clean upon completing a paint job. Be sure to keep roller frames clean as well. Remove a roller cover from the frame as soon as you're done painting so it doesn't stick to the frame. Buy good-quality roller frames that come apart for easy cleaning.

Clean brushes the easy way

Cleaning brushes need not be a messy ordeal and, if you do it properly, can add years of life to your brushes.

❶ Upon completing a paint job, brush out as much paint as possible on the wall, ceiling, or on old newspaper. Then use an absorbent rag to wipe as much of the remaining paint from the bristles as possible.

❷ Soak a small area of a clean rag with the appropriate solvent (paint thinner for alkyd or water for latex), and wipe the bristles again. If you take a few moments to do this carefully, there should be very little paint left on your brush at this point.

❸ Rinse the brush in solvent or water, and wipe the bristles clean one more time.

❹ Finish by washing your brush in a bucket of warm water and several squirts of liquid dishwashing soap.

☞ DON'T
pour solvent down the drain

Don't pour that used solvent or solvent-contaminated water down your drain, where it can contaminate water supplies. Recycle it as described on the next page. Or save it for special collection day; call your local sanitation or environmental protection agency for details.

USE NATURAL BRISTLES FOR
ALKYD; SYNTHETIC ONES
FOR LATEX

BRUSH OFF EXCESS PAINT ON
NEWSPAPER BEFORE CLEANING

NEVER LOAD MORE THAN ONE-THIRD
OF THE BRISTLES WITH PAINT

CLEAN OFF ALKYD PAINT
WITH PAINT THINNER; LATEX
WITH WATER

STORE BRUSH WRAPPED IN
ORIGINAL CARDBOARD JACKET
OR FOLDED PAPER

REMOVE OLD,
HARDENED ALKYD PAINT BY
SIMMERING IN VINEGAR

SOFTEN STIFF NATURAL
BRISTLES WITH HAIR
CONDITIONER

Recycle dirty solvents

Save and reuse solvents, such as turpentine and mineral spirits, by pouring used solvents into glass jars and closing the lid. Don't mix different types of solvents, and be sure to clearly label the jar's contents! Eventually, the dirt and pigments will settle to the base of the jars, whereupon you can pour off the solvent into a clean (marked) container for use in the future.

Store brushes in jackets

When you buy a good-quality brush, it will come packaged in a cardboard brush jacket. Don't discard this jacket. Use it to preserve the brush shape while it's being stored.

Don't toss stir sticks

It's a nuisance to not have a stir stick on hand when you need it. Avoid this by simply wiping stir sticks clean after each use. The thin dried film of paint that remains won't affect paint in the next can you stir.

Skim off the congealed paint

On opening a previously used can of alkyd paint, you might find a skin on the paint surface. Professional painters have long known that this is no problem. Just cut around the perimeter of the skin with a knife, and then carefully lift the skin from the can and discard it. Thoroughly stir the paint, and you're ready to start brushing. You may need to thin the paint slightly to ease application. Follow the paint manufacturer's instructions on the paint can label for thinning. Paint additives, such as Penetrol from the Flood Company, work well to thin alkyd paints. For latex paints, use Floetrol (also made by Flood).

Preserve leftover paint

When you store leftover paint in its original can, you often get rust and paint flakes in the paint. To avoid this, you can pour the paint into a plastic bottle or a glass jar with a screw lid. But don't let any paint get on the threads of the lid or you won't be able to reopen the container. If you do get paint on the threads, rubbing a little petroleum jelly on them will keep the lid from sticking.

Here's another clever way to keep leftover paint fresh: Pour the paint into a resealable plastic food-storage bag. Squeeze the air out before you seal the bag; then put the bag into the original paint can and tap the lid closed.

Revive a crusty paintbrush

If your paintbrush is hardened with dried oil-base paint, give it a vinegar bath. Place it in a pot of white vinegar and simmer it for 10 minutes. Rinse the bristles with water, and use a brushcomb to clear out any remaining particles. Finally, hang the brush until it dries.

Soften a stiff paintbrush

Even when you clean them carefully, natural-bristle paintbrushes may dry out and become stiff. A quick soak in 1 tablespoon of hair conditioner mixed with 1 pint (475ml) of warm water will soften up a clean, stiff brush.

Grandpa says...

"Even when you thoroughly seal a can of alkyd paint, there is enough oxygen sealed inside to form a skin. Try this old painter's trick. Just before you put the lid in place, take a deep breath and blow into the can. The carbon dioxide you exhale often displaces enough oxygen to prevent the skin."

Wood, Fasteners, and Other Supplies

When you get ready to tackle an improvement project, it's a great feeling to discover that you have all the supplies you'll need without having to head off to the hardware store or home center. However, the feeling fades quickly if you discover the supplies are no longer usable. Here's how to store them.

Store wood in a dry place

Dry wood stock won't warp unless is becomes damp or wet. If your shop is dry, then you just need to find a convenient spot to store the wood. If your floor is damp, it's best to build a rack to keep the wood off the floor. Otherwise, store the boards vertically. That way, only the bottom edge can be affected by moisture—not enough to cause significant warping.

"Sticker" green wood

If you want to air-dry green wood, it's best to "sticker" the boards outside, where they'll get a lot of air circulation. Start the stack on top of some bricks or pressure-treated blocks to keep the bottom of the stack off the ground. Stickering means putting a short piece of scrap wood—a sticker—crosswise every 24 inches (60 cm) across

the boards to keep them separated, further promoting air circulation. The stickers must all be the same thickness—about 1/2 inch (13 mm) is good—to keep the pile level. And the stickers should all be directly above one another to support the load without causing warping. Keep the pile covered with a tarp weighted down by some bricks or a sheet of plywood.

Store screws and nails in airtight containers

Most workshops are subject to moisture and temperature swings that cause condensation. Store nails, screws, and other fasteners in airtight containers. You can purchase transparent bins of various sizes for this purpose—or use empty coffee cans. They, too, come in various sizes. The large ones are tall enough for storing spade bits as

well. Just remember to use a marker to label the contents on the lid so you can find what you need quickly.

Store glue at the right temperature

Different glues have different storage requirements. Super glues (cyanoacrylate adhesive such as Krazy Glue, Superglue, or Miracle Glue), for example, will last a lot longer once opened if you keep them in the refrigerator or freezer. White (craft glue) and yellow (carpenter's wood glue) glues, on the other hand, should not be frozen. The same goes for cartridges of latex caulk and latex adhesives. Flammable adhesives, such as contact cement and spray adhesives, are more tolerant of freeze-thaw cycles but should not be stored near a heat source (including sunlight).

Cap adhesives and caulks after each use

Tightly cap all glue tubes, glue bottles, and adhesive and caulking cartridges after each use. If you lose the cap provided with the product, find a wire connector of suitable size and screw it onto the applicator tip to form a good seal.

Index

Windshields, 332

Winter squash, storing, 18

Wood
avoiding antiques storage in, 81
on clocks, cleaning, 154
green, air-drying, 356
pressure-treated, for outdoor structures, 286–87, 311, 312
storing, 356

Wood blinds, 150

Wooden baseball bats, 124, 125

Wooden bowls, 31

Wooden floors, 247
cleaning, 246
minimizing gaps in, 248–49
repairing nicks and scratches in, 248
restoring shine to, 247
selecting, 248

Wooden furniture
brass hardware on, 143–44
cabinets and bookcases, 144
chairs, 144
chest of drawers, 141
dusting, 138
insect infestations in, 141
leveling, 142
moving, 143
preventing deterioration of, 139
regluing veneers on, 142–43
removing candle wax from, 140
removing water rings from, 141–42
selecting, 140
stripping, 143
waxing vs. polishing, 138–39

Wooden kitchen tools, 30–31, 32

Wooden musical instruments, winterizing, 131

Wooden outdoor structures, 310–12

Wooden play sets, 313

Wooden toys, storing, 95

Wood finishes, for decks, 285

Wood-finish kitchen cabinets, 157

Wood roofs, 270

Wood siding
patching, 269
and trim, staining, 264–65

Woodstoves, 261

Woodwinds, 136

Workbenches, 344

Workshops, 344–45

Wrapping materials, storing, 163

Wreaths, storing, 163

Wrist strap, antistatic, for protecting computer, 205

X

Xbox systems, faulty power cords on, 224

Y

Yard maintenance, 290–92

Yard watering systems, 316

Z

Zippers, 47